T0231425

Cost-Sensitive
Machine
Learning

Chapman & Hall/CRC
Machine Learning & Pattern Recognition Series

SERIES EDITORS

Ralf Herbrich and Thore Graepel
Microsoft Research Ltd.
Cambridge, UK

AIMS AND SCOPE

This series reflects the latest advances and applications in machine learning and pattern recognition through the publication of a broad range of reference works, textbooks, and handbooks. The inclusion of concrete examples, applications, and methods is highly encouraged. The scope of the series includes, but is not limited to, titles in the areas of machine learning, pattern recognition, computational intelligence, robotics, computational/statistical learning theory, natural language processing, computer vision, game AI, game theory, neural networks, computational neuroscience, and other relevant topics, such as machine learning applied to bioinformatics or cognitive science, which might be proposed by potential contributors.

PUBLISHED TITLES

MACHINE LEARNING: An Algorithmic Perspective
Stephen Marsland

HANDBOOK OF NATURAL LANGUAGE PROCESSING,
Second Edition
Nitin Indurkhya and Fred J. Damerau

UTILITY-BASED LEARNING FROM DATA
Craig Friedman and Sven Sandow

A FIRST COURSE IN MACHINE LEARNING
Simon Rogers and Mark Girolami

COST-SENSITIVE MACHINE LEARNING
Balaji Krishnapuram, Shipeng Yu, and Bharat Rao

Chapman & Hall/CRC
Machine Learning & Pattern Recognition Series

Cost-Sensitive Machine Learning

Edited by
Balaji Krishnapuram
Shipeng Yu
Bharat Rao

CRC Press
Taylor & Francis Group
Boca Raton London New York

CRC Press is an imprint of the
Taylor & Francis Group, an **informa** business

A CHAPMAN & HALL BOOK

CRC Press
Taylor & Francis Group
6000 Broken Sound Parkway NW, Suite 300
Boca Raton, FL 33487-2742

© 2012 by Taylor & Francis Group, LLC
CRC Press is an imprint of Taylor & Francis Group, an Informa business

No claim to original U.S. Government works

Printed in the United States of America on acid-free paper
Version Date: 20111107

International Standard Book Number: 978-1-4398-3925-6 (Hardback)

Visit the Taylor & Francis Web site at
http://www.taylorandfrancis.com

and the CRC Press Web site at
http://www.crcpress.com

Contents

List of Figures

List of Tables

Preface

As generally seen as a special topic under artificial intelligence, machine learning has become a mature field over the last several decades. It has been used by researchers and practitioners in a variety of application domains to discover patterns, predict outcomes, or simply mine knowledge from the data. In a nutshell, a machine learning algorithm takes some input data as *training data*, conducts *model fitting* with specific probabilistic or statistical methodologies, and outputs a *model* which encapsulates the knowledge or intelligence it obtained from the training data. The model can be applied to newly obtained data (sometimes called *test data*) and generate outputs or results on these data (depending on the applications these can be called predictions, classifications, etc). These basic steps can be iterated in many algorithm designs to consider user input/feedback (e.g., reinforcement learning), share information (e.g., transfer learning), and integrate knowledge (e.g., ensemble learning).

Most machine learning algorithms are designed to minimize a loss function based on the training data, or to maximize the probability of the observations in the training data. In practical machine learning applications, however, an important aspect that every practitioner needs to take into account is the *cost* that associates with the algorithm. Depending on different application scenarios this can mean one or a combination of the following things:

- Cost of acquiring training data

- Cost of data annotation/labeling and cleaning

- Computational cost for model fitting, validation, and testing

- Cost of collecting features/attributes for test data

- Cost of user feedback collection

- Cost of incorrect prediction/classification

For a machine learning algorithm to work well in practice, it is important to optimize the model fitting performance and at the same time minimize the cost associated with the learning process. In other words, the machine learning algorithm needs to be *sensitive* to the cost that it is dealing with, and in the better case take the cost into account in the model fitting process. This leads to *cost-sensitive machine learning*, a relatively new research topic in machine learning. It is becoming increasingly popular, both in terms of academic research and real-world applications that seek to minimize modeling costs. This book provides an overview of the current research efforts and problems in the area and discusses several real-world problems that incorporate the cost of learning into the modeling process.

Many fields in machine learning attempt to solve cost-sensitive learning with simplifying assumptions. For example, in semi-supervised learning, class-labels are assumed to be expensive and features are implicitly assumed to have zero cost. In active learning, labels are again assumed to be expensive; however the learner may ask an oracle to reveal a label for unlabeled data for selected examples. Active feature acquisition assumes that obtaining features is expensive and the learner identifies instances for which complete information is most informative to classify a particular test sample. Inductive transfer learning and domain adaptation methods assume that training data for a particular task are expensive or that other data from other domains may be cheaper. Cascaded classifier architectures are primarily designed in order to reduce the cost of acquiring features to classify a sample.

There is a common thread linking all of these different research communities. In particular, all these learning methods are motivated by the need to minimize the modeling and/or predictive costs. Going beyond just minimizing data acquisition costs, recently, the need to trade off different types of costs in the data modeling process has become increasingly apparent in various applications such as web ad placement, computer-aided medical diagnosis, computer vision, information extraction, natural language processing, marketing, etc., and several high-impact application papers have started to address this need. However, to the best of our knowledge, this is the first book to address all of these related topics in a cohesive manner, and explicitly address the tradeoffs between the various costs and benefits.

Structure of the Book

The proposed book will consist of two parts, each containing several chapters. The first part consisting of the first five chapters of the book reviews the theoretical underpinnings of cost sensitive machine learning. The first three chapters are devoted to well-established machine learning approaches to reduce data acquisition costs during training, while the next two chapters deal with approaches to reduce costs when the systems are asked to make predictions for new samples. This part highlights the often implicit assumptions in various fields of research that were not fully understood in the past, which we emphasize in an effort to spur focused research on several open problems.

Burr Settles provides an overview of the vast literature on active learning in Chapter 1. After first describing the problem, Burr surveys the main theoretical approaches that have been adopted, and provides a unified view that will help graduate students and new researchers understand the common themes and open problems in this area of research. In Chapter 2, Xueyuan Zhou, Ankan Saha, and Vikas Sindhwani survey the state-of-the-art techniques in the very actively researched (and still somewhat controversial) topic of semi-supervised learning, clearly highlighting the open challenges. Bin Cao, Yu Zhang, and Qiang Yang summarize the current approaches to transfer learning and multi-task learning in Chapter 3.

In Chapter 4, Vikas C. Raykar describes recent advances in the design of cascaded classifiers that attempt to reduce the cost of acquiring features during prediction time by making a decision after acquiring the most important information where possible. In Chapter 5, Josh Attenberg, Prem Melville, Foster Provost, and Maytal Saar-Tsechansky discuss an alternative approach that dynamically decides which features to acquire at test time in an effort to further optimize costs.

The second part of the book describes real-world applications that effectively trade off different types of costs. These applications are at the cutting edge of the technological developments in this area, and while they utilize the traditional machine learning approaches described in the first part, they also advance beyond the constraining assumptions by analyzing the application needs from first principles.

In Chapter 6, Sudheendra Vijayanarasimhan and Kristen Grauman survey the latest advances in the research on reducing annotation costs for visual category learning. This chapter clearly shows how multiple instance learning, active learning, semi-supervised learning, learning with noisy labels, etc. are all used in this application domain. Addressing the topic of medical decision support in Chapter 7, Xiang Sean Zhou and his co-authors discuss how to reduce error costs in medical imaging by systematically analyzing both the costs of medical tests and the costs of errors. In Chapter 8, Deepak Agarwal identifies key problems from computational advertising that benefit from cost-sensitive learning including sponsored search, contextual matching, and display advertising. Similarly, in Chapter 9, Martin Szummer and Filip Radlinski highlight the need for cost-sensitive machine learning in information retrieval. Demonstrating the commercial importance of the unified view of the topic, these four chapters survey the rapid developments in important applications from leading companies as well as academic research labs funded by the industry.

Acknowledgments

The idea of editing a book on the topic was first proposed at the workshop on cost-sensitive learning at NIPS in 2008. We are grateful to Oksana Yakhnenko and Lawrence Carin for co-organizing this workshop, and John Shawe-Taylor, Andreas Krause, and Volker Tresp for their invited talks. We are also grateful to all the authors who contributed their papers to make this workshop successful. Pleasantly surprised by the prodigious growth in this area of research, we heeded the advice and suggestions from the audience of the workshop. We are grateful to all the participants, and particularly want to thank Ashish Kapoor and Burr Settles for their time and participation.

We are particularly indebted to Amber Donley, Michele Dimont, and Randi Cohen for the excellent support from Taylor & Francis. It is no exaggeration to state that this book would be impossible without their patience and help. We are also grateful to Ralf Herbrich and Thore Graepel for their guidance and encouragement as the series editors.

We would like to thank our employer, Siemens Medical Solutions, USA and many colleagues who helped us formalize ideas around this topic over the years. Finally, we are very grateful to our families for their love and support.

Balaji Krishnapuram, Shipeng Yu, and Bharat Rao

Contributors

Deepak Agarwal
Yahoo! Research
Sunnyvale, California

Josh Attenberg
Polytechnic Institute of New York
    University
Brooklyn, New York

Bin Cao
Department of Computer Science
    and Engineering
Hong Kong University of Science and
    Technology
Hong Kong

Maneesh Dewan
Siemens Healthcare
Malvern, Pennsylvania

Hendrik Ditt
Siemens Healthcare
Forchheim, Germany

Ute Feuerlein
Siemens Healthcare
Forchheim, Germany

Kristen Grauman
Department of Computer Science
University of Texas at Austin
Austin, Texas

Stefan Grosskopf
Siemens Healthcare
Forchheim, Germany

Martin Harder
Siemens Healthcare
Erlangen, Germany

Bing Jian
Siemens Healthcare
Malvern, Pennsylvania

Arun Krishnan
Siemens Healthcare
Malvern, Pennsylvania

Lars Lauer
Siemens Healthcare
Erlangen, Germany

Prem Melville
IBM T. J. Watson Research Center
Yorktown Heights, New York

Heiko Meyer
Siemens Healthcare
Erlangen, Germany

Zhigang Peng
Siemens Healthcare
Malvern, Pennsylvania

Foster Provost
Stern School of Business
New York University
New York, New York

Filip Radlinski
Microsoft
Vancouver, British Columbia
Canada

Vikas C. Raykar
Siemens Healthcare
Malvern, Pennsylvania

Maytal Saar-Tsechansky
Red McCombs School of Business
University of Texas at Austin
Austin, Texas

Ankan Saha
Department of Computer Science
University of Chicago
Chicago, Illinois

Raphael Schwarz
Siemens Healthcare
Erlangen, Germany

Burr Settles
Machine Learning Department
Carnegie Mellon University
Pittsburg, Pennsylvania

Vikas Sindhwani
IBM T. J. Watson Research Center
Yorktown Heights, New York

Martin Szummer
Microsoft Research
Cambridge, UK

Sudheendra Vijayanarasimhan
Department of Computer Science
University of Texas at Austin
Austin, Texas

Qiang Yang
Department of Computer Science
   and Engineering
Hong Kong University of Science and
   Technology
Hong Kong

Yiqiang Zhan
Siemens Healthcare
Malvern, Pennsylvania

Yu Zhang
Department of Computer Science
   and Engineering
Hong Kong University of Science and
   Technology
Hong Kong

Xiang Sean Zhou
Siemens Healthcare
Malvern, Pennsylvania

Xueyuan Zhou
Department of Computer Science
University of Chicago
Chicago, Illinois

Part I

Theoretical Underpinnings of Cost-Sensitive Machine Learning

Chapter 1

Algorithms for Active Learning

Burr Settles

Machine Learning Department, Carnegie Mellon University, Pittsburgh, Pennsylvania

1.1   Introduction

Active learning (sometimes called "query learning") is a subfield of machine learning concerned with minimizing annotation and training costs. More precisely, the goal of active learning is to minimize the cost of obtaining labels for data, by selectively interacting with the labeling source. By contrast, the traditional "passive" approach to supervised learning is to acquire a large random sample of training instances to be labeled before any learning begins. The key hypothesis is that if the learning algorithm is allowed to *choose* the most informative data instances to be labeled for training—to be "curious," so to speak—it will perform better with less data (and lower costs).

This is a desirable property for modern machine learning applications, because in order to perform well they must usually be trained on many labeled instances. If we are lucky, the training labels may come at little or no cost, such as the the "spam" flag users mark on unwanted email messages, or the five-star rating they might assign to their favorite music or films in an online database.

Learners could use these flags and ratings to better filter junk email and suggest new music or movies, but in such cases the labels are provided virtually for free. Unfortunately, for most interesting learning and data modeling tasks, instance labels can be very difficult or expensive to obtain. Active learning can be quite valuable in these sorts of problems, since it aims to reduce the cost associated with the annotations necessary for training. Consider these examples:

- *Speech Recognition.* Accurate labeling of speech utterances is time consuming and requires trained linguists. In fact, annotation at the word level can take 10 times longer than the actual audio (e.g., 1 minute of speech takes 10 minutes to label), and annotating phonemes can take 400 times as long (e.g., nearly 7 hours). The problem is compounded for rare languages or dialects [67]. Active learning has been shown to expedite this process by achieving high accuracy while reducing the number of utterances that need to be annotated by humans [61].

- *Computational Biology.* The discovery and characterization of biological networks is a slow and expensive process, requiring hundreds (even thousands) of lab experiments to iteratively refine a working hypothesis. If machine learning is used to induce hypotheses from experimental data, then active learning can be a way to select which experiments should be executed next, facilitating discovery and reducing the cost of laboratory materials. Such methods have been shown to be useful in protein engineering [17] and the induction of metabolic pathways [30, 31].

- *Internet Classification and Filtering.* Learning to classify text documents (e.g., web pages or news feeds) and other kinds of online media (e.g., image, audio, or video files) usually requires that humans assign each instance a label, like "relevant" vs. "not relevant." Annotating thousands of these can become tedious and even redundant. Active learning has been employed in virtually all of these media types over the years, demonstrating that more accurate classification systems can be learned by selectively choosing the training instances [26, 35, 54, 64, 65].

In the most common active learning setting, a learner may pose *queries* in the form of unlabeled instances to be labeled by an *oracle*. The oracle is often thought of as a human annotator or domain expert, but could also be the empirical result of a scientific experiment or sensor measurement; the oracle is simply the label source for the learning task at hand. By interacting with the oracle in this way, the learner attempts to get the most out of each labeled instance in order to reduce data costs without sacrificing accuracy.

1.1.1　Preliminaries

To formalize our discussion a bit, consider a variation on a standard supervised learning problem. The learner is presented with labeled instances, each denoted by the pair $\langle x, y \rangle$. Its goal, then, is to learn a function $f : X \to Y$ to properly assign a label y to each new instance x it encounters in the future. For *classification* tasks, these labels come from a discrete set of known classes $y \in \mathcal{Y}$. For example, suppose we want a system to scan through a collection of emails determine which ones to assign to the "spam" class for filtering. For *regression* tasks, the label is a continuous value $y \in \mathbb{R}$, such as a five-star rating on books or movies.

Let $\mathcal{L} = \{\langle x, y \rangle^{(1)}, \ldots, \langle x, y \rangle^{(L)}\}$ be a labeled training set composed of instance-label pairs. We usually assume that an active learner has access to a small initial $\mathcal{L}$ from which to begin learning. Let us use θ to denote the model induced by the learning algorithms (e.g., a set of parameters). The active learning task is to select the "best" query instance $x^* \in X$ to be labeled by the oracle, and have $\langle x^*, \text{oracle}(x^*) \rangle$ added to $\mathcal{L}$ for subsequent learning. Let $\phi(x, \theta)$ be some *utility measure*, which is used to evaluate how informative x would be to the current learner θ if it were labeled and added to the training set. Section 1.2 discusses a variety of utility measures used by different active learning strategies, but for the time being let us simply assume that higher values of ϕ imply more informative instances. The fundamental *active learning cycle* is described by the algorithm in Table 1.1.

TABLE 1.1: The general active learning cycle.

given: labeled training set $\mathcal{L}$, utility measure ϕ

1	**repeat**
2	$\quad \theta = \text{train}(\mathcal{L})$;
3	$\quad x^* = \text{argmax}_x \, \phi(x, \theta)$;
4	$\quad \mathcal{L} = \mathcal{L} \cup \langle x^*, \text{oracle}(x^*) \rangle$;
5	**until** some stopping criterion ;

1.1.2 Active Learning Scenarios

A key consideration for using active learning in practice is: "Where do query instances come from?" Line 3 in Table 1.1 indicates that the learner should select the instance with the highest utility according to ϕ, but over what set of candidates? This section briefly touches on three basic learning scenarios in which queries can be tractably posed: (i) query synthesis, (ii) stream-based selective sampling, and (iii) pool-based sampling. These scenarios are illustrated by the diagram in Figure 1.1.

One of the first active learning scenarios to be studied is learning with *membership queries* [2]. In this setting, the learner may request labels for any unlabeled point in the instance space X, typically assuming that queries can be generated de novo. This can be problematic if X is represented by unbounded continuous features though, because our search space for queries is infinite!

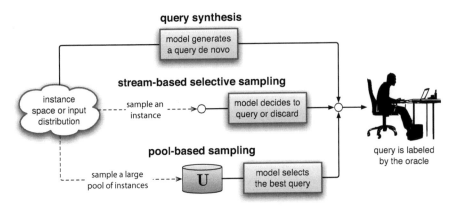

FIGURE 1.1: The three main active learning scenarios.

Even if the instance space is finite, it may be very large and intractable to evaluate ϕ for every possible $x \in X$.

Fortunately, there are are at least two methods for synthesizing query instances that are often tractable and efficient. One such approach is a generalization of binary search. If X is a simple one-dimensional instance space, and the learning task is binary classification, the optimal query is simply the midpoint of the two consecutive training examples with differing labels (if we assume no label noise), which iteratively bisects the ambiguous section of the instance space. Conceptual variants of this approach have been proposed to synthesize examples in higher-dimensional spaces [2, 4, 46]. A second approach is relevant if $\phi(x, \theta)$ is differentiable with respect to the input features that describe the instance space, which is applicable in both classification and regression problems. In such cases, a gradient ascent algorithm can be used to search for the x that maximizes the utility measure of interest [9, 12]. The specifics of these synthesis approaches are usually dependent on the problem or learning algorithm, and further details are beyond the scope of this chapter.

Query synthesis can be reasonable for many problems, but labeling such arbitrary queries can be awkward, especially if the oracle is a human domain expert. For example, when synthesizing queries for human oracles in a computer vision task—handwritten digit classification—Lang and Baum [34] found that many query images generated by the learner contained no recognizable symbols: only artificial hybrid characters that had no natural semantic meaning. Similarly, one could imagine that synthetic queries for natural language processing tasks might be composed of text or speech streams that amount to gibberish. The central problem is that there may be many informative points in X which are highly improbable, so for synthesized queries to be meaningful the active learner should also know something about the underlying input distribution $P(X)$. This is often unavailable or difficult to model, and as a result, the synthesis scenario has mostly been the subject of theoretical study. It has been employed successfully for a few applications in robotics [9] and computational biology [31], where sufficient information about the input distribution are known, and queries correspond to meaningful experiments.

An alternative to synthesizing queries is a scenario based on *selective sampling* [10, 11]. The key assumption is that obtaining an unlabeled instance is free (or very inexpensive relative to its labeling), so it can first be sampled from the actual $P(X)$, and then the learner can decide whether or not to request its label. This approach is sometimes called *stream-based* active learning, as unlabeled instances are provided in a stream (drawn one at a time from a data source) and the learner must decide whether to query or discard it. If the input distribution is uniform, queries from selective sampling may well seem as arbitrary as query synthesis. However, if the distribution is non-uniform and (more importantly) unknown, we have some guarantee that queries will still be sensible, since they come from a real underlying distribution.

The decision whether or not to query an instance can be framed several ways. One approach is to evaluate samples using the utility measure ϕ and make a biased random decision, such that higher utility scores are more likely to be queried [16]. Another approach is to compute an explicit *region of uncertainty* [10], i.e., a partition of the instance space that is still ambiguous to the learner, and only query instances that fall within this region. A naïve way of doing this is to set a minimum threshold on ϕ which defines the region. Instances whose score is above this threshold are then queried. Another more principled approach is to define the region that is still unknown to the overall model class, i.e., to the set of hypotheses consistent with the current labeled training set called the *version space* [42]. In other words, if any two hypotheses of the same model class (but different parameter settings) agree on all the labeled data, but disagree on some unlabeled instance, then that instance lies within the region of uncertainty. Calculating this region completely and explicitly is computationally expensive, however, and it must be maintained after each new query. As a result, approximations are used in practice.

The stream-based scenario has been the subject of much theoretical analysis in active learning [3, 20], but it has also been studied in several real-world applications, including part-of-speech tagging [16], sensor scheduling [33], and learning ranking functions for information retrieval [64]. Fujii et al. [21] employ selective sampling for active learning in word sense disambiguation, e.g., determining if the word "bank" means land alongside a river or a financial institution in a given context. The approach not only reduces labeling costs, but also limits the size of $\mathcal{L}$, which in turn speeds up inference in non-parametric methods like nearest-neighbor learning.

For many real-world learning problems, it is reasonable to collect a large amount of unlabeled data at once. This motivates *pool-based sampling* [35], which assumes the learner has access to both a labeled set $\mathcal{L}$ and a large pool of unlabeled data $\mathcal{U} = \{x^{(1)}, \ldots, x^{(U)}\}$, composed of unlabeled instances drawn from $P(X)$. Queries are selectively drawn from this pool, which is usually assumed to be closed (i.e., static or non-changing), although this is not strictly necessary. Typically, instances are queried in a greedy fashion such that $x^* = \text{argmax}_{x \in \mathcal{U}} \, \phi(x, \theta)$. If $\mathcal{U}$ is very large, Monte Carlo sampling is sometimes used to reduce the size of the candidate set to be evaluated.

Pool-based sampling has generally received less theoretical attention, but it has been the scenario of choice in many applied empirical studies, such as in text classification [35, 39, 60, 27], information extraction [58, 53], image classification and retrieval [59, 65], video classification and retrieval [63, 26], speech recognition [61], and cancer diagnosis [37] to name only a few. It is perhaps the most common active learning scenario in practice.

The main difference between stream-based and pool-based active learning is that the former scans through the data sequentially and makes query decisions individually, whereas the latter evaluates and ranks the entire collection in order to select the *best* query. While the pool-based scenario appears to be much more common among application papers, one can imagine settings where the stream-based approach is more appropriate. For example, when memory or processing power may be limited, as with mobile and embedded devices, or when the input data are so vast they cannot even fit into memory at once. It is also worth noting that some authors [43, 58] use "selective sampling" to refer to pool-based sampling. Under this interpretation, the term merely signifies that queries are made with a select set of instances sampled from a real data distribution. However, in most of the literature selective sampling refers to the stream-based scenario as described above. For ease of discourse, and because of its practical applicability, we will assume the pool-based scenario for most of what follows in this chapter.

1.1.3 An Illustrative Example

Before diving into query frameworks in detail, let us consider a simple example of active learning. Figure 1.2 shows the potential of the pool-based scenario in a way that is easy to visualize. Imagine a toy dataset generated from two Gaussians centered at $(-2,0)$ and $(2,0)$ with standard deviation $\sigma = 1$, each representing a different class distribution. Figure 1.2(a) shows a resulting dataset of 400 instances (200 sampled from each class); instances are represented as points in a 2D feature space. In a realistic problem setting, each instance x might be available but its label y is unknown. Figure 1.2(b) shows what might happen using a traditional "passive" supervised learning approach, where 30 instances are randomly sampled i.i.d. from the pool and labeled for training. The line represents the linear decision boundary of a logistic regression model (i.e., where the posterior equals 0.5) trained using these 30 points. Notice that most of the labeled instances in this training set are far from zero on the horizontal axis, which is where the Bayes optimal decision boundary should be. As a result, this classifier only achieves 70% accuracy on the remaining unlabeled points.

Figure 1.2(c), however, shows an active learning approach. If we use the

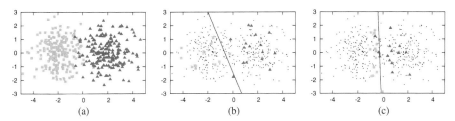

FIGURE 1.2: An example of pool-based active learning. (a) A toy dataset of 400 instances, evenly sampled from two class Gaussians. The instances are represented as points in a 2D feature space. (b) A logistic regression model trained with 30 labeled instances randomly drawn from the problem domain. The line represents the decision boundary of the classifier (70% accuracy). (c) A logistic regression model trained with 30 actively queried instances (90%).

simple utility measure $\phi(x, \theta) = 1 - P_\theta(\hat{y}|x)$, where $\hat{y}$ denotes the most likely label under the model, then the learner will iteratively query the unlabeled instance closest to the decision boundary (i.e., it prefers instances with confidence closest to 0.5). This method is called *uncertainty sampling* (Section 1.2.1), and the intuition is that the model can adequately explain instances in other parts of the input space, but the data points closest to the boundary are most ambiguous and thus the most informative. As a result, the learner avoids requesting labels for redundant or irrelevant instances at the extremes, and can achieve 90% accuracy with 30 labeled instances.

The rest of this chapter is organized as follows. In the next section, we will take a closer look at several query strategy frameworks in the active learning literature, and discuss specific utility functions that are commonly used within each framework. Note that as a gentle introduction to active learning algorithms this chapter is not an exhaustive review, although we will cover the most common algorithms and the intuitions behind them. Next we will take a unified view, seeing how these varied approaches can all be seen as approximations of a single utility measure that aims to maximize data likelihood. Finally, we will briefly touch on some more recent topics regarding active learning in practice.

1.2 Query Strategy Frameworks

Regardless of the problem setting, active learners must have the ability to evaluate the utility of a query, which can either be generated de novo or sampled from a given distribution $P(X)$. This section provides an overview of the general frameworks that are used—including derivations of specific utility measures—as well as some algorithmic details of how they can be implemented in practice. To keep the discussion as general as possible, we will generally avoid implementation details for any particular learning algorithm or model class. Fortunately, most active learning frameworks are fairly modular, and we can present utility measures at a more abstract level. The only consistent assumption is that the learner being used has some way of estimating the posterior probability $P_\theta(y|x)$. That is, the probability of the label y given an instance x under the model θ. From this point on, we will use $\phi_A(x)$ to denote the utility measure for some query selection algorithm A. From here on, we will also drop the θ argument from ϕ for brevity.

1.2.1   Uncertainty Sampling

Perhaps the simplest and most commonly used query framework is *uncertainty sampling* [35], which was used in the example from Section 1.1.3. In this framework, an active learner queries the instance about which it is least certain how to label. This approach is often straightforward for probabilistic models. For example, when using a probabilistic model for binary classification, uncertainty sampling simply queries the instance whose posterior probability of being in the positive class is closest to 0.5. For non-probabilistic classifiers, this is equivalent to selecting instances that are closest to the decision boundary between the positive and negative classes.

For learning problems with three or more classes, or for structured learning problems, a more general uncertainty sampling variant might query the instance whose best prediction is the *least confident*:

$$\phi_{LC}(x) = 1 - P_\theta(\hat{y}|x),$$

where $\hat{y} = \text{argmax}_y \, P_\theta(y|x)$, or the class label with the highest posterior probability under the model θ. One way to interpret this uncertainty measure is the expected 0/1-loss, i.e., the model's belief that it will mislabel x. This sort of strategy has been popular, for example, with statistical sequence models in information extraction tasks [15, 53]. This is because the most likely label sequence (and its associated likelihood) can be efficiently computed using dynamic programming.

However, the criterion for the least confident strategy only considers information about the most probable label. Thus, it effectively "throws away" information about the remaining label distribution. To correct for this, some researchers use a different multi-class uncertainty sampling variant called *margin sampling* [48]:

$$\phi_M(x) = P_\theta(\hat{y}_2|x) - P_\theta(\hat{y}_1|x),$$

where $\hat{y}_2$ and $\hat{y}_1$ are the second and first most probable class labels under the model, respectively. Margin sampling aims to correct for a shortcoming in least confident strategy by incorporating the posterior of the second most likely label. Instances with large margins, where $P_\theta(\hat{y}_1|x) \gg P_\theta(\hat{y}_2|x)$, are

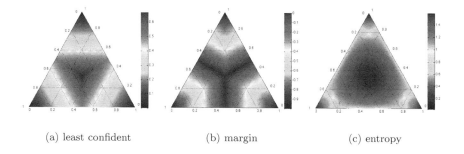

(a) least confident   (b) margin   (c) entropy

FIGURE **1.3**: Heatmaps illustrating the query behavior of common uncertainty-based utility measures in a three-label classification problem. Simplex corners indicate where one label has very high probability, with the opposite edge showing the probability range for the *other* two classes when that label has very low probability. Simplex centers represent a uniform posterior distribution, where there is most ambiguity. The most informative distributions for querying radiate outward from the centers.

thought to be easy since the classifier has little doubt in its ability to differentiate between the two most probable labels. Instances with small margins are more ambiguous, however, so knowing the true label should help the model discriminate more effectively between them in the future. However, for problems with very large label sets, the margin approach still ignores much of the output distribution for the remaining classes.

A more general uncertainty sampling strategy uses the *entropy* [56] of the posterior as an uncertainty measure:

$$\phi_H(x) = -\sum_y P_\theta(y|x) \log P_\theta(y|x),$$

where y ranges over all possible labelings. Entropy is an information-theoretic measure that represents the amount of information needed to "encode" a distribution. As such, it is often thought of as a measure of uncertainty or impurity in machine learning. In binary classification, entropy-based sampling can be reduced to the margin and least confident strategies above; in fact these are all symmetric functions centered at 0.5 in the binary case, so they will yield the same results in practice. However, the entropy-based approach generalizes to probabilistic multi-label classifiers and probabilistic models of more complex structured instances, such as sequences [53] and trees [28].

To see the differences among these approaches, Figure 1.3 presents a visualization of the different uncertainty-based utility measures for a three-label classification task. In all cases, the *most* informative instance would lie at the center of the triangle, because this represents where the posterior label distribution is most uniform (and thus least certain under the model). Similarly, the *least* informative instances are at the three corners, where one of the classes has extremely high probability (and thus little model uncertainty). The main differences lie in the rest of the probability space. For example, the entropy measure does not particularly favor instances where only one of the labels is *un*likely (i.e., along the outer side edges), because the model is fairly certain about what is *not* the true label. The least confident and margin measures, on the other hand, consider such instances to be useful if the model cannot distinguish between the remaining two classes. Empirical comparisons of these measures [32, 49, 53] have yielded mixed results, suggesting that the best strategy may be application dependent (however, all strategies still generally outperform passive baselines). Intuitively, though, entropy seems appropriate if the objective function is to minimize log-loss, while the other two (particularly margin) are more appropriate if we aim to reduce classification error, since they prefer instances that would help the model better discriminate among specific classes.

Uncertainty sampling strategies may also be employed with non-probabilistic classifiers. Similar approaches have been applied to active learning with nearest-neighbor (a.k.a. "memory-based" or "instance-based") classifiers [21, 36], by allowing each neighbor to vote on the class label of x, with the proportion of these votes representing the posterior label probability. Uncertainty sampling is also applicable to *regression* problems (i.e., learning tasks where the output variable is a continuous value rather than from a set of discrete class labels). In this setting, the learner may simply query the unlabeled instance for which the model has the highest output variance in its prediction, which corresponds to the model trying to minimize a squared-loss objective. Under a Gaussian assumption, the entropy of a random variable is a monotonic function of its variance, so this approach is very much in the same spirit as entropy-based uncertainty sampling for classification. Closed-form approximations of output variance can be computed for a variety of models, including Gaussian random fields [14] neural networks [38], and locally weighted linear regression [12]. Active learning for regression problems has a long history in the statistics literature, generally referred to as *optimal experimental design* [18]. Such approaches shy away from uncertainty sampling in lieu of more sophisticated strategies, which we will explore further in Section 1.2.4.

1.2.2   Query-by-Committee

Another common query selection framework is the *query-by-committee* (QBC) algorithm [55]. The QBC approach involves maintaining a committee $\mathcal{C} = \{\theta^{(1)}, \ldots, \theta^{(C)}\}$ of classifiers which are all induced on the current labeled set $\mathcal{L}$, but represent competing hypotheses. Each committee member is then allowed to vote on the labelings of query candidates. The utility function in this case is a measure of disagreement among the committee members, rather than the uncertainty of a single classifier.

The fundamental premise behind the QBC framework is minimizing the

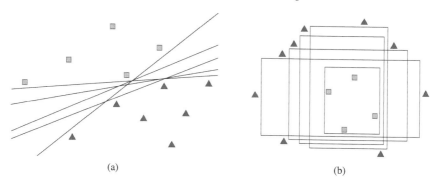

(a)   (b)

FIGURE 1.4: Version space examples for (a) linear and (b) axis-parallel box classifiers. All committee members are hypotheses that are consistent with the labeled training data (indicated by shaded polygons), but each represents a different model in the version space.

version space $\mathcal{V} \subset \Theta$, which is (as described in Section 1.1.2) a subset of the hypothesis space Θ whose classifiers are all consistent with the current labeled training data. Figure 1.4 illustrates the concept of version spaces for (a) linear functions and (b) axis-parallel box classifiers in different binary classification tasks. If we view machine learning as a search for the "best" model $\theta \in \mathcal{V}$, then our goal in active learning is to constrain the size of the version space as much as possible (so that the search can be more precise) with as few labeled instances as possible. This is exactly what QBC aims to do by querying the most controversial instances, which in turn constrain the size of the version space. In order to implement a QBC selection algorithm, we must:

i. be able to construct a committee $\mathcal{C}$ that represents or approximates different regions of the version space $\mathcal{V}$, and

ii. have some measure of disagreement among committee members.

The first task might be accomplished by sampling a committee of any two random hypotheses that are consistent with $\mathcal{L}$ [55]. For generative model classes like Naive Bayes or hidden Markov models, this can be done more generally by randomly sampling an arbitrary number of models from some posterior distribution $P(\theta|\mathcal{L})$. For example, the Normal and Dirichlet distributions over model parameters have been used [16, 39]. For other model classes, such as discriminative or non-probabilistic classifiers, standard *ensemble learning* methods (e.g., bagging and boosting) can be used to generate a committee [1, 40, 44]. There is no general agreement in the literature on the appropriate committee size, which may in fact vary by model class or application. However, even small committee sizes (e.g., two or three) have been shown to work well in practice [39, 53, 55].

For measuring the level of disagreement there are many approaches. Perhaps the most common is *vote entropy* [16]:

$$\phi_{VE}(x) = -\sum_y \frac{V(y,x)}{C} \log \frac{V(y,x)}{C},$$

where $V(y,x)$ is the number of "votes" that a label y receives from among the committee members' predictions on x, and C is the committee size. This can be thought of as a QBC generalization of entropy-based uncertainty sampling, where $P(y|x) \equiv V(y,x)/C$. This is preferable to vanilla uncertainty sampling because a single model's posterior label estimate (and thus information content) can be flawed. Vote entropy takes a Bayesian approach by integrating over several plausible hypotheses, smoothing out variance in its parameter estimates. Derivations of other information-theoretic measures like Kullback-Leibler divergence [39] and Jensen-Shannon divergence [41] have also been used to measure disagreement, as well as the other uncertainty measures discussed in Section 1.2.1, by pooling committee members' predictions to estimate class posteriors [32]. Note also that in the definition of vote entropy above, such posterior estimates are based on committee members that cast "hard" votes for their respective label predictions. They might also cast "soft" votes using their posterior label probabilities, which in turn could be weighted by an estimate of each committee member's accuracy or probability.

Aside from the QBC framework, several other query strategies attempt to minimize the version space as well. It turns out that uncertainty sampling for support vector machines (i.e., querying instances closest to the classification boundary) is a form of version space search, since the SVM objective function aims to maximize the distance between the decision boundary and the two classes. In essence, SVMs try to be at the "center" of the version space, so selecting the nearest data points should approximately bisect $\mathcal{V}$ [51, 60]. Cohn et al. [10] describe a selective sampling algorithm for a committee of two neural networks, the "most specific" and "most general" models, which lie at two extremes of the version space given the current training set $\mathcal{L}$, and query points where they disagree. Certain query synthesis algorithms [2, 31] can also be interpreted as synthesizing instances de novo that most constrain the size of the version space.

While QBC was motivated by this version space argument [55], $\mathcal{V}$ only exists if the labeled data are actually separable by the model class (e.g., if using linear discriminant functions, the data must be linearly separable and noise-free). This is clearly not always the case. Furthermore, for non-classification tasks like regression there is not really a notion of version space at all! However, there is a more general information-theoretic interpretation of QBC. Recall that we want to select a query x whose (as yet unknown) output y contains the most information about the choice of model parameters $\theta \in \Theta$ (i.e., most reduces the entropy or uncertainty about the model itself). With some abuse of notation, let $I(Y; \Theta)$ be this definition of mutual information. Consider the well-known information-theoretic identity:

$$
\begin{aligned}
I(Y; \Theta) &= H(\Theta) - \mathbb{E}_Y[H(\Theta|y)] \\
&= H(Y) - \mathbb{E}_\Theta[H(Y|\theta)],
\end{aligned}
$$

where H denotes entropy. If we assume that $H(\Theta) \propto |\mathcal{V}|$—both are measures of uncertainty about or complexity of the hypothesis search—the first equality justifies our search for queries that reduce $|\mathcal{V}|$ in expectation over possible labelings. If a proper version space does not exist, however, consider the second identity. This states that we want to query instances which are uncertain (i.e., where $H(Y)$ is high), but in such a way that there is disagreement among the competing hypotheses. If the choices of θ largely agree on y, then $\mathbb{E}_\Theta[H(Y|\theta)]$ will be very close to $H(Y)$, and the information content is deemed to be low; the more they disagree, the lower the second term is and the higher the overall information content. However, since the hypothesis space Θ can be intractably large, we use a committee $\mathcal{C} \approx \Theta$ as a subset approximation.

Under this interpretation, QBC can also be employed in regression settings, i.e., by measuring disagreement as the variance among the committee members' predictions on continuous output variables [7]. By integrating over a set of hypotheses and identifying queries that lie in controversial regions of the instance space, the learner attempts to collect data that reduces variance over both the output predictions and the parameters of the model itself (as opposed to uncertainty sampling, which focuses only on the output variance of a single hypothesis).

1.2.3 Expected Error Reduction

The utility measures we have discussed so far do not directly optimize the objective function against which the learner will ultimately be evaluated, such as the error on future test instances. Although uncertainty sampling and QBC have been effective for many tasks, they may still underperform by querying outliers, or by expending labeling effort to eliminate areas of the hypothesis space that have little to no effect on the error rate.

An alternative, decision-theoretic approach is *expected error reduction*, which aims to measure how much a labeled query is likely to improve the error rate. The idea is to estimate the expected future error of a model after the query has been labeled and added to the training set: $\mathcal{L} \cup \langle x, y \rangle$. We do not know the true label y in advance, but we can instead calculate the error as an expectation over the possible labelings under the current model θ. To estimate the error rate, we can use the unlabeled instances in $\mathcal{U}$ as a sort of validation set, under the usually reasonable assumption that it is representative of the test distribution. Thus, an instance which minimizes the expected future error (sometimes called *risk*) is the query with the highest utility.

One such approach is to optimize for the expected $0/1$-loss over $\mathcal{U}$:

$$\phi_{0/1}(x) = -\sum_y P_\theta(y|x) \left(\sum_{u=1}^{U} 1 - P_{\theta^{+\langle x,y \rangle}}(\hat{y}|x^{(u)}) \right),$$

where $\theta^{+\langle x,y \rangle}$ refers to the the new model after it has been retrained with the tuple $\langle x, y \rangle$ added to $\mathcal{L}$. Recall that the utility function ϕ is meant to be maximized, so the leading minus sign in the equation above makes it equivalent to minimizing the expected $0/1$-loss over $\mathcal{U}$. This utility measure corresponds to selecting the instance that will reduce the expected total number of incorrect predictions or, conversely, increase the number of correct predictions. A different approach is to optimize for the expected log-loss:

$$\phi_{\log}(x) = -\sum_y P_\theta(y|x) \left(-\sum_{u=1}^{U} \sum_{y'} P_{\theta^{+\langle x,y \rangle}}(y'|x^{(u)}) \log P_{\theta^{+\langle x,y \rangle}}(y'|x^{(u)}) \right),$$

which is equivalent to reducing the expected entropy over $\mathcal{U}$. Another interpretation of this utility measure is to maximize the expected log-likelihood of the unlabeled data under the model (by allowing the two leading minus signs to cancel out).

This framework has been studied in several classification problems [24, 47, 68] and has the advantage of being near-optimal in terms of error reduction. All that is required is an appropriate error function and a way to estimate posterior label probabilities, and strategies in this framework have been used with a variety of models including Naive Bayes [47], Gaussian random fields [68], logistic regression [24], and support vector machines [43]. In theory, the general approach can be employed not only to optimize loss or likelihood functions, but also to try and optimize any performance measure of interest, such as precision, recall, F-measure, or area under the ROC curve.

In most cases, unfortunately, expected error reduction is also the most computationally expensive active learning framework. Not only does it require estimating the expected future error over $\mathcal{U}$ for each query, but a new model must be incrementally retrained for each possible query labeling, which in turn iterates over the entire pool. This leads to a drastic increase in run-time complexity. For non-parametric model classes, the incremental training procedure is efficient [68], making this approach fairly practical.[1] For many other model classes, this is not the case. For example, a binary logistic regression model would require $O(ULG)$ time complexity simply to choose the next query, where U is the size of the unlabeled pool $\mathcal{U}$, L is the size of the current training set $\mathcal{L}$, and G is the number of gradient computations required by the optimization procedure until convergence. A classification task with three or more labels using a maximum entropy classifier [5] would require $O(M^2ULG)$

---

[1] The bottleneck in non-parametric models generally is not retraining, but inference.

time complexity, where M is the number of class labels. For a sequence labeling task using a Markov model like linear-chain conditional random fields [57], the complexity explodes to $O(TM^{T+2}ULG)$, where T is the length of an input sequence. Because of this, the applications of the expected error reduction framework have mostly only considered simple binary classification tasks. Moreover, because the approach is often still impractical, researchers must resort to Monte Carlo sampling from the pool to reduce the U term in the previous analysis [47], or use approximate training techniques to reduce the G term [24]. It is also possible that parallelized, distributed computing can help alleviate these problems to a certain extent.

1.2.4 Variance Reduction

Minimizing the expectation of a loss function directly can be expensive, and in general cannot be done in closed form. However, we can still reduce generalization error *indirectly* by minimizing output variance, which sometimes does have a closed-form solution. Consider a regression problem, where the learning objective is to minimize standard error (i.e., squared loss). We can take advantage of the fact that a learner's expected future error can be decomposed in the following way [22]:

$$\mathbb{E}_T\left[(\hat{y}-y)^2|x\right] = \mathbb{E}\left[(y-\mathbb{E}[y|x])^2\right]$$
$$+ (\mathbb{E}_{\mathcal{L}}[\hat{y}] - \mathbb{E}[y|x])^2$$
$$+ \mathbb{E}_{\mathcal{L}}\left[(\hat{y}-\mathbb{E}_{\mathcal{L}}[\hat{y}])^2\right],$$

where $\mathbb{E}_{\mathcal{L}}[\cdot]$ is an expectation over the labeled set $\mathcal{L}$, $\mathbb{E}[\cdot]$ is an expectation over the conditional density $P(y|x)$, and $\mathbb{E}_T$ is an expectation over both. Here also $\hat{y}$ is shorthand for the model's predicted output for a given instance x, while y indicates the true label for that instance.

The first term on the right-hand side of this equation is *noise*, i.e., the variance of the true label y given only x, which does not depend on the model or training data. Such noise may result from stochastic effects of the method used to obtain the labels, for example, or because the feature representation is inadequate. The second term is the *bias*, which represents the error due to the model class itself, e.g., if a linear model is used to learn a function that is only approximately linear. This component of the overall error is invariant given a fixed model class. The third term is the model's *variance*, which is the remaining component of the learner's squared loss with respect to the target function. Minimizing the variance, then, is guaranteed to minimize the future generalization error of the model (since the learner itself can do nothing about the noise or bias components).

This general approach—querying data instances whose labeling is expected to minimize output variance—is inspired by the area of statistics known as *optimal experimental design*, or OED [8, 18]. For example, consider the approximation of the output variance $\sigma_{\hat{y}}^2$ for artificial neural networks [38]:

$$\sigma_{\hat{y}}^2(x) \approx \left[\frac{\partial \hat{y}}{\partial \theta}\right]^{\mathsf{T}} \left[\frac{\partial^2}{\partial \theta^2} S_\theta(\mathcal{L})\right]^{-1} \left[\frac{\partial \hat{y}}{\partial \theta}\right] \approx \nabla x^{\mathsf{T}} F^{-1} \nabla x,$$

where $S_\theta(\mathcal{L})$ is the squared error of the current model θ on the training set $\mathcal{L}$. In the equation above, the first and last terms are computed using the gradient of the model's predicted output with respect to model parameters, written in shorthand (on the right) as ∇x. The middle term is the inverse of a covariance matrix representing a second-order expansion around the objective function S with respect to θ, written in shorthand as F. This is known as the *Fisher information matrix* [50], and we will discuss this more in a bit.

Suffice it to say that if we can derive an expression for $\langle \tilde{\sigma}_{\hat{y}}^2 \rangle^{+x}$, the estimated mean output variance across the input distribution after the neural network has been retrained on the query x and its label, then a *variance reduction* query selection strategy is simply:

$$\phi_{VR}(x) = -\langle \tilde{\sigma}_{\hat{y}}^2 \rangle^{+x},$$

where the leading minus sign is again simply to make ϕ a maximizing utility measure. For certain model classes, this variance can be estimated efficiently in closed form [9, 12, 23], although details are model specific and omitted here for the sake of generality. This means, however, that the explicit model retraining required for the error reduction framework in Section 1.2.3 is no longer necessary for variance reduction active learning strategies. Furthermore, since the objective is usually a smooth function that is differentiable with respect to input features, gradient methods can be used to search for the best query in cases where de novo synthesis is reasonable.

A key ingredient of OED approaches such as this is Fisher information, which is sometimes written $I(\theta)$ to make its relationship with model parameters explicit. Formally, Fisher information is the variance of the *score*, which is the partial derivative of the log-likelihood function with respect to parameters:

$$I(\theta) = n \int_x P(x) \int_y P_\theta(y|x) \frac{\partial^2}{\partial \theta^2} \log P_\theta(y|x),$$

where there are n independent samples drawn from the input distribution. This measure is convenient because its inverse sets a lower bound on the variance of the model's parameter estimates; this result is known as the Cramér-Rao inequality [13]. In other words, to minimize the variance over its parameter estimates, an active learner should select data that maximize its Fisher information (or minimizes the inverse thereof). When there is only one parameter in the model, this strategy is straightforward. But for models of K parameters, Fisher information takes the form of a $K \times K$ covariance matrix (denoted by F), and deciding on a scalar value to optimize is less clear. In the OED literature, there are three main types of optimal designs in such cases:

- *A-optimality* minimizes the *trace* of the inverse information matrix,

- *D-optimality* minimizes the *determinant* of the inverse matrix, and

- *E-optimality* minimizes the maximum *eigenvalue* of the inverse matrix.

E-optimality does not correspond to an obvious utility function, and is not often used in the machine learning literature (though there are some exceptions [19]). *D*-optimality, it turns out, is related to minimizing the expected posterior entropy [8]. Since the determinant is often thought of as a measure of volume, the *D*-optimal design criterion essentially aims to minimize the volume of the (noisy) version space, with boundaries estimated via entropy, which makes it analogous to the QBC framework (Section 1.2.2).

A-optimal designs are considerably more popular, and aim to reduce the *average* variance of parameter estimates by focusing on values along the diagonal of the information matrix. A common variant of *A*-optimal design is to minimize $\text{tr}(AF^{-1})$—the trace of the product of A and the inverse of the information matrix F—where A is a square, symmetric "reference" matrix. As a special case, consider a matrix of rank one: $A = \mathbf{c}\mathbf{c}^\mathsf{T}$, where $\mathbf{c}$ is some vector of length K (i.e., the same length as the model's parameter vector). In this case we have $\text{tr}(AF^{-1}) = \mathbf{c}^\mathsf{T}F^{-1}\mathbf{c}$, and minimizing this value is sometimes called *c*-optimality. Note that, if we let $\mathbf{c} = \nabla x$, this criterion results in the equation for output variance $\sigma_{\hat{y}}^2(x)$ in neural networks defined earlier in this section. Minimizing this variance measure can be achieved by simply querying on instance x, so this form of *c*-optimal criterion can be viewed as a formalism for uncertainty sampling (Section 1.2.1): the most informative instance is the one for which the model has the highest variance in its prediction.

Recall that we are interested in reducing variance across the input distribution (not merely for a single point in the instance space), thus the A matrix should encode the whole instance space, not a single point. Such solutions have been derived for regression with neural networks [38], as well as classification with logistic regression [49, 66]. The basic idea is this: consider letting the reference matrix $A = I_{\mathcal{U}}(\theta)$, i.e., the Fisher information of the unlabeled pool of instances $\mathcal{U}$, and letting $F = I_x(\theta)$, i.e., the Fisher information of some query instance x. Using *A*-optimal design, we can derive a utility measure for active learning called the *Fisher information ratio* [66]:

$$\phi_{FIR} = -\text{tr}\left(I_{\mathcal{U}}(\theta)I_x(\theta)^{-1}\right).$$

Here once again the leading minus sign is so that ϕ acts as a maximizer. The equation above provides us with a ratio given by the inner product of the two matrices, which can be interpreted as the model's output variance across the input distribution (approximated by $\mathcal{U}$) that is not accounted for by x. Querying the instance which maximizes this utility function is analogous to minimizing the future output variance once x has been labeled, thus indirectly reducing generalization error. The advantage here over error reduction (Section 1.2.3) is that the model need not be retrained: the information matrices give us an approximation of output variance that simulates retraining. This general framework has been applied to classification with logistic regression [27, 49, 66] and has even been generalized to more complex sequence labeling problems with exponential models like conditional random fields [53].

There are some practical disadvantages to these variance-reduction methods, however, in terms of computational complexity. Estimating output variance requires inverting a $K \times K$ matrix for each new instance, where K is the number of parameters in the model, resulting in a time complexity of $O(UK^3)$, where U is the size of the query pool $\mathcal{U}$. This quickly becomes intractable for large K, which is a common occurrence in, say, natural language processing tasks. One can alleviate these problems by using principal component analysis to reduce the dimensionality of the parameter space [27], or by approximating the matrix with its diagonal vector [53], which can be inverted in only $O(K)$ time. However, these methods are still empirically much slower than simple utility measures like uncertainty sampling or QBC.

1.2.5   Density-Weighted Methods

A motivation for the estimated error and variance reduction frameworks is that they attempt to reduce error over the entire input distribution, rather than individual instances. As a result, they are less prone to querying outliers than simpler query strategies like uncertainty sampling and QBC. Figure 1.5 illustrates this problem for a binary linear classifier using uncertainty sampling. The least certain instance lies on the classification boundary, but is not "representative" of other instances in the distribution, so knowing its label is unlikely to improve accuracy on the data as a whole. QBC may exhibit similar behavior, by spending time querying possible outliers simply because they are controversial. By utilizing the unlabeled pool $\mathcal{U}$ when estimating future errors and output variances, the estimated error and variance reduction strategies implicitly avoid these problems. The drawback is usually a significant computational expense that may not be worth the potential gains. Fortunately, we can also overcome these problems by modeling the input distribution explicitly during query selection, which can be significantly faster.

One such example is the *information density* framework, which is a general density-weighting technique. The main idea is that informative instances should not only be those with high information content, but also those which are "representative" of the underlying distribution (i.e., inhabit dense regions of the input space). An example utility measure is:

$$\phi_{ID}(x) = \phi_A(x) \times \left(\frac{1}{U} \sum_{u=1}^{U} \text{sim}(x, x^{(u)}) \right)^{\beta}.$$

Here, $\phi_A(x)$ represents the utility of x according to some "base" query strategy A, such as an uncertainty sampling or QBC approach. The second term weights the informativeness of x by its average similarity to all other instances

FIGURE 1.5: An illustration of when uncertainty sampling can be a poor strategy for classification. Shaded polygons represent labeled instances in $\mathcal{L}$, and circles represent unlabeled instances in $\mathcal{U}$. Since A is on the decision boundary, it would be queried as the most uncertain. However, querying B is likely to result in more information about the data distribution as a whole.

in the input distribution (as approximated by $\mathcal{U}$), subject to a parameter β that controls the relative importance of the density term. A variant of this might first use a clustering algorithm on $\mathcal{U}$ and then compute average similarity to instances in the same cluster, which may be faster.

This and similar approaches have been employed in a variety of machine learning applications [21, 39, 45, 53, 62]. Results in these studies are reported to be superior to methods that do not consider density or representativeness in their utility measures. Furthermore, if the density terms are pre-computed and cached for efficient lookup later, the time required to select the next query is essentially no different than the base informativeness measure (e.g., uncertainty sampling) [53]. This is advantageous for conducting active learning interactively with oracles in real time.

1.3 A Unified View

To put these various query selection frameworks in perspective, let us consider a single, well-motivated utility measure ϕ_ℓ with the objective of maximizing data likelihood. We can show that all the query frameworks we have discussed here contain a popular utility function that approximates this measure. Under the assumptions that $\mathcal{U}$ is a good approximation of the input distribution $P(X)$, and that the optimal sequence of queries is obtained by greedily selecting queries that maximize ϕ_ℓ at each iteration of the active learning cycle, then our likelihood-based objective function is:

$$\phi_\ell(x) = \sum_{u=1}^{U} \log P_{\theta^{+\langle x,y \rangle}}\left(y^{(u)} | x^{(u)}\right),$$

where again $\theta^{+\langle x,y \rangle}$ denotes a new model after the query and its associated label have been added to $\mathcal{L}$. Note that we are using the log-likelihood—a monotonic function of likelihood—as a common mathematical convenience.

Unfortunately, as we have already seen, the true label y is not known for either the query x, nor is the label $y^{(u)}$ known for the pool instances $x^{(u)} \in \mathcal{U}$. If we assume that the current model's predictions for these values are sufficiently accurate, then we can compute both as expectations under the corresponding models:

$$\phi_\ell(x) \approx \sum_y P_\theta(y|x) \left(\sum_{u=1}^{U} \sum_{y'} P_{\theta+\langle x,y \rangle}(y'|x^{(u)}) \log P_{\theta+\langle x,y \rangle}(y'|x^{(u)}) \right),$$

which is equivalent to the $\phi_{\log}$ utility measure in the error-reduction framework from Section 1.2.3. If we make a slightly different approximation, by computing an expectation for the label of query x, but using only the most probable label for $x^{(u)}$, then we arrive at the $\phi_{0/1}$ utility measure from the same section. Maximizing the equation above is equivalent to minimizing the expected total future entropy. Since the entropy of a random variable is a monotonic function of its variance, the ϕ_{VR} and ϕ_{FIR} utility measures in the variance reduction framework of Section 1.2.4 are also approximations to likelihood-based objective in cases where the proper assumptions hold.

As noted earlier, utility measures based on reducing error or variance are quite computationally expensive in general. If we take a different view, though, we can derive an equivalent objective function which aims to maximize the *information gain* of the query x, and then simplify things further. By using the shorthand $H_\theta(Y|x)$ to denote the conditional entropy of the label for x under the model θ, we can rewrite this utility measure as:

$$\phi_\ell(x) \approx \sum_{u=1}^{U} H_\theta(Y|x^{(u)}) - \sum_{u=1}^{U} \sum_y P_\theta(y|x) H_{\theta+\langle x,y \rangle}(Y|x^{(u)}).$$

The left term is the total label entropy of $\mathcal{U}$ under the current θ, which is fixed and constant for all queries. The right term is the expected future entropy if x were to be labeled and added to $\mathcal{L}$. Therefore, if we drop the first term and do some rearranging we can arrive at the same approximation $\phi_{\log}$. Clearly this formulation is not any more tractable, though; it has the same computational complexity issues as before. However, if we make the simplifying assumption that $H_\theta(Y|x) \approx H_\theta(Y|x^{(u)})$, or that x is fairly representative of each $x^{(u)} \in \mathcal{U}$, then we can drop the sums from the equation and consider only the entropies of the query instance x. This leaves us with:

$$\phi_\ell(x) \approx H_\theta(Y|x) - \sum_y P_\theta(y|x) H_{\theta+\langle x,y \rangle}(Y|x).$$

Furthermore, we can assume the expected future entropy $H_{\theta+\langle x,y \rangle}(Y|x)$ to be zero since the oracle will provide its true label, so we can also drop the second term which leaves only $H_\theta(Y|x)$. This is exactly the ϕ_H utility measure from the uncertainty sampling framework in Section 1.2.1. Entropy-based uncertainty sampling, then, is an approximation for $\phi_{\log}$ and therefore ϕ_ℓ as well.

By a similar proof we can show that the least confident utility measure ϕ_{LC} makes the corresponding assumptions to approximate the $\phi_{0/1}$ utility measure from the same section.

Under this interpretation, the ϕ_{VE} function from the QBC framework in Section 1.2.2 is very similar to ϕ_H. Namely, it makes the assumptions that x is representative of $\mathcal{U}$ and that the expected future vote entropy of the query point is zero. The crucial difference is that QBC methods replace the point estimate θ with a distribution over possible hypotheses $\theta \in \mathcal{C}$, approximating the version space with a committee. This Bayesian flavor helps mitigate problems caused by the first assumption in this section: that prediction under the model θ is a good estimate of the true label distribution.

Finally, let us consider how density-weighted methods make a similar approximation, but mitigate the overly strong assumption that x is sufficiently representative of the input distribution. By rewriting the equation for information gain above, we get:

$$\phi_\ell(x) \approx \sum_{u=1}^{U} \left(H_\theta(Y|x^{(u)}) - \sum_{y} P_\theta(y|x) H_{\theta + \langle x, y \rangle}(Y|x^{(u)}) \right).$$

The expression inside the summand represents the expected reduction in entropy for each instance in the pool if x is the selected query. Let us hold to the assumption that the expected future entropy of x is zero since the oracle provides the label, so the reduction in entropy is simply given by $H_\theta(Y|x)$. However, let us make a less stringent assumption about the rest of the input distribution: the reduction in entropy for all other $x^{(u)} \in \mathcal{U}$ is proportional to its similarity with x. By this notion, we can substitute the parenthetical above with $H_\theta(Y|x) \times \text{sim}(x, x^{(u)})$:

$$\phi_\ell(x) \approx \sum_{u=1}^{U} \left(H_\theta(Y|x) \times \text{sim}(x, x^{(u)}) \right).$$

With some trivial rearranging of terms, this is precisely the information density measure ϕ_{ID} from Section 1.2.5, if we use ϕ_H as the base utility measure, set $\beta = 1$, and ignore the constant $\frac{1}{U}$. Hence, ϕ_{ID} can also be interpreted as an approximation to $\phi_{\log}$, and thus our ideal likelihood-based measure ϕ_ℓ.

1.4 Summary and Outlook

The main points of this chapter include:

- Active learning is a useful tool for reducing label acquisition costs in machine learning applications. This is accomplished by allowing the learner to interact with an *oracle* (i.e., labeling source) by posing *queries* in the form of unlabeled data to be annotated for training. Usually, this is done in an iterative loop called the active learning cycle.

- There are three basic problem settings in which queries can be posed. The first scenario is *query synthesis*, in which the learning can generate a query de novo which optimizes some utility function ϕ. In cases where generating instances from scratch is unreasonable or intractable, *stream-based selective sampling* draws unlabeled data one at a time from a real underlying data distribution, and the learner decides whether to query or discard each example in sequence. For the common scenario in which a large number of instances can be obtained at once, *pool-based sampling* assumes a pool $\mathcal{U}$ which can be inspected, and the instance with the highest utility is queried each iteration.

- Several query strategy frameworks exist, each containing a variety of utility measures and exhibiting different properties. *Uncertainty sampling* is the simplest and often most tractable framework, based on the intuition that the learner would get the most utility out of instances it cannot confidently label. *Query-by-committee* takes a different view, by attempting to query instances that will most constrain the version space. The *expected error reduction* framework explicitly optimizes an evaluation metric of interest (such as the estimated future error rate on the unlabeled data), often at great computational expense. *Variance reduction* strategies, which come from statistical theories of optimal experimental design, try to accomplish this task indirectly by reducing the output variance of its predictions. *Density-weighted methods* are intuitively and computationally simpler, avoiding queries that are outliers by combining a density measure with efficient utility measures.

- With a few basic assumptions, the common utility measures from all query frameworks can be viewed as approximations to an ideal (but unachievable) strategy which maximizes data likelihood under the model.

Active learning is often also combined with other cost-saving machine learning strategies (e.g., semi-supervised learning, multiple-instance learning, and other methods discussed elsewhere in this book) to even further reduce data acquisition and annotation costs. Note, however, that the discussion of active learning in this chapter—indeed, in most of the active learning literature— has made several basic assumptions that do not always hold in practice.

For example, we often assume that queries are made one at a time, so that the classifier is able to take advantage of each newly labeled data point incrementally. Consider a machine learning system assisting in the design and interpretation of high-throughput biology experiments, where hundreds or thousands of data points can be collected simultaneously. In this "batch" active learning setting, a myopic approach might simply rank the candidate queries from $\mathcal{U}$ by their utility, and select the most informative instances starting at the top until the query budget is exhausted. However, a non-myopic approach would consider the information content of the batch *as a whole*, incorporating diversity into the query set to ensure that they are not only informative, but also non-redundant [6, 25, 27].

Another often-violated assumption is that all query options are equally costly. For example, when labeling audio segments for a speech recognition task, if one is twice as long as the other you might expect the first to be twice as expensive to label. To deal with this situation well, it may be necessary to incorporate variable notions of cost into the active learning strategy. Sometimes these costs are known beforehand [29, 31], but sometimes they are not and the learner must try to predict them [54]. There may also be competing notions of cost, such as those incurred by misclassification vs. labeling. At what point is the cost of obtaining more training data greater than the savings that would result from the learner's improvement?

New work has begun to address these and other practical issues, although a detailed exposition is beyond the scope of this introductory chapter. The interested reader should consult the literature survey by Settles [52] and http://active-learning.net for a periodically updated review and collection of resources on these and other advanced topics in active learning.

References

[1] N. Abe and H. Mamitsuka. Query learning strategies using boosting and bagging. In *Proceedings of the International Conference on Machine Learning (ICML)*, pages 1–9. Morgan Kaufmann, 1998.

[2] D. Angluin. Queries and concept learning. *Machine Learning*, 2:319–342, 1988.

[3] M.F. Balcan, S. Hanneke, and J. Wortman. The true sample complexity of active learning. In *Proceedings of the Conference on Learning Theory (COLT)*, pages 45–56. Springer, 2008.

[4] E. Baum. Neural net algorithms that learn in polynomial time from examples and queries. *IEEE Transactions on Neural Networks*, 2(1), 1991.

[5] A.L. Berger, V.J. Della Pietra, and S.A. Della Pietra. A maximum entropy approach to natural language processing. *Computational Linguistics*, 22(1):39–71, 1996.

[6] K. Brinker. Incorporating diversity in active learning with support vector machines. In *Proceedings of the International Conference on Machine Learning (ICML)*, pages 59–66. AAAI Press, 2003.

[7] R. Burbidge, J.J. Rowland, and R.D. King. Active learning for regression based on query by committee. In *Proceedings of Intelligent Data Engineering and Automated Learning (IDEAL)*, pages 209–218. Springer, 2007.

[8] K. Chaloner and I. Verdinelli. Bayesian experimental design: A review. *Statistical Science*, 10(3):237–304, 1995.

[9] D. Cohn. Neural network exploration using optimal experiment design. In *Advances in Neural Information Processing Systems (NIPS)*, volume 6, pages 679–686. Morgan Kaufmann, 1994.

[10] D. Cohn, L. Atlas, and R. Ladner. Improving generalization with active learning. *Machine Learning*, 15(2):201–221, 1994.

[11] D. Cohn, L. Atlas, R. Ladner, M. El-Sharkawi, R. Marks II, M. Aggoune, and D. Park. Training connectionist networks with queries and selective sampling. In *Advances in Neural Information Processing Systems (NIPS)*. Morgan Kaufmann, 1990.

[12] D. Cohn, Z. Ghahramani, and M.I. Jordan. Active learning with statistical models. *Journal of Artificial Intelligence Research*, 4:129–145, 1996.

[13] T.M. Cover and J.A. Thomas. *Elements of Information Theory*. Wiley, 2006.

[14] N. Cressie. *Statistics for Spatial Data*. Wiley, 1991.

[15] A. Culotta and A. McCallum. Reducing labeling effort for stuctured prediction tasks. In *Proceedings of the National Conference on Artificial Intelligence (AAAI)*, pages 746–751. AAAI Press, 2005.

[16] I. Dagan and S. Engelson. Committee-based sampling for training probabilistic classifiers. In *Proceedings of the International Conference on Machine Learning (ICML)*, pages 150–157. Morgan Kaufmann, 1995.

[17] S. Danziger, J. Zeng, Y. Wang, R. Brachmann, and R. Lathrop. Choosing where to look next in a mutation sequence space: Active learning of informative p53 cancer rescue mutants. *Bioinformatics*, 23(13):i104–i114, 2007.

[18] V. Federov. *Theory of Optimal Experiments*. Academic Press, 1972.

[19] P. Flaherty, M. Jordan, and A. Arkin. Robust design of biological experiments. In *Advances in Neural Information Processing Systems (NIPS)*, volume 18, pages 363–370. MIT Press, 2006.

[20] Y. Freund, H.S. Seung, E. Shamir, and N. Tishby. Selective samping using the query by committee algorithm. *Machine Learning*, 28:133–168, 1997.

[21] A. Fujii, T. Tokunaga, K. Inui, and H. Tanaka. Selective sampling for example-based word sense disambiguation. *Computational Linguistics*, 24(4):573–597, 1998.

[22] S. Geman, E. Bienenstock, and R. Doursat. Neural networks and the bias/variance dilemma. *Neural Computation*, 4:1–58, 1992.

[23] C. Guestrin, A. Krause, and A.P. Singh. Near-optimal sensor placements in Gaussian processes. In *Proceedings of the International Conference on Machine Learning (ICML)*, pages 265–272. ACM Press, 2005.

[24] Y. Guo and R. Greiner. Optimistic active learning using mutual information. In *Proceedings of International Joint Conference on Artificial Intelligence (IJCAI)*, pages 823–829. AAAI Press, 2007.

[25] Y. Guo and D. Schuurmans. Discriminative batch mode active learning. In *Advances in Neural Information Processing Systems (NIPS)*, number 20, pages 593–600. MIT Press, 2008.

[26] A. Hauptmann, W. Lin, R. Yan, J. Yang, and M.Y. Chen. Extreme video retrieval: joint maximization of human and computer performance. In *Proceedings of the ACM Workshop on Multimedia Image Retrieval*, pages 385–394. ACM Press, 2006.

[27] S.C.H. Hoi, R. Jin, and M.R. Lyu. Large-scale text categorization by batch mode active learning. In *Proceedings of the International Conference on the World Wide Web*, pages 633–642. ACM Press, 2006.

[28] R. Hwa. Sample selection for statistical parsing. *Computational Linguistics*, 30(3):73–77, 2004.

[29] A. Kapoor, E. Horvitz, and S. Basu. Selective supervision: Guiding supervised learning with decision-theoretic active learning. In *Proceedings of International Joint Conference on Artificial Intelligence (IJCAI)*, pages 877–882. AAAI Press, 2007.

[30] R.D. King, J. Rowland, S.G. Oliver, M. Young, W. Aubrey, E. Byrne, M. Liakata, M. Markham, P. Pir, L.N. Soldatova, A. Sparkes, K.E. Whelan, and A. Clare. The automation of science. *Science*, 324(5923):85–89, 2009.

[31] R.D. King, K.E. Whelan, F.M. Jones, P.G. Reiser, C.H. Bryant, S.H. Muggleton, D.B. Kell, and S.G. Oliver. Functional genomic hypothesis generation and experimentation by a robot scientist. *Nature*, 427(6971):247–52, 2004.

[32] C. Körner and S. Wrobel. Multi-class ensemble-based active learning. In *Proceedings of the European Conference on Machine Learning (ECML)*, pages 687–694. Springer, 2006.

[33] V. Krishnamurthy. Algorithms for optimal scheduling and management of hidden Markov model sensors. *IEEE Transactions on Signal Processing*, 50(6):1382–1397, 2002.

[34] K. Lang and E. Baum. Query learning can work poorly when a human oracle is used. In *Proceedings of the IEEE International Joint Conference on Neural Networks*, pages 335–340. IEEE Press, 1992.

[35] D. Lewis and W. Gale. A sequential algorithm for training text classifiers. In *Proceedings of the ACM SIGIR Conference on Research and Development in Information Retrieval*, pages 3–12. ACM/Springer, 1994.

[36] M. Lindenbaum, S. Markovitch, and D. Rusakov. Selective sampling for nearest neighbor classifiers. *Machine Learning*, 54(2):125–152, 2004.

[37] Y. Liu. Active learning with support vector machine applied to gene expression data for cancer classification. *Journal of Chemical Information and Computer Sciences*, 44:1936–1941, 2004.

[38] D. MacKay. Information-based objective functions for active data selection. *Neural Computation*, 4(4):590–604, 1992.

[39] A. McCallum and K. Nigam. Employing EM in pool-based active learning for text classification. In *Proceedings of the International Conference on Machine Learning (ICML)*, pages 359–367. Morgan Kaufmann, 1998.

[40] P. Melville and R. Mooney. Diverse ensembles for active learning. In *Proceedings of the International Conference on Machine Learning (ICML)*, pages 584–591. Morgan Kaufmann, 2004.

[41] P. Melville, S.M. Yang, M. Saar-Tsechansky, and R. Mooney. Active learning for probability estimation using Jensen-Shannon divergence. In *Proceedings of the European Conference on Machine Learning (ECML)*, pages 268–279. Springer, 2005.

[42] T. Mitchell. Generalization as search. *Artificial Intelligence*, 18:203–226, 1982.

[43] R. Moskovitch, N. Nissim, D. Stopel, C. Feher, R. Englert, and Y. Elovici. Improving the detection of unknown computer worms activity using active learning. In *Proceedings of the German Conference on AI*, pages 489–493. Springer, 2007.

[44] I. Muslea, S. Minton, and C.A. Knoblock. Selective sampling with redundant views. In *Proceedings of the National Conference on Artificial Intelligence (AAAI)*, pages 621–626. AAAI Press, 2000.

[45] H.T. Nguyen and A. Smeulders. Active learning using pre-clustering. In *Proceedings of the International Conference on Machine Learning (ICML)*, pages 79–86. ACM Press, 2004.

[46] R. Nowak. The geometry of generalized binary search. Department of electrical and computer engineering, University of Wisconsin–Madison, 2009.

[47] N. Roy and A. McCallum. Toward optimal active learning through sampling estimation of error reduction. In *Proceedings of the International Conference on Machine Learning (ICML)*, pages 441–448. Morgan Kaufmann, 2001.

[48] T. Scheffer, C. Decomain, and S. Wrobel. Active hidden Markov models for information extraction. In *Proceedings of the International Conference on Advances in Intelligent Data Analysis (CAIDA)*, pages 309–318. Springer-Verlag, 2001.

[49] A.I. Schein and L.H. Ungar. Active learning for logistic regression: An evaluation. *Machine Learning*, 68(3):235–265, 2007.

[50] M.J. Schervish. *Theory of Statistics*. Springer, 1995.

[51] G. Schohn and D. Cohn. Less is more: Active learning with support vector machines. In *Proceedings of the International Conference on Machine Learning (ICML)*, pages 839–846. Morgan Kaufmann, 2000.

[52] B. Settles. Active learning literature survey. Computer Sciences Technical Report 1648, University of Wisconsin–Madison, 2009.

[53] B. Settles and M. Craven. An analysis of active learning strategies for sequence labeling tasks. In *Proceedings of the Conference on Empirical Methods in Natural Language Processing (EMNLP)*, pages 1069–1078. ACL Press, 2008.

[54] B. Settles, M. Craven, and L. Friedland. Active learning with real annotation costs. In *Proceedings of the NIPS Workshop on Cost-Sensitive Learning*, pages 1–10, 2008.

[55] H.S. Seung, M. Opper, and H. Sompolinsky. Query by committee. In *Proceedings of the ACM Workshop on Computational Learning Theory*, pages 287–294, 1992.

[56] C.E. Shannon. A mathematical theory of communication. *Bell System Technical Journal*, 27:379–423, 623–656, 1948.

[57] C. Sutton and A. McCallum. An introduction to conditional random fields for relational learning. In L. Getoor and B. Taskar, editors, *Introduction to Statistical Relational Learning*. MIT Press, 2006.

[58] C.A. Thompson, M.E. Califf, and R.J. Mooney. Active learning for natural language parsing and information extraction. In *Proceedings of the International Conference on Machine Learning (ICML)*, pages 406–414. Morgan Kaufmann, 1999.

[59] S. Tong and E. Chang. Support vector machine active learning for image retrieval. In *Proceedings of the ACM International Conference on Multimedia*, pages 107–118. ACM Press, 2001.

[60] S. Tong and D. Koller. Support vector machine active learning with applications to text classification. In *Proceedings of the International Conference on Machine Learning (ICML)*, pages 999–1006. Morgan Kaufmann, 2000.

[61] G. Tür, D. Hakkani-Tür, and R.E. Schapire. Combining active and semi-supervised learning for spoken language understanding. *Speech Communication*, 45(2):171–186, 2005.

[62] Z. Xu, R. Akella, and Y. Zhang. Incorporating diversity and density in active learning for relevance feedback. In *Proceedings of the European Conference on IR Research (ECIR)*, pages 246–257. Springer-Verlag, 2007.

[63] R. Yan, J. Yang, and A. Hauptmann. Automatically labeling video data using multi-class active learning. In *Proceedings of the International Conference on Computer Vision*, pages 516–523. IEEE Press, 2003.

[64] H. Yu. SVM selective sampling for ranking with application to data retrieval. In *Proceedings of the International Conference on Knowledge Discovery and Data Mining (KDD)*, pages 354–363. ACM Press, 2005.

[65] C. Zhang and T. Chen. An active learning framework for content based information retrieval. *IEEE Transactions on Multimedia*, 4(2):260–268, 2002.

[66] T. Zhang and F.J. Oles. A probability analysis on the value of unlabeled data for classification problems. In *Proceedings of the International Conference on Machine Learning (ICML)*, pages 1191–1198. Morgan Kaufmann, 2000.

[67] X. Zhu and A. Goldberg. *Introduction to Semi-Supervised Learning*. Synthesis Lectures on Artificial Intelligence and Machine Learning. Morgan & Claypool, 2009.

[68] X. Zhu, J. Lafferty, and Z. Ghahramani. Combining active learning and semi-supervised learning using Gaussian fields and harmonic functions. In *Proceedings of the ICML Workshop on the Continuum from Labeled to Unlabeled Data*, pages 58–65, 2003.

Chapter 2

Semi-Supervised Learning: Some Recent Advances

Xueyuan Zhou

Department of Computer Science, University of Chicago, Chicago, Illinois

Ankan Saha

Department of Computer Science, University of Chicago, Chicago, Illinois

Vikas Sindhwani

IBM T. J. Watson Research Center, Yorktown Heights, New York

2.1 Introduction

Let us begin by recalling the familiar supervised learning framework. A large number of raw data objects, $\{x_i\}_{i=1}^n$, are typically collected by an automated process, such as a crawler in a web-page classification setting, a camera in video surveillance applications, or a microphone recorder for speech recognition problems. Given an example x, we assume that there is an unknown true conditional distribution $P(y|x)$ over an output space $y \in \mathcal{Y}$. By human annotation effort, the desired outputs for a random subset of objects is obtained by sampling $y_i \sim P(y|x_i), 1 \leq i \leq l$, where l, the number of labeled examples, is very often far smaller than the total data collected. Next, a typically high-dimensional numerical representation $\Psi(x) \in \mathcal{X} \subset \mathbb{R}^d$ is chosen for the raw data, and a supervised learning model based on labeled samples is induced as a proxy for the true underlying conditional distribution, i.e., $P(y|x) = P(y|\Psi(x), \theta)$, where the model parameters θ are tuned to fit the labeled examples while being regularized sufficiently to avoid overfitting.

The dominant cost and the primary bottleneck in this end-to-end process is the collection of high-quality human annotations which directly bounds the expected generalization performance of the supervised model. The performance-versus-cost curve is highly domain specific. Cost per label may be measured in terms of time and/or monetary resources required for a human to manually probe an object x and arrive at an accurate judgment for an appropriate label y, which naturally tends to increase with the complexity of the input and output spaces, as well as the amount of domain expertise needed to resolve ambiguity consistently.

The tantalizing prospect of utilizing unbounded amounts of unlabeled data in lieu of labeled examples, and thereby lower the cost of learning, has sparked more than a decade of vigorous research in machine learning leading to several principles, associated algorithms, and theoretical justifications for semi-supervised learning. This effort has been well documented in comprehensive surveys and tutorials [55, 27, 33], two dedicated books [11, 57], and several influential papers. The objective of this chapter is to survey recent advances in semi-supervised learning not sufficiently covered in existing introductory expositions, and outline a set of challenges that offer research opportunities to significantly advance the state of the art in this field. In particular, we emphasize the need for theoretical developments to complement algorithmic advances in semi-supervised learning. We review some recent work on applying semi-supervised learning to problems with complex structured outputs where the need for reducing human labeling cost is even greater. Finally, we conclude this chapter with a discussion and a list of outstanding open questions in semi-supervised learning.

2.1.1 Principles of Semi-Supervised Learning

Let $P_{\mathcal{XY}}$ represent the full joint distribution on $\mathcal{X} \times \mathcal{Y}$. In its idealized form, semi-supervised learning (SSL) is the study of how the marginal probability distribution on the input space $P_{\mathcal{X}}$, from which unlabeled examples are assumed to have been abundantly drawn, can be exploited for better function learning. If there is no identifiable relationship between the marginal $P_{\mathcal{X}}$ and the conditional $P(y|x)$, then the value of unlabeled data is questionable. Different families of SSL algorithms arise by making different assumptions on the relationship between $P_{\mathcal{X}}$ and $P(y|x)$.

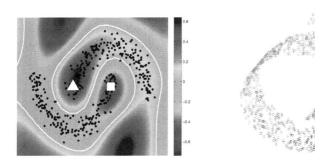

FIGURE 2.1: [Left] The popular two moons problem in semi-supervised learning depicting two labeled examples, unlabeled data shaped as two moons, and the contours of a low-density separator learned by a semi-supervised learning algorithm (Laplacian Regularized Least Squares). [Right] An example of three-dimensional data supported near a two-dimensional "swissroll" manifold.

- *Cluster Assumption*: The marginal $P_\mathcal{X}$ has a clear multi-model structure that reveals "clusters" in the input space, and $P(y|x)$ is piecewise constant with respect to these clusters. In other words, if two data points are in the same cluster, then they are highly likely to have the same class label. An equivalent statement can be made in terms of the *low-density separation principle* which states that the decision boundary should pass through a region of low density and therefore avoid cutting a data cluster.

- *Manifold Assumption*: The marginal $P_\mathcal{X}$ is supported on a low-dimensional manifold embedded in a high-dimensional ambient space. The conditional distribution $P(y|x)$ is smooth, as a function of x, with respect to this low-dimensional manifold structure.

Figure 2.1 gives a geometric depiction of these assumptions. The presence of such structure in real-world high-dimensional data, being in the form of non-Gaussian clusters or low-dimensional manifolds, is a conjecture backed by strong intuition and empirical evidence. For almost any imaginable source of meaningful high-dimensional data, the subset of input configurations possible is only a tiny fraction of the total volume available. For example, in speech production, the articulatory organs can be modeled as a collection of tubes. The space of speech sounds is therefore a low-dimensional manifold parameterized by lengths and widths of the tubes. Likewise, pictures of an object taken from varying angles form a three-dimensional submanifold of the very high-dimensional image space of raw pixels.

The cluster and manifold assumptions motivate different forms of *data-dependent regularization* that can be defined using unlabeled examples and be imposed on a hypothesis space of functional dependencies between inputs and outputs. When working with finite, high-dimensional samples, supervised learners typically trade off empirical loss against *data-independent* measures of smoothness that enforce prediction outputs to be similar if the *ambient* distance between the associated inputs is small. In a semi-supervised setting, these smoothness functionals can instead be defined using an *intrinsic* notion that is based on the structure of the marginal distribution. In other words, function outputs are similar on two points connected by path of high-density of unlabeled data, i.e., the two points lie in the same cluster, or in the case of the manifold assumption, they are in proximity when distance is measured by geodesics on the data manifold.

A conceptually different principle of SSL naturally arises in learning problems where each data point has multiple representations or "views." For example, a web page may be represented by its textual content, or the anchor text on links pointing to/from it; or a video stream may be considered as being composed of an audio view and an image view. Let $x = (x^1, x^2)$ be two views of a data point. Then, it is clear that if the true conditional distribution can be redundantly represented in both views, i.e., $P(y|x) \sim P(y|x^1)$ and $P(y|x) \sim P(y|x^2)$, then the individual estimates must "agree," i.e., $P(y|x^1) \sim P(y|x^2)$. In other words, function estimation may be posed jointly in multiple views and *co-regularized* [36] to discard combinations of dependencies that disagree. The disagreement rate can be measured using unlabeled data and in fact, in some formal settings, can be shown to bound the misclassification error [15]. The Co-Training framework initially proposed in [7] has been among the first efforts that provided a widely successful semi-supervised algorithm with theoretical justifications. The framework employs two assumptions that allow unlabeled examples in multiple views to be utilized effectively: (a) the assumption that the target functions in each view agree on labels of most examples (compatibility assumption) and (b) the assumption that the views are independent given the class label (independence assumption). The first assumption allows the complexity of the learning problem to be reduced by the constraint of searching over compatible functions; and the second assumption allows high performance to be achieved since it becomes unlikely for compatible classifiers trained on independent views to agree on an incorrect label. The cotraining idea has since become synonymous with a greedy agreement-maximization algorithm that is initialized by supervised classifiers in each view and then iteratively retrained on boosted labeled sets, based on high-confidence predictions on the unlabeled examples. The original implementation [7] runs this algorithm on Naive-Bayes classifiers defined in each view. More recently, extensions of kernel methods (SVMs, Regularized Least Squares, Gaussian Processes) have been proposed [36, 37, 48] that explicitly formulate joint regularizers and priors for maximizing agreement, leading to convex optimization problems.

2.1.2 Semi-Supervised Learning Algorithms

The principles and assumptions of SSL can be implemented in different algorithmic frameworks, each with its own optimization and efficiency concerns. Here, we prefer to present some of the SSL algorithms as extended Tikhonov regularization problems. This allows us to emphasize the central role of data-dependent regularization in SSL and point out several issues that turn out to cut across various other frameworks as well.

We use the standard notations in the literature for SSL. Let $X_L = \{x_1, \cdots, x_l\}$ be the set of labeled data, whose labels are given as $Y_L = \{y_1, \cdots, y_l\}$, and let $X_U = \{x_{l+1}, \cdots, x_{l+u}\}$ be the set of unlabeled data, whose labels $Y_U = \{y_{l+1}, \cdots, y_{l+u}\}$ are unknown. Let feature vectors be $x_i \in \mathcal{X} = \mathbb{R}^d$ which are drawn *iid* from a fixed unknown distribution $P_{\mathcal{X}}$, with density $p(x)$, $y_i \in \mathcal{Y}$ (e.g., $\mathcal{Y} = \mathbb{R}$ for regression and $\mathcal{Y} = \{\pm 1\}$ for binary classification), and (x_i, y_i) follows a joint probability distribution $P_{\mathcal{X}\mathcal{Y}}$ with density $p(x, y)$. We also let $n = l + u$ in the context of SSL. The goal of an inductive SSL algorithm is to estimate a function $f(x)$ on the whole domain given X_L, Y_L, and X_U. In a transductive setting, the goal is to estimate $f(x)$ on X_U, i.e., the vector Y_U.

First, let us recall the framework of Reproducing Kernel Hilbert Spaces (RKHS) in which non-parametric function estimation can be elegantly posed. Let $k : \mathcal{X} \times \mathcal{X} \mapsto \mathbb{R}$ be a kernel function, i.e., a positive semi-definite function which for any finite collection of data points $\{x_i\}_{i=1}^l$ generates a positive semi-definite Gram matrix K where $K_{ij} = k(x_i, x_j)$. There is a one-to-one correspondence between kernels k and RKHS $\mathcal{H}_k$ defined by taking the span of the functions, $\mathcal{H}_0 = \{k(x, \cdot), x \in \mathcal{X}\}$, endowing the resulting space with an inner product, $\langle \sum_{i=1}^p \alpha_i k(x_i, \cdot), \sum_{j=1}^q \beta_j k(x_j, \cdot) \rangle_{\mathcal{H}_k} = \sum_{i,j=1}^{p,q} \alpha_i \beta_j k(x_i, x_j)$ and setting $\mathcal{H}_k$ as the closure of $\mathcal{H}_0$. Then, the kernel function satisfies the reproducing property, i.e., $\langle f, k(x, \cdot) \rangle_{\mathcal{H}_k} = f(x)$ for any $f \in \mathcal{H}_k$. Conversely, any Hilbert space with the nice property that evaluation operators on it, $E_x : f \mapsto f(x)$ for any fixed x, are continuous, is an RKHS possessing a reproducing kernel. Stated informally, this property simply means that if two functions $f, g \in \mathcal{H}_k$ are close (i.e., $\|f - g\|_{\mathcal{H}_k}$ is small), then $f(x)$ and $g(x)$ are guaranteed to be close at all points $x \in \mathcal{X}$. The reproducing property underlies the classical Representer Theorem that says that any infinite-dimensional optimization problem of the form,

$$\operatorname*{argmin}_{f \in \mathcal{H}_k} \mathcal{L}(f(x_1), y_1, f(x_2), y_2, \ldots f(x_l), y_l) + \gamma \|f\|_{\mathcal{H}_k}^2,$$

where $\mathcal{L}$ is an arbitrary empirical loss function (need not be additive, or convex), $\|\cdot\|_{\mathcal{H}_K}$ is the norm in the RKHS, and $\lambda > 0$ is a real-valued regularization parameter, has a minimizer with a finite dimensional representation,

$$f(x) = \sum_{i=1}^l \alpha_i k(x, x_i).$$

When $\mathcal{L}$ is taken to be an average of hinge losses over the labeled data points, $\frac{1}{l}\sum_{i=1}^{l}\max\left(0, 1 - y_i f(x_i)\right)$, the resulting problem of estimating the finite dimensional coefficients α_i leads to the SVM algorithm. Other popular choices for loss functions are the squared loss or the logistic loss leading to Regularized Least Squares and Regularized Logistic Regression, respectively. Furthermore, for certain choices of kernels, e.g., the Gaussian kernel, $k(x, z) = e^{-\frac{\|x - z\|^2}{2\sigma^2}}$, $\mathcal{H}_k$ is universal and can approximate square integrable functions to arbitrary accuracy. Thus, kernel methods offer rich hypothesis spaces for non-parametric learning with tractable optimization procedures.

We now consider semi-supervised kernel methods. It is natural to extend the regularized risk minimization problem as follows,

$$\underset{f \in \mathcal{H}_k}{\operatorname{argmin}} \frac{1}{l} \sum_{i=1}^{l} \mathcal{L}(f(x_i), y_i) + \gamma_A \|f\|^2_{\mathcal{H}_k} + \gamma_I \Omega_I\left(f(x_1) \ldots f(x_n)\right), \quad (2.1)$$

where a second regularization term $\Omega_I(\cdot)$ involving unlabeled data is introduced to attempt to bias the learning process toward satisfying an SSL assumption. The Representer Theorem clearly extends to this setting so that the solution is given by the extended expansion, $f(x) = \sum_{i=1}^{n} \alpha_i k(x, x_i)$, which runs over both labeled and unlabeled examples. We now review the typical forms that this regularizer takes for implementing the low-density, manifold and multiview assumptions.

- *Low-Density/Cluster Assumption*: The regularizer below was introduced by Vapnik [45] in the context of Transductive SVMs (TSVMs) and first implemented by [23] followed by several other related efforts (see [12] for a review). It may be interpreted as an attempt to maximize the margin while choosing the optimal labeling for unlabeled data.

$$\Omega_I(f(x_1) \ldots f(x_n)) = \frac{1}{u} \sum_{j=l+1}^{n=l+u} \min_{y_i \in \{-1,+1\}} \max(0, 1 - y_i f(x_i)) \quad (2.2)$$

By noting that $\min_{y_i \in \{-1,+1\}} \max(0, 1 - y_i f(x_i)) = \max(0, 1 - |f(x_i)|)$, it may be seen that the loss increases when the absolute value approaches zero, or in other words, the decision boundary gets too close to an unlabeled data point. Thus, this penalty directly implements the low-density separation principle. However, since this term is non-convex, the full optimization problem becomes hard to optimize and tends to be susceptible to local minima. Furthermore, a class balancing constraint needs to be added to steer the algorithm away from degenerate solutions lumping all unlabeled data in one class. We point the reader to the review article [12] and references therein for a careful comparison of various non-convex optimization strategies.

- *Manifold Regularization*: In Manifold Regularization [6, 35], a nearest neighbor graph G is constructed by mapping each random variable x_i to a vertex of the graph and a similarity measure between two random variables to the weight on the edge connecting these two vertices. The graph G serves as a discrete proxy for the data manifold. By defining a similarity weight W_{ij} for any two points x_i and x_j, we can define graph Laplacian L as $L = D - W$, where D is a diagonal matrix with $D_{ii} = \sum_j W_{ij}$, and W is the weight matrix for the graph G. The Laplacian L of this graph provides a natural intrinsic measure of data-dependent smoothness,

$$\Omega_I(f(x_1)\ldots f(x_n)) = \mathbf{f}^T L\mathbf{f} = \frac{1}{2}\sum_{i,j=1}^{n=l+u} W_{ij}(f(x_i) - f(x_j))^2, \quad (2.3)$$

where $\mathbf{f} = [f(x_1)\ldots f(x_n)]$. From the Representer Theorem, the minimizer has the form $f^\star(x) = \sum_{i=1}^n \alpha_i k(x, x_i)$ involving both labeled and unlabeled data. For the squared loss, the Laplacian Regularized Least Squares algorithm [6] estimates $\alpha = [\alpha_1 \ldots \alpha_n]^T$ by solving the linear system $[JK + l\gamma_I LK + l\gamma_A I]\alpha = Y$ where K is the Gram matrix of k with respect to both labeled and unlabeled examples, I is the $n \times n$ identity matrix, J is a diagonal matrix with first l diagonal entries equaling 1 and the rest being 0 valued, and Y is the $n \times 1$ label vector with $Y_i = 0, i > l$. Manifold Regularization algorithms may be seen as providing an out-of-sample extension for graph-transduction methods as the following, which directly optimize for a function whose domain is the nodes of the data adjacency graph,

$$\operatorname*{argmin}_{f\in\mathbb{R}^n} \gamma \mathbf{f}^T L\mathbf{f} + \sum_{i=1}^l (f_i - y_i)^2$$

A large family of graph regularizers can be defined based on spectral transformations on the Laplacian [39]. Manifold Regularization also corresponds to adjusting an ambient kernel to take data geometry into account. An explicit formula for the transformed kernel is given in [35]. The transformed kernel can then be used with any supervised learner.

- *Co-Regularization [37]*: Let us consider a two-view problem, $x = (x^1, x^2)$, and define corresponding kernels, $k^1(x, z) = k^1(x^1, z^1)$, $k^2(x, z) = k^2(x^2, z^2)$. Let H^1, H^2 be associated RKHSs. Then, we can consider the sum space of functions, $\mathcal{H} = \{f : \mathcal{X} \mapsto \mathbb{R} | f(x) = f^1(x) + f^2(x), f^1 \in \mathcal{H}^1, f^2 \in \mathcal{H}^2\}$. A natural complexity measure on this space is the following,

$$\|f\|_{\mathcal{H}}^2 = \min_{\substack{f=f^1+f^2 \\ f^i\in\mathcal{H}^i, i=1,2}} \|f^1\|_{\mathcal{H}^1}^2 + \|f^2\|_{\mathcal{H}^2}^2 + \gamma_I \frac{1}{n}\sum_{i=1}^n (f^1(x_i) - f^2(x_i))^2,$$

which measures norms in individual view functions and also their disagreement. It turns out that a kernel function can be derived for which $\mathcal{H}$ is the corresponding RKHS with the norm given above. An explicit formula is given in [37]. This turns co-regularization into standard supervised learning with a specific multi-view co-regularization kernel. [48] derive a closely related result for a transductive setting. These results can be generalized to multiple views with view-dependent weights on the final combined predictor.

2.2   Semi-Supervised Prediction for Structured Outputs

The enhancement of supervised learning algorithms to deal with prediction problems involving rich and complex output spaces has been another major strand of research in machine learning. Complex output structure arises in speech recognition, various forms of object recognition tasks and also in a wide range of natural language tasks like Part of Speech (POS) tagging and parsing among other tasks. Several supervised algorithms have been proposed to make use of the internal structure through Markovian and graphical model assumptions. Although the last decade has seen a surge in algorithms and approaches pertaining to SSL [11] for standard classification and regression problems, relatively less progress has been made in *semi-supervised structured output prediction*. The need for such algorithms is obvious: the difficulty of obtaining high-quality labels is even more exaggerated since the output is much more complex than a scalar valued label. We now review some recent advances in this area.

2.2.1   Structured Output Prediction

Structured output prediction consists of learning and inference with structured input-output pairs $(\mathbf{x}, \mathbf{y}) \in \mathcal{X} \times \mathcal{Y}$. Here $\mathbf{y}$ is a structured label, in particular when $\mathbf{y}$ is a sequence it can be expressed as $(y_1, y_2, \ldots y_l)$ where l is the length of the sequence. For example, in Part of Speech (POS) tagging, $\mathbf{y}$ can be the POS tag sequence of a sentence $\mathbf{x}$; in handwritten character recognition, $\mathbf{y}$ can be the sequence of digits corresponding to a sequence of handwritten characters $\mathbf{x}$. We assume that the feasible set of labels $\mathcal{Y}(\mathbf{x}) \subset \mathcal{Y}$ is finite for a given $\mathbf{x}$.

A standard framework of learning structured models is by developing functions $h : \mathcal{X} \to \mathcal{Y}$ as

$$h(\hat{\mathbf{x}}) = \operatorname*{argmax}_{\mathbf{y} \in \mathcal{Y}} F(\mathbf{x}, \mathbf{y}; \mathbf{w})$$

$$= \operatorname*{argmax}_{\mathbf{y} \in \mathcal{Y}} \mathbf{w}^\top \phi(\mathbf{x}, \mathbf{y})$$

where F is a scoring function parameterized by a weight vector $\mathbf{w}$. For computational tractability and feasibility, F is broken as a linear combination of weights $\{w_k\}$ and functions $\{\phi_k(\mathbf{x}_i, y_{j-1}, y_j)\}$ that are defined on individual positions of the output sequence. This is also done to take advantage of Markovian dependence that is generally assumed over the output sequences. We refer readers to [42, 2, 44] for more details.

Given a set of supervised input label pairs $\{(\mathbf{x}_i, \mathbf{y}_i)\}_{i=1}^n$, structured prediction models define a regularized risk minimization problem,

$$J(\mathbf{w}) = C \sum_{i=1}^{n} \mathcal{L}(\mathbf{x}_i, \mathbf{y}_i; \mathbf{w}) + \frac{\lambda}{2} \|\mathbf{w}\|^2, \qquad (2.4)$$

where $\mathcal{L}(\mathbf{x}_i, \mathbf{y}_i; \mathbf{w})$ is an empirical loss term defined on the labeled input/output pairs. Naturally different loss functions lead to different optimization problems and different models. When the loss function is the structured conditional logistic loss $\mathcal{L}(\mathbf{x}_i, \mathbf{y}_i; \mathbf{w}) = -\log p(\mathbf{y}_i|\mathbf{x}_i, \mathbf{w})$, the corresponding model (under appropriate graphical model structure and tractability assumptions) is known as Conditional Random Field [24].

Here we focus on the structured max-margin loss $\mathcal{L}(\mathbf{x}_i, \mathbf{y}; \mathbf{w}) = \max_{\mathbf{y} \in \mathcal{Y}} \{\ell_{\mathbf{y}}^i - \langle \mathbf{w}, \psi_{\mathbf{y}}^i \rangle\}$ where $\psi_{\mathbf{y}}^i = \phi(\mathbf{x}_i, \mathbf{y}_i) - \phi(\mathbf{x}_i, \mathbf{y})$ is the distance of the score of the true input-label pair from any other pair and $\ell_{\mathbf{y}}^i = \ell(\mathbf{y}_i, \mathbf{y})$ is a loss function measuring how bad a label $\mathbf{y}$ is compared to the true label $\mathbf{y}_i$. The general choice of ℓ is the Hamming loss. The corresponding optimization problem formulation is given by

$$\min_{\mathbf{w}, \boldsymbol{\xi}} \quad C \sum_{i=1}^{n} \xi_i + \frac{\lambda}{2} \|\mathbf{w}\|^2 \qquad (2.5)$$
$$\text{s.t.} \quad \forall i, \forall \mathbf{y}, \langle \mathbf{w}, \psi_{\mathbf{y}}^i \rangle \geq \ell_{\mathbf{y}}^i - \xi_i$$
$$\forall i, \xi_i \geq 0.$$

This problem is intractable due to the presence of exponential number of constraints; the above-mentioned Markovian assumptions help in sparsifying the solution space to polynomial. The optimization problem is generally solved in the dual using one of numerous techniques like cutting plane algorithms (which led to structured SVMs) [44], message passing [42], or gradient-based approaches [43]. Note that since the vectors $\psi(\mathbf{x}, \mathbf{y})$ are defined with respect to both inputs and labels, the dual involves taking dot products of such "joint" features which leads to the use of joint kernels $K((\mathbf{x}_1, \mathbf{y}_1), (\mathbf{x}_2, \mathbf{y}_2)) = \langle \psi(\mathbf{x}_1, \mathbf{y}_1), \psi(\mathbf{x}_2, \mathbf{y}_2) \rangle$. These joint kernels can be used for efficient evaluation of the dual objective and the corresponding optimization and lend all the benefits of kernelization to structured prediction.

Unfortunately, there has been very limited work on SSL for structured data. [1] try to adapt Manifold Regularization approaches by adding an *intrinsic* regularizer, which depends on the geometry of the data to the objective function. This is based on the assumption that the structured outputs for two *similar* inputs are close to each other based on some notion of proximity in the complex output space. While both the assumptions are standard in the realm of SSL and make sense for structured data, [1] try to build a graph on cliques of the input instead of the inputs themselves. Also since standard approaches in structured learning depend heavily on joint kernels [2], the authors are forced to pad up the unlabeled data with all possible labels in the label space to generate labeled examples. As a result, for any given input $\hat{\mathbf{x}}$, the correct label $\hat{\mathbf{y}}$ gets padded with the same weight as a label which does not match the correct label at any of the positions in the input. Other approaches [9] try to adapt standard semi-supervised algorithms like co-learning into structured domains and further it analogously to co-regression and co-SVMs. Some recent work has involved latent variables where the labels corresponding to the unlabeled data are treated as latent variables and are marginalized over [47].

There has also been asymptotic analysis of semi-supervised structured prediction [16] where semi-supervision is explored from the setting of completely unlabeled examples and also from the more helpful setting of structured inputs (sequences or graphs) with partial labels provided.

Before going into details of some of the approaches used in semi-supervised structured prediction, it would be apt to point out how the standard techniques and assumptions of semi-supervised learning are extended to structured output prediction. In [58], the authors attempt to extend the low density/cluster assumption on structured outputs by defining transductive structured SVMs. They extend the standard structured SVM formulation of [44] to include slack variables for the unlabeled inputs. The underlying assumption is that for each unlabeled $\mathbf{x}_i$, there exists a label $\mathbf{y}_i$ such that all other labels $\mathbf{y}$ do not violate the score of $(\mathbf{x}_i, \mathbf{y}_i)$ by more than the slack. Thus the new objective looks like

$$\min_{\mathbf{w}, \boldsymbol{\xi}, \hat{\boldsymbol{\xi}}} \ C_l \sum_{i=1}^{l} \xi_i + C_u \sum_{i=l+1}^{l+u} \hat{\xi}_i + \frac{\lambda}{2} \|\mathbf{w}\|^2$$

$$\text{s.t.} \quad \forall i = \{1, \ldots, l\}, \quad \forall \mathbf{y}, \langle \mathbf{w}, \psi_{\mathbf{y}}^i \rangle \geq \ell_{\mathbf{y}}^i - \xi_i$$

$$\forall j = \{l+1, \ldots, l+u\}, \quad \exists \hat{\mathbf{y}}, \forall \mathbf{y}, \langle \mathbf{w}, \psi_{\mathbf{y}}^j \rangle \geq \ell(\hat{\mathbf{y}}, \mathbf{y}) - \hat{\xi}_j$$

$$\forall i, \xi_i \geq 0, \quad \forall j, \hat{\xi}_j \geq 0.$$

The corresponding optimization problem can be solved in the dual by using a conjugate gradient descent technique [58].

The co-regularization framework is extended to the structured setting in [10]. Just as in co-regularization, the general idea is to minimize the number of errors on the labeled examples by the views and maximize the agreement on the unlabeled examples. The joint decision function $f(\mathbf{x}, \mathbf{y})$ is given by the sum of the functions on both views. As usual we need the score of the classifier f on the true label $\mathbf{y}^*$ to be more than the score on any other label $\mathbf{y}$ by a certain margin. However, for each view and each unlabeled example, the same kind of margin difference should hold between the scores of the $(\mathbf{x}, \hat{\mathbf{y}}^v)$

predicted by the view v and any other $(\mathbf{x}, \mathbf{y})$ pair. For details, we refer the readers to [10].

Finally, variations of the key ideas in Manifold Regularization framework have also been applied to the structured case. We describe the corresponding graph construction and the analogous intrinsic regularizer in the next section.

2.2.2 Graph-Based Semi-Supervised CRFs

As described before, CRFs are structured prediction models which maximize the conditional log likelihood of the labeled structured data. These can be described by

$$\min_{\mathbf{w}} -\sum_i -\log p(\mathbf{y}_i|\mathbf{x}_i; \mathbf{w}) + \frac{\lambda}{2} \|\mathbf{w}\|^2$$

where the conditional probability is modeled as an exponential family which factors over the underlying graphical model of the structured data.

$$p(\mathbf{y}_i|\mathbf{x}_i; \mathbf{w}) = \frac{\exp(\langle \mathbf{w}, F(\mathbf{x}, \mathbf{y}) \rangle)}{Z(\mathbf{x}; \mathbf{w})} = \frac{\exp(\sum_k \sum_j w_k f_k(y_i^{j-1}, y_i^j, \mathbf{x}_i))}{Z(\mathbf{x}; \mathbf{w})},$$

where Z is a normalization term called the partition function.

The setting is, however, a semi-supervised one now; thus in addition to labeled data $\{\mathbf{x}_i, \mathbf{y}_i\}_{i=1}^l$, we have unlabeled data $\{\mathbf{x}_j\}_{j=l+1}^{l+u}$. For specificity, we consider the problem of POS tagging of sentences. In [40], the authors leverage information from the unlabeled data by generating a similarity graph over trigrams extracted from all the input sentences (both labeled as well as unlabeled). The graph is endowed with symmetric weights on the edges. For each vertex, its k-nearest neighbors are connected to itself by edges having non-zero weights while the remaining vertices are connected via edges having zero weights. The graph over trigrams $G = (V, E)$ helps capture the structure in the local sequence contexts. The vertices $V = V_l \bigcup V_u$ correspond to the labeled as well as unlabeled data. It is also observed empirically over the entire dataset, that local neighborhoods of trigrams in the graph have significant coherence thus re-affirming the notion of syntactic similarity. This further motivates the similarity graph construction, as the goal is to capture certain local structures and similarities in unlabeled data in general.

However since no labels are available for the unlabeled data, it is not possible to directly use the unlabeled data for training. Instead, the similarity graph can be used to generate a data-dependent regularizer which takes note of the internal local structures existing in both labeled and unlabeled data. The algorithm consists of five main steps:

- At every iteration, once the CRF parameters are obtained, they are used to calculate the marginal probabilities of the trigrams in the labeled data, i.e., $p(y_i^j|\mathbf{x}_i; \mathbf{w}_m)$ where $\mathbf{w}_m$ refers to the weight parameter obtained after the mth iteration of the algorithm. Note that while the data is drawn from a probability distribution on the sequences, the similarity graph is on the trigrams and thus evaluation of this marginal probability at every step is essential.

- This is followed by the calculation of the posterior probabilities of every *type* of trigram from its example *tokens* in the training and test data. If $T(i, j)$ refers to the trigram occurring at the position j in the ith sentence, and $T^{-1}(u)$ is the set of occurrences of the trigram u, the type level posterior is obtained by calculating the average of the token probabilities corresponding to that trigram type.

- A convex minimization problem is next solved to smooth these marginals. Given the marginals $\{q(\mathbf{u})\}$ corresponding to trigram type $\mathbf{u}$, we smooth it by minimizing

$$C(\mathbf{q}) = \sum_{\mathbf{u} \in V_l} \|q_{\mathbf{u}} - r_{\mathbf{u}}\|^2 + \lambda_1 \sum_{\substack{\mathbf{u} \in V \\ \mathbf{v} \in \mathcal{N}(\mathbf{u})}} w_{\mathbf{u},\mathbf{v}} \|q_{\mathbf{u}} - q_{\mathbf{v}}\|^2 + \lambda_2 \sum_{\mathbf{u} \in V} \|q_{\mathbf{u}} - U\|^2$$

subject to q being a distribution. Here $r_{\mathbf{u}}$ is the empirical marginal label distribution of trigram $\mathbf{u}$ in labeled data, $\mathcal{N}(\mathbf{u})$ is the set of neighbors of the trigram $\mathbf{u}$ in the similarity graph, $w_{\mathbf{u},\mathbf{v}}$ is the weight on the edges connecting trigrams $\mathbf{u}$ and $\mathbf{v}$ and U is the uniform distribution. Thus the first term forces the distribution of trigrams to conform to the distribution over labeled data, at the same time it enforces neighboring distributions to be similar and also requires the distributions to be close to the uniform distribution, unless forced by the other terms. Note that the second term is the Laplacian regularizer applied in Manifold Regularization. The importance of the terms is controlled by the hyperparameters λ_1 and λ_2.

- Once the type posterior marginals are computed, they are interpolated with the CRF marginals by taking a weighted average, where the weights reflect the confidence in the CRF parameters and the smoothed posteriors. To enforce the Markovian assumption over the unlabeled sentences, these interpolated marginals are combined with the CRF transition probabilities by Viterbi decoding, thus obtaining the best possible tags for the unlabeled data. These newly labeled data are then added to the already labeled data and the CRF is retrained. This process is continued until convergence.

This work improves the prediction accuracy over unseen test data by a significant amount and also has the advantage of being an inductive algorithm. It is generally used as a domain adaptation technique with improved performances on labeling the target domain.

There has been other recent work to extend semi-supervision to CRFs [22, 30] which adds a low conditional entropy regularization term corresponding to the unlabeled data. Such a regularization is justified, since it is equivalent to maximizing the KL divergence of the empirical distribution of the unlabeled data with the conditional distribution of labels given unlabeled data, thus allowing the labels with high probability to gain prominence.

On the other hand, [29] looks at fast training of semi-supervised CRFs using a boosting technique called virtual evidence boosting [28], that does not require graph-based assumptions and tries to maximize the pseudolikelihood of the data assuming hidden labels. We skip the details for brevity.

2.2.3   Structured Prediction with Hidden Structure

A recent line of work [54] looks at structured output prediction with hidden structure by building on the well-known discriminative Max-Margin Markov Networks (M^3N) [42] approach for structured learning. The problem posed is similar to [47], although the latter is restricted to structured SVMs.

The original prediction problem is posed as

$$h(\mathbf{x}) = \underset{\mathbf{y} \in \mathcal{Y}}{\operatorname{argmax}} \int p(\mathbf{w}) F(\mathbf{x}, \mathbf{y}; \mathbf{w}) d\mathbf{w}, \tag{2.6}$$

where a prior $p_0(\mathbf{w})$ is assumed over $\mathbf{w}$ and p is obtained by optimizing

$$\underset{p(\mathbf{w}) \in \mathfrak{C}, \boldsymbol{\xi} \in \mathbb{R}^n_+}{\min} KL(p(\mathbf{w}) \| p_0(\mathbf{w})) + U(\boldsymbol{\xi}),$$

where $U(\boldsymbol{\xi})$ is an additive function over the slack variables introduced for optimization (generally chosen to be $C \sum_i \xi_i$ for some constant C) and

$$\mathfrak{C} = \left\{ p(\mathbf{w}) : \int p(\mathbf{w}) [\langle \mathbf{w}, \psi^i_{\mathbf{y}} \rangle - \ell^i_{\mathbf{y}}] d\mathbf{w} \geq -\xi_i, \quad \forall i, \forall \mathbf{y} \right\}$$

represents the feasible distribution space. Using p_0 as the standard Gaussian distribution, we can retrieve p in the form isomorphic to the dual of M^3N. For more details of the optimum $\mathbf{w}$, we refer readers to [53].

This model can be extended into the realm of SSL in the case of structured outputs with hidden parts. Consider that the label of a structured input $\mathbf{x}$ consists of an observed part $\mathbf{y}$ and a hidden part $\mathbf{z}$ such that the conditional probability factorizes according to the following condition

$$p(\mathbf{y}, \mathbf{z}, \mathbf{w} | \mathbf{x}) = p(\mathbf{w}, \mathbf{z} | \mathbf{x}) p(\mathbf{y} | \mathbf{x}, \mathbf{w}, \mathbf{z})$$

and $p(\mathbf{y} | \mathbf{x}, \mathbf{w}, \mathbf{z}) = \frac{1}{Z} \exp \{ -F(\mathbf{x}, \mathbf{y}, \mathbf{z}; \mathbf{w}) \}$ decomposes similar to an undirected graphical model. The corresponding model [54], called the *Partially Observed Maximum Entropy Discrimination Markov Network* (PoMEN), predicts its label similar to (2.6)

$$h(\mathbf{x}) = \underset{\mathbf{y} \in \mathcal{Y}}{\operatorname{argmax}} \sum_{\mathbf{z}} \int p(\mathbf{w}, \mathbf{z}) F(\mathbf{x}, \mathbf{y}, \mathbf{z}; \mathbf{w}) d\mathbf{w}$$

Denoting $\bar{\mathbf{z}} = \{\mathbf{z}_1, \mathbf{z}_2, \ldots \mathbf{z}_n\}$ to denote the hidden label parts for all the inputs, we specify a prior distribution $p_0(\mathbf{w}, \bar{\mathbf{z}})$ over all hidden labels. Denoting $p(\mathbf{w}, \mathbf{z})$ as the marginalization of $p(\mathbf{w}, \bar{\mathbf{z}})$, we can set up the corresponding regularized risk minimization problem

$$\min_{p(\mathbf{w},\bar{\mathbf{z}}\in\mathfrak{C}_1,\boldsymbol{\xi}\in\mathbb{R}^n_+)} KL(p(\mathbf{w})\|p_0(\mathbf{w})) + U(\boldsymbol{\xi}), \qquad (2.7)$$

where the feasible distribution set

$$\mathfrak{C}_1 = \left\{ p(\mathbf{w}, \bar{\mathbf{z}}) : \sum_{\mathbf{z}} \int p(\mathbf{w}, \mathbf{z})[\langle \mathbf{w}, \boldsymbol{\gamma}^i_{\mathbf{y}} \rangle - \ell^i_{\mathbf{y}}] d\mathbf{w} \geq -\xi_i, \quad \forall i, \forall \mathbf{y} \right\}$$

and $\boldsymbol{\gamma}^i_{\mathbf{y}} = \phi(\mathbf{x}_i, \mathbf{y}_i, \mathbf{z}, \mathbf{w}) - \phi(\mathbf{x}_i, \mathbf{y}, \mathbf{z}, \mathbf{w})$ is the difference in the features corresponding to true and any other observed labels.

2.2.4 Optimization for PoMEN

In order to make the learning problem tractable, the probability distributions of the hidden variables in p and p_0 are assumed to be *iid* and independent of $\mathbf{w}$. Thus $p(\mathbf{w}, \bar{\mathbf{z}}) = p(\mathbf{w}) \prod_{i=1}^n p(\mathbf{z}_i)$ and similarly for p_0. For many practical problems, such an assumption is realistic.

An alternating coordinate descent scheme can be used to optimize the objective function. When we hold $\bar{\mathbf{z}}$ fixed and optimize over $\mathbf{w}$, the corresponding optimization problem is solved in the dual since it is isomorphic to the M^{3}N dual and thus existing techniques for M^{3}N [42, 44] can be used for minimization.

On the other hand, holding $\mathbf{w}$ and $\bar{\mathbf{z}}_{-i} = \{\mathbf{z}_1, \mathbf{z}_2, \ldots \mathbf{z}_{i-1}, \mathbf{z}_{i+1}, \ldots, \mathbf{z}_n\}$ fixed and varying individual $\mathbf{z}_i$s can be solved in the dual by taking gradients of the objective. Assuming the prior $p_0(\mathbf{z}_i)$ as an exponential family, we can use approximate inference to calculate the gradients of the dual and thus optimize the objective.

The above model is similar to learning structured SVMs with hidden variables [47] which also assumes a hidden part $\mathbf{z}_i$ corresponding to each structured example. The key difference lies in the fact that unlike PoMEN, the latter model maximizes over the hidden variables for prediction. Thus

$$h(\mathbf{x}) = \underset{\mathbf{y}\in\mathcal{Y},\mathbf{z}\in\mathcal{Z}}{\operatorname{argmax}} F(\mathbf{x}, \mathbf{y}, \mathbf{z}; \mathbf{w}).$$

In this case, at each point, the labeled part of the output $\mathbf{y}$ is padded with the unlabeled part $\mathbf{z}$ and all maximization is performed over both $\mathbf{y}$ and $\mathbf{z}$. This leads to an optimization problem similar to M^{3}N over $\mathbf{w}$ with each maximization now jointly over $\mathbf{y}$ and $\mathbf{z}$. The corresponding objective function can be written as the difference of two convex functions which enables the use of Convex-Concave Procedure (CCCP) for obtaining its minima. We refer the reader to [47] for more details.

2.3 Theoretical Analysis

The setting of few labeled samples with a huge amount of easily obtained unlabeled ones is attractive in practice. Many methods are introduced to take advantage of unlabeled data based on different assumptions. Empirical results on standard datasets also show the advantages of SSL algorithms when labeled data is limited.

However, despite the success of various SSL algorithms, the theoretical understanding of SSL is still unsatisfactory. Among various aspects of the theoretical study of SSL, in this chapter we focus on the large sample analysis, or the asymptotic analysis of SSL algorithms. Although there have been several studies on the asymptotic analysis of SSL, e.g., [49, 25, 32, 52], complete asymptotic analyses for various popular SSL algorithms are largely missing. The asymptotic analysis is of great importance not only from a theoretical point of view, but also has huge impacts on practical applications. One example is that a surprising finding in [31] shows when labeled points are fixed, but when the number of unlabeled points increases to infinity, the solution of a popular SSL algorithm [56] degenerates to a constant function on unlabeled points, which provides no information about labels. The algorithms in [50, 4] suffer from essentially the same problem. This example highlights the need for large sample analysis of SSL. Algorithms that at first glance appear to be intuitively reasonable and empirically perform well for moderate-sized datasets need to also be well behaved in the limit of growing data sizes. This is particularly important also because SSL is, in a sense, designed for large-scale learning, i.e., most practical large-scale data analysis scenarios necessitate the use of unlabeled data since human labeling effort is unlikely to keep pace with the rate of data collection.

2.3.1 Asymptotic Analysis for Semi-Supervised Learning

Asymptotic analysis is a key component for a better understanding of SSL algorithms. Particularly, analyses of consistency and convergence rate will shed light on how they work in practice. In supervised learning, consistency deals with the problem of whether an estimator converges in probability to the true function as the number of labeled points increases to infinity, while the convergence rate shows how fast the estimator converges to its limit as the number of samples increases.

Compared to the asymptotic analysis for supervised learning, where the number of labeled points, l is large, the asymptotic analysis for SSL has another large sample factor: unlabeled points size. This means the asymptotic analysis of any SSL algorithm should involve the limit analysis of two sequences, l as the number of labeled points, and u as the number of unlabeled points. We can fix one of them and study the asymptotics of the other, or study the asymptotics for both of them at the same time. Among these settings, the following two are particularly important for both the theoretical studies and practical applications:

- I: Fixed X_L, Increasing X_U

- II: Increasing X_L, Increasing X_U

In each setting, two key questions are what the limit of these estimators are, and how fast the estimators converge to their limits. Next, we review several works in settings I and II. Due to the limited space, the review is far from being comprehensive. However, we hope we can shed light on the importance of asymptotic analysis. Particularly, as an example, we show how an asymptotic analysis in setting I can expose unobvious weaknesses of a popular and intuitively reasonable algorithm. Most importantly, the theoretical analysis guides us to a solution that works well in practice.

2.3.2   Setting I: A Case Study

Instead of a general review for analyses in setting I, we use an example study for the next algorithm [56] to show its importance. A similar analysis also applies to the algorithm in [50].

$$\min_f \quad \sum_{i=1}^{n=l+u} W_{ij}(f(x_i) - f(x_j))^2 \tag{2.8}$$

$$\text{s.t.} \quad f(x_i) = y_i, \; i = 1, \cdots, l,$$

where W_{ij} is a similarity measure between x_i and x_j, for instance a Gaussian weight defined as $W_{ij} = e^{-\|x_i - x_j\|^2/t}$, and $f \in \mathbb{R}^{l+u}$, a function on all the sample points. The intuitive idea behind this optimization problem is that if x_i and x_j are similar, the estimated function on them should be similar. This is implemented by penalizing the weighted function value difference between data pairs.

Although the idea is appealing for transductive SSL and the empirical results also show its advantages compared to supervised learning algorithms, it is shown in [31] that the solution of problem (2.8) degenerates to a constant on unlabeled points in the limit of infinite unlabeled points with fixed labeled points. This study involves the asymptotic analysis in setting I. The cause of this problem comes from the objective function, which can be rewritten as

$$\frac{1}{2} \sum_{i=1}^{n=l+u} W_{ij}(f(x_i) - f(x_j))^2 = f^T L f, \tag{2.9}$$

where L is the unnormalized graph Laplacian, see e.g., [46], and we treat vector f as the evaluation of $f(x)$ on sample points (i.e., $f_i = f(x_i)$). In the rest of this chapter, we will use f to mean either the vector f, or the continuous function $f(x)$ when the meaning is clear from the context. With a proper scaling, the limit of this regularizer for a smooth function $f(x)$ given infinite sample points [8] is

$$f^T L f \to J(f) = \int_{\mathbb{R}^d} \|\nabla f(x)\|^2 p^2(x) dx, \qquad (2.10)$$

where $p(x)$ is the probability density function of the sample. In [31], it is shown when $d = 1$, the space equipped with semi-norm $J(f)$ is an RKHS, the kernel of which is a continuous function. The solution of problem (2.8) is a continuous well-behaved function, and the labels recovered by the solution is meaningful. However, when $d \geq 2$, the solution is an indicator function (up to a change of sign) on labeled points, which is constant everywhere except on the labeled points.

With the help of this asymptotic analysis, the essential cause is found to be that the semi-normed space is too rich and the solution is forced to be the discontinuous indicator function in higher dimensions. An improved learning algorithm is introduced in [51], where instead of using regularizer $f^T L f$, an iterated graph Laplacian regularizer $f^T L^m f$ is used with a positive integer m, corresponding to a semi-norm in a higher-order Sobolev space. In order to reduce the influence of noises, the following regularized least squares problem is used in [51] instead of an interpolation problem:

$$\min_{f \in \mathbb{R}^{l+u}} \sum_{i=1}^{l} (f(x_i) - y_i)^2 + \lambda f^T L^m f. \qquad (2.11)$$

As unlabeled set size increases, λ should decrease accordingly to maintain a meaningful limit of L, see, e.g., [3, 26, 21]. Based on the limit analyses of graph Laplacians, iterated graph Laplacian regularization in SSL is shown to be a parallel partner of thin plate splines in regression, both of which use a proper order Sobolev semi-norm as the penalty term in higher dimensions. Note that the power of the Laplacian was also observed as an important hyperparameter in Manifold Regularization [6, 35].

An important observation in [51] is that in the finite sample case, the semi-normed space with $f^T L f$ is indeed an RKHS, however, in the limit of infinite unlabeled points when $d \geq 2$, the semi-normed space with $J(f)$ becomes a non-RKHS. Without a careful asymptotic analysis, this hidden but important issue can easily be overlooked.

2.3.3 Setting II: Some Results

In this section, we review the asymptotic studies of several SSL algorithms that are related to setting II. In [16], an asymptotic analysis is studied for both the normal as well as the structured output setting for generative models with the definition of semi-supervision slightly different in the structured case. This study allows the sizes of X_L as well as X_U increase to infinity but the ratio

$\lambda = l/(l + u)$ remains constant. In particular, the authors look at questions of consistency of the corresponding models in the limit of infinite data as well as the accuracy of prediction of the corresponding models in terms of labeled and unlabeled data. In the sequel $n = l + u$ refers to the total number of samples (labeled as well as unlabeled). If not mentioned otherwise, capital variables X and Y refer to random input and output variables (non-structured or structured, which will be clear from the context).

For generative models, the model is typically learned [11] by maximizing the joint likelihood of the data:

$$\hat{\mathbf{w}}_n = \operatorname*{argmax}_{\mathbf{w}} \sum_{i=1}^{l} \log p(X_i, Y_i; \mathbf{w}_i) + \sum_{i=l+1}^{l+u} \log p(X_i; \mathbf{w}).$$

However, the authors consider a stochastic setting where each example is labeled with probability λ (which keeps the total number of labeled examples l in expectation). The corresponding objective becomes

$$\hat{\mathbf{w}}_n = \operatorname*{argmax}_{\mathbf{w}} \sum_{i=1}^{l} Z_i \log p(X_i, Y_i; \mathbf{w}_i) + \sum_{i=l+1}^{l+u} (1 - Z_i) \log p(X_i; \mathbf{w}),$$

where $Z_i \sim Ber(\lambda)$ are Bernoulli random variables with parameter λ. Assuming the data generated by the ground truth (corresponding to model $\mathbf{w}^*$), the question of consistency boils down to whether the empirical model $\hat{\mathbf{w}}_n \to \mathbf{w}^*$ as $n \to \infty$. If the distribution generating the data is identifiable (i.e., $p(X, Y; \mathbf{w}) - p(X, Y; \mathbf{w}')$ is not identically 0 whenever $\mathbf{w} \neq \mathbf{w}'$), then using ideas from stochastic composite likelihood [17], the authors show that the model $\hat{\mathbf{w}}_n$ is indeed consistent whenever the space of models is compact.

Let us denote $V_1 = \nabla_{\mathbf{w}}^* \log p(X, Y; \mathbf{w}^*)$ and $V_2 = \nabla_{\mathbf{w}}^* \log p(X; \mathbf{w}^*)$ as the gradients of the joint and marginal probabilities with respect to the true model and $Var_{\mathbf{w}^*}(\mathbf{v})$ as the variance of any vector $\mathbf{v}$ under $p(,: \mathbf{w}^*)$. Denoting $\Sigma = \lambda Var_{\mathbf{w}^*}(V_1) + (1 - \lambda) Var_{\mathbf{w}^*}(V_2)$, the authors can again extend their analysis of stochastic composite likelihood to show that the following convergence in distribution takes place:

$$\sqrt{n}(\hat{\mathbf{w}}_n - \mathbf{w}^*) \xrightarrow{\mathcal{D}} \mathcal{N}(0, \Sigma^{-1}),$$

i.e., the distribution of the empirical maximizer is asymptotically normal and $\hat{\mathbf{w}}_n$ can be characterized in terms of the remaining parameters. This also proves that the asymptotic variance is a good proxy for finite sample measures like error rates and empirical mean square error which is also validated empirically.

In the structured case, the authors define semi-supervised data in a modified way. They assume that certain fractions of the label sequence Y may be labeled whereas the rest may be unlabeled. This leads to stochastic policies for labeling sequences $\mathcal{P}(Y_i) \subseteq \{Y_i^1 \ldots Y_i^m\}$ which determines what part of the sequence (of length m) is labeled. This leads to the corresponding objective function:

$$\hat{\mathbf{w}}_n = \underset{\mathbf{w}}{\text{argmax}} \sum_{i=1}^{n} \log p(X_i, \mathcal{P}(Y_i); \mathbf{w}_i).$$

Using a similar stochastic model as the previous case, we assume that $\mathcal{P}(Y)$ takes values $\chi_j(Y)$, $j = \{1, \ldots k\}$ with probabilities $\lambda_1, \ldots \lambda_k$. This is a straightforward generalization of the non-structured case. For example, $\chi_1(Y)$ can be $\emptyset$ which corresponds to no labels, $\chi_k(Y)$ can be the complete labeling of the sequence Y and $\chi_p(Y)$ might correspond to the labeling for the first half of Y for some $p < k$. Thus the corresponding stochastic objective becomes

$$\hat{\mathbf{w}}_n = \underset{\mathbf{w}}{\text{argmax}} \sum_{i=1}^{n} \sum_{j=1}^{k} Z_i^j \log p(X_i, \chi_j(Y_i); \mathbf{w}_i), \qquad (2.12)$$

where Z_i^j are random variables with $\mathbb{E}(Z_i^j) = \lambda_j$ and $\forall i, \sum_j Z_i^j = 1$. Note that Z_i^j are not independent of j for a given i. Under analogous definitions of identifiability of $\chi_1, \ldots \chi_k$ we can show that the maximizer of (2.12) is consistent and approaches the true model as $n \to \infty$. Analogous results for accuracy of prediction hold as well for the structured case as for the non-structured case which is outside the scope of this text. We refer the interested readers to [16].

Next we turn to the error bound analysis of several SSL algorithms in a nonparametric model setting. Regularization in certain RKHS is one of the most popular kernel-based SSL methods. It solves a regression problem with a kernel-based regularizer penalty term. The general form of transductive RKHS models is

$$\hat{f} = \arg \inf_{f \in \mathbb{R}^{l+u}} \left[\frac{1}{l} \sum_{i=1}^{l} \mathcal{L}(f(x_i), y_i) + \lambda f^T K^{-1} f \right], \qquad (2.13)$$

where $\mathcal{L}(\cdot, \cdot)$ is a convex loss function, K is a $(l+u) \times (l+u)$ matrix with $K(i, j) = k(x_i, x_j)$ and $k(\cdot, \cdot)$ being the reproducing kernel of an RKHS, and λ is a tuning parameter for the balance between the convex loss and penalty $f^T K^{-1} f$.

In [49], asymptotics for problem (2.13) using spectral decomposition-based unsupervised kernel design is studied. The estimator of this problem is shown to converge to its limit almost surely given a mild condition when unlabeled points increase ($u \to \infty$). Moreover, when X_L is a set of l samples drawn uniformly from $l + u$ samples, a generalization bound of errors on unlabeled points is also given by [49, Theorem 4.1] as

$$\mathbb{E}_{X_L}\left[\frac{1}{u} \sum_{x_i \notin X_L} \mathcal{L}(\hat{f}_i(X_L), y_i)\right]$$

$$\leq \inf_{f \in \mathbb{R}^{l+u}} \left[\frac{1}{l+u} \sum_{i=1}^{l+u} \mathcal{L}(f_i, y_i) + \lambda f^T K^{-1} f + \frac{\gamma^2 \text{tr}(K)}{2\lambda l(l+u)} \right]. \qquad (2.14)$$

The analysis is based on the convergence of empirical feature vectors to feature vectors in the underlying RKHS by strong law of large numbers, which is an insightful way of studying these algorithms. The generalization bound also suggests the design of transductive kernels using unlabeled data.

Although the almost sure convergence is established in this study, the limit estimator is unknown, which can be an uninformative function. Therefore, if the estimator is useless, i.e., the limit is quite different from the true function, then the generalization error bound given in [49] does not provide much useful information. In practice, this inconsistency can happen easily without a careful design of the optimization problem. One example is the graph Laplacian regularization in Section (2.3.2), which is also discussed in [49].

The various kernels used in [49] in fact are closely related to the graph Laplacian, since they share the same or closely related eigenvalues and eigenvectors. The special transform acts as a low pass filter, which is also closely related to Diffusion maps method [14]. In [49], the dependence of errors on the number of unlabeled points u is not clear.

Other variations on the theme of graph Laplacian regularization have also been considered. Consider choosing an estimator by minimizing the following general regularized empirical risk,

$$\mathcal{R}(f) = \sum_{i=l+1}^{l+u} \sum_{j=1}^{l} K_t(x_i, x_j)(y_j - f(x_i))^2 + \gamma \sum_{i,j=1}^{l+u} K_t(x_i, x_j)(f(x_i) - f(x_j))^2,$$

(2.15)

where $K_t(x, y)$ is a symmetric kernel function depending on the bandwidth t (e.g., a Gaussian with bandwidth t), the second term is the graph Laplacian regularizer $2f^T L f$, and γ is a tuning parameter. When $\gamma = 0$, the problem becomes the standard nonparametric kernel smoother. The minmax rate of convergence for this problem is studied in [25]. The main result is that the pointwise mean square error (MSE) for this SSL problem has the same leading term as a regular supervised kernel smoother, which means unlabeled points do not help *asymptotically*. This is not surprising if we have no assumption on unlabeled points. Based on this analysis, several assumptions on the relations between the margin density $p(x)$ and the regression function $f(x)$ are made to take advantage of unlabeled points, and a faster rate therefore can be obtained.

However, the typical setting of SSL is when the number of labeled points is limited, which means l should be relatively small and fixed or slowly increasing compared to the fast increasing u. In another word, the asymptotic analysis of unlabeled points is more important to SSL. Therefore, the asymptotic leading term as a function of l should be seen as a constant in the MSE. This suggests the possibility that in certain small labeled set cases, more unlabeled points can improve errors greatly.

Eigenvectors of graph Laplacians are used in SSL in [5], as in the following least squares problem:

$$\hat{\beta} = \arg\min_{\beta} \sum_{i=1}^{l}(y_i - \sum_{j=1}^{p}\beta_j v_j(x_i))^2, \qquad (2.16)$$

where v_j is the jth eigenvector of a graph Laplacian (unnormalized or normalized graph Laplacian), and only the first p eigenvectors are used when the corresponding eigenvalues are in increasing order. Notice that the graph Laplacian is constructed on both the labeled and unlabeled data, so unlabeled data do not explicitly appear in the least squares problem, but hide inside the eigenvectors v_j.

In [52], an asymptotic analysis shows that if we are given infinite unlabeled points, this method achieves the following error rate (asymptotic integrated mean squares error) as a function of l when $f(x)$ is smooth:

$$\tilde{O}(l^{-\frac{2}{d+2}}), \qquad (2.17)$$

where d is the intrinsic dimensionality of the domain for the samples, and the notation $\tilde{O}$ includes a logarithmic factor and the optimal number of eigenvectors to be used:

$$\tilde{O}(l^{\frac{d}{d+2}}). \qquad (2.18)$$

The error rate is the same as the optimal rate of nonparametric regressions on the intrinsic domain, up to a logarithmic factor. This is consistent with the finding that without any assumptions on unlabeled points, unlabeled points do not help *asymptotically*. When there are finite unlabeled points, the error rate should be slower, as a function of l and u, which is not studied in [52]. Note that this method does not suffer the degeneracy issue compared to the graph Laplacian regularization problem (2.8).

Different from the above regression problems, semi-supervised classification under cluster assumption is studied in [32], where a generalization error bound is given. The cluster excess risk, which is the excess risk within clusters, is shown to be

$$\tilde{O}(\frac{u^{-\alpha}}{1-\theta}) + e^{-l(\theta\delta)^2/2}, \qquad (2.19)$$

where $\alpha > 0$, $\delta > 0$, $0 < \theta < 1$. The estimation procedure is based on two steps: estimating clusters using unlabeled points, then labeling the estimated clusters using labeled points. The analysis shows that unlabeled points are helpful for classification given the cluster assumption [33, 32]. For large u, the first error term from estimations of clusters is negligible, and the risk is the same as labeling several known clusters using l labeled points. A framework is also developed in [38] for evaluating the performance gains with SSL under the cluster assumption using finite sample error bounds, which involves finite labeled and unlabeled points.

Most of these studies show that in a distribution-free setting, unlabeled points do not help asymptotically, while in [32, 38] SSL under cluster assumption is studied. However, there is little work on the rigorous and complete analyses for the commonly used SSL algorithms. The possible technical difficulty is that both the common assumptions for SSL as well as their specific implementations in concrete algorithms need to be jointly investigated.

2.3.4 Discussion

The existing asymptotic analyses provide some insights on several SSL algorithms; however, they are far from being complete and satisfactory. For instance, a complete consistency and convergence rate analysis for the popular graph Laplacian regularization is still missing. Generally, a complete analysis should have two components. First, the consistency of an estimator. This consistency should be meaningful in terms of both labeled and unlabeled points. When we have infinite labeled points, the consistency is similar to the one studied in supervised learning, i.e., whether an estimator converges to the true unknown function in a certain sense in the limit of infinite labeled data. However, when we have a fixed and finite labeled set, but infinite unlabeled points, the notion of "consistency" is unique to SSL. One way to define this consistency is that the estimator converges to the "best" one among a chosen family of estimators given a fixed number of labeled points, in terms of certain criteria. Second, the convergence rate should be a two-dimensional function of both l and u. This rate function can provide insight into the relation between labeled and unlabeled data in learning. Consistency should be established before convergence rate, otherwise the rate does not provide much useful information. A complete analysis will more efficiently guide practical applications.

One difficulty for an asymptotic analysis is how to formulate the assumptions in a reasonable way. Several analyses use a distribution-free setting, for instance [49, 25, 52]. Cluster assumption is formulated by level set in [32]. In order to show how much unlabeled data can help, we need a more rigorous study on assumptions for SSL.

Another feature of SSL is that there is a variety of algorithms based on different assumptions. These algorithms can be very different from one another, even based on the same assumptions. For instance, instead of L_2 setup, L_1 optimization can be used, AdaBoost with different weak classifiers can also be used in SSL, and unlabeled data also show improvement in structured learning. Besides the huge differences between algorithms, even a seemingly minor difference can result in totally different large sample behaviors. For instance, Manifold Regularization [6] only differs from graph Laplacian Regularization [56, 50] by one term, i.e., an ambient RKHS norm. The result is that the former is well defined in setting I, while the latter is not. This shows that asymptotic analyses for these algorithms are quite different from each other.

2.4 New Directions

One may argue that over the years, supervised learning has become a "technology" in the sense that a practitioner, with sufficient feature engineering and sufficient human input, can often get supervised methods to work well "out of the box" across a variety of problems. Despite its ubiquitous applicability and various demonstrations of empirical success, the same cannot be stated yet for SSL. This is because of a number of issues and challenges that arise in practice. We list five challenges in this section that in our opinion can significantly advance the state of the art and bring SSL closer to routine deployment.

- *Model Selection*: In settings with limited labeled data, model selection can be highly challenging. This is particularly exaggerated also because semi-supervised models introduce numerous additional hyperparameters whose choice is a priori not clear on a given new domain. For example, apart from the kernel parameters, Manifold Regularization needs to tune (a) ambient and intrinsic regularization parameters, (b) parameters for construction of the graph Laplacian (e.g., the choice of k in k-NN graphs), (c) parameters for the construction of the graph regularizer (e.g., m in iterated Laplacians L^m). Similarly, Transductive SVMs work well in practice when an accurate estimate of the class ratios is available to enforce the balance constraint.

- *Scalability*: Arguably, large-scale learning is only meaningful when coupled with SSL since human annotation effort cannot keep pace with growing data sizes in most applications. Despite the obvious need for scalable methods, very little work has been done to scale non-linear semi-supervised methods to massive real-world problems. Furthermore, the limit of infinite unlabeled data may expose unobvious issues concerning consistency of the algorithm and whether one can realistically expect performance to improve by learning with larger and larger unlabeled datasets. For example, a standard formulation for graph transduction at first glance appears to be a natural SSL algorithm that also scales well as it reduces to solving sparse linear systems. However, as we have discussed, its limiting solution is not meaningful. [18] work with the limiting solution for a generalized eigenvector formulation for graph Laplacian-based SSL instead, and note that the limiting eigenfunctions can be computed in closed form if the data density follows a parameteric/product form, leading to a large-scale algorithm. Scalability aside, for methods such as TSVM, non-convexity poses a serious hurdle. For example, [13] show that the globally optimal solution of the TSVM problem is actually far better than what most practical methods are able to achieve. Fast algorithms have been proposed [34] for linear TSVMs.

Three related themes are (a) online learning [20] which also closely relates to the use of efficient general purpose stochastic optimization algorithms, (b) the use of parallel computing (see, e.g., [19]) for SSL on modern distributed and multicore platforms, and (c) the intersection of SSL with Sparse Learning [41] for building compact models that can be efficiently applied to large test sets.

- *Structured Output prediction*: The problem of semi-supervised structured prediction is naturally motivated as structured data is in generally much more complicated and time consuming to manually annotate, whereas input data is abundant and easy to obtain. We have elaborated on various approaches used to tackle semi-supervised structured learning in Section (2.2), but it should be evident that there is room for significant further progress both in terms of algorithmic advances as well as theoretical underpinnings.

- *Theoretical Analysis*: The asymptotic analysis for SSL can shed light on various SSL algorithms and guide their applications. However, existing analyses are far from being satisfactory. There are two important questions for any SSL algorithm. First, what the estimators are. This is the problem of consistency, including how to define consistency. Second, how fast an empirical estimator converges to its limit, including how to define convergence. The rate should involve both l and u. Without consistency, no matter how fast the convergence rates are, it does not provide any guarantee.

- *Combinations with other cost-reducing learning strategies*: Semi-supervised learning can be combined with numerous other strategies such as active learning, transfer learning, and other forms of weakly supervised learning. The theoretical basis of such combinations and the design of optimal joint strategy for cost-effective learning is an open area of research.

We expect the SSL research community to devote significant effort in the near future in these directions.

References

[1] Yasemin Altun, David McAllester, and Mikhail Belkin. Maximum margin semi-supervised learning for structured variables. In Y. Weiss, B. Schölkopf, and J. Platt, editors, *Advances in Neural Information Processing Systems 18*, pages 33–40. MIT Press, Cambridge, MA, 2006.

[2] G. Bakir, T. Hofmann, B. Schölkopf, A. Smola, B. Taskar, and S. V. N. Vishwanathan. *Predicting Structured Data*. MIT Press, Cambridge, MA, 2007.

[3] M. Belkin. Problems of learning on manifold. PhD thesis, University of Chicago, 2003.

[4] M. Belkin, I. Matveeva, and P. Niyogi. Regularization and semi-supervised learning on large graphs. In John Shawe-Taylor and Yoram Singer, editors, *COLT*, volume 3120 of Lecture Notes in Computer Science, pages 624–638. Springer, 2004.

[5] M. Belkin and P. Niyogi. Semi-supervised learning on Riemannian manifolds. *Machine Learning, Special Issue on Clustering*, 56:209–239, 2004.

[6] M. Belkin, P. Niyogi, and V. Sindhwani. Manifold regularization: A geometric framework for learning from labeled and unlabeled examples. *Journal of Machine Learning Research*, 7:2399–2434, 2006.

[7] A. Blum and T. Mitchell. Combining labeled and unlabeled data with co-training. In *COLT*, pages 92–100, 1998.

[8] Olivier Bousquet, Olivier Chapelle, and Matthias Hein. Measure based regularization. In Sebastian Thrun, Lawrence Saul, and Bernhard Schölkopf, editors, *Advances in Neural Information Processing Systems 16*. MIT Press, Cambridge, MA, 2004.

[9] Ulf Brefeld. Semi-supervised structured prediction models. PhD thesis, Humboldt-Universität zu Berlin, 2008.

[10] Ulf Brefeld and Tobias Scheffer. Semi-supervised learning for structured output variables. In *23rd International Conference on Machine Learning (ICML)*, 2006.

[11] O. Chapelle, B. Schölkopf, and A. Zien, editors. *Semi-Supervised Learning*. MIT Press, Cambridge, MA, 2006. http://www.kyb.tuebingen.mpg.de/ssl-book.

[12] O. Chapelle, V. Sindhwani, and S.S. Keerthi. Optimization techniques for semi-supervised support vector machines. *Journal of Machine Learning Research*, 9:203–233, 2006.

[13] Olivier Chapelle, Vikas Sindhwani, and S. Sathiya Keerthi. Branch and bound for semi-supervised support vector machines. In B. Schölkopf, J. Platt, and T. Hoffman, editors, *Advances in Neural Information Processing Systems 19*, pages 217–224, MIT Press, Cambridge, MA, 2007.

[14] R. R. Coifman and S. Lafon. Diffusion maps. *Applied and Computational Harmonic Analysis*, 21(1):5–30, 2006.

[15] S. Dasgupta, M. Littman, and D. McAllester. PAC generalization bounds for co-training. In *NIPS*, 2001.

[16] Joshua V. Dillon, K. Balasubramanian, and G. Lebanon. Asymptotic analysis of generative semi-supervised learning. In *International Conference on Machine Learning (ICML)*, 2010.

[17] Joshua V. Dillon and Guy Lebanon. Stochastic composite likelihood. *Journal of Machine Learning Research*, 11:2597–2633, 2010.

[18] Rob Fergus, Yair Weiss, and Antonio Torralba. Semi-supervised learning in gigantic image collections. In Y. Bengio, D. Schuurmans, J. Lafferty, C. K. I. Williams, and A. Culotta, editors, *Advances in Neural Information Processing Systems 22*, pages 522–530. 2009.

[19] A. Ghoting, R. Krishnamurthy, E. Pednault, B. Reinwald, V. Sindhwani, S. Tatikonda, Y. Tian, and S. Vaithyanathan. Declarative machine learning on mapreduce. In *IEEE International Conference on Data Engineering (ICDE)*, 2011.

[20] Andrew B. Goldberg, Ming Li, and Xiaojin Zhu. Online manifold regularization: A new learning setting and empirical study. In *Proceedings of the 2008 European Conference on Machine Learning and Knowledge Discovery in Databases, ECML08*, 2008.

[21] M. Hein. Geometrical aspects of statistical learning theory. PhD thesis, Wissenschaftlicher Mitarbeiter am Max-Planck-Institut für biologische Kybernetik in Tübingen in der Abteilung, 2005.

[22] Feng Jiao, Shaojun Wang, Chi-Hoon Lee, Russell Greiner, and Dale Schuurmans. Semi-supervised conditional random fields for improved sequence segmentation and labeling. In *Association for Computational Linguistics (ACL)*, 2006.

[23] T. Joachims. Transductive inference for text classification using support vector machines. In *International Conference on Machine Learning*, 1999.

[24] J. D. Lafferty, A. McCallum, and F. Pereira. Conditional random fields: Probabilistic modeling for segmenting and labeling sequence data. In *Proceedings of International Conference on Machine Learning*, volume 18, pages 282–289. Morgan Kaufmann, San Francisco, CA, 2001.

[25] John Lafferty and Larry Wasserman. Statistical analysis of semi-supervised regression. In J.C. Platt, D. Koller, Y. Singer, and S. Roweis, editors, *Advances in Neural Information Processing Systems 20*, pages 801–808. MIT Press, Cambridge, MA, 2008.

[26] S. Lafon. Diffusion maps and geodesic harmonics. PhD thesis, Yale University, 2004.

[27] F. Liang, Sayan Mukherjee, and Mike West. The use of unlabeled data in predictive modeling. *Statistical Science*, 22:189–205, 2007.

[28] Lin Liao, Tanzeem Choudhury, Dieter Fox, and Henry Kautz. Training conditional random fields using virtual evidence boosting. In *Proceedings of the International Joint Conference on Artificial Intelligence (IJCAI)*, 2007.

[29] Maryam Mahdaviani and Tanzeem Choudhury. Fast and scalable training of semi-supervised crfs with application to activity recognition. In J.C. Platt, D. Koller, Y. Singer, and S. Roweis, editors, *Advances in Neural Information Processing Systems 20*, pages 977–984. MIT Press, Cambridge, MA, 2008.

[30] Gideon S. Mann and Andrew Mccallum. Efficient computation of entropy gradient for semi-supervised conditional random fields. In *Proceedings NAACL-Short '07 Human Language Technologies 2007: The Conference of the North American Chapter of the Association for Computational Linguistics*, pages 109–112. Association for Computational Linguistics Stroudsburg, PA, 2007.

[31] Boaz Nadler, Nathan Srebro, and Xueyuan Zhou. Statistical analysis of semi-supervised learning: The limit of infinite unlabelled data. In Y. Bengio, D. Schuurmans, J. Lafferty, C. K. I. Williams, and A. Culotta, editors, *Advances in Neural Information Processing Systems 22*, pages 1330–1338. 2009.

[32] Philippe Rigollet. Generalization error bounds in semi-supervised classification under the cluster assumption. *Journal of Machine Learning Research*, 8:1369–1392, 2007.

[33] M. Seeger. Learning with labeled and unlabeled data. Technical report, 2000. http://www.dai.ed.ac.uk/~seeger/papers.html.

[34] V. Sindhwani and S.S. Keerthi. Large scale semi-supervised linear SVMs. In *29th Annual International ACM SIGIR*. 2006.

[35] V. Sindhwani, P. Niyogi, and M. Belkin. Beyond the point cloud: From transductive to semi-supervised learning. In *International Conference on Machine Learning*, 2005.

[36] V. Sindhwani, P. Niyogi, and M. Belkin. A co-regularization approach to semi-supervised learning with multiple views. In *International Conference on Machine Learning*, 2005.

[37] V. Sindhwani and D. Rosenberg. An RKHS for multi-view learning and manifold co-regularization. In *International Conference on Machine Learning*, 2008.

[38] Aarti Singh, Robert Nowak, and Xiaojin Zhu. Unlabeled data: Now it helps, now it doesn't. In D. Koller, D. Schuurmans, Y. Bengio, and L. Bottou, editors, *Advances in Neural Information Processing Systems 21*, pages 1513–1520. 2009.

[39] A. Smola and I.R. Kondor. Kernels and regularization on graphs. In *COLT*, 2004.

[40] Amarnag Subramanya, Slav Petrov, and Fernando Pereira. Efficient graph-based semi-supervised learning of structured tagging models. *Empirical Methods in Natural Language Processing (EMNLP)*, 2010.

[41] S. Sun and J. Shawe-Taylor. Sparse semi-supervised learning using conjugate functions. *Journal of Machine Learning Research*, 11:2423–2455, 2010.

[42] B. Taskar, C. Guestrin, and D. Koller. Max-margin Markov networks. In S. Thrun, L. Saul, and B. Schölkopf, editors, *Advances in Neural Information Processing Systems 16*, pages 25–32. MIT Press, Cambridge, MA, 2004.

[43] Ben Taskar, Simon Lacoste-Julien, and Michael Jordan. Structured prediction, dual extragradient and Bregman projections. *Journal of Machine Learning Research*, 7:1627–1653, 2006.

[44] I. Tsochantaridis, T. Joachims, T. Hofmann, and Y. Altun. Large margin methods for structured and interdependent output variables. *Journal of Machine Learning Research*, 6:1453–1484, 2005.

[45] V. Vapnik. *Statistical Learning Theory*. Wiley-Interscience Press, New York, 1998.

[46] Ulrike von Luxburg. A tutorial on spectral clustering. *Statistics and Computing*, 17(4):395–416, 2007.

[47] Chun-Nam John Yu and T. Joachims. Learning structural SVMs with latent variables. In *International Conference on Machine Learning (ICML)*, 2009.

[48] Shipeng Yu, Balaji Krishnapuram, Romer Rosales, Harald Steck, and R. Bharat Rao. Bayesian co-training. In J.C. Platt, D. Koller, Y. Singer, and S. Roweis, editors, *Advances in Neural Information Processing Systems 20*, pages 1665–1672. MIT Press, Cambridge, MA, 2008.

[49] Tong Zhang and Rie Ando. Analysis of spectral kernel design based semi-supervised learning. In Y. Weiss, B. Schölkopf, and J. Platt, editors, *Advances in Neural Information Processing Systems 18*, pages 1601–1608. MIT Press, Cambridge, MA, 2006.

[50] Dengyong Zhou, Olivier Bousquet, Thomas Navin Lal, Jason Weston, and Bernhard Schölkopf. Learning with local and global consistency. In Sebastian Thrun, Lawrence Saul, and Bernhard Schölkopf, editors, *Advances in Neural Information Processing Systems 16*. MIT Press, Cambridge, MA, 2004.

[51] Xueyuan Zhou and Mikhail Belkin. Semi-supervised learning by higher order regularization. In Geoffrey Gordon, David Dunson, and Miroslav Dudík, editors, *The 14th International Conference on Artificial Intelligence and Statistics*, 2011.

[52] Xueyuan Zhou and Nathan Srebro. Error analysis of Laplacian eigenmaps for semi-supervised learning. In Geoffrey Gordon, David Dunson, and Miroslav Dudík, editors, *The 14th International Conference on Artificial Intelligence and Statistics*, 2011.

[53] Jun Zhu and Eric P. Xing. Maximum entropy discrimination Markov networks. *Journal of Machine Learning Research*, 10:2531–2569, 2009.

[54] Jun Zhu, Eric P. Xing, and Bo Zhang. Partially observed maximum entropy discrimination Markov networks. In D. Koller, D. Schuurmans, Y. Bengio, and L. Bottou, editors, *Advances in Neural Information Processing Systems 21*, pages 1977–1984, 2009.

[55] X. Zhu. Semi-supervised learning literature survey. Technical report, 2008. `http://pages.cs.wisc.edu/~jerryzhu/research/ssl/semireview.html`.

[56] X. Zhu, Z. Ghahramani, and J. Lafferty. Semi-supervised learning using Gaussian fields and harmonic function. In *The Twentieth International Conference on Machine Learning (ICML)*, 2003.

[57] Xiaojin Zhu and Andrew B. Goldberg. *Introduction to Semi-Supervised Learning*. Synthesis Lectures on Artificial Intelligence and Machine Learning 3:1, 1–130. Morgan and Claypool Publishers, 2009.

[58] A. Zien, U. Brefeld, and T. Scheffer. Transductive support vector machines for structured variables. In *International Conference on Machine Learning*, pages 1183–1190, 2007.

Chapter 3

Transfer Learning, Multi-Task Learning, and Cost-Sensitive Learning

Bin Cao

Department of Computer Science and Engineering, Hong Kong University of Science and Technology, Hong Kong

Yu Zhang

Department of Computer Science and Engineering, Hong Kong University of Science and Technology, Hong Kong

Qiang Yang

Department of Computer Science and Engineering, Hong Kong University of Science and Technology, Hong Kong

3.1   Introduction

In this chapter we discuss transfer learning and multi-task learning problems, and relate them to cost-sensitive learning. In many machine learning problems, the learning problem in one or more domains of interest, known as target domains, may be very difficult to solve due to a lack of high-quality labeled training data, but we may have some related knowledge from one or more different but similar domains. In such cases, we may find some common knowledge between these domains to help improve the learning performance in some chosen target domains, or improve the performance of learning in all related domains. Learning under these circumstances is called transfer learning or multi-task learning (see a survey by Pan and Yang [42]).

This learning paradigm has been inspired by human learning activities in that people often apply the knowledge gained from previous learning tasks to help learn a new task. For example, a baby can be observed to first learn how to recognize his parents before using this knowledge to help him learn how to recognize other people. Transfer learning and multi-task learning can be formulated under two different settings: *symmetric* and *asymmetric* [61]. In the symmetric setting, we are interested in improving the performance of all tasks simultaneously; in this case we have multi-task learning. But at other times we are interested in improving the performance of some target task using the information knowledge from the other auxiliary or source tasks, typically after the source tasks have been learned. In this case we generally refer to the learning setting as transfer learning.

When the costs of different losses are considered, transfer and multi-task learning can be further formulated more specifically depending on the different objectives to optimize. In transfer learning, cost-sensitive learning can be seen as the process in which we focus on reducing the the costs on the interested target tasks, whereas in multi-task learning, we further consider the costs as evenly distributed over all tasks under consideration. In the following, we first consider the transfer learning model where there is only one target learning task. We then consider the symmetric multi-task model where tasks have equal weights.

3.2   Notations

We first introduce the notations we will use in later sections. In general, we use lowercase, italic letters like a, b, c to represent scalars and bold letters like $\mathbf{u}, \mathbf{v}, \mathbf{w}$ to represent vectors. Uppercase letters in bold like $\mathbf{A}, \mathbf{B}, \mathbf{C}$ represent matrices. Lowercase letters with parentheses such as $f(), g(), h()$ are used to

TABLE 3.1: Notations.

$\mathcal{D}$	A dataset
$\mathcal{X}$	A feature space
$\mathcal{H}$	A hypothesis space
$\text{tr}(\mathbf{A})$	Trace of matrix $\mathbf{A}$
p	A probability distribution
$\mathbb{E}_p[\cdot]$	Expectation with respect to distribution P
$\mathcal{S}$	The source task (domain)
$\mathcal{T}$	The target task (domain)
p_s	Distribution on the training/source data
p_t	Distribution on test/target data
$\mathbb{E}_{\mathcal{D}}[\cdot]$	Expectation over dataset $\mathcal{D}$
min	Minimize
max	Maximize

represent functions. More specific notations are shown in Table 3.1. Other notations will be introduced when they appear.

3.3   Transfer Learning Models

Cost-sensitive learning can be seen as placing a heavier importance weight on *some* selected instances and features than others. In transfer learning, these weight assignments correspond to sampling-based approaches that are used in covariate shift, which we introduce below. These learning approaches share many similarities with classical cost-sensitive learning methods.

Transfer learning attempts to learn useful knowledge from a source task and generalize this knowledge in a target task. This learning paradigm breaks a common assumption made by most machine learning methods, which states that the training and test data are drawn from the same feature space and the same distribution. When the distribution changes, most statistical models need to be rebuilt from scratch using newly collected training data. In many real-world applications, it is expensive or even impossible to re-collect the needed training data and rebuild the models. Therefore, we expect to transfer the knowledge from the source tasks to the target task to reduce the effort of labeling. These learning problems include domain adaptation, sample selection bias, covariate shift, and self-taught learning [10, 16, 9, 48]. These approaches are similar in their common goal of knowledge reuse, and different in their specific assumptions made in their learning algorithms to handle the knowledge transfer.

In the following, we review several major methodologies that have been developed to solve the transfer learning problem. These methodologies can be classified in three categories: sampling-based approaches, representation-based approaches and task-regularization-based approaches.

3.3.1 Sampling-Based Approach

Sampling-based approaches find their roots in statistical sampling methods, where the aim is to draw selected instances from a particular distribution. When directly drawing samples from the distribution is difficult, samples are drawn from some initial distributions and then are adapted to approximate the original distribution. These adaptation algorithms can be utilized to correct the distribution difference for transfer learning.

3.3.1.1 Importance Sampling as Cost-Sensitive Learning

The intuitive idea behind sampling-based approaches is the following. Although the source and the target tasks are different, there are certain parts of the data that can still be reused together with a few labeled data in the target task. Most instance-based transfer approaches are motivated by importance sampling. To see how importance sampling methods may help in this setting, we first review the problem of empirical risk minimization (ERM) [59]. In general, we might want to learn the optimal parameters θ^* of the model by minimizing the expected risk,

$$\theta^* = \arg\min_{\theta \in \Theta} \; \mathbb{E}[l(\boldsymbol{x}, y, \theta)],$$

where $l(\boldsymbol{x}, y, \theta)$ is a loss function that depends on the parameter θ. However, since it is hard to estimate the probability distribution p, we choose to minimize the ERM instead,

$$\theta^* = \arg\min_{\theta \in \Theta} \; \frac{1}{n} \sum_{i=1}^{n} l(\boldsymbol{x}_i, y_i, \theta),$$

where n is the size of the training data.

In the *transfer learning* setting, we want to learn an optimal model for the target task by minimizing the expected risk,

$$\theta^* = \arg\min_{\theta \in \Theta} \; \mathbb{E}_{(\boldsymbol{x}, y) \sim p_t}[l(\boldsymbol{x}, y, \theta)],$$

where $(\boldsymbol{x}, y) \sim p_t$ means that the data $(\boldsymbol{x}, y)$ samples follow the distribution given by p_t. When no labeled data in the target domain are observed in the training data, we have to learn a model from the source domain data instead. If $p_s(\boldsymbol{x}, y) = p_t(\boldsymbol{x}, y)$, then we may simply learn the model by solving the following optimization problem for use in the target domain,

$$\theta^* = \arg\min_{\theta \in \Theta} \; \mathbb{E}_{(\boldsymbol{x}, y) \sim p_s}[l(\boldsymbol{x}, y, \theta)].$$

Otherwise, when $p_s(\boldsymbol{x}, y) \neq p_t(\boldsymbol{x}, y)$, we need to modify the above optimization problem to learn a consistent model for the target domain, as follows:

$$
\begin{aligned}
\mathbb{E}_{(\boldsymbol{x},y)\sim p_t}[l(\boldsymbol{x}, y, \theta)] &= \int p_t(\boldsymbol{x}, y)\, l(\boldsymbol{x}, y, \theta)\mathrm{d}\mathbf{x}\mathrm{d}y \\
&= \int \frac{p_t(\boldsymbol{x}, y)}{p_s(\boldsymbol{x}, y)} p_s(\boldsymbol{x}, y)\, l(\boldsymbol{x}, y, \theta)\mathrm{d}\mathbf{x}\mathrm{d}y \\
&= \mathbb{E}_{(\boldsymbol{x},y)\sim p_s}\left[\frac{p_t(\boldsymbol{x}, y)}{p_s(\boldsymbol{x}, y)} l(\boldsymbol{x}, y, \theta)\right].
\end{aligned}
$$

Therefore, by adding different importance weights to each instance with the corresponding weight $\beta(\boldsymbol{x}, y) := \frac{p_t(\boldsymbol{x},y)}{p_s(\boldsymbol{x},y)}$, we can learn a consistent model for the target domain.

3.3.1.2   Estimating the Importance Weight

The key problem in the sampling-based algorithm is how to estimate the importance weights. In the following, we discuss two recently developed methods.

Under the covariate shift setting, we have the assumption that the conditional distribution is invariant, namely, $p_s(y|\boldsymbol{x}) = p_t(y|\boldsymbol{x})$. Thus the difference between $p_s(\boldsymbol{x}, y)$ and $p_t(\boldsymbol{x}, y)$ is caused by $p_s(\boldsymbol{x})$ and $p_t(\boldsymbol{x})$ and $\frac{p_t(\boldsymbol{x},y)}{p_s(\boldsymbol{x},y)} = \frac{p_s(\boldsymbol{x})}{p_t(\boldsymbol{x})}$. If we can estimate $\frac{p(\boldsymbol{x}_s)}{p(\boldsymbol{x}_t)}$ for each instance, we can solve the *covariate shift* problems via cost-sensitive learning.

There are various ways to estimate $\frac{p_t(\boldsymbol{x})}{p_s(\boldsymbol{x})}$. The most intuitive idea is to estimate p_t and p_s first and then compute the ratio. This basic solution is used in early works for solving the sample selection bias problem [67]. However, this method needs to estimate the density function of distributions, which can be infeasible in high-dimensional spaces. Therefore, directly estimating the importance weight $\frac{p_t(\boldsymbol{x})}{p_s(\boldsymbol{x})}$ is a more preferable approach [58]. The idea is to estimate the weighting function $\beta(\boldsymbol{x})$ that can approximate the ratio. Formally, we would want to minimize the following objective function:

$$
\min \ \ \mathrm{div}\big(p_t(\boldsymbol{x}),\ \beta(\boldsymbol{x}) \cdot p_s(\boldsymbol{x})\big), \tag{3.1}
$$

where $\mathrm{div}(,)$ is a type of divergence on distributions.

Sugiyama et al. propose an algorithm known as Kullback-Leibler Importance Estimation Procedure (KLIEP), which uses the Kullback-Leibler divergence as the objective function [52]. The objective then becomes

$$
\min \ \ \mathrm{D}_{\mathrm{KL}}\big(p_t(\boldsymbol{x}) \ || \ \beta(\boldsymbol{x}) \cdot p_s(\boldsymbol{x})\big).
$$

According to the definition of Kullback-Leibler divergence,

$$
\begin{aligned}
D_{KL}\big(p_t(\boldsymbol{x}) \,\|\, w(\boldsymbol{x}) \cdot p_s(\boldsymbol{x})\big) &= \int p_t(\boldsymbol{x}) \log \frac{p_t(\boldsymbol{x})}{p_s(\boldsymbol{x})\beta(\boldsymbol{x})} \mathrm{dx} \\
&= \int p_t(\boldsymbol{x}) \log \frac{p_t(\boldsymbol{x})}{p_s(\boldsymbol{x})} \mathrm{dx} - \int p_t(\boldsymbol{x}) \log \beta(\boldsymbol{x}) \mathrm{dx}.
\end{aligned}
$$

In the above equations, since the first term is independent of $\beta(\boldsymbol{x})$, the optimization problem can be converted to a maximization problem for the second term:

$$
\max \int p_t(\boldsymbol{x}) \log \beta(\boldsymbol{x}) \mathrm{dx}.
$$

KLIEP further assumes the weighting function has a special form, such that

$$
w(\boldsymbol{x}) = \sum_l \alpha_l \varphi_l(\boldsymbol{x}),
$$

where α_l are parameters to be learned from the data samples and $\{\varphi_l(\boldsymbol{x})\}$ are a set of basis functions such that $\varphi_l(\boldsymbol{x}) \geq 0$ for all $\boldsymbol{x}$. The optimization problem can be converted to the following convex optimization problem given finite training samples:

$$
\begin{aligned}
\max \;& \sum_{\boldsymbol{x} \in \mathcal{D}_t} \log\Big(\sum_l \alpha_l \varphi_l(\boldsymbol{x})\Big), \\
s.t. \;& \sum_{\boldsymbol{x} \in \mathcal{D}_t} \sum_l \alpha_l \varphi_l(\boldsymbol{x}) = n_s \text{ and } \alpha_l \geq 0,
\end{aligned}
\tag{3.2}
$$

where n_s is the number of data in the source domain and the constraint comes from $\int p_t(\boldsymbol{x})\beta(\boldsymbol{x}) \mathrm{dx} = 1$.

It is possible to consider other types of divergence instead of KL-divergence. Recently, researchers have made the connection between distributions and kernel methods. This connection is based on the finding that there exists a bijection[1] μ between the space of all probability measures and the marginal polytope induced by the feature map $\Phi(\boldsymbol{x})$ if F is an reproducing-kernel Hilbert space (RKHS) with a universal kernel $k(\boldsymbol{x}, \boldsymbol{x}') = \langle \Phi(\boldsymbol{x}), \Phi(\boldsymbol{x}') \rangle$ [24].

Huang et al. [28] propose a kernel-mean matching (KMM) algorithm to learn $\beta(\boldsymbol{x})$ directly by matching the means between the source domain data and the target domain data in a reproducing-kernel Hilbert space (RKHS):

$$
\min_\beta \; \|\mu(p_t) - \mathbb{E}_{x \sim p_t}[\beta(\boldsymbol{x}) \cdot \Phi(\boldsymbol{x})]\|.
$$

The additional constraint of the optimization problem is similar to KLIEP, which is $\beta(\boldsymbol{x}) \geq 0$ and $\mathbb{E}_{x \sim p_s}[\beta(\boldsymbol{x})] = 1$.

---

[1] A bijection is a function f from a set X to a set Y with the property that, for every y in Y, there is exactly one x in X such that $f(x) = y$.

KMM can be rewritten as the following quadratic programming (QP) optimization problem:

$$\min_{\boldsymbol{\beta}} \quad \frac{1}{2}\boldsymbol{\beta}^T \mathbf{K}\boldsymbol{\beta} - \kappa^T \boldsymbol{\beta}$$

$$s.t. \quad \beta_i \in [0, B] \ \ and \ \ |\sum_{i=1}^{n_s} \beta_i - n_s| \leq n_s \epsilon,$$

where B is the upper bound for the importance weights. $\mathbf{K} = \begin{bmatrix} \mathbf{K}_{s,s} & \mathbf{K}_{s,t} \\ \mathbf{K}_{t,s} & \mathbf{K}_{t,t} \end{bmatrix}$ and $\mathbf{K}_{t,t}$ are kernel matrices for the source domain data and the target domain data, respectively. $\kappa_i = \frac{n_s}{n_t} \sum_{j=1}^{n_t} k(\boldsymbol{x}_i, \boldsymbol{x}_{t_j})$, where $\boldsymbol{x}_i$ is an instance from either the source or target domain, while $\boldsymbol{x}_{t_j}$ is an instance from the target domain.

Different from KLIEP, which estimates the weighting function, KMM directly estimates the weight vector $\boldsymbol{\beta}$ of training samples. When doing this, the out-of-sample problem introduces difficulty in using cross-validation to set the parameters in the kernel function. This is not a problem of KLIEP, since it can be integrated with cross-validation to perform model selection automatically in two steps: (1) estimating the weights of the source domain data; (2) training models on the reweighted data. Both KMM and KLIEP avoid estimating the distribution of $\boldsymbol{x}$, which is not a trivial problem to solve when the data dimension is high. It has been shown that KMM is equivalent to an alternative version of KLIEP [58].

It is also possible to combine the estimation of importance weights with the learning problem in a unified framework. Bickel et al. [9] derive a kernel-logistic regression classifier based on this idea. Besides sample re-weighting techniques, Dai et al. [17] extend a traditional Naive Bayesian classifier for the transductive transfer learning problems, where unlabeled data are available at training time. For more information on importance sampling and reweighting methods for covariate shift or sample selection bias, readers can refer to a recently published book [47] by Quionero-Candela et al.

The covariate shift assumption does not hold when $p_s(y|\boldsymbol{x}) \neq p_t(y|\boldsymbol{x})$. In this case, we can consider label information to improve the estimation of the importance weights. This would require that some labeled data for the target task be available. Similar to the previous case, directly estimating the joint probability is an intuitive method, but it suffers from the data sparseness problem. An alternative approach is to learn the weights through a boosting-style algorithm, as is done in TrAdaBoost [18].

TrAdaBoost [18] is an extension of the AdaBoost algorithm to the transfer learning problem. The original AdaBoost algorithm sequentially trains some weak learners so that the subsequently built classifiers are tweaked in favor of those instances misclassified by previous classifiers [22]. The cost of misclassification increases in each next round. TrAdaBoost revises the weighting scheme to filter out the training data that are very different from the test data

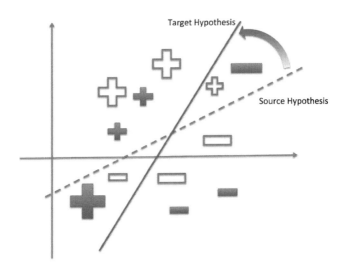

FIGURE 3.1: A toy example to show the weighting scheme for TrAdaBoost. Solid plus and minus points represent the target task and the hollow plus and minus points represent the source task. The symbols $+/-$ indicate positive and negative instances. The size of the points stands for their corresponding weights.

by automatically adjusting the weights of training instances. The algorithm of TrAdaBoost is shown in Algorithm 1.

At each boosting step, TrAdaBoost increases the relative weight of target instances that are misclassified, as is shown in Figure 3.1. When a source instance is misclassified, its weight is decreased, instead of increased as in classical boosting algorithms. In this way, TrAdaBoost makes use of the source instances that are similar to the target data while distancing from those that are dissimilar. Since class labels are taken into consideration, we can use $p(\boldsymbol{x}, y)$ to represent similarity between sample instances in source and target domains, allowing the final classifier to be more accurate and robust. For a more detailed description, please see [18].

3.3.2   Feature-Representation-Based Approach

The feature-representation-based approaches to the transfer learning problem aim at finding "good" feature representations to minimize domain divergence and classification or regression model error. Strategies to find "good" feature representations are different for different types of the source task data. If many labeled data in the source domain are available, supervised learning

---

Algorithm 1 TrAdaBoost

Input: Two labeled datasets $\mathcal{D}_t = \{(\boldsymbol{x}_i, y_i)\}_{i=1}^{n}$ and $\mathcal{D}_s = \{(\boldsymbol{x}_j, y_j)\}_{j=n+1}^{n+m}$, the unlabeled dataset $\mathcal{D}_u = \{\boldsymbol{x}_k\}$, a base learning algorithm *Learner*, and the maximum number of iterations T.

Output: A hypothesis $h_f(\boldsymbol{x})$

Initialize the initial weight vector.

for $t = 1, \ldots, T$ **do**

　1. Set $\beta^t \leftarrow \beta^t / (\sum_i \beta_i^t)$

　2. Call *Learner*, providing it the combined training set with the weight w^t and the unlabeled dataset $\mathcal{D}_u$. Then, get back a hypothesis $h_t : \mathcal{X} \rightarrow \{-1, +1\}$.

　3. Calculate the error of h_t by

$$\epsilon_t = \sum_{i=n+1}^{n+m} \frac{\beta_i^t \|h_t(\boldsymbol{x}_i) - y_i\|}{\sum_{i=n+1}^{n+m} \beta_i^t}$$

Set $\alpha_t = \epsilon_t / (1 - \epsilon_t)$ and $\alpha = 1/(1 + \sqrt{2 \ln n / T})$.

Update the new weight vector:

$$\beta_i^{t+1} = \begin{cases} \beta_i^t \alpha^{\|h_t(\boldsymbol{x}_i) - y_i\|} & \text{if } 1 \leq i \leq n \\ \beta_i^t \alpha_t^{-\|h_t(\boldsymbol{x}_i) - y_i\|} & \text{if } n + 1 \leq i \leq n + m \end{cases}$$

and the hypothesis

$$h_f(x) = \begin{cases} 1, & \prod_{t=\lceil T/2 \rceil}^{T} \alpha_t^{-h_t(x)} \geq \prod_{t=\lceil T/2 \rceil}^{T} \alpha_t^{-\frac{1}{2}} \\ 0, & \text{otherwise} \end{cases}$$

end for

---

methods can be used to construct a feature representation. This is similar to common feature-representation-based approach in multi-task learning, to be discussed in Section 3.4.1.

　Formally, the loss function of representation-based approach can be defined as

$$\min_{\theta} \; \text{div}\big(p_t(f_\theta(\boldsymbol{x})), \; p_s(f_\theta(\boldsymbol{x}))\big),$$

where f_θ is a function to map $\boldsymbol{x}$ to a new feature representation.

　This objective is similar to Equation 3.1 in that they both try to minimize the divergence between transformation of distributions. They differ in that feature-representation-based approaches use transformation on features.

　We should note that the above objective is only a necessary condition for a successful transfer learning algorithm, because we can always find a trivial mapping function that makes the distributions are identical. Often, we need other constraints or objectives at the same time to avoid such trivial mappings.

If no labeled data are available in the source domain, we can exploit what is known as self-taught learning [48], which is a type of unsupervised learning method that can be used to construct a new feature representation. In self-taught learning, the label space differences between the source and target domains may be large, which implies the auxiliary information of the source domain cannot be used directly. This situation is similar to the inductive transfer-learning setting where the labeled data in the source domain are unavailable. Thus, the key is to find the overlap of the two feature spaces either through a mapping function or through a subspace.

As an example of feature-representation-based approach, consider a sentiment classification problem, which aims to find the orientation of product reviews based on their content. For the sentiment classification problem, Blitzer et al. [11] propose the structural correspondence learning (SCL) algorithm to exploit domain adaptation techniques for sentiment classification. SCL uses an alternating structural optimization (ASO) algorithm as the optimization algorithm, which was proposed by Ando and Zhang [3]. SCL tries to construct a set of related tasks to model the relationship between pivot features and non-pivot features. The non-pivot features with similar weights among the source and target tasks tend to have similar discriminative power in a low-dimensional latent space, which can be used to transfer the classification knowledge.

Another example is transfer learning via dimensionality reduction, which is proposed by Pan et al. [43]. In this work, Pan et al. exploit the Maximum Mean Discrepancy Embedding (MMDE) method, originally designed for dimensionality reduction, to learn a low-dimensional space to reduce the difference of distributions between different domains for transfer learning. In particular,

$$\min_{\beta} \ \|\mathbb{E}_{x \sim p_s}[\Phi(\boldsymbol{x})] - \mathbb{E}_{x \sim p_t}[\Phi(\boldsymbol{x})]\|.$$

The aim of MMDE is that, besides minimizing the gap between the two distributions, MMDE also maximizes the information to be kept in the kernel space, which is represented by the trace of the kernel matrix.

In the same spirit, Si et al. in [51] consider a linear mapping function for f and using the Bregman-divergence as the divergence function, where the objective function can be formulated as follows:

$$\min_{W} \ \mathrm{D}_{\mathrm{Breg}}\big(p_t(f_{\mathbf{W}}(\boldsymbol{x}))\|p_s(f_{\mathbf{W}}(\boldsymbol{x}))\big) + \lambda \cdot l(\mathbf{W}).$$

In this equation, $\mathbf{W}$ is a linear mapping from a high-dimensional space to a low-dimensional space and $l(\mathbf{W})$ is a general subspace learning objective function.

The feature-representation-based approaches are also used in multi-task learning problems, which we review in Section 3.4.1.

TABLE 3.2: Cross-domain sentiment classification examples.

	Electronics	Video Games
P	Compact; easy to operate; very good picture quality; looks sharp!	A very good game! It is action packed and full of excitement. I am very much hooked on this game.
P	I purchased this unit from Circuit City and I was very excited about the quality of the picture. It is really nice and sharp.	Very realistic shooting action and good plots. We played this and were hooked.
N	It is also quite blurry in very dark settings. I will never buy HP again.	The game is so boring. I am extremely unhappy and will probably never buy UbiSoft again.

3.3.3   Application Example: Cross-Domain Sentiment Classification

We take *sentiment classification* as an example which aims to determine whether a product review document reflects a positive or a negative view. Sentiment classification is very useful in online shopping applications, since it allows vendors to know which products are liked by the customers and for what reasons. Many machine learning techniques have been developed for sentiment classification, which have shown good performance when there are sufficient labeled data for training in one specific domain.

Sentiment classification is a domain-dependent task. Table 3.2 gives some examples on domain differences of sentiment terms. Table 3.2 shows several user review sentences from two domains: electronics and video games. In the electronics domain, we may use words like "compact," "sharp" to express our positive sentiment, and "blurry" to express our negative sentiment. While in the video game domain, words like "hooked" and "realistic" indicate positive opinion and the word "boring" indicates negative opinion. Due to the mismatch between domain-specific words, a sentiment classifier trained in one domain may not work well when directly applied to other domains. Thus, cross-domain sentiment classification algorithms are highly desirable for reducing the domain dependency and manually labeling cost.

Among the cross-domain sentiment classification algorithms, most adopt the feature-representation-based approaches. As we see in Table 3.2, some sentiment terms are shared across domains while some are domain dependent. Thus, they can be used to map between two domains. One example is the work by Blitzer et al. [11], who propose the structural correspondence learning (SCL) algorithm to exploit domain adaptation techniques for sentiment classification. As we mentioned above, the SCL algorithm first identifies the common features that are shared among different domains as the pivot features. It then uses unlabeled data and the pivot features from both source

TABLE 3.3: Results on sentiment classification.

Dataset	No Transfer	SCL	SFA	Bound
Book → DVD	77.3%	78.5%	81.4%	82.6%
DVD → Book	74.1%	77.6%	77.1%	81.4%
Kitchen → Electronic	82.8%	85.1%	85.0%	84.6%
Electronic → Kitchen	85.0%	85.1%	86.8%	87.1%

and target domains to find a mapping between the features from these domains, by which a common feature space is constructed. Extending this idea, Pan et al. [44] develop a spectral feature alignment (SFA) algorithm to align domain-specific words from different domains into unified clusters, with the help of domain-independent words as a bridge. Compared to SCL, SFA can discover a robust representation for cross-domain data by fully exploiting the relationship between the domain-specific and domain-independent words via simultaneously co-clustering them in a common latent space. Table 3.3 shows some experimental results on sentiment classification [44]. We can observe that the domain adaptation algorithms achieve better performance than the baseline without considering out-of-domain data. The bound indicates the performance of the gold standard, which is an in-domain classifier trained with labeled data from the target domain.

3.4 Multi-Task Learning Models

Transfer learning is focused on learning in the target domain, where the source domains are only used as auxiliary information. In contrast, multi-task learning seeks to improve the generalization performance of each learning task with the help of the other related tasks [14, 7, 53]. As we mentioned in the beginning of the chapter, most existing multi-task learning methods consider all tasks to have the same importance. In this setting, we review some existing methods for multi-task learning problems, which can be further categorized into five sets: common representation approach, task regularization approach, task clustering approach, hierarchical Bayesian approach, and task relationship learning approach.

3.4.1 Common-Representation-Based Approach

The "representation" here mostly denotes data representation. Neural network is the earliest model in this category. Note that a multi-task neural network is just a conventional multilayer feed-forward neural network that captures the commonality of the tasks when learning. In a multi-task neural network, the hidden layer corresponds to common data representation after some linear or nonlinear transformation. Following this strategy, Liao and Carin [38] extend radial basis function networks for multi-task learning. In their work, the hidden layer is treated as a common representation for each task. Since the radial basis function network has an analytical solution, it can use the data points in multiple tasks to determine the form of the RBF function in the hidden layer, which can be learned via active learning.

Argyriou et al. [4, 5] propose a multi-task feature learning method to learn the common representation for multi-task learning under a regularization framework:

$$\xi(\mathbf{U}, \mathbf{A}) = \sum_{i=1}^{k} \sum_{j=1}^{n_i} l(y_j^i, \mathbf{a}_i^{\mathrm{T}} \mathbf{U}^{\mathrm{T}} \mathbf{x}_j^i) + \gamma ||\mathbf{A}||_{2,1}^2, \tag{3.3}$$

where $l(\cdot, \cdot)$ denotes the loss function, $\mathbf{U}$ is the common transformation to find common representation, $\mathbf{a}_i$ is the model parameters for task T_i, $\mathbf{A} = (\mathbf{a}_1, \ldots, \mathbf{a}_k)$, and $||\mathbf{A}||_{2,1} = \sum_j ||\mathbf{A}^j||_2$ denotes $l_{1,2}$ norm of a matrix $\mathbf{A}$, where $\mathbf{A}^j$ denotes jth row of $\mathbf{A}$. The $l_{1,2}$ norm in regularization function will lead to zero-row in $\mathbf{A}$, which is equivalent to feature selection on $\mathbf{U}^T \mathbf{x}_j^i$, because of the sparsity property of l_1 norm. An alternating method is used to learn the model parameters.

The common representation in multi-task neural network and multi-task feature learning is some form of transformation on the original data representation. Obozinski et al. [41] propose a feature selection method for multi-task learning, the formulation of which is similar to Equation (3.3) but without $\mathbf{U}$. This can be viewed as a multi-task extension of LASSO [55]. Jebara [31] extends the maximum entropy discrimination (MED) method to multi-task learning [29]. MED solves the feature and kernel selection problems in multi-task learning settings, in which a selected subset of features and the kernel combination coefficients are shared by the tasks.

3.4.2 Task Regularization Approach

The task-regularization methods are all under the regularization framework, which consists of two objective function terms: an empirical loss on the training data of each task, and a regularization term that encodes the relationship between tasks for reducing the model complexity.

Evgeniou and Pontil [21] propose a multi-task extension of SVM, which minimizes the following objective function:

$$\xi(\{\mathbf{w}_i\}) = \sum_{i=1}^{k} \sum_{j=1}^{n_i} l(y_j^i, \mathbf{w}_i^{\mathrm{T}} \mathbf{x}_j^i) + \lambda_1 \sum_{i=1}^{k} ||\mathbf{w}_i||_2^2 + \lambda_2 \sum_{i=1}^{k} ||\mathbf{w}_i - \frac{1}{k} \sum_{j=1}^{k} \mathbf{w}_j||_2^2. \tag{3.4}$$

The first and second terms of Equation (3.4) denote the empirical error and 2-norm of parameter vectors, respectively, which are the same as those of single-task SVMs. However, the third term is designed to penalize large deviation between each parameter vector and the mean parameter vector of all tasks, which enforces the parameter vectors in all tasks are similar to each other.

In [20], Evgeniou et al. extend the work in [21] and propose a multi-task kernel, by which the formulation of multi-task kernel methods can be reduced to that in single-task kernel methods.

Similar to [20], by utilizing an unweighted task network to encode the relatedness between tasks, Kato et al. [32] propose a different multi-task learning method, which is also based on SVM. The formulation can be written as

$$\min \quad \xi(\{\mathbf{w}_i\}) = \sum_{i=1}^{k} \sum_{j=1}^{n_i} l(y_j^i, \mathbf{w}_i^\mathrm{T} \mathbf{x}_j^i) + \lambda_1 \sum_{i=1}^{k} ||\mathbf{w}_i||_2^2 + \lambda_2 \rho$$

$$s.t. \quad ||\mathbf{w}_{i_k} - \mathbf{w}_{j_k}||_2^2 \le \rho \text{ for } T_{i_k} \text{ and } T_{j_k} \text{ are related,}$$

which means the difference of the parameter vectors of any two related tasks is small.

3.4.3   Task Clustering Approach

Thrun and O'Sullivan [54] were the first to propose a task clustering method for multi-task learning. The main idea is to cluster all tasks into several clusters, in which the related tasks are assumed to share similar representations. The base learner in [54] is weighted K-Nearest-Neighbor classifier, in which each feature is given a weight for computing a distance metric, which are then used in clustering.

Different from [54], Bakker and Heskes [6] propose a Bayesian multi-task neural network, which has a structure that is the same as that of conventional multi-task neural network in which the input-to-hidden-layer weights are shared by all tasks. Different from the multi-task neural network, the hidden-layer-to-output-layer weights $\mathbf{A}_i$ for each task have a common prior.

Task-clustering methods require the number of clusters to be given, which is difficult for many real-world applications, Xue et al. [61] propose a task clustering multi-task learning method, which utilizes a nonparametric Bayesian model, the Dirichlet process (DP), as a basic mechanism to cluster tasks without knowing the number of clusters. For each task, they use logistic regression to model the data:

$$p(y_j^i | \mathbf{x}_j^i, \mathbf{w}_i) = \sigma(y_j^i \mathbf{w}_i^\mathrm{T} \mathbf{x}_j^i).$$

Then we add a DP prior to $\mathbf{w}_i$ as

$$\mathbf{w}_i \sim \mathrm{DP}(\alpha_0, G_0),$$

where α_0 denotes the concentration parameter and G_0 denotes the base measure.

Researchers have also considered a task clustering approach under the regularization framework. Jacob et al. [30] propose a regularization method by incorporating the cluster structure as a regularization term. In [30], researchers introduce a cluster indicator matrix and integrate the cluster structure and empirical loss in the same objective function. A limitation of this method is that the number of clusters in multiple tasks must be given as a prior.

3.4.4   Hierarchical Bayesian Approach

The hierarchical Bayesian model is well studied in the statistics community and widely used in many applications. Heskes [27] proposes a Bayesian multi-task neural network method for multi-task learning, in which the hidden-to-output weights for each task have a prior whose parameters are shared by all tasks. This model is similar to that in [6].

Micchelli and Pontil [40] were the first to employ a Gaussian process (GP)[50] in multi-task learning. Lawrence and Platt [35] generalize the informative vector machine (IVM)[36], which is a sparse extension of GP, to multi-task learning. In this method, the parameters in the kernel function are shared by all tasks. Thus, the formulation in multi-task IVM is identical to that of single-task IVM with the covariance matrix being a block matrix. Each sub-diagonal matrix of this block matrix corresponds to the covariance matrix for each task.

Yu et al. [64] propose a hierarchical Bayesian model, which utilizes a GP for each task for multi-task regression. The nonparametric GP prior for each task is identical and the mean and covariance matrices have a conjugate prior in this model. Then, an EM algorithm is used to learn the mean and covariance matrix. Since the learned kernel matrix has no parametric form, when making a prediction, approximate estimation of kernel function is needed. Since all tasks share the same GP prior, the hierarchical model is affected by outlier tasks, which motivates a robust extension [66, 72] by utilizing a t-process (TP) model. Different from the above methods, which are mostly based on GP, Zhang et al. [68] describe a latent variable model for multi-task learning. For each task T_i, the classifier or regressor is parameterized by some parameters $\boldsymbol{\theta}_i$. Then, the parameters $\boldsymbol{\theta}_i$ in different tasks are assumed to satisfy a latent variable model

$$\boldsymbol{\theta}_i = \boldsymbol{\Lambda}\mathbf{s}_i + \mathbf{e}_i$$
$$\mathbf{e}_i \sim \mathcal{N}(\mathbf{0}, \boldsymbol{\Psi}).$$

From this formula, we can see $\boldsymbol{\Lambda}$ and $\boldsymbol{\Psi}$ are shared by all tasks. By changing the probabilistic form of $\mathbf{s}_i$, this model is flexible to describe many variants in multi-task learning, such as independent tasks, noisy tasks, clusters of tasks, tasks having sparse representations, duplicated tasks, and evolving tasks.

3.4.5   Task Relationship Learning Approach

In multi-task learning, a central issue is how to characterize the task relationships between different tasks. Most existing methods solve this problem by making an assumption on the task relationship, e.g., all task are similar or share the same data representation. Some methods utilize some a priori knowledge in some specific domains. However, in most cases, model assumption is hard to verify directly from the data. Moreover, in most applications, the a priori knowledge about task relationships does not exist. In these cases, we hope to learn task relationships from the data directly. Task clustering approaches can be viewed as a way to learn task relationships, although the learned relationship is only "local" since they mostly ignore the negative correlations that may exist between different tasks in different task clusters. The multi-task GP model proposed in [12] is the first to learn the global task relationships in the form of a task covariance matrix. In the following, we briefly review this method.

The multi-task GP model in [12] directly models the task covariance matrix $\boldsymbol{\Sigma}$ by incorporating it into the GP prior, as follows:

$$\langle f_j^i, f_s^r \rangle = \Sigma_{ir} k(\mathbf{x}_j^i, \mathbf{x}_s^r), \tag{3.5}$$

where $\langle \cdot, \cdot \rangle$ denotes the covariance of two random variables, f_j^i is the latent function value for the jth data point $\mathbf{x}_j^i$ in the ith task, Σ_{ir} is the (i, r)th element of $\boldsymbol{\Sigma}$, and $k(\cdot, \cdot)$ is a kernel function. The output y_j^i given f_j^i is distributed as

$$y_j^i | f_j^i \sim \mathcal{N}(f_j^i, \sigma_i^2),$$

which defines the likelihood for $\mathbf{x}_j^i$. Here y_j^i is the label for $\mathbf{x}_j^i$ and σ_i^2 is the noise level of the ith task. One advantage of the formulation in [12] is its analytical form for the marginal likelihood. This is similar to conventional GP models where inference can be done efficiently. However, the model suffers from several drawbacks. One drawback is that when the number of tasks is large, the low-rank approximation used to reduce its computational cost may limit its expressive power. Another limitation is that, since the log-likelihood is non-convex with respect to $\boldsymbol{\Sigma}$ or to its low-rank approximation, the solution found by parameter-learning algorithms may be very sensitive to the initial value of $\boldsymbol{\Sigma}$ with no guarantee of the optimal solution.

To overcome the drawbacks of multi-task GP and also develop methods to learn the task relationships in other models, Zhang and Yeung developed a method called multi-task relationship learning method [71] that learns the task relationship under the regularization framework:

$$\min_{\mathbf{W}, \mathbf{b}, \boldsymbol{\Omega}} \quad \sum_{i=1}^{m} \frac{1}{n_i} \sum_{j=1}^{n_i} (y_j^i - \mathbf{w}_i^{\mathrm{T}} \mathbf{x}_j^i - b_i)^2 + \frac{\lambda_1}{2} \operatorname{tr}(\mathbf{W}\mathbf{W}^{\mathrm{T}}) + \frac{\lambda_2}{2} \operatorname{tr}(\mathbf{W}\boldsymbol{\Omega}^{-1}\mathbf{W}^{\mathrm{T}})$$

$$\text{s.t.} \quad \boldsymbol{\Omega} \succeq 0$$

$$\operatorname{tr}(\boldsymbol{\Omega}) \leq 1, \tag{3.6}$$

where $\mathbf{w}_i$ and b_i are the model parameters for the ith task and $\mathbf{W} = (\mathbf{w}_1, \dots, \mathbf{w}_m)$. This method can be viewed as maximum a posteriori (MAP) solution of the following probabilistic model:

$$\mathbf{W} \quad \sim \quad \left(\prod_{i=1}^{m} \mathcal{N}(\mathbf{w}_i \mid \mathbf{0}_d, \epsilon_i^2 \mathbf{I}_d)\right) q(\mathbf{W}) \qquad (3.7)$$

$$y_j^i \mid \mathbf{x}_j^i, \mathbf{w}_i, b_i \quad \sim \quad \mathcal{N}(\mathbf{w}_i^T \mathbf{x}_j^i + b_i, \varepsilon_i^2), \qquad (3.8)$$

where $\mathcal{N}(\mathbf{m}, \boldsymbol{\Sigma})$ denotes the multivariate (or univariate) normal distribution with mean $\mathbf{m}$ and covariance matrix (or variance) $\boldsymbol{\Sigma}$. The novelty lies in the prior $q(\mathbf{W})$ on $\mathbf{W}$ which belongs to matrix variate distribution [25]. When $q(\mathbf{W}) = \mathcal{MN}_{d \times m}(\mathbf{0}, \mathbf{I} \otimes \boldsymbol{\Omega})$ where $\mathcal{MN}_{d \times m}(\mathbf{M}, \mathbf{A} \otimes \mathbf{B})$ denotes the matrix variate normal distribution[2] with mean $\mathbf{M} \in \mathbb{R}^{d \times m}$, row covariance matrix $\mathbf{A} \in \mathbb{R}^{d \times d}$ and column covariance matrix $\mathbf{B} \in \mathbb{R}^{m \times m}$, the MAP solution will lead to Problem (3.6). Here $\boldsymbol{\Omega}$ is the column covariance matrix of $\mathbf{W}$ where each column represents each task and hence $\boldsymbol{\Omega}$ can represent the task covariance. Moreover, when $q(\mathbf{W}) = \mathcal{MN}_{d \times m}(\mathbf{0}, \boldsymbol{\Sigma} \otimes \mathbf{I})$, the MAP solution will become the multi-task feature learning formulation presented in [4, 5].

3.4.6 Application Examples of Multi-Task Learning

Multi-task learning has many applications in machine learning areas, e.g., computer vision, information retrieval, bioinformatics. We will review some of these applications in the following.

- *Face Recognition*: Heisele et al. [26] propose a multi-task learning method for face recognition. This method first detects the components of a face and then combines the component features and a whole face for face recognition. Lapedriza et al. [34] propose a multi-task feature extraction method for face recognition. In this method, face recognition is treated as a target task, while other face tasks such as facial expression recognition are complementary tasks to help improve the performance of face recognition. This method works by maximizing the mutual information between low-dimensional representation and subject labels in face recognition while minimizing the mutual information between low-dimensional representation and labels in complementary tasks using quadratic mutual information [56].

- *Image Classification*: Quattoni et al. [46] propose a method for image classification using a prototype representation. In this method, unlabeled data are used first to learn prototype representation, then used to select prototypes learned in the previous stage by learning from some previous supervised learning tasks. They then use the selected prototypes for the target task. Ahmed et al. [1] propose a method for visual

---

[2]The probability density function is defined as $p(\mathbf{X} \mid \mathbf{M}, \mathbf{A}, \mathbf{B}) = \frac{\exp\left(-\frac{1}{2}\operatorname{tr}\left(\mathbf{A}^{-1}(\mathbf{X}-\mathbf{M})\mathbf{B}^{-1}(\mathbf{X}-\mathbf{M})^T\right)\right)}{(2\pi)^{md/2}|\mathbf{A}|^{m/2}|\mathbf{B}|^{d/2}}$.

recognition via using multi-task neural network, in which the target task and pseudo-tasks share a common representation via a common hidden layer. This method also proposes to generate pseudo-tasks for visual recognition tasks. Kienzle and Chellapilla [33] propose a biased regularization method for personalized handwriting recognition, in which the parameters of SVM in source tasks provide a bias of the target task. This bias is added to the regularization term of SVM for target task as a prior.

- *Object Detection*: Torralba et al. [57] propose a method for multiclass object detection. Different from previous methods in object detection that train a classifier for individual object detection, this method solves multi-class object detection simultaneously by using shared features in multi-class objects, which can also reduce the number of features used in object detection.

- *Image Segmentation*: An et al. [2] utilize the Dirichlet process and kernel stick-breaking process to segment multiple images simultaneously. The Dirichlet process is used as a prior of base measure in the kernel stick-breaking process and the kernel stick-breaking process is used to incorporate the spatial information contained in images to help the segmentation and cluster image features in multiple images into several clusters to complete image segmentation. This work can be viewed as a way for multi-task clustering.

- *Collaborative Filtering*: Yu et al. [65] unify content-based filtering and collaborative filtering (CF) in a framework by using the task clustering method, in which the parameters for each user profile share the same DP prior. Yu and Tresp [63] propose using a multi-task learning method to solve the CF problem. In this model, the low-rank matrix approximation, which is used widely in CF, can be reformulated as a similar formulation in regularization framework in multi-task learning. The methods in [13, 70] utilize the useful information in multiple domains to improve the performance on each domain by learning domain relations in the form of a covariance matrix.

- *Age Estimation*: In [73], Zhang and Yeung formulate the age estimation problem as a multi-task learning problem, where each task corresponds to estimating ages based on the images of one person, and propose a multi-task extension of warped GP to solve this problem.

- *Text Classification*: Raina et al. [49] propose a transfer learning method for binary text classification problem. This method places a Gaussian prior on the parameters of logistic regression for target task and it learns the covariance matrix of the covariance matrix from source tasks. Do and Ng [19] also propose a logistic regression-based method for text classification for multi-class problems.

- *Bioinformatics*: Xu et al. [60] use multi-task learning to solve the protein subcellular location prediction problem. Liu et al. [39] use the multi-task feature learning method [4, 5] for cross-platform siRNA efficacy prediction, and Zhang et al. [69] identify common mechanisms of responses to therapeutic targets. Puniyani et al. [45] utilize the multi-task feature selection method on multi-population GWA mapping problems, and Lee et al. [37] extend multi-task feature selection method by learning the hyperparameters for solving the eQTL detection problem. Bickel et al. [8] provide a multi-task learning method based distribution matching for HIV therapy screening.

- *Finance*: Ghosn and Bengio [23] apply a multi-task learning method for stock selection. Different from previous methods, which use one neural network to predict the return of one stock, the method in [23] learns several stocks in one neural network, in which the hidden layer is shared by all stocks and can be viewed as a common representation for all stocks. Experimental results show the generalization ability of a multi-task neural network is much better than various benchmarks.

- *Robot Inverse Dynamics*: The methods in [15, 62] apply the multi-task GP regression model in [12] for robot inverse dynamics that can improve the performance over previous methods.

3.5   Conclusion and Future Work

In this chapter, we have discussed transfer learning and multi-task learning frameworks and related them to cost-sensitive learning. Transfer and multi-task learning approaches are useful when a learning problem is difficult to solve in some target domains, but some related knowledge can be found in some other domains. In such cases, we may find some common knowledge to link these domains to help improve the learning performance. We have systematically reviewed typical approaches to transfer and multi-task learning problems in inductive learning settings. In particular, we have pointed out that transfer learning can be seen as a type of cost-sensitive learning where the costs are associated with the instances in both the source and target domains, and heavier weights can also be associated with the target domain.

Many successful learning algorithms have been proposed for situations where the covariate shift assumption holds. However, this is not the case when covariate shift assumption fails. One future work is to explore if there may exist some weaker assumptions under which successfully transfer learning algorithms could still be applied. From a cost-sensitive learning perspective, another future work is to study how the task-associated costs, such as misclassification costs, can be properly distributed across different domains in isolating the common knowledge that can be transferred between the tasks. Since the task relationship can be encoded as the task covariance matrix, a related problem is how to best estimate the covariance between the tasks that corresponds to the costs. To achieve this goal, we must have a good understanding of the task structures in addition to the data features.

References

[1] A. Ahmed, K. Yu, W. Xu, Y. Gong, and E. P. Xing. Training hierarchical feed-forward visual recognition models using transfer learning from pseudo-tasks. In *Proceedings of the 10th European Conference on Computer Vision*, pages 69–82, Marseille, France, 2008.

[2] Q. An, C. Wang, I. Shterev, E. Wang, L. Carin, and D. B. Dunson. Hierarchical kernel stick-breaking process for multi-task image analysis. In *Proceedings of the Twenty-Fifth International Conference on Machine Learning*, pages 17–24, Helsinki, Finland, 2008.

[3] R. K. Ando and T. Zhang. A framework for learning predictive structures from multiple tasks and unlabeled data. *Journal of Machine Learning Research*, 6, 2005.

[4] A. Argyriou, T. Evgeniou, and M. Pontil. Multi-task feature learning. In B. Schölkopf, J. C. Platt, and T. Hoffman, editors, *Advances in Neural Information Processing Systems 19*, pages 41–48, Vancouver, British Columbia, Canada, 2006.

[5] A. Argyriou, T. Evgeniou, and M. Pontil. Convex multi-task feature learning. *Machine Learning*, 73(3):243–272, 2008.

[6] B. Bakker and T. Heskes. Task clustering and gating for Bayesian multitask learning. *Journal of Machine Learning Research*, 4:83–99, 2003.

[7] J. Baxter. A Bayesian/information theoretic model of learning to learn via multiple task sampling. *Machine Learning*, 28(1):7–39, 1997.

[8] S. Bickel, J. Bogojeska, T. Lengauer, and T. Scheffer. Multi-task learning for HIV therapy screening. In *Proceedings of the Twenty-Fifth International Conference on Machine Learning*, pages 56–63, Helsinki, Finland, 2008.

[9] S. Bickel and T. Scheffer. Discriminative learning under covariate shift. *Journal of Machine Learning Research*, 10:2137–2155, 2009.

[10] J. Blitzer, K. Crammer, A. Kulesza, F. Pereira, and J. Wortman. Learning bounds for domain adaptation. *Advances in Neural Information Processing Systems*, 20:129–136, 2007.

[11] J. Blitzer, R. McDonald, and F. Pereira. Domain adaptation with structural correspondence learning. In *Proceedings of the 2006 Conference on Empirical Methods in Natural Language Processing*, pages 120–128, Sydney, Australia, July 2006. Association for Computational Linguistics.

[12] E. Bonilla, K. M. A. Chai, and C. Williams. Multi-task Gaussian process prediction. In J.C. Platt, D. Koller, Y. Singer, and S. Roweis, editors, *Advances in Neural Information Processing Systems 20*, pages 153–160, Vancouver, British Columbia, Canada, 2007.

[13] B. Cao, N. N. Liu, and Q. Yang. Transfer learning for collective link prediction in multiple heterogenous domains. In *Proceedings of the 27th International Conference on Machine Learning*, pages 159–166, Haifa, Israel, 2010.

[14] R. Caruana. Multitask learning. *Machine Learning*, 28(1):41–75, 1997.

[15] K. M. A. Chai, C. K. I. Williams, S. Klanke, and S. Vijayakumar. Multi-task Gaussian process learning of robot inverse dynamics. In D. Koller, D. Schuurmans, Y. Bengio, and L. Bottou, editors, *Advances in Neural Information Processing Systems 21*, pages 265–272, Vancouver, British Columbia, Canada, 2008.

[16] C. Cortes, M. Mohri, M. Riley, and A. Rostamizadeh. Sample selection bias correction theory. In *Proceedings of the International Conference on Algorithmic Learning Theory*. Springer, pages 38–53, 2008.

[17] W. Dai, G.-R. Xue, Q. Yang, and Y. Yu. Transferring Naive Bayes classifiers for text classification. In *Proceedings of The National Conference on Artifical Intelligence*, pages 540–545, 2007.

[18] W. Dai, Q. Yang, G.-R. Xue, and Y. Yu. Boosting for transfer learning. In *Proceedings of the 24th International Conference on Machine Learning*, pages 193–200, Corvalis, OR, 2007, ACM Press, New York.

[19] C. Do and A. Ng. Transfer learning for text classification. In Y. Weiss, B. Schölkopf, and J. Platt, editors, *Advances in Neural Information Processing Systems 18*, pages 299–306, Vancouver, British Columbia, Canada, 2006.

[20] T. Evgeniou, C. A. Micchelli, and M. Pontil. Learning multiple tasks with kernel methods. *Journal of Machine Learning Research*, 6:615–637, 2005.

[21] T. Evgeniou and M. Pontil. Regularized multi-task learning. In *Proceedings of the Tenth ACM SIGKDD International Conference on Knowledge Discovery and Data Mining*, pages 109–117, Seattle, WA, 2004.

[22] Y. Freund. Boosting a weak learning algorithm by majority. In *Proceedings of the Third Annual Workshop on Computational Learning Theory*, pages 202–216, New York, 1990.

[23] J. Ghosn and Y. Bengio. Multi-task learning for stock selection. In M. Mozer, M. I. Jordan, and T. Petsche, editors, *Advances in Neural Information Processing Systems 9*, pages 946–952, Denver, CO, 1996.

[24] A. Gretton, K. M. Borgwardt, M. Rasch, B. Schölkopf, and A. J. Smola. A kernel method for the two-sample-problem. *Journal of Machine Learning Research*, 1:1–10, 2008.

[25] A. K. Gupta and D. K. Nagar. *Matrix Variate Distributions*. Chapman & Hall, New York, 2000.

[26] B. Heisele, T. Serre, M. Pontil, T. Vetter, and T. Poggio. Categorization by learning and combining object parts. In T. G. Dietterich, S. Becker, and Z. Ghahramani, editors, *Advances in Neural Information Processing Systems 14*, pages 1239–1245, Vancouver, British Columbia, Canada, 2001.

[27] T. Heskes. Solving a huge number of similar tasks: A combination of multi-task learning and a hierarchical Bayesian approach. In *Proceedings of the Fifteenth International Conference on Machine Learning*, pages 233–241, Madison, WI, 1998.

[28] J. Huang, A. J. Smola, A. Gretton, K. M. Borgwardt, and B. Schölkopf. Correcting sample selection bias by unlabeled data. In B. Schölkopf, J. Platt, and T. Hoffman, editors, *Advances in Neural Information Processing Systems 19*, pages 601–608. MIT Press, Cambridge, MA, 2007.

[29] T. Jaakkola, M. Meila, and T. Jebara. Maximum entropy discrimination. In S. A. Solla, T. K. Leen, and K.-R. Müller, editors, *Advances in Neural Information Processing Systems 12*, pages 470–476, Denver, CO, 1999.

[30] L. Jacob, F. Bach, and J.-P. Vert. Clustered multi-task learning: A convex formulation. In D. Koller, D. Schuurmans, Y. Bengio, and L. Bottou, editors, *Advances in Neural Information Processing Systems 21*, pages 745–752, Vancouver, British Columbia, Canada, 2008.

[31] T. Jebara. Multi-task feature and kernel selection for SVMs. In *Proceedings of the Twenty-First International Conference on Machine Learning*, pages 55–62, Banff, Alberta, Canada, 2004.

[32] T. Kato, H. Kashima, M. Sugiyama, and K. Asai. Multi-task learning via conic programming. In J. C. Platt, D. Koller, Y. Singer, and S. Roweis, editors, *Advances in Neural Information Processing Systems 20*, pages 737–744, Vancouver, British Columbia, Canada, 2007.

[33] W. Kienzle and K. Chellapilla. Personalized handwriting recognition via biased regularization. In *Proceedings of the Twenty-Third International Conference on Machine Learning*, pages 457–464, Pittsburgh, PA, 2006.

[34] À. Lapedriza, D. Masip, and J. Vitrì. On the use of independent tasks for face recognition. In *Proceedings of the IEEE Computer Society Conference on Computer Vision and Pattern Recognition*, pages 1–6, Anchorage, Alaska, 2008.

[35] N. D. Lawrence and J. C. Platt. Learning to learn with the informative vector machine. In *Proceedings of the Twenty-First International Conference on Machine Learning*, Banff, Alberta, Canada, 2004.

[36] N. D. Lawrence, M. Seeger, and R. Herbrich. Fast sparse Gaussian process methods: The informative vector machine. In S. Becker, S. Thrun, and K. Obermayer, editors, *Advances in Neural Information Processing Systems 15*, pages 609–616, Vancouver, British Columbia, Canada, 2002.

[37] S. Lee, J. Zhu, and E. Xing. Adaptive multi-task lasso: With application to eQTL detection. In J. Lafferty, C. K. I. Williams, J. Shawe-Taylor, R.S. Zemel, and A. Culotta, editors, *Advances in Neural Information Processing Systems 23*, pages 1306–1314, 2010.

[38] X. Liao and L. Carin. Radial basis function network for multi-task learning. In Y. Weiss, B. Schölkopf, and J. Platt, editors, *Advances in Neural Information Processing Systems 18*, pages 795–802, Vancouver, British Columbia, Canada, 2005.

[39] Q. Liu, Q. Xu, V. W. Zheng, H. Xue, Z. Cao, and Q. Yang. Multi-task learning for cross-platform siRNA efficacy prediction: An in-silico study. *BMC Bioinformatics*, 11, page 181, 2010.

[40] T. P. Minka and R. W. Picard. Learning how to learn is learning with point sets. MIT Media Lab note, 1997, revised in 1999.

[41] G. Obozinski, B. Taskar, and M. Jordan. Multi-task feature selection. Technical report, Department of Statistics, University of California, Berkeley, June 2006.

[42] S. Pan and Q. Yang. A survey on transfer learning. *IEEE Transactions on Knowledge and Data Engineering*, 22(10):1345–1359, 2010.

[43] S. J. Pan, J. T. Kwok, and Q. Yang. Transfer learning via dimensionality reduction. In *Proceedings of the Twenty-Third AAAI Conference on Artificial Intelligence*, pages 677–682, 2008.

[44] S. J. Pan, X. Ni, J.-T. Sun, Q. Yang, and Z. Chen. Cross-domain sentiment classification via spectral feature alignment. *Proceedings of the 19th International Conference on World Wide Web*, 2010.

[45] K. Puniyani, S. Kim, and E. P. Xing. Multi-population GWA mapping via multi-task regularized regression. *Bioinformatics [ISMB]*, 26(12):208–216, 2010.

[46] A. Quattoni, M. Collins, and T. Darrell. Transfer learning for image classification with sparse prototype representations. In *Proceedings of the IEEE Computer Society Conference on Computer Vision and Pattern Recognition*, pages 1–8, Anchorage, AK, 2008.

[47] J. Quionero-Candela, M. Sugiyama, A. Schwaighofer, and N. D. Lawrence. *Dataset Shift in Machine Learning*. MIT Press, Cambridge, MA, 2009.

[48] R. Raina, A. Battle, H. Lee, B. Packer, and A. Y. Ng. Self-taught learning: Transfer learning from unlabeled data. In *Proceedings of the 24th International Conference on Machine Learning*, pages 759–766, New York, 2007.

[49] R. Raina, A. Y. Ng, and D. Koller. Constructing informative priors using transfer learning. In *Proceedings of the Twenty-Third International Conference on Machine Learning*, pages 713–720, Pittsburgh, Pennsylvania, 2006.

[50] C. E. Rasmussen and C. K. I. Williams. *Gaussian Processes for Machine Learning*. MIT Press, Cambridge, MA, 2006.

[51] S. Si, D. Tao, and B. Geng. Bregman Divergence-Based Regularization for Transfer Subspace Learning. *IEEE Transactions on Knowledge and Data Engineering*, 22(7):929–942, July 2010.

[52] M. Sugiyama. Covariate shift adaptation by importance weighted cross-validation. *Journal of Machine Learning Research*, 8:985–1005, 2007.

[53] S. Thrun. Is learning the n-th thing any easier than learning the first? In D. S. Touretzky, M. Mozer, and M. E. Hasselmo, editors, *Advances in Neural Information Processing Systems 8*, pages 640–646, Denver, CO, 1995.

[54] S. Thrun and J. O'Sullivan. Discovering structure in multiple learning tasks: The TC algorithm. In *Proceedings of the Thirteenth International Conference on Machine Learning*, pages 489–497, Bari, Italy, 1996.

[55] R. Tibshirani. Regression shrinkage and selection via the lasso. *Journal of the Royal Statistical Society. Series B(Methodological)*, 58(1):267–288, 1996.

[56] K. Torkkola. Feature extraction by non-parametric mutual information maximization. *Journal of Machine Learning Reasearch*, 3:1415–1438, 2003.

[57] A. B. Torralba, K. P. Murphy, and W. T. Freeman. Sharing features: Efficient boosting procedures for multiclass object detection. In *Proceedings of the IEEE Computer Society Conference on Computer Vision and Pattern Recognition*, pages 762–769, Washington, DC, 2004.

[58] Y. Tsuboi, H. Kashima, S. Hido, S. Bickel, and M. Sugiyama. Direct density ratio estimation for large-scale covariate shift adaptation. In *Proceedings of the SIAM International Conference on Data Mining*, pages 443–454, Atlanta, GA, 2008.

[59] V. N. Vapnik. *Statistical Learning Theory*. Wiley, New York, 1998.

[60] Q. Xu, S. Pan, H. Xue, and Q. Yang. Multitask learning for protein subcellular location prediction. *IEEE/ACM Transactions on Computational Biology and Bioinformatics*, pages 41–75, 2010.

[61] Y. Xue, X. Liao, L. Carin, and B. Krishnapuram. Multi-task learning for classification with Dirichlet process priors. *Journal of Machine Learning Research*, 8:35–63, 2007.

[62] D.-Y. Yeung and Y. Zhang. Learning inverse dynamics by Gaussian process regression under the multi-task learning framework. In G. S. Sukhatme, editor, *The Path to Autonomous Robots*, pages 131–142. Springer, New York, 2009.

[63] K. Yu and V. Tresp. Learning to learn and collaborative filtering. In *NIPS Workshop on Inductive Transfer: 10 Years Later*, Vancouver, British Columbia, Canada, 2005.

[64] K. Yu, V. Tresp, and A. Schwaighofer. Learning Gaussian processes from multiple tasks. In *Proceedings of the Twenty-Second International Conference on Machine Learning*, pages 1012–1019, Bonn, Germany, 2005.

[65] K. Yu, V. Tresp, and S. Yu. A nonparametric hierarchical bayesian framework for information filtering. In *Proceedings of the 27th Annual International ACM SIGIR Conference on Research and Development in Information Retrieval*, pages 353–360, Sheffield, UK, 2004.

[66] S. Yu, V. Tresp, and K. Yu. Robust multi-task learning with *t*-processes. In *Proceedings of the Twenty-Fourth International Conference on Machine Learning*, pages 1103–1110, Corvalis, OR, 2007.

[67] B. Zadrozny. Learning and evaluating classifiers under sample selection bias. In *Proceedings of the Twenty-First International Conference on Machine Learning*, pages 114, Banff, Alberta, Canada, 2004.

[68] J. Zhang, Z. Ghahramani, and Y. Yang. Learning multiple related tasks using latent independent component analysis. In Y. Weiss, B. Schölkopf, and J. Platt, editors, *Advances in Neural Information Processing Systems 18*, pages 1585–1592, Vancouver, British Columbia, Canada, 2005.

[69] K. Zhang, J. W. Gray, and B. Parvin. Sparse multitask regression for identifying common mechanism of response to therapeutic targets. *Bioinformatics [ISMB]*, 26(12):97–105, 2010.

[70] Y. Zhang, B. Cao, and D.-Y. Yeung. Multi-domain collaborative filtering. In *Proceedings of the 26th Conference on Uncertainty in Artificial Intelligence*, pages 725–732, Catalina Island, CA, 2010.

[71] Y. Zhang and D.-Y. Yeung. A convex formulation for learning task relationships in multi-task learning. In *Proceedings of the 26th Conference on Uncertainty in Artificial Intelligence*, pages 733–742, Catalina Island, CA, 2010.

[72] Y. Zhang and D.-Y. Yeung. Multi-task learning using generalized t process. In *Proceedings of the 13rd International Conference on Artificial Intelligence and Statistics*, pages 964–971, Chia Laguna Resort, Sardinia, Italy, 2010.

[73] Y. Zhang and D.-Y. Yeung. Multi-task warped Gaussian process for personalized age estimation. In *Proceedings of the 23rd IEEE Computer Society Conference on Computer Vision and Pattern Recognition*, pages 2622–2629, San Francisco, CA, 2010.

Chapter 4

Cost-Sensitive Cascades

Vikas C. Raykar

Siemens Healthcare, Malvern, Pennsylvania

4.1   Features Incur a Cost

In many applications the features used for classification are *acquired on demand*. Usually a set of features can be acquired as a group. However each feature group incurs a certain cost. This cost could be either computational (fast detectors), financial (expensive medical tests), or human discomfort (biopsy).

- *Computational*—For many real-time applications like face detection [19, 21] and computer-aided diagnosis [5, 23, 14] an important requirement is that run time of the classifier should be quite small to meet the real-time requirements. While computing the final classifier decision is not the bottleneck, computing the required features can be computationally very expensive. This can be due to two reasons: either (1) the classifier uses a lot (generally thousands) of cheap features or (2) computing certain group of features involves sophisticated computationally intensive image processing algorithms.

- *Financial*—In certain medical applications some tests are very expensive. For example in survival prediction for lung cancer [4, 14] the clinical

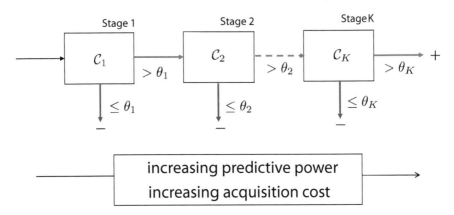

FIGURE 4.1: Illustration of a cascade of K classifiers, each stage using features with increasing predictive power and also increasing acquisition cost. Based on a threshold θ_j each stage $\mathcal{C}_j$ can either accept and pass a sample into the next stage for further feature acquisition or it can reject the sample immediately and classify it as negative.

features are already available and have zero acquisition cost while acquiring the blood biomarkers is generally very expensive.

- **Human discomfort**—Certain medical tests generally used for cancer detection can cause extreme discomfort for the patient (e.g., biopsy).

4.2   Cascade of Classifiers

This motivates the design of a *cascade of classifiers* (see Figure 4.1), each stage using features with *increasing predictive power* and also *increasing acquisition cost*. Each stage of the cascade can either accept and pass a sample into the next stage for further feature acquisition and further classification analysis or it can reject the sample immediately—classifying it as a negative class sample—thus avoiding any further (downstream) feature acquisition cost. Typically we would like the first stage of our classifier to use the cheapest features and the most expensive features at the later stage.

We will denote a K stage cascade by $[\mathcal{C}_1, \mathcal{C}_2, \ldots, \mathcal{C}_K]$. The features for any instance $\mathbf{x} \in \mathbb{R}^d$ are divided into K distinct sets—$\mathbf{x} = [\mathbf{x}^1, \mathbf{x}^2, \ldots, \mathbf{x}^K]$. This feature grouping is usually done based on the cost required to acquire these features. Let t_j be an estimate of the cost it takes to acquire/compute feature subset $\mathbf{x}^j$. Typically the cascade is ordered by the feature acquisition time t_j, i.e., we would like the first stage of our classifier to use the cheapest features and the most expensive features at the later stage. Based on the feature set $\mathbf{x}^j$ the classifier in jth stage of the cascade $\mathcal{C}_j$ computes a score $f_{\mathcal{C}_j}(\mathbf{x}^j)$ where f belong to a suitable class of discriminating functions. If the score $f_{\mathcal{C}_j}(\mathbf{x}^j) > \theta_j$ then it passes that instance to the next stage of the cascade for further feature acquisition and classification. If $f_{\mathcal{C}_j}(\mathbf{x}^j) \leq \theta_j$ the instance is immediately classified as negative. The threshold θ_j is generally chosen such that the early stages are designed to have high sensitivity and the later stages to have a high specificity.

Since the earliest stages use the cheapest features those examples which can be classified easily with only few features will be discarded quite early on without the need for further feature acquisition. Thus the cascade structure is inherently designed to reduce the average feature computation cost. In general, cascaded classifier design is used to reduce run time of the overall classifier by reducing the number of samples which need the computation of more expensive features. However, this process of cascaded classification may reduce accuracy of classification somewhat, but at the same time we do not want to sacrifice accuracy too much.

How to Draw a ROC for a Cascade?

Generally a binary classifier predicts the label of an instance $\mathbf{x}$ as positive $\hat{y} = 1$ if $f(\mathbf{x}) > \theta$ and $\hat{y} = 0$ if $f(\mathbf{x}) \leq \theta$. *Sensitivity* (or True Positive Fraction) is the fraction of positive instances that are correctly classified as positive, i.e., it is an estimate of $\Pr[\hat{y} = 1 | y = 1]$. Similarly *specificity* (or 1-False Positive Fraction) is the fraction of negative instances that are correctly classified as negative, i.e., it is an estimate of $\Pr[\hat{y} = 0 | y = 0]$. The Receiver Operating Characteristic (ROC) curve is a plot of sensitivity (on the Y-axis) vs. 1-specificity (on the X-axis) as the threshold θ is varied from $-\infty$ to ∞ and essentially characterizes the tradeoff between the two kinds of errors. Generally the thresholds $\theta_1, \ldots, \theta_K$ for the cascade are chosen such that the *early stages have a high sensitivity* and the *later stages have a high specificity*. High sensitivity is essential in the early stages because any example missed at this stage can never be detected.

One common way to visualize the ROC for a cascade is to plot the ROC for the last stage only (see the ROC for stage 3 in the figure below). Once the threshold for each stage is chosen we can also draw a combined ROC plot (as shown in the figure below) with only the relevant range of thresholds for each stage. The area under this ROC curve can be used to guide the automated threshold selection procedure.

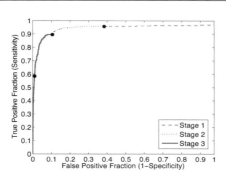

If d_j and $1 - f_j$ are the sensitivity and the specificity for the examples that pass through the jth stage of the cascade then the overall sensitivity and the specificity are given by $\prod_{j=1}^{K} d_j$ and $1 - \prod_{j=1}^{K} f_j$, respectively.

Different Cascade Scenarios

Conventionally each stage of the cascade uses only a subset of features. However the later stages can use the features used by the previous stages since they are already computed. Raykar et al. [14] describe the following three cascade scenarios.

- **Scenario 1** Each stage $\mathcal{C}_j$ of the cascade uses only the subset $\mathbf{x}^j$ of the features. Each cascade $\mathcal{C}_j$ is from a family of linear discriminating functions, where for any $\mathbf{x} \in \mathbb{R}^d$, $f_{\mathcal{C}_j}(\mathbf{x}) = \mathbf{w}_j^\top \mathbf{x}^j$.

- **Scenario 2** Each stage $\mathcal{C}_j$ uses the subset $\left[\mathbf{x}^1, \ldots, \mathbf{x}^j\right]$ of the features, i.e., the stage j can also use the features from all the previous stages since they are already computed. In this case $f_{\mathcal{C}_j}(\mathbf{x}) = \sum_{k=1}^{j} \mathbf{w}_k^\top \mathbf{x}^k$. This scenario is related to the ChainBoost embedded cascade [25] where a standard boosting algorithm is used to design a classifier and then thresholds are incorporated after each stage. This creates as many stages as weak learners.

- **Scenario 3** This is the same as the previous scenario, with the important difference that the weights for each stage are separate and not shared with the previous stage as in scenario 2. Hence $f_{\mathcal{C}_j}(\mathbf{x}) = \sum_{k=1}^{j} \mathbf{w}_{jk}^\top \mathbf{x}^k$.

4.3   Successful Applications of Cascaded Architectures

Two kinds of cascades are commonly reported in the literature—*detection/attentional cascades* and *cost sensitive classification cascades*.

4.3.1   Detection/Attentional Cascades

The detection cascades are typically designed in scenarios where we have a large number of relatively cheap features—all of them having roughly the same computational cost. There is no explicit notion of different costs for different feature groups. Also the design of these cascades reflect the fact that during testing the majority of the candidates passing through the cascade will be negative and the positive candidate is a rare event.

A lot of work on designing cascades is based on the Viola-Jones cascade framework [21, 19] and is developed for building rapid real-time object detection systems. In a typical object detection system a large number of subwindows in a given image are scanned at different scales and locations. For each such subwindow a large number of features are computed. A trained classifier is used to label each such subwindow. The Viola-Jones cascade for face detection is a method for combining successively more complex classifiers into a cascade which allows background regions to be quickly discarded while spending more computation on promising face-like regions. Each stage of the cascade is an AdaBoost classifier with decision stump as the base learner and has its own threshold. The cascade architecture was one of the key components[1] which allowed face detection to be performed at frame rate. Since then various improvements and other cost-sensitive modifications over the Viola-Jones cascade have been proposed [20, 3, 10, 1, 17, 7, 12, 26].

4.3.2   Cost-Sensitive Classification Cascades

The cost-sensitive classification cascades generally incorporate the notion of computation cost explicitly into the cascade design. These cascades are generally ordered by the feature acquisition time and we would like the first stage of the classifier to use the cheapest features and the most expensive features at the later stage. Generally it is also true that more expensive features have better predictive power.

Classification cascades have been successfully employed in computer-aided diagnosis (CAD) systems [5, 23, 14] which detect abnormal or malignant lesions from medical images. In [5] the authors applied a cascade architecture to the problem of automatically detecting polyps from multi-slice CT images. In

---

[1]The other two being the integral representation of the image and the feature selection mechanism provided by AdaBoost.

their system feature computation was the most expensive component in the pipeline and they obtained a significant improvement in the processing time by employing a three-stage cascade. Raykar et al. [14] designed a four-stage cascade for 2-year survival prediction for advanced non-small cell lung cancer patients treated with chemo/radiotherapy. The task was to predict whether the patient will survive for more than 2 years. They considered four groups of features which are known to be predictive for this problem.

Open Question: How Many Stages?

The detection cascades generally have a large number of stages. For example the face detection system in [21] had 38 stages in the cascade. However it has been observed by [5] for classification cascades the more stages in the cascade the higher risk for the system to be unstable—this is especially the case when we have a small training set. Hence for classification cascades it is preferable to have a small number of stages for better generalization performance. It is also not clear whether the generalization guarantees provided by AdaBoost carry over to cascade architectures.

4.4 Training a Cascade of Classifiers

We are given the training data $\mathcal{D} = \{(\mathbf{x}_i, y_i)\}_{i=1}^N$ containing N instances, where $\mathbf{x}_i \in \mathbb{R}^d$ is the d-dimensional feature vector and $y_i \in \{0, 1\}$ is the corresponding known label. The features for any instance $\mathbf{x}_i$ are divided into K distinct sets: $\mathbf{x}_i = [\mathbf{x}_i^1, \mathbf{x}_i^2, \ldots, \mathbf{x}_i^K]$. This feature grouping is usually done based on the cost required to acquire these features. Let t_j be an estimate of the cost it takes to acquire/compute feature subset $\mathbf{x}^j$. We will also assume that the order of the cascade is fixed. Typically the cascade is ordered by the feature acquisition time t_j, i.e., we would like the first stage of our classifier to use the cheapest features.

Training the cascade implies (a) learning the parameters of the classifier for each stage of the cascade $f_{\mathcal{C}_1}, \ldots, f_{\mathcal{C}_K}$ and (b) choosing the thresholds for each stage $\theta_1, \ldots, \theta_K$ to *minimize the error* on unseen data and also *minimizing the average cost* per instance. Satisfying all these tradeoffs is known to be an extremely hard problem. Various approximate training strategies have been used. The greedy sequential strategy learns one stage at a time hence requiring that the thresholds for the previous stages are fixed. The joint strategy learns all the stages simultaneously and also decouples the training process from the threshold selection process by relaxing the hard cascade into a soft probabilistic cascade.

4.4.1 Sequential Training of Each Stage

Conventionally detection cascades are trained in a *sequential manner*. Only examples for which the classifier score is greater than a certain threshold pass through the next stage of the cascade. Each stage of the classifier is trained using *only* those examples which pass through all the previous stages. As a result the sequential design needs the thresholds $\theta_1, \ldots, \theta_{j-1}$ for previous stages to be fixed before the classifier parameters of the next stage $\mathcal{C}_j$ are learned.

The choice of the thresholds is a design choice and can be chosen in an ad hoc fashion based on the domain knowledge and various cost constraints. We can also choose the thresholds by doing an exhaustive grid search over a range of thresholds for each stage such that some performance metric (like the area under the ROC curve and/or the average computational cost) is optimized. For each choice of the thresholds we have to retrain the cascade. This can be very expensive if the number of stages is large and the threshold selection is done over a fine grid. For example, for a five-stage cascade if we have to search over 10 thresholds for each stage in sequential training we have to train the cascade roughly 10^5 times. A hierarchical grid search can be less computationally demanding.

In the Viola-Jones cascade a strategy to sequentially add more stages was presented [21]. The user selects the maximum acceptable false positive rate and the minimum acceptable sensitivity for each stage based on the overall design goals. Each stage of the cascade was trained using an AdaBoost with the number of features used being increased until the target was met on an independent validation set. If the overall target false positive rate is not yet met then another layer is added to the cascade. The negative set for training subsequent layers is obtained by collecting all false detections found by running the current detectors on a set of images which do not contain any instances of the positive class.

The Viola-Jones in general requires extensive manual supervision. Several modifications of this basic sequential framework have been proposed [18, 11, 17, 12, 2, 24]. Some strategies have been proposed for better selection of thresholds as a post-processing step [11].

4.4.2 Joint Training of All Stages

Sequential greedy learning of each stage is globally suboptimal. Also in sequential training we have to focus on optimally choosing the thresholds for each stage to maximize a certain performance metric, since the training process depends on the choice of the thresholds. There has been some recent work that trains a cascade of classifiers by simultaneously optimizing all its stages [5, 14, 15, 9]. Dundar et al. [5] describe their method using an SVM classifier in each stage of the cascade while the approach of Raykar et al. [14] is probabilistic and uses logistic regression as the base classifier. The approaches

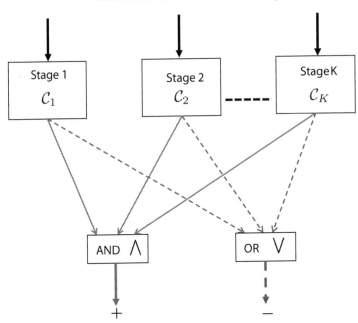

FIGURE 4.2: Soft cascade and the probabilistic AND-OR framework.

of Saberian et al. [15] and Lefakis et al. [9] are based on the original AdaBoost architecture. However, all these approaches rely on the AND-OR interpretation of a cascade structure described below.

The approach of Raykar et al. [14] relies on the idea of optimizing soft cascades. In particular, instead of optimizing a deterministic hard cascade, they optimize a stochastic soft cascade (see Figure 4.2) where each stage accepts or rejects samples according to a probability distribution induced by the previous stage-specific classifier. In logistic regression for each stage the probability for the positive class is written as a logistic sigmoid acting on the linear classifier f_{C_j}, i.e., $p_{C_j}(y = 1|\mathbf{x}, \mathbf{w}) = \sigma\left(f_{C_j}(\mathbf{x})\right)$. The logistic sigmoid function—also known as the squashing function—is defined as $\sigma(z) = 1/(1 + e^{-z})$. For any $\mathbf{x}, \mathbf{w} \in \mathbb{R}^d$ the linear discriminating function is defined as $f_{C_j}(\mathbf{x}) = \mathbf{w}_j^\top \mathbf{x}^j$.

- **Probabilistic AND model for positives** For the overall soft cascade system, an instance $\mathbf{x}$ is classified as positive if *all* the K stages in the cascade predict it as positive. The probability that all stages predict it as positive can be written as

$$p(y = 1|\mathbf{x}, \mathbf{w}) = \prod_{j=1}^{K} p_{C_j}(y = 1|\mathbf{x}, \mathbf{w}) = \prod_{j=1}^{K} \sigma\left(f_{C_j}(\mathbf{x})\right). \qquad (4.1)$$

Note that this is equivalent to the probabilistic AND ($\bigwedge$) model.

- **Probabilistic OR model for negatives** An instance $\mathbf{x}$ is classified as negative if *at least one* of the K classifiers predicts it as negative. Hence

$$p(y = 0|\mathbf{x}, \mathbf{w}) = 1 - \prod_{j=1}^{K} \sigma\left(f_{\mathcal{C}_j}(\mathbf{x})\right). \tag{4.2}$$

Note that this is equivalent to the probabilistic OR ($\bigvee$) model.

Based on the above two models Raykar et al. [14] describe a maximum likelihood estimator to estimate the parameters of each stage of the cascade. Define $p_i = p(y_i = 1|\mathbf{x}_i, \mathbf{w}) = \prod_{j=1}^{K} \sigma\left(f_{\mathcal{C}_j}(\mathbf{x}_i)\right)$—the probability that the ith instance $\mathbf{x}_i$ is positive. Assuming that the training instances are independent the log-likelihood can then be written as

$$l(\mathbf{w}) = \log p(\mathcal{D}|\mathbf{w}) = \sum_{i=1}^{N} y_i \log p_i + (1 - y_i) \log(1 - p_i). \tag{4.3}$$

The maximum likelihood estimate for $\mathbf{w}$ is given by maximizing the log likelihood, i.e., $\widehat{\mathbf{w}}_{\mathrm{ML}} = \arg\max_{\mathbf{w}} \log p(\mathcal{D}|\mathbf{w})$. The Bayesian extension and optimization details to the above model are described in [14].

Note that the hard and soft cascades demonstrate somewhat different properties. For example, *the sequential ordering of the cascade is not important for a soft cascade*, although it certainly matters for the hard cascade. In other words, even if we switch the order of the stages of the soft cascade the overall accuracy is not affected, but the ordering of the cascade is crucial when considering the cost. This relaxation is a device to ease the training process and as such the order definitely matters during testing.

Nevertheless, in order to optimize all stages of a cascade simultaneously to optimize accuracy we need a strategy that allows us to model the interrelationships between the stages. In other words, we want a mathematical method that explicitly accounts for the fact that it is sufficient for a sample to be rejected at any stage of the classifier, we do not have to force multiple stages to reject it. This means that the joint design of cascades can potentially allow each stage to focus on a different type of false positive and thus improve overall accuracy as compared to a traditional one-stage-at-a-time cascade design which ignores this information.

In the sequential framework since each stage is trained independently the latter stages have a much smaller training set. In contrast the joint approach uses all the available data to train all the stages. The joint training provides implicit mutual feedback from one stage to all other stages.

Decoupling Threshold Selection from Classifier Design

The joint training methods [14, 5] essentially decouple the classifier design and the threshold selection. If we directly incorporate the thresholds, then during training we have to solve a discrete optimization problem which is not easy. Although the eventual test set will have to be evaluated using a hard cascade which explicitly thresholds and thus rejects a subset of samples at each stage, the joint training methods propose to *design* the parameters of this system by instead optimizing a surrogate cascade of soft-classifiers. Rather than a hard rejection, the stages of the surrogate system optimized during training only provide a probability that the sample is negative. In intuitive physical terms, this soft cascade may be viewed as stochastically rejecting a sample at any stage based on the posterior class probability evidenced by the classifier for that stage.

4.5   Tradeoff between Accuracy and Cost

An crucial motivation for adopting cascade structure is that we have limited cost. In some applications the cost may be a deciding factor and the user may be willing to sacrifice some accuracy. There is not much work which tries to explicitly measure or minimize run time although they may implicitly assume that cascaded classifier design reduces run time by its very nature. One exception is the method proposed by Raykar et al. [14] which can be tuned to reflect this tradeoff between cost and accuracy. Because of the notion of soft cascades they were able to write an estimate of the average cost for each example and incorporate that in the cascade design.

We would like to design the cascade (or find the maximum likelihood estimate) subject to the constraint of the expected cost for a new instance

$$E_{p(\mathbf{x})}\left[\mathcal{T}(\mathbf{x})\right] \leq c, \tag{4.4}$$

where $\mathcal{T}$ is the cost for a new instance $\mathbf{x}$. The expectation is over the unknown test distribution. Since we do not know $p(\mathbf{x})$ we can use an estimate of this quantity based on the training set. Consider a training instance $\mathbf{x}_i$. The first stage takes cost t_1 to compute the set of features $\mathbf{w}_1$. Once the features are computed it declares it as positive with probability $\sigma\left(f_{\mathcal{C}_1}(\mathbf{x}_i)\right)$. This means that $\mathbf{x}_i$ passes through to the second stage of the cascade with probability $\sigma\left(f_{\mathcal{C}_1}(\mathbf{x}_i)\right)$. The second stage now takes cost t_2 to acquire the set of features $\mathbf{w}_2$. The second stage declares it a positive with probability $\sigma\left(f_{\mathcal{C}_2}(\mathbf{x}_i)\right)$. Hence it passes through to the third stage of the cascade with probability $\sigma\left(f_{\mathcal{C}_1}(\mathbf{x}_i)\right)\sigma\left(f_{\mathcal{C}_2}(\mathbf{x}_i)\right)$. So given the parameters of the cascade an estimate of the expected cost can be written as

$$T(\mathbf{w}) = \frac{1}{N} \sum_{i=1}^{N} \left[t_1 + \sum_{j=2}^{K} t_j \prod_{l=1}^{j-1} \sigma \left(f_{\mathcal{C}_l}(\mathbf{x}_i) \right) \right]. \tag{4.5}$$

The optimization problem is modified to incorporate this constraint regarding the expected cost, i.e.,

$$\widehat{\mathbf{w}} = \arg\max_{w} l(\mathbf{w}) \quad \text{subject to} \quad T(\mathbf{w}) \leq c. \tag{4.6}$$

In practice we solve the following unconstrained optimization problem

$$\widehat{\mathbf{w}}_\beta = \arg\max_{w} l(\mathbf{w}) - \beta T(\mathbf{w}), \tag{4.7}$$

where β controls the tradeoff between accuracy and cost. Experimental results on three clinically relevant problems showed the effectiveness of this approach in achieving the desired tradeoff between accuracy and feature acquisition cost [14]. Saberian et al. [15] recently proposed a similar algorithm called FCBoost that accounts for both accuracy and computational complexity specifically for detection cascades.

4.6 Conclusions and Future Work

In this chapter we presented an overview of how cascaded classifiers can deal with the cost aspects of various learning tasks. While we mainly focused on binary classification tasks the notion of a cascaded architecture has also been extended to other learning paradigms like multiple instance learning [26, 23] and structured learning [6, 22]. We end the chapter by pointing out a couple of open problems for future research.

Open Question: How to Decide the Cascade Order?

One assumption we have made is that prior to training the cascade the ordering of the different stages in the cascade is fixed. Typically the cascade is ordered by the feature acquisition time, i.e., we would like the first stage of our classifier to use the cheapest features and the most expensive features at the later stage. Generally it true that more expensive features have better predictive power. However, this may not be the most optimal strategy in terms of both accuracy and cost.

Open Question: Granularity of Feature Grouping?

Cascading is a passive one-size-fits-all strategy that is not adapted for *each example*. Feature cost has been considered in the framework of cost-sensitive learning [13, 8, 16] approaches described in this book. For example, Ji and Carin [8] propose the medical diagnosis problem introduced earlier as a cost-sensitive classification problem and solve it via a partially observable Markov decision process.

References

[1] L. Bourdev and J. Brandt. Robust object detection via soft cascade. In *Proceedings of the IEEE International Conference on Computer Vision and Pattern Recognition (CVPR'05)*, pages 236–243, 2005.

[2] S. C. Brubaker, J. Wu, J. Sun, M. D. Mullin, and J. M. Rehg. On the design of cascades of boosted ensembles for face detection. *International Journal of Compuer Vision*, 77:65–86, 2008.

[3] L. Ce and H.-Y. Shum. Kullback-Leibler boosting. In *Proceedings of the IEEE International Conference on Computer Vision and Pattern Recognition (CVPR'07)*, pages 587–594, 2003.

[4] C. Dehing-Oberije, D. De Ruysscher, et al. Tumor volume combined with number of positive lymph node stations is a more important prognostic factor than TNM stage for survival of non-small-cell lung cancer patients treated with (chemo)radiotherapy. *International Journal of Radiation Oncology-Biology-Physics*, 70(4):1039–1044, 2007.

[5] M. Dundar and J. Bi. Joint optimization of cascaded classifiers for computer aided detection. In *Proceedings of the IEEE International Conference on Computer Vision and Pattern Recognition (CVPR'07)*, 1–8, 2007.

[6] G. Heitz, S. Gould, A. Saxena, and D. Koller. Cascaded classification models: Combining models for holistic scene understanding. In *Advances in Neural Information Processing Systems 21*, pages 641–648. 2009.

[7] X. Hou, C.-L. Liu, and T. Tan. Learning boosted asymmetric classifiers for object detection. In *Proceedings of the IEEE International Conference on Computer Vision and Pattern Recognition (CVPR'06)*, pages 330–338, 2006.

[8] S. Ji and L. Carin. Cost-sensitive feature acquisition and classification. *Pattern Recognition*, 40(5):1474–1485, 2007.

[9] L. Lefakis and F. Fleuret. Joint cascade optimization using a product of boosted classifiers. In *Advances in Neural Information Processing Systems 23*, pages 1315–1323, 2010.

[10] S. Z. Li and Z. Zhang. Floatboost learning and statistical face detection. *IEEE Transactions on Pattern Analysis and Machine Intelligence*, 26(9):1112–1123, 2004.

[11] H. Luo. Optimization design of cascaded classifiers. In *Proceedings of the IEEE International Conference on Computer Vision and Pattern Recognition (CVPR'05)*, pages 480–485, 2005.

[12] H. Masnadi-Shirazi and N. Vasconcelos. High detection-rate cascades for real-time object detection. In *Proceedings of the IEEE International Conference on Computer Vision and Pattern Recognition (CVPR'07)*, pages 14–21, 2007.

[13] P. Melville, M. Saar-Tsechansky, F. Provost, and R. Mooney. An expected utility approach to active feature-value acquisition. In *ICDM '05: Proceedings of the Fifth IEEE International Conference on Data Mining*, pages 745–748, 2005.

[14] V. C. Raykar, B. Krishnapuram, and S. Yu. Designing efficient cascaded classifiers: Tradeoff between accuracy and cost. In *Proceedings of the 16th ACM SIGKDD International Conference on Knowledge Discovery and Data Mining (KDD'10)*, pages 853–860, 2010.

[15] M. Saberian and N. Vasconcelos. Boosting classifier cascades. In *Advances in Neural Information Processing Systems 23*, pages 2047–2055, 2010.

[16] V. S. Sheng and C. X. Ling. Partial example acquisition in cost-sensitive learning. In *KDD '07: Proceedings of the 13th ACM SIGKDD International Conference on Knowledge Discovery and Data Mining*, pages 638–646, 2007.

[17] J. Sochman and J. Matas. WaldBoost—Learning for time constrained sequential detection. In *Proceedings of the IEEE International Conference on Computer Vision and Pattern Recognition (CVPR'05)*, pages 150–156, 2005.

[18] J. Sun, J. M. Rehg, and A. Bobick. Automatic cascade training with perturbation bias. In *Proceedings of the IEEE International Conference on Computer Vision and Pattern Recognition (CVPR'04)*, pages 276–283, 2004.

[19] P. Viola and M. J. Jones. Rapid object detection using a boosted cascade of simple features. In *Proceedings of the IEEE International Conference on Computer Vision and Pattern Recognition (CVPR'01)*, pages 511–518, 2001.

[20] P. Viola and M. J. Jones. Fast and robust classification using asymmetric AdaBoost and a detector cascade. In *Advances in Neural Information Processing Systems*, pages 1311–1318, 2002.

[21] P. Viola and M. J. Jones. Robust real-time face detection. *International Journal of Computer Vision*, 57(2):137–154, 2004.

[22] D. Weiss and B. Taskar. Structured prediction cascades. In *Proceedings of the Thirteenth International Conference on Artificial Intelligence and Statistics (AISTATS) 2010, JMLR: W&CP 9*, pages 916–923, 2010.

[23] D. Wu, J. Bi, and K. Boyer. A min-max framework of cascaded classifier with multiple instance learning for computer aided diagnosis. In *Proceedings of the IEEE International Conference on Computer Vision and Pattern Recognition (CVPR'09)*, 2009.

[24] J. Wu, S. C. Brubaker, M. D. Mullin, and J. M. Rehg. Fast asymmetric learning for cascade face detection. *IEEE Transactions on Pattern Analysis and Machine Intelligence*, 30:369–382, 2008.

[25] R. Xiao, L. Zhu, and H. J. Zhang. Rapid object detection using a boosted cascade of simple features. In *Proceedings of the Ninth IEEE International Conference on Computer Vision and Pattern Recognition (CVPR'03)*, pages 709–715, 2003.

[26] C. Zhang and P. Viola. Multiple-instance pruning for learning efficient cascade detectors. In *Advances in Neural Information Processing Systems 20*, pages 1681–1688, 2008.

Chapter 5

Selective Data Acquisition for Machine Learning

Josh Attenberg

Polytechnic Institute of New York University, Brooklyn, New York

Prem Melville

IBM T.J. Watson Research Center, Yorktown Heights, New York

Foster Provost

Stern School of Business, New York University, New York

Maytal Saar-Tsechansky

Red McCombs School of Business, University of Texas at Austin

5.1   Introduction

In many applications, one must invest effort or money to acquire the data and other information required for machine learning and data mining. Careful selection of the information to acquire can substantially improve generalization performance per unit cost. The costly information scenario that has received the most research attention (see Chapter 10) has come to be called "active learning," and focuses on choosing the instances for which target values (labels) will be acquired for training. However, machine learning applications offer a variety of different sorts of information that may need to be acquired.

This chapter focuses on settings and techniques for selectively acquiring information beyond just single training labels (the values of the target variable) for selected instances in order to improve a model's predictive accuracy. The different kinds of acquired information include feature values, feature labels, entire examples, values at prediction time, repeated acquisition for the same data item, and more. For example, Figure 5.1 contrasts the acquisition of training labels, feature values, and both. We will discuss all these sorts of information in detail. Broadening our view beyond simple active learning not only expands the set of applications to which we can apply selective acquisition strategies, but it also highlights additional important problem dimensions and characteristics, and reveals fertile areas of research that to date have received relatively little attention.

In what follows we start by presenting two general notions that are employed to help direct the acquisition of various sorts of information. The first is to prefer to acquire information for which the current state of modeling is *uncertain*. The second is to acquire information that is estimated to be the most valuable to acquire.

After expanding upon these two overarching notions, we discuss a variety of different settings where information acquisition can improve modeling. The purpose of examining various different acquisition settings in some detail is to highlight the different challenges, solutions, and research issues. As just one brief example, distinct from active learning, active acquisition of feature values may have access to additional information, namely instances' labels—which enables different sorts of selection strategies.

More specifically, we examine the acquisition of feature values, feature labels, and prediction-time values. We also examine the specific, common setting where information is not perfect, and one may want to acquire additional information specifically to deal with information quality. For example, one may want to acquire the same data item more than once. In addition, we emphasize that it can be fruitful to expand our view of the sorts of acquisition actions we have at our disposal. Providing specific variable values is only one sort of information "purchase" we might make. For example, in certain cases, we may be able to acquire entire examples of a rare class or distinguishing words for document classification. These alternative acquisitions may give a better return on investment for modeling.

Finally, and importantly, most research to date has considered each sort of information acquisition independently. However, why should we believe that only one sort of information is missing or noisy? Modelers may find themselves in situations where they need to acquire various pieces of information, and somehow must prioritize the different sorts of acquisition. This has been addressed in a few research papers for pairs of types of information, for example for target labels and feature labels ("active dual supervision"). We argue that a challenge problem for machine learning and data mining research should be to work toward a unified framework within which arbitrary information acquisitions can be prioritized, to build the best possible models on a limited budget.

5.2 Overarching Principles for Selective Data Acquisition

In general selective data acquisition a learning algorithm can request the value of particular missing data, which is then provided by an oracle at some cost. There may be more than one oracle, and oracles are not assumed to be perfect. The goal of selective data acquisition is to choose to acquire data that are most likely to improve the system's use-time performance on a specified modeling objective in a cost-effective manner. We will use q to refer to the query for a selected piece of missing data. For instance, in traditional active learning this would correspond to querying for the missing label of a selected instance; while in the context of active feature-value acquisition, q is the request for a missing feature value. We will focus primarily (but not exclusively) on *pool-based* selective data acquisition, where we select a query from a pool of available candidate queries, e.g., the set of all missing feature-values that can be acquired on request.

Note that in most cases, selection from the pool is performed in epochs, whereby at each phase, a batch of one or more queries are performed simultaneously. The combinatorial problem of selecting the most useful such batches (and overall dataset) from such a pool of candidates makes direct optimization an NP-hard problem. Typically, a first-order Markov relaxation is performed, whereby the most promising data are selected greedily one at a time from the pool. While not guaranteeing a globally optimal result set (regardless of what selection criterion is being used), such sequential data access often works well in practice while making the selection problem tractable.

We begin by discussing two general principles that are applicable for the selective acquisition of many different types of data. These overarching principles must be instantiated specifically to suit the needs of each acquisition setting. While individual instantiations may differ considerably, both principles have advantages and disadvantages that hold in general, which we discuss below. In reviewing these techniques, we often refer to the familiar active learning setting; we will see how the principles do and do not apply to the other settings as the chapter unfolds.

5.2.1 Uncertainty Reduction

The most commonly used method for non-uniform sample selection for machine learning is to select data items for which the current model is most uncertain.

This notion is the basis for the most commonly used individual active learning technique, Uncertainty Sampling [44], as well as closely related (and in some cases identical) techniques, such as selecting data points closest to a separating hyperplane, Query-by-Committee, and variance reduction [79]. Specifically, with Uncertainty Sampling the active learner requests labels for examples that the currently held model is least certain about how to classify.

Uncertainty Reduction techniques are based on the assumption that predictive errors largely occur in regions of the problem space where predictions are most ambiguous. The intent is that by providing supplemental information in these regions, model confidence can be improved, along with predictive performance. Despite the typical reference to the classic 1994 paper [44], even Uncertainty Sampling itself has become a framework within which different techniques are implemented. For example, exactly how one should measure uncertainty is open to interpretation; the following three calculations of uncertainty all have been used [79, 55, 78]:

$$1 - P(\hat{y}|x) \tag{5.1}$$

$$P(\hat{y_1}|x) - P(\hat{y_2}|x) \tag{5.2}$$

$$-\sum_i P(\hat{y}_i|x) \log(P(\hat{y}_i|x)), \qquad (5.3)$$

where $P(\hat{y}|x)$ is the highest posterior probability assigned by the classifier to a class, while $P(\hat{y}_1|x)$ and $P(\hat{y}_2|x)$ are the probabilities assigned to the first and second most probable classes as predicted by the classifier.

Uncertainty Reduction is widely used with some success in the research literature, though we will discuss situations where Uncertainty Reduction fails to make beneficial selections. The same uncertainty-based heuristic can be applied more broadly to acquiring other forms of data. For instance, when feature values are missing, one can attempt to impute the missing values from those that are present, and choose to acquire values where the model is least certain of the imputed values.

The advantages of Uncertainty Reduction are:

- Evaluating and selecting queries based on uncertainty is computationally efficient in many settings. For instance, Uncertainty Sampling for training labels only requires applying the classifier to predict the posterior class probabilities of examples in the unlabeled pool. There is no retraining of models required in order to select queries. Note that, in other settings, such as acquiring feature values, the complexity may be considerably higher depending on how one choses to measure uncertainty.

- Uncertainty Reduction techniques are often adopted because of their ease of implementation. For example, Uncertainty Sampling requires computing one of the uncertainty scores described above which are simply applications of the existing model in order to make predictions on an unlabeled instance.

- In the active learning literature, Uncertainty Reduction techniques have been applied across many problems with reasonable success.

The disadvantages of Uncertainty Reduction are:

- While often effective in practice, Uncertainty Reduction does not directly attempt to optimize a classifier's generalization performance. As such it can often choose queries that may reduce model uncertainty, but not result in improvement on test set predictions. Notably, when applied to obtaining example labels, Uncertainty Sampling is prone to selecting outliers [79]. These could be instances the model is uncertain about, but are not representative of instances in the test set. The selection of outliers can be addressed by using the uncertainty scores to form a sampling distribution [72, 73]; however, sampling also can reduce the effectiveness of Uncertainty Reduction techniques by repeatedly selecting marginally informative examples. In other settings, Uncertainty

Reduction may reduce uncertainty about values that are not discriminative, such as acquiring values for a feature that is uncorrelated to the class.

- While Uncertainty Sampling is often favored for ease of implementation, in settings beyond the acquisition of single training labels, estimating uncertainty is often not as straightforward. For example, how should you measure the uncertainty of an instance label, given a current model and many contradictory labels for the same instance from different oracles [82]?

- In general, selective data acquisition assumes that the response to each query comes at a cost. In realistic settings, these costs may vary for each type of acquisition and even for each query. Notably, some examples are more difficult for humans to label than others, and as such may entail a higher cost in terms of annotation time. Similarly, some features-values are more expensive to obtain than others, e.g., if they are the result of a more costly experiment. Uncertainty Reduction methods do not naturally facilitate a meaningful way to tradeoff costs with potential benefits of each acquisition. One ad hoc approach of attempting this is to divide the uncertainty score with the cost for each query, and make acquisitions in order of the resulting quantity [80, 32]. This is a somewhat awkward approach to incorporating costs, as uncertainty per unit cost is not necessarily proportional to potential benefit to the resulting model.

- As mentioned above, uncertainty can be defined in different ways even for the same type of acquisition, such as a class label. Different types of acquisitions, such as feature values, require very different measures of uncertainty. Consequently, when considering more than one type of acquisition simultaneously, there is no systematic way to compare two different measures of uncertainty, since they are effectively on different scales. This makes it difficult to construct an Uncertainty Reduction technique that systematically decides which type of information is most beneficial to acquire next.

5.2.2   Expected Utility

Selecting data that the current model is uncertain about may result in queries that are not useful in discriminating between classes. An alternative to such uncertainty-based heuristics is to directly estimate the expected improvement in generalization due to each query. In this approach, at every step of selective data acquisition, the next query selected is the one that will result in the highest estimated improvement in classifier performance per unit cost. Since the true values of the missing data are unknown prior to acquisition, it is necessary to estimate the *potential* impact of every query for all possible outcomes.[1] Hence, the decision-theoretic optimal policy is to ask for missing data which, once incorporated into the existing data, will result in the greatest increase in classification performance in *expectation*. If w_q is the cost of the query q, then its Expected Utility of acquisition can be computed as

$$EU(q) = \int_v P(q = v) \frac{\mathcal{U}(q = v)}{w_q}, \tag{5.4}$$

where $P(q = v)$ is the probability that query q will take on value v, and $\mathcal{U}(q = v)$ is the utility to the model of knowing that q has the value v. This utility can be defined in any way to represent a desired modeling objective. For example, $\mathcal{U}$ could be defined as classification error. In this case, this approach is referred to as *Expected Error Reduction*. When applied more generally to arbitrary utility functions we refer to such a selection scheme as *Expected Utility* or *Estimated Risk Minimization*. Note that, in Equation 5.4 the true values of the marginal distribution $P(.)$ and the utility $\mathcal{U}(.)$ on the test set is unknown. Instead, empirical estimates of these quantities are used in practice. When the missing data can only take on discrete values, the expectation can be easily computed by piecewise summation over the possible values. While for continuous values, computation of expected utility can be performed using Monte Carlo methods.

The advantages of Expected Utility are:

- Since this method is directly trying to optimize the objective on which the model will be evaluated, it avoids making acquisitions that do not improve this objective even if it reduces uncertainty or variance in the predictions.

- Incorporating different acquisition costs is also straightforward in this framework. The tradeoff of utility versus cost is handled directly, as opposed to relying on an unknown indirect connection between uncertainty and utility.

- This approach is capable of addressing multiple types of acquisition simultaneously within a single framework. Since the measure of utility is independent of the type of acquisition and only dependent on the resulting classifier, we can estimate the expected utility of different forms of acquisitions in the same manner. For instance, we can use such an approach to estimate the utility of acquiring class labels and feature values in tandem [71]. The same framework can also be instantiated to yield a holistic approach to active dual supervision, where the Expected Utility of an instance or feature label query can be computed and compared on the same scale [2]. By evaluating different acquisitions in the

---

[1] For instance, in the case of binary classification, the possible outcomes are a *positive* or *negative* label for a queried example.

same units, and by measuring utility per unit cost of acquisition, such a framework facilitates explicit optimization of the tradeoffs between the costs and benefits of the different types of acquisitions. between the costs and benefits of the different types of acquisitions.

The disadvantages of Expected Utility are:

- A naïve implementation of the Expected Utility framework is computationally intractable even for data of moderate dimensionality. The computation of Expected Utility (Equation 5.4) requires iterating over all possible outcomes of all candidate queries. This often means training multiple models for the different values a query may take on. This combinatorial computational cost can often be prohibitive. The most common approach to overcome this, at the cost of optimality, is to subsample the set of available queries, and only compute Expected Utility on this smaller candidate set [71]. This method has also been demonstrated to be feasible for classifiers that can be rapidly trained incrementally [70]. Additionally, dynamic programming and efficient data structures can be leveraged to make the computation tractable [8]. The computation of the utility of each outcome of each query, while being the bottleneck, is also fully parallelizable. As such large-scale parallel computing has the potential of making the computational costs little more than that of training a single classifier.

- As mentioned above, the terms $P(.)$ and $\mathcal{U}(.)$ in the Expected Utility computation must be estimated from available data. However, the choice of methods to use for these estimations is not obvious. Making the correct choices can be a significant challenge for a new setting, and can make a substantial difference in the effectiveness of this approach [71].

- Typically, the estimators used for $P(.)$ and $\mathcal{U}(.)$ are based on the pool of available training data, for instance, through cross-validation. The available training examples themselves are often acquired through an active acquisition process. Here, due to the preferences of the active process, the distribution of data in the training pool may differ substantially from that of the native data population and as a result, the estimations of $P(.)$ and $\mathcal{U}(.)$ may be arbitrarily inaccurate in the worst case.

- Additionally, it should be noted that despite the *emperical risk minimization* moniker, Expected Utility methods do not in general yield the globally optimal set of selections. This is due to several simplifications: first, the myopic, sequential acquisition policy mentioned above where the benefit for each individual example is taken in isolation, and second, the utilization of empirical risk as a proxy for actual risks.

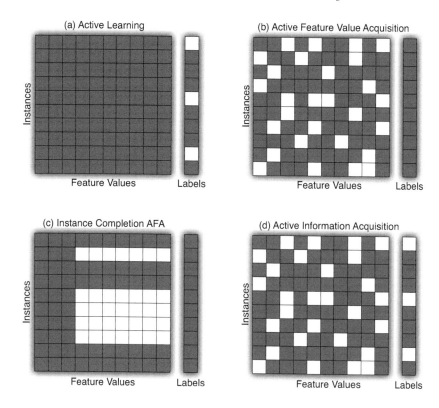

FIGURE 5.1: Different data acquisition settings.

5.3   Active Feature-Value Acquisition

In this section we begin by discussing active feature-value acquisition (AFA), the selective acquisition of single feature values for training. We then review extensions of these policies for more complex settings in which feature values, different sets thereof, as well as class labels can be acquired at a cost simultaneously. We discuss some insights on the challenges and effective approaches for these problems as well as interesting open problems.

As an example setting for active feature-value acquisition, consider consumers' ratings of different products being used as predictors to estimate whether or not a customer is likely to be interested in an offer for a new product. At any given time, only a subset of any given consumer's "true" ratings of her prior purchases are available, and thus many feature values are missing, potentially undermining inference. To improve this inference, it is possible to offer consumers incentives so as to reveal their preferences—for example, rating other prior purchases. Thus, it is useful to devise an intelligent acquisition policy to select which products and which consumers are most cost-effective to acquire. Similar scenarios arise in a variety of other domains, including when databases are being used to estimate the likelihood of success of alternative medical treatments. Often the feature values of some predictors, such as of medical tests, are not available; furthermore, the acquisition of different tests may incur different costs.

This general active feature-value acquisition setting, illustrated in Figure 5.1(b), differs from active learning in several important ways. First, policies for acquiring training labels assign one value to an entire prospective instance acquisition. Another related distinction is that the impact on induction from obtaining an entire instance may require a less precise measure to that required to estimate the impact from acquiring merely a single feature value. In addition, having multiple missing feature values gives rise to myriad settings regarding the level of granularity at which feature values can be acquired and the corresponding cost [102, 47, 57, 56, 38]. For example, in some applications, such as when acquiring consumers' demographic and lifestyle data from syndicated data providers, only the complete set of all feature values can be purchased at a fixed cost. In other cases, such as the recommender systems and treatment effectiveness tasks above, it may be possible to purchase the value of a single variable, such as by running a medical test. And there are intermediate cases, such as when different subsets (e.g., a battery of medical tests) can be acquired as a bundle. Furthermore, different sets may incur different costs; thus, while very few policies do so, it is beneficial to consider such costs when prioritizing acquisition. In the remainder of this section, we discuss how we might address some of these problem settings, as well as interesting open challenges.

A variety of different policies can be envisioned for the acquisition of individual feature values at a fixed cost, following the Expected Utility framework we discussed in Section 1.2 and [47, 56, 71]. As such, Expected Utility AFA policies aim to estimate the expected benefit from an acquisition by the change in some loss/gain function in expectation.

For feature value acquisitions the expected utility framework has several important advantages, but also some limitations. Because different features (such as medical tests) are very likely to incur different costs perhaps the most salient advantage for AFA is the ability to incorporate cost information when prioritizing acquisitions. The Expected Utility framework also allows us to prioritize among acquisitions of individual features as well as different sets thereof. However, the expected value framework would guarantee the acquisition of the optimal single feature value in expectation, only if the true distributions of values for each missing feature were known, and the loss/gain function, $\mathcal{U}$, were to capture the actual change in the model's generalization accuracy following an acquisition. In settings where many feature values are missing these estimations may be particularly challenging. For example, empirical estimation of the model's generalization performance over instances with many missing values may not accurately approximate the magnitude or even the direction of change in generalization accuracy. Perhaps a more important consideration regarding the choice of gain function, $\mathcal{U}$, for feature value acquisition is the sequential, myopic nature of these policies. Similar to most information acquisition policies, if multiple features are to be acquired, a myopic policy, which aims to estimate the benefit from each prospective acquisition in isolation, is not guaranteed to identify the optimal *set* of acquisitions, even if the estimations listed above were precise. This is because the expected contribution of an individual acquisition is estimated with respect to the current training data, irrespective of other acquisitions which will be made. Interestingly, due to this myopic property, selecting the acquisition which yields the best estimated improvement in generalization accuracy often does not yield the best results; rather, other measures have been shown to be empirically more effective [71], for example, log gain. Specifically, when a model is induced from a training set T, let $\hat{P}(c_k|x_i)$ be the probability estimated by the model that instance x_i belongs to class c_k; and $\mathbb{I}$ is an indicator function such that $\mathbb{I}(c_k, x_i) = 1$ if c_k is the correct class for x_i and $\mathbb{I}(c_k, x_i) = 0$, otherwise. Log gain (LG) is then defined as:

$$LG(x_i) = -\sum_{k=1}^{K} \mathbb{I}(c_k, x_i) \log \hat{P}(c_k|x_i). \tag{5.5}$$

Notably, LG is sensitive to changes in the model's estimated probability of the correct class. As such, this policy promotes acquisitions which increase the likelihood of correct class prediction, once other values are acquired.

We have discussed the computational cost which the Expected Utility framework entails and the need to reduce the consideration set to a small subset of all prospective acquisitions. For AFA, drawing from the set of prospective acquisitions uniformly at random [71] may be used; however, using fast heuristics to identify feature values that are likely to be particularly informative per unit cost can be more effective. For example, a useful heuristic is to draw a subset of prospective acquisitions based on the corresponding features' predictive values [71] or to prefer acquisitions from particularly informative instances [56].

A related setting, illustrated in Figure 5.1(c), is one in which for all instances the same subset of feature values are known, and the subset of all remaining feature values can be acquired at a fixed cost. Henceforth, we refer to this setting as *instance completion*. Under some conditions, this problem bears strong similarity to the active learning problem. For example, consider a version of this problem in which only instances with complete feature values are used for induction [102, 103]. If the class labels of prospective training examples are unknown or are otherwise not used to select acquisition, this problem becomes very similar to active learning in that the value from acquiring a complete training instance must be estimated. For example, we can use measures of prediction uncertainty (cf. Section 5.2 to prioritize acquisitions [103].

Note however that the active feature-value acquisition setting may have additional information that can be brought to bear to aid in selection: the known class labels of prospective training examples. The knowledge of class labels can lead to selection policies that prefer to acquire features for examples on which the current model makes mistakes [57]. An extreme version of the instance completion problem is when there are no known feature values and the complete feature set can be acquired as a bundle for fixed cost (see Section 5.7 below).

5.3.1   Acquiring Feature Values and Class Labels

We noted earlier that an important benefit of the AFA Expected Utility framework is that it allows comparing among the benefits from acquiring feature values, sets thereof, as well as class labels—and thus can consider selecting these different sorts of data simultaneously [71]. This setting is shown in Figure 5.1(d). Note, however, that considering different types of acquisitions simultaneously also presents new challenges. In particular, recall the need for a *computationally fast* heuristic to select a subset of promising prospective acquisitions to be subsequently estimated by the Expected Utility policy. Assuming uniform costs, in most cases acquiring a class label is likely to be significantly more cost-effective than acquiring a single feature value. However, if the consideration set were to be sampled uniformly at random, when class labels constitute a minority in this pool, many informative class labels may not even be considered for acquisition. One heuristic that has been shown to perform well is to infer a crude measure of a class label's benefit by the benefits of the corresponding instance's known feature values. Specifically, the probability of drawing a prospective feature-value acquisition is proportional to the cost-normalized variant of the corresponding feature's information gain $IG(F, L)$ [63] for class variable L; the likelihood of considering a class label can then be made proportional to the sum of the cost-normalized information gains of all the instance's missing feature values [71].

One important setting in which arbitrary subsets of feature values can be acquired at different costs has not been explored extensively. It may be natural to extend the Expected Utility framework to consider sets of categorical features. However, estimating the joint probability distribution of all possible sets of values may render such a policy hopelessly inefficient. To our knowledge, there has been some work on the acquisition of sets of values during inference [8]. However, the complexity of the estimation for induction is substantially more significant.

Lastly, integral to designing and evaluating information acquisition policies is a solid understanding of the best *costless* alternatives for dealing with unknown feature values [45]. For example, unknown feature values may be replaced with estimates via imputation or, in some cases, ignored during induction [28, 75]. For the most part, the literature on selective data acquisition has not developed to consider (systematically) alternative costless solutions. Nonetheless, acquisition policies ought to estimate an acquisition's value as compared to the best costless solution (imputing the value; ignoring that variable all together; taking a Bayesian approach). Perhaps more importantly, the conclusions of empirical comparisons among policies and, consequently, the perceived effectiveness of different policies, may be affected substantively by which (if any) costless solutions are employed.

5.4   Labeling Features versus Examples

In selective data acquisition, we can acquire more information about our data instances as in active feature-value acquisition. However, there are other types of class-indicative data that are informative data that may be useful for building predictive models. In such a setting, where myriad forms supervision can be compiled into building predictive models, it becomes important to examine acquisition costs and benefits, allocating budget to those data most valuable to the task at hand. Consider, for example, the task of *sentiment detection*, where given a piece of text as input, the desired output is a label that indicates whether this text expresses a positive or negative opinion. This problem can be cast as a typical binary text classification task, where a learner is trained on a set of documents that have been labeled based on the sentiment expressed in them [60]. Alternatively, one could provide *labeled features*: for example, in the domain of movie reviews, words that evoke positive sentiment (e.g., "captivating," "suspenseful," etc.) may be labeled positive, while words that evoke negative sentiment (e.g., "predictable," "unimaginative," etc.) may be labeled negative. Through this kind of annotation a human conveys prior linguistic experience with a word by a sentiment label that reflects the emotion that the word evokes.

The setting where individual semantic features provide useful class indicators arises broadly, notably in Natural Language Processing tasks where, in addition to labeled documents, it is possible to provide domain knowledge in the form of words or phrases [100] or more sophisticated linguistic features that associate strongly with a class. Such feature supervision can greatly reduce the number of labels required to build high-quality classifiers [24, 84, 54]. In general, example and feature supervision are complementary rather than redundant. As such they can also be used together. This general setting of learning from both labels on examples and features is referred to as *dual supervision* [84].

In this section we provide a brief overview of learning from labeled features, as well as learning from both labeled features and labeled examples. We will also discuss the challenges of active learning in these settings, and some approaches to overcome them.

5.4.1 Learning from Feature Labels

Providing feature-class associations through labeling features can be viewed as one approach to expressing background, prior or domain knowledge about a particular supervised learning task. Methods to learn from such feature labels can be divided into approaches that use labeled features along with unlabeled examples, and methods that use both labeled features and examples. Since, we focus primarily on text classification in this section, we will use *words* and *documents* interchangeably with *features* and *examples*. However, incorporating background knowledge into learning has also been studied outside the context of text classification, as in knowledge-based neural networks [90] and knowledge-based SVMs [29, 42].

5.4.1.1 Labeled Features and Unlabeled Examples

A simple way to utilize feature supervision is to use the labels on features to label examples, and then use an existing supervised learning algorithm to build a model. Consider the following straightforward approach. Given a representative set of words for each class, create a *representative document* for each class containing all the representative words. Then compute the cosine similarity between unlabeled documents and the representative documents. Assign each unlabeled document to the class with the highest similarity, and then train a classifier using these *pseudo-labeled examples*. This approach is very convenient as it does not require devising a new model, since it can effectively leverage existing supervised learning techniques such as Naïve Bayes [46]. Given that it usually take less time to label a word than it takes to label a document [24], this is a cost-effective alternative.

An alternative to approaches of generating and training with pseudo-labeled examples, is to directly use the feature labels to constrain model predictions. For instance, a label y for feature x_i can be translated into a soft constraint, $P(y|x_i) > 0.9$, in a multinomial logistic regression model [24]. Then the model parameters can be optimized to minimize some distance, e.g. Kullback-Leibler divergence from these reference distributions.

5.4.1.2 Dual Supervision

In dual supervision models, labeled features are used in conjunction with labeled examples. Here too, labeled features can be used to generate pseudo-labeled examples, either by labeling unlabeled examples [97] or relabeling duplicates of the training examples [77]. These pseudo-labeled examples can be combined with the given labeled examples, using weights to down-weight prior knowledge when more labeled examples are available. Such methods can be implemented within existing frameworks, such as boosting logistic regression [77], and weighted margin support vector machines [97].

Generating pseudo-labeled examples is an easy way to leverage feature labels within the traditional supervised learning framework based on labeled examples. Alternatively one can incorporate both forms of supervision directly into one unified model [54, 84]. Pooling Multinomials is one such classifier, which builds a generative model that explains both labeled features and examples. In Pooling Multinomials unlabeled examples are classified just as in multinomial Naïve Bayes classification [52], by predicting the class with the maximum likelihood, given by $argmax_{c_j} P(c_j) \prod_i P(w_i|c_j)$, where $P(c_j)$ is the prior probability of class c_j, and $P(w_i|c_j)$ is the probability of word w_i appearing in a document of class c_j. In the absence of background knowledge about the class distribution, the class priors $P(c_j)$ are estimated solely from the training data. However, unlike regular Naïve Bayes, the conditional probabilities $P(w_i|c_j)$ are computed using both the labeled examples and the set of labeled features. Given two models built using labeled examples and labeled features, the multinomial parameters of such models are aggregated through a convex combination, $P(w_i|c_j) = \alpha P_e(w_i|c_j) + (1 - \alpha)P_f(w_i|c_j)$; where $P_e(w_i|c_j)$ and $P_f(w_i|c_j)$ represent the probability assigned by using the example labels and feature labels, respectively, and α is a weight indicating the level of confidence in each source of information. At the crux of this framework is the generative labeled-features model, which assumes that the feature-class associations provided by human experts are implicitly arrived at by examining many latent documents of each class. This assumption translates in into several constraints on the model parameter, which allows one to exactly derive the conditional distributions $P_f(w_i|c_j)$ that would generate the latent documents [54].

5.4.2 Active Feature Labeling

While traditional active learning has primarily focused on selecting unlabeled *instances* to be labeled, the dual-supervision setting adds an additional aspect to active learning where labels may be acquired for features as well. In this section we focus on the task of active learning applied to feature-label acquisition, illustrated by Figure 5.2.

5.4.2.1 Uncertainty-Based Approaches

Feature and instance labels contribute very differently to learning a model, and as such, standard active learning approaches may not be directly applicable to feature label acquisition. Nevertheless, heuristic approaches based on the principle of Uncertainty Sampling have been applied to acquire feature labels, with varying degrees of success. As in traditional Uncertainty Sampling, Feature Uncertainty Sampling requests labels for *features* for which the current model has the highest degree of uncertainty.

Much like instance uncertainty, feature uncertainty can be measured in different ways, depending on the underlying method used for incorporating

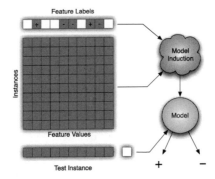

FIGURE 5.2: Active feature labeling.

feature supervision. For instance, when using a learner that produces a linear classifier, we can use the magnitude of the weights on the features as a measure of uncertainty [85], where lower weights indicate less certainty. In the case of Pooling Multinomials, which builds a multinomial Naïve Bayes model, we can directly use the model's conditional probabilities of each feature f given a class. Specifically, feature uncertainty can be measured by absolute log-odds ratio, $abs\left(\log\left(\frac{P(f|+)}{P(f|-)}\right)\right)$. The smaller this value, the more uncertain the model is about the feature's class association. Then in every iteration of active learning, features with the lowest certainty scores are selected for labeling.

Though Uncertainty Sampling for features seems like an appealing notion, it may not lead to better models. If a classifier is uncertain about a feature, it may have insufficient information about this feature and may indeed benefit from learning its label. However, it is also quite likely that a feature has a low certainty score because it does not carry much discriminative information about the classes. For instance, in the context of sentiment detection, one would expect that neutral/non-polar words will appear to be uncertain words. For example, words such as "the," which are unlikely to help in discriminating between classes, are also likely to be considered the most uncertain. In such cases, Feature Uncertainty ends up squandering queries on such words ending up with performance inferior to random feature queries. What works significantly better in practice is *Feature Certainty*, which acquires labels for features in *descending* order of the uncertainty scores [85, 58]. Alternative uncertainty-based heuristics have also been used with different degrees of success [25, 31].

5.4.2.2   Expected Feature Utility

Selecting features that the current model is uncertain about may results in queries that are not useful in discriminating between classes. On the other hand, selecting the most certain features is also suboptimal, since queries may be wasted simply confirming confident predictions, which is of limited utility to the model. An alternative to such certainty-based heuristics is to directly estimate the expected value of acquiring each feature label. This can be done by instantiating the Expected Utility framework described in Section 5.2.2 for this setting. This results in the decision-theoretic optimal policy, which is to ask for feature labels which, once incorporated into the data, will result in the highest increase in classification performance in *expectation*.

More precisely, if f_j is the label of the jth feature, and q_j is the query for this feature's label, then the Expected Utility of a feature query q_j can be computed as:

$$EU(q_j) = \sum_{k=1}^{K} P(f_j = c_k)\mathcal{U}(f_j = c_k), \tag{5.6}$$

where $P(f_j = c_k)$ is the probability that f_j will be labeled with class c_k, and $\mathcal{U}(f_j = c_k)$ is the utility to the model of knowing that f_j has the label c_k. As in other applications of this framework, the true values of these two quantities are unknown, and the main challenge is to accurately estimate these quantities from the data currently available.

A direct way to estimate the utility of a feature label is to measure expected classification accuracy. However, small changes in the probabilistic model that result from acquiring a single additional feature label may not be reflected by a change in accuracy. As in active feature-value acquisition (see Section 5.3) one can use a finer-grained measure of classifier performance, such as log gain defined in Equation 5.5. Then the utility of a classifier, $\mathcal{U}$, can be measured by summing the log gain for all instances in the training set.

In Equation 5.6, apart from the measure of utility, we also do not know the true probability distribution of labels for the feature under consideration. This too can be estimated from the training data, by seeing how frequently the word appears in documents of each class. For Pooling Multinomials, one can use the model parameters to estimate the feature label distribution, $\hat{P}(f_j = c_k) = \frac{P(f_j|c_k)}{\sum_{k=1}^{K} P(f_j|c_k)}$. Given the estimated values of the feature-label distribution and the utility of a particular feature query outcome, we can now estimate the Expected Utility of each unknown feature, selecting the features with the highest Expected Utility for labeling.

As in other settings, this approach can be computationally intensive if Expected Utility estimation is performed on all unknown features. In the worst case this requires building and evaluating models for each possible outcome of each unlabeled feature. In a setting with m features and K classes, this approach requires training $O(mK)$ classifiers. However, the complexity of the approach can be significantly alleviated by only applying Expected Utility evaluation to a subsample of all unlabeled features. Given a large number of features with no true class labels, selecting a sample of available features uniformly at random may be suboptimal. Instead one can subsample features based on a fast and effective heuristic like Feature Certainty [85]. Figure 5.3 shows the typical advantage one can see using such a decision-theoretic approach versus uncertainty-based approaches.

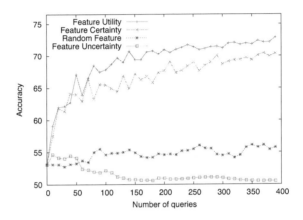

FIGURE 5.3: Comparison of different approaches for actively acquiring feature labels, as demonstrated on the Pooling Multinomials classifier applied to the *Movies* [60] dataset.

5.4.3   Active Dual Supervision

Since dual supervision makes it possible to learn from labeled examples and labeled features simultaneously, one would expect more labeled data of either form to lead to more accurate models. Figure 5.4 illustrates the influence of increased number of instance labels and feature labels independently, and also in tandem. The figure presents an empirical comparison of three schemes: Instances-then-features, Features-then-instances, and Passive Interleaving. As the name suggests, *Instances-then-features*, provides labels for randomly selected instances until all instances have been labeled, and then switches to labeling features. Similarly, *Features-then-instances* acquires labels for randomly selected features first and then switches to getting instance labels. In *Passive Interleaving* we probabilistically switch between issuing queries for randomly chosen instance and feature labels.

We see from Figure 5.4 that fixing the number of labeled features, and increasing the number of labeled instances steadily improves classification accuracy. This is what one would expect from traditional supervised learning curves. More interestingly, the results also indicate that we can fix the number of instances and improve accuracy by labeling more features. Finally, results on Passive Interleaving show that though both feature labels and example labels are beneficial by themselves, dual supervision which exploits the interaction of examples and features does in fact benefit from acquiring both types of labels concurrently.

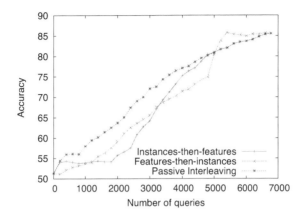

FIGURE 5.4: Comparing the effect of instance and feature label acquisition in dual supervision.

In the sample results above, we selected instances and/or features to be labeled uniformly at random. Based on previous work in active learning one would expect that we can select instances to be labeled more efficiently, by having the learner decide from which instances it is most likely to benefit. The results in the previous section show that actively selecting features to be labeled is also beneficial. Furthermore, the Passive Interleaving results suggest that an ideal active dual supervision scheme would actively select both instances and features for labeling. This setting is illustrated in Figure 5.5.

One could apply an Uncertainty Sampling approach to this problem. However, though uncertainty scores can be used to order examples or features by themselves, there is no principled way to compare an uncertainty score computed for an example with a score for a feature. This is because these scores are based on different heuristics for examples and features, and are not in comparable units. One alternative is to apply uncertainty-based active learning schemes to select labels for examples and features separately. Then, at each iteration of active dual supervision, randomly choose to acquire a label for either an example or feature, and probe the corresponding active learner. Such an Active Interleaving approach is in general more effective than the active learning of either instances or features in isolation [85]. While easy to implement, and effective in practice, this approach is dependent on the ad hoc selection of the *interleave probability* parameter, which determines how frequently to probe for an example versus a feature label. This approach is

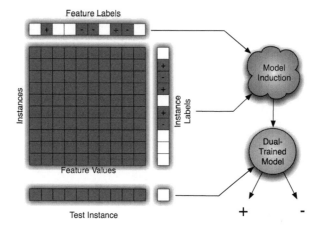

FIGURE 5.5: Active dual supervision.

indeed quite sensitive to the choice of this interleave probability [85]. An ideal active scheme should, instead, be able to assess if an instance or feature would be more beneficial at each step, and select the most informative instance or feature for labeling.

Fortunately, the Expected Utility method is very flexible, capable of addressing both types of acquisition within a single framework. Since the measure of utility is independent of the type of supervision and only dependent on the resulting classifier, we can estimate the expected utility of different forms of acquisitions in the same manner. This yields a holistic approach to active dual supervision, where the Expected Utility of an instance or feature label query, q, can be computed as

$$EU(q) = \sum_{k=1}^{K} P(q = c_k)\frac{\mathcal{U}(q = c_k)}{\omega_q}, \tag{5.7}$$

where ω_q is the cost of the query q, $P(q = c_k)$ is the probability of the instance or feature queried being labeled as class c_k, and utility $\mathcal{U}$ can be computed as in Equation 5.5. By evaluating instances and features in the same units, and by measuring utility per unit cost of acquisition, such a framework facilitates explicit optimization of the tradeoffs between the costs and benefits of the different types of acquisitions. As with Feature Utility, query selection can be sped up by subsampling both examples and features, and evaluating the Expected Utility on this candidate set. It has been demonstrated that such a holistic approach does indeed effectively manage the tradeoffs between the costs and benefits of the different types of acquisitions, to deterministically select informative examples or features for labeling [2]. Figure 5.6 shows the

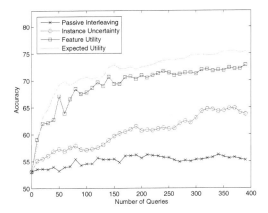

FIGURE 5.6: The effectiveness of Expected Utility instantiated for active dual supervision, compared to alternative label acquisition strategies.

typical improvements of this unified approach to active dual supervision over active learning for only example or feature labels.

5.5 Dealing with Noisy Acquisition

We have discussed various sorts of information that can be acquired (actively) for training statistical models. Most of the research on active/selective data acquisition either has assumed that the acquisition sources provide perfect data or has ignored the quality of the data sources. Let's examine this more critically. Here, let's call the values that we will acquire "labels." In principle these could be values of the dependent variable (training labels), feature labels, feature values, etc., although the research to which we refer has focused exclusively on training labels.

In practical settings, it may well be that the labeling is not 100% reliable—due to imperfect sources, contextual differences in expertise, inherent ambiguity, noisy information channels, or other reasons. For example, when building diagnostic systems, even experts are found to disagree on the "ground truth": "no two experts, of the 5 experts surveyed, agreed upon diagnoses more than 65% of the time. This might be evidence for the differences that exist between sites, as the experts surveyed had gained their expertise at different locations. If not, however, it raises questions about the correctness of the expert data" [62]. The quality of selectively acquired data recently has received greatly increased attention, as modelers increasingly have been taking ad-

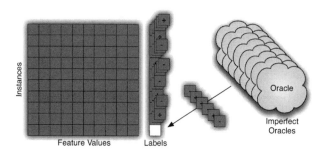

FIGURE 5.7: Multiple noisy oracles.

vantage of low-cost human resources for data acquisition. Micro-outsourcing systems, such as Amazon's Mechanical Turk (and others), are being used routinely to provide data labels. The cost of labeling using such systems is much lower than the cost of using experts to label data. However, with the lower cost can come lower quality.

Surveying all the work on machine learning and data mining with noisy data is beyond the scope of this chapter. The interested reader might start with some classic papers [86, 51, 83]. We will discuss some work that has addressed strategies for the *acquisition* of data specifically from noisy sources to improve data quality for machine learning and data mining (the interested reader should also see work on information fusion [18].

5.5.1 Multiple Label Acquisition: Round-Robin Techniques

If data acquisition costs are relatively low, a natural strategy for addressing data quality is to acquire the same data point multiple times, as illustrated in Figure 5.7. This assumes that there is at least some independence between repeated acquisitions of the same data point, with the most clean-cut case being that each acquisition is an independent random draw of the value of the variable, from some noisy labeling process. We can define the class of *generalized round-robin* (GRR) labeling strategies. [82]: request a label for the data point that currently has the fewest labels. Depending on the process by which the rest of the data are acquired/selected, GRR can be instantiated differently. If there is one fixed set of data points to be labeled, GRR becomes the classic *fixed round-robin*: cycle through the data points in some order obtaining another label for each. If a new data point is presented every k labels, then GRR becomes the common strategy of acquiring a fixed number of labels on each data point [88, 87].

Whether one ought to engage in round-robin repeated labeling depends on several factors [82], which are clarified by Figure 5.8. Here we see a set of

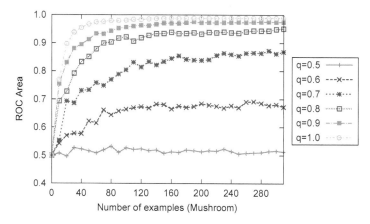

FIGURE 5.8: Learning curves under different quality levels of training data (q is the probability of a label being correct).

learning curves[2] for the classic mushroom classification problem from the UCI repository [12]. The mushroom domain provides a useful illustration because with perfect labels and a moderate amount of training, predictive models can achieve perfect classification. Thus, we can examine the effect of having noisy labels and multiple labels. The several curves in the figure show learning curves for different labeling qualities—here simply the probability that a labeler will give the correct label for this binary classification problem. As the labeler quality deteriorates, not only does the generalization performance suffer, but importantly the rate of change of the generalization performance as a function of the number of labeled data suffers markedly.

Thus, we can summarize the conditions under which we should consider repeated labeling [82]:

1. What is the relative cost of acquiring labels for data points, as compared to the cost of acquiring the "unlabeled" part of the data item? The cheaper the labels are, relatively speaking, the more one can afford to acquire for each unlabeled data point.

2. How steep is the (single-label) learning curve? Specifically, if the rate of change of generalization performance (however measured) is high, as a function of labeling new instances, it may instead be best to label new instances rather than to get additional labels for already labeled instances. As illustrated in Figure 5.8, learning curves generally are steeper when relatively few data points have been labeled, and when the labeling is relatively good.

---

[2]Generalization accuracy estimated using cross-validation with a classification tree model.

3. How steep is the gradient of generalization performance as a function
   of increasing the number of labelers? This is a complicated function of
   the individual labeler quality and the independence of the labelers. For
   the former, note that at the extremes one will see no improvement with
   increasing the number of labelers—when the labelers are either perfect
   or they are completely random. The largest improvement per label comes
   for mid-range quality. With respect to independence, obviously repeated
   labeling is wasted in the trivial scenario that the labelers all provide the
   same labels for the same data points, and maximal value will come when
   the errors the labelers make are completely independent. In Figure 5.8,
   getting additional (non-trivial) labels for the already labeled data points
   would correspond to moving up to a higher-quality curve.

5.5.2   Multiple Label Acquisition: Selecting Examples to Re-label

The round-robin techniques described above repeatedly label (relabel) data
instances indiscriminantly. However, if we have the opportunity to monitor the
repeated labeling process, intuitively it seems that we would want to select
cases carefully for relabeling. For example, all else equal we would rather get
another label on a case with label multiset $\{+,-,-,+\}$ than one with label multiset $\{+,+,+,+\}$. Why? Because we are less certain about the true label in
the former case than in the latter. As in other settings, we can formulate our
strategy as one of uncertainty reduction (cf. Section 5.2); a difference is that
here we examine the uncertainty embodied by the current label multiset. It
is important to distinguish here between how mixed up the label set is, as
measured for example by its entropy, and our uncertainty in the underlying
label. For example, a label multiset with 600 +s and 400 −s has high entropy,
but if we are expecting high-noise labelers we may be fairly certain that this
is a +. Thus, we should compute careful statistical estimates of the certainty
of the label multiset, in order to select the highest uncertainty sets for relabeling; doing so gives consistently better performance than round-robin repeated
labeling [82, 35]. Let's call that the *label uncertainty*.

For selective repeated labeling, the label uncertainty is only one sort of
information that can be brought to bear to help select cases to relabel. Alternatively, one can learn a predictive model from the current set of relabeled
data, and then examine the uncertainty in the *model* for each case, for example how close the probability estimated by a model or ensemble of models
is to the classification threshold, using the measures introduced earlier for
uncertainty sampling (Section 5.2). Let's call this *model uncertainty* or MU.
Model uncertainty also can identify important cases to relabel; however, its
performance is not as consistent as using label uncertainty [82]. Interestingly,
these two notions of uncertainty are complementary and we can combine them
and prefer selecting examples for which both the label multiset and the model

are uncertain of the true class, for example by using the geometric mean of the two measures [82]. This *label-and-model uncertainty* is significantly superior to using either sort of uncertainty alone and therefore also is superior to round-robin repeated labeling [82].

Although model uncertainty uses the same measures as Uncertainty Sampling, there is a major difference. The difference is that to compute MU the model is applied back to the cases from which it was trained; mislabeled cases get systematically higher model uncertainty scores [35]. Thus, model uncertainty actually is more closely akin to methods for finding labeling errors [14]: it selects cases to label because they are mislabeled, in a "self-healing" process, rather than because the examples are going to improve a model in the usual active-learning sense. This can be demonstrated by instead using cross-validation, applying the model to held-out cases (active-learning style) and then relabeling them; we see that most of MU's advantage disappears [35].

5.5.3 Using Multiple Labels and the Dangers of Majority Voting

Once we have decided to obtain multiple labels for some or all data points, we need to consider how we are going to use multiple labels for training. The most straightforward method is to integrate the multiple labels into a single label by taking an average (mode, mean, median) of the values provided by the labelers. Almost all research in machine learning and data mining uses this strategy, specifically taking the majority (plurality) vote from multiple classification labelers.

While being straightforward and quite easy to implement, the majority vote integration strategy is not necessarily the best. Soft labeling can improve the performance of the resultant classifiers, for example by creating an example for each class weighted by the proportion of the votes [82]. Indeed, soft labeling can be made "quality aware" if knowledge of the labeler qualities is available (cf. a quality-aware label uncertainty calculation [35]). This leads to a caution for researchers studying strategies for acquiring data and learning models with noisy labelers: showing that our new learning strategy improves modestly over majority voting may not be saying as much as we think, since simply using a better integration strategy (e.g., soft labeling) also shows modest improvements over majority voting (in many cases).

A different, important danger of majority voting comes when labelers can have varying quality: a low-quality labeler will "pull down" the majority quality when voting with higher-quality labelers. With labelers who make independent errors, there is a rather narrow range of quality under which we would want to use majority voting [43, 82]. An alternative is to use a quality-aware technique for integrating the labels.

5.5.4   Estimating the Quality of Acquisition Sources

If we want to eliminate low-quality sources or to take their quality into account when coalescing the acquired data, we will have to know or estimate the quality of the sources—the labelers. The easiest method for estimating the quality of the labelers is to give them a reasonably large quantity of "gold standard" data, for which we know the truth, so that we can estimate error statistics. Even ignoring changes in quality over time, the obvious drawback is that this is an expensive undertaking. We would prefer not to waste our labeling budget getting labels on cases for which we already know the answer.

Fortunately, once we have acquired multiple labels on multiple data points, even without knowing any true labels we can estimate labeler quality using a maximum likelihood expectation maximization (EM) framework [19]. Specifically, given as input a set of N objects, $o_1, \ldots, o_N$, we associate with each a *latent* true class label $T(o_n)$, picked from one of the L different possible labels. Each object is annotated by one or more of the K labelers. To each labeler (k) we assign a *latent* "confusion matrix" $\pi_{ij}^{(k)}$, which gives the probability that worker (k), when presented with an object of true class i, will classify the object into category j. The EM-based technique simultaneously estimates the latent true classes and the labeler qualities. Alternatively, we could estimate the labeler confusion matrices using a Bayesian framework [16], and can extend the frameworks to the situation where some data instances are harder to label correctly than others [96], and to the situation where labelers differ systematically in their labels (and this bias can then be corrected to improve the integrated labels) [36]. Such situations are not just figments of researchers' imaginations. For example, a problem of contemporary interest in online advertising is classifying web content as to the level of objectionability to advertisers, so that they can make informed decisions about whether to serve an ad for a particular brand on a particular page. Some pages may be classified as objectionable immediately; other pages may be much more difficult, either because they require more work or because of definition nuances. In addition, labelers do systematically differ in their opinions on objectionability: one person's R-rating may be another's PG-rating.

If we are willing to estimate quality in tandem with learning models, we could use an EM procedure to iterate the estimation of the quality with the learning of models, with estimated-quality-aware supervision [67, 68].

5.5.5   Learning to Choose Labelers

We possibly can be even more selective. As illustrated in Figure 5.9, we can select from among labelers as their quality becomes apparent, choosing particularly good labelers [22, 99] or eliminating low-quality labelers [23, 20]. Even without repeated labeling, we can estimate quality by comparing the labelers' labels with the predictions from the model learned from all the labeled examples—effectively treating the model predictions as a noisy version of the truth [20]. If we do want to engage in repeated labeling, we can compare labelers with each other and keep track of confidence intervals on their qualities; if the upper limit of the confidence interval falls too low, we can avoid using that expert in the future [23].

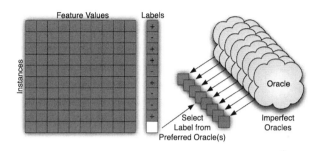

FIGURE 5.9: Selecting oracle(s).

What's more, we can begin to consider that different labelers may have different sorts of expertise. If so, it may be worthwhile to model labeler quality conditioned on the data instance, working toward selecting the labeler best suited to each specific instance [22, 99].

5.5.6   Where to Go from Here?

Research on selective data acquisition with noisy labelers is still in its infancy. Little has been done to compare labeler selection strategies with selective repeated labeling strategies and with sophisticated label integration strategies. Moreover, little work has addressed integrating all three. It would be helpful to have procedures that simultaneously learn models from multiple labelers, estimate the quality of the labelers, combine the labels accordingly, all the while selecting which examples to relabel, and which labelers to apply to which examples. Furthermore, learning with multiple, noisy labelers is a strict generalization of traditional active learning, which may be amenable to general selective data acquisition methods such as expected utility [22] (cf. Section 5.2). Little has been done to unify theoretically or empirically the notions of repeated labeling, quality-aware selection, and active learning.

Most of these same ideas apply beyond the acquisition of training labels, to all the other data acquisition scenarios considered in this chapter: selectively acquired data may be noisy, but the noise may be mitigated by repeated labeling and/or estimating the quality of labelers. For example, we may want to get repeated feature values when their acquisition is noisy, for example, because they are the result of error-prone human reporting or experimental procedures.

5.6   Prediction Time Information Acquisition

Traditional active information acquisition is focused on the gathering of instance labels and feature values at training time. However, in many realistic settings, we may also have the need or opportunity to acquire information when the learned models are used (call this "prediction time"). For example, if features are costly at training time, why would these features not incur a similar cost at prediction time? Extending the techniques of active feature-value acquisition, we can address the problem of procuring feature values at prediction time. This additional information, can, in turn, potentially offer greater clarity into the state of the instance being examined, and thereby increase predictive performance, all at some cost. In an analogous setting to prediction time active feature value acquisition, if an oracle is available to provide class labels for instances at training time, the same oracle may be available at test time, providing a supplement to error-prone statistical models, with the intent of reducing the total misclassification cost experienced by the system consuming the class predictions. This objective of this section is to develop motivating settings suitable for predictive time information acquisition, and to explore effective techniques for gathering information cost-effectively.

5.6.1   Active Inference

At first blush, it might seem that prediction-time acquisition of training labels would not make sense: if labels are available for the instances being processed, then why perform potentially error-prone statistical inference in the first place? While "ground truth" labels are likely to be preferable to statistical prediction, all things being equal, such an equal comparison ignores the cost-sensitive context in which the problem is likely to exist. Acquisition of ground truth labels may be more costly than simply making a model-based prediction; however, it may nonetheless be more *cost-effective* to acquire particular labels at this heightened cost depending on the costs incurred from making certain errors in prediction. We refer to this prediction-time acquisition of label information as *Active Inference*.

More formally, given a set of n discrete classes, $c_j \in \mathcal{C}$, $j = 1, \ldots, n$, and some cost function, $\text{cost}(c_k|c_j)$, yielding the penalty for predicting a label c_k for an example whose true label is c_j, the optimal model-based prediction for a given x is then: $c = \arg \min_c \sum_j \hat{P}(c_j|x) \text{cost}(c|c_j)$, where $\hat{P}(c_j|x)$ represents a model's estimated posterior probability of belonging in class c_j given an instance x. The total expected cost on a given set $\mathbb{T}$ of to-be-classified data is then:

$$\mathcal{L}_{\mathrm{T}} = \sum_{x \in \mathrm{T}} \phi(x) \min_c \sum_j \hat{P}(c_j|x)\mathrm{cost}(c|c_j). \tag{5.8}$$

Where $\phi(x)$ is the number of times a given example x appears during test time. Note that unless stated otherwise, $\phi(x) = 1$, and can therefore simply be ignored. This is the typical case for pool-based test sets where each instance to be labeled is unique.

Given a budget, B, and a cost structure for gathering labels for examples at prediction time, $C(x)$, the objective of an active inference strategy is to then select a set of examples for which to acquire labels, $\mathcal{A}$, such that the expected cost incurred is minimized, while adhering to the budget constraints:

$$\mathcal{A} = \arg \min_{\mathcal{A}' \subset \mathrm{T}} \sum_{x \in \mathrm{T} \setminus \mathcal{A}'} \phi(x) \min_c \sum_j \hat{P}(c_j|x)\mathrm{cost}(c|c_j) \tag{5.9}$$

$$+ \sum_{x \in \mathcal{A}'} C(x)$$

$$\mathrm{s.t.}\ B \geq \sum_{x \in \mathcal{A}'} C(x).$$

Given a typical setting of evaluating a classifier utilizing only local feature values on a fixed set of test instances drawn without replacement from $P(x)$, choosing the optimal inference set, $\mathcal{A}$ is straightforward. Since the labels of each instance are considered to be i.i.d., the utility for acquiring a label on each instance given in the right side of Equation 5.9 can be calculated independently, and since the predicted class labels are uncorrelated, greedy selection can be performed until either the budget is exhausted or further selection is no longer beneficial. However, there are settings where active inference is both particularly useful and particularly interesting: while performing *collective inference*, where network structure and similarity among neighbors is specifically included while labeling, and *online classification*, where instances are drawn with replacement from some hidden distribution. The remainder of this section is dedicated to the details of these two special cases.

5.6.1.1 Active Collective Inference

By leveraging the correlation among the labels of connected instances in a network, collective inference can often achieve predictive performance beyond that which is possible through classification using only local features. However, when performing collective inference in settings with noisy local labels (e.g., due to imperfect local label predictions, limitations of approximate inference, or other noise), the blessing of collective inference may become a curse; incorrect labels are propagated, effectively multiplying the number of mistakes that are made. Given a trained classifier and a test network, the intent of

Active Collective Inference is to carefully select those nodes in a network for which to query an oracle for a "gold standard" label that will be hard set when performing collective inference, such that the collective generalization performance is maximally improved [66].

Unlike the traditional content-only classification setting, in collective classification the label, y, of a given to a particular example, x, depends not only on the features used to represent x, but on the labels and attributes of x's neighbors in the network being considered. This makes estimation of the benefits of acquiring a single example's label for active inference challenging; the addition may alter the benefits of all other nodes in the graph, and approximation is generally required in order to make inference tractable. Furthermore, as in other data acquisition tasks (Section 5.2) finding the optimal set is known to be an NP-hard problem as it necessitates the investigation of all possible candidate active inference sets [9, 10, 11]. Because of the computational difficulties associated with finding the optimal set of instances to acquire for active inference, several approximation techniques have been devised that enable a substantial reduction in misclassification cost while operating on a limited annotation budget.

First among the approximation techniques for active collective inference are so-called *connectivity metrics*. These metrics rely solely on the graphical structure of the network in order to select those instances with the greatest level of connectivity within the graph. Measures such as closeness centrality (the average distance from node x to all other nodes), and betweenness centrality (the proportion of shortest paths passing through a node x) yield information about how central nodes are in a graph. By using graph k-means and utilizing cluster centers, or simply using measures such as degree (the number of connections), locally well-connected examples can be selected. The intent of connectivity-based active inference is to select those nodes with the greatest *potential* influence, without considering any of the variables or labels used in collective inference [66].

Approximate Inference and Greedy Acquisition attempts to optimize the first-order Markov relaxation of the active inference utility given in Equation 5.9. Here, the expected utility of each instance is assessed and the instance with the most promise is used to supplement $\mathcal{A}$. The utility for acquiring a particular x then involves an expected value computation over all possible label assignments for that x, where the value given to each label assignment is the expected network misclassification cost given in Equation 5.8. The enormous computational load exerted here is eased somewhat through the use of approximate inference [9, 10, 11].

An alternative approach to active collective inference operates by building a collective model in order to predict whether or not the predictions at each node are correct, $P(c|x)$. The effectiveness of acquiring the label for a particular x_i is assumed to be a function of the gradient of $P(c|x_j)$ with respect to a change in $P(c|x_i)$ for all $x_j \in \mathbb{T}$, and the change in prediction correctness for the x_i being considered. It is important to consider both whether a change in the label of an x_i can change many (in)correct labels, as well as how likely it is that x_i is already correctly classified. Appropriate choice of the functional form of $P(c|x)$ leads to efficient analytic computation at each step. This particular strategy is known as *viral marketing acquisition*, due to its similarity with assumptions used in models used for performing marketing in network settings. Here the effectiveness of making a particular promotion is a function of how that promotion influences the target's buying habits, and how that customer's buying habits influence others [9, 10, 11].

Often, the mistakes in prediction caused by collective inference tend to take the form of closely linked "islands." Focusing on eliminating these islands, *reflect and correct* attempts to find centers of these incorrect clusters and acquire their labels. In order to do so, reflect and correct relies on the construction of a secondary model utilizing specialized features believed to indicate label effectiveness. Local, neighbor-centric, and global features are derived to build a predictive model used to estimate the probability that a given x_i's label is incorrect. Built using the labeled network available at test time, this "correctness model" is then applied to the collective inference results at test time. Rather than directly incorporating the utility of annotating an x_i to reduce the overall misclassification cost given in Equation 5.8, reflect and correct leverages an uncertainty-like measurement, seeking the example likely to be misclassified with the greatest number of misclassified neighbors. This is akin to choosing the center of the largest island of incorrectness [9, 10, 11].

5.6.1.2 Online Active Inference

Many realistic settings involve online prediction; performing classification on instances drawn sequentially and with replacement from some hidden distribution. Example applications include query classification, traffic analysis at web servers, classification of web pages seen in ad server logs and web logs, and marketing decisions faced in online advertising. Because instances may be seen repeatedly as time progresses, the expected frequency of occurrence for each instance x may be non-zero. As a result, the expected misclassification cost given in Equation 5.8 may be heavily influenced by the frequency of certain examples and the cumulative cost their repetition imparts.

For many of the problems faced on the web, this problem imparted by repeated encounters with certain xs becomes particularly acute; heavy-tailed distributions imply that even though a great many unique instances may be encountered, a handful of instances may impart a majority of the total possible misclassification cost. Fortunately, it is often possible to defer the predictive model's predictions to an oracle, sacrificing a one-time labeling cost in order to minimize future misclassification costs for particular examples. The task on this *online active inference* is then to select those instances from the example stream for "gold standard" labeling offering the greatest reduction in "impression-sensitive" expected loss given in Equation 5.8 while factoring in label acquisition costs and adhering to a limited budget [3].

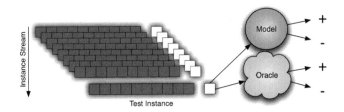

FIGURE 5.10: Online active inference: Presented with an incoming example, a system must decide if it is to sent a model's predicted label to an end system, or pass the example to an oracle for more reliable, albeit more expensive annotation.

A typical use case of online active inference is seen in Figure 5.10. For each example x seen in the stream, the active inference system computes an expected label acquisition benefit, $EU(x) = \left[\hat{\phi}(x) \min_c \sum_j \hat{P}(c_j|x) \mathrm{cost}(c|c_j) \right] - C(x)$, where $C(x)$ is the label acquisition cost for x. As in other active inference settings, an ideal system would seek the $x \in \mathcal{A}$ optimizing $\sum_{x \in \mathcal{A}} EU(x)$ constrained such that $\sum_{x \in \mathcal{A}} C(x) \leq B$.

However, the online, stream-based setting imparts several complications when making the above optimization. First, the estimated probability, $P(x)$, and associated $\phi(x)$ is unknown a priori, and must be estimated on the fly. This estimation relies on the established field of univariate density estimation, or using the feature values of each x in order to compute a conditional density of each x. Second, each time a given x is encountered, this instance's expected misclassification cost is reduced. Accurate utility measurements require that this reduction in expected cost should be extrapolated to the future. A third complication stems from how the budget, B, is set. A budget-per-instance, a one-time fixed budget, and periodic fixed budgets yield different objective functions, complicating the task faced in online active inference.

A fourth and particularly insidious difficulty stems from the fact that $P(x)$ is unknown. This implies that a system sampling a stream of examples from $P(x)$ may not even know the set of unique xs that can potentially be encountered; as a consequence, the set of utilities under consideration. However, it is possible to build a distribution on the expected utility values conditioned on the probability of at least one occurrence during the time period under consideration. An appropriate lower bound, τ, can then be chosen whereby labeling all examples with a utility greater than τ gathers as many of the highest utility examples as is possible while exhausting the available budget during that time period [3].

While labeling for the purpose of online active inference, it is also appealing to consider how these labeled examples reduce overall cost via incorporation into the training set and updating the underlying model. Indeed, it is reasonable to consider how to allocate a single budget in order to achieve the best overall performance, while taking into account both active learning and active inference. While it is interesting to consider how expected utility-optimizing techniques for active learning can be incorporated into the same scale as the proposed technique for online active inference, it can be shown that the examples with the highest $EU(x)$ are the same examples selected by a generalized uncertainty sampling strategy for active learning. This implies that the selections made through active inference potentially offer valuable information for the task of model improvement while explicitly reducing misclassification cost [3].

5.6.2 Prediction Time Active Feature-Value Acquisition

In many domains we can acquire additional information for selected test instances that may help improve our classification performance on the test set. When this additional information comes at a cost, or is potentially noisy, it is best to actively select the instances that are most likely to benefit from acquiring additional information. This problem of prediction-time Active Feature-Value Acquisition is analogous to AFA during induction as discussed in Section 5.3. This setting has been studied in the context of customer targeting models [37], where, when making a decision for a customer, additional information may be purchased, if necessary, to make a more informed decision.

At the time of classifier induction, class labels are available for all instances including the incomplete instances. This information can be used effectively to estimate the potential value of acquiring more information for the incomplete instances. However, this label information is obviously not present during prediction on test instances. Yet, we must evaluate the benefit of acquiring additional features for an incomplete instance versus making a prediction using only incomplete feature information.

However, uncertainty-based heuristics are still applicable in this setting. In particular, given a set of incomplete test instances, one can apply a previously trained classifier to predict the class membership probabilities of these instances, using only the feature values that are known. The uncertainty of these predictions can be computed using a measure such as unlabeled margin in Equation 5.2. Then all the feature values for the most uncertain instances can be acquired until the acquisition budget is exhausted.

The above Uncertainty Sampling strategy aims to obtain more information about an uncertain prediction, with the hope that it will allow a more certain prediction, which in turn is assumed to result in a more accurate prediction. Even if more certain predictions are likely to be more accurate, acquiring additional information on the most uncertain instance may not result in the highest payoff. For example, if an instance is inherently ambiguous. Alternatively, we can select additional features values only if they are *expected* to reduce the uncertainty in classification after acquisition. Again, this can be viewed as a special case of the Expected Utility framework, where utility $\mathcal{U}$ in Equation 5.4 can be measured by the log of the unlabeled margin [37].

Another factor to be taken into consideration at prediction time is the cost of misclassifying an instance. Often misclassification costs are non-symmetric, such as the cost of misclassifying a malignant tumor as being benign. In such cases, one needs to weigh the cost of acquisitions with the cost of misclassification for each test instance. When acquisition and misclassification costs can be represented in the same units, we can selectively acquire feature values, so as to minimize the sum of the acquisition cost and expected misclassification cost [81].

Just as misclassification costs associated with different types of errors may not be uniform, it is also often possible to acquire arbitrary subsets of feature values, each at a different cost, a setting that has not been extensively explored in the research literature. It may be natural to extend the Expected Utility framework to consider sets of categorical features. However, estimating the joint probability distribution of all possible sets of values may render such a policy hopelessly inefficient. To overcome the constraints of this computational complexity, one may consider only potentially relevant feature subsets for acquisition, by combining innovative data structures and dynamic programming for incrementally updating the search space of informative subsets as new evidence is acquired—exploiting dependencies between missing features so as to share information value computations between different feature subsets, making the computation of the information value of different feature subsets tractable [8].

Finally, if we know that feature values can be acquired at test time, it would make sense to account for this at the time of classifier induction. For example, by avoiding expensive features at induction that may result in a more accurate model, but are not worth the cost at prediction time. Such a setting can be addressed in a budgeted learning framework where a learner can spend a fixed learning budget b_l to acquire training data, so as to produce a classifier that spends at most b_c per test instance [38].

5.7 Alternative Acquisition Settings

There are other sorts of data that can be acquired at a cost to improve machine learning, besides the values for individual variables for the construction of predictive models. This section covers some alternative settings for applying a modeling budget. This section begins with a treatment of the active collection of feature values for the purpose of performing unsupervised learning. Here, additional information may be acquired in order to improve the quality of tasks such as clustering.

This section then continues to investigate the selection of entire examples by class, in order that the training data comprise a "better" proportion of the constituent classes. We then discuss the related scenario where a human can be deployed to *search* for relevant information, for example, instances belonging to a given class, as well as feature values and feature labels. Finally, we present the important and often-ignored fact that in many practical situations, learned models are applied in a decision-making context, where maximizing the accuracy (or some other decision-agnostic measure) of one model is not the ultimate goal. Rather, we want to optimize decision making. Decision-focused strategies may acquire different data from model-focused strategies.

5.7.1 Information Acquisition for Unsupervised Learning

Almost all work in information acquisition has addressed supervised settings. However information may also be acquired for unstructured tasks, such as clustering. Interestingly, different clustering approaches may employ different types of information which may be potentially acquired at a cost, such as constraints as well as feature values.

Most clustering policies assume that each instance is represented by a vector of feature values. As is the case in supervised learning, clustering is undermined when the instance representation is incomplete and can therefore benefit from effective policies to improve clustering through cost-effective acquisition of information. Consider for example data on consumers' preferences. Clustering can be applied to these data in order to derive natural groupings of products based on customer preferences, such as for data-driven discovery of movie genres [6]. Clustering has also been used to help produce product/service recommendations to consumers [30]. In all these cases, performance can be improved with cost-effective acquisition of information.

Let us first consider the Expected Utility framework for clustering. At the outset it may appear that, given clustering algorithms typically aim to optimize some objective function, changes in the value of this function can be used to reflect the utility $\mathcal{U}$ from prospective feature-value acquisitions. However, recall that typically only different clustering assignments yield changes in the corresponding clustering algorithm's objective function. Yet, as noted in [91], a costly feature-value acquisition may alter the value of algorithm's objective function, without changing the assignment of even a single instance into a different cluster. For the popular K-means clustering algorithm, for example, such an approach may select feature values that alter cluster centroid locations (decreasing the total distances between instances and their respective centroids); however, these changes may not change the cluster assignments significantly or at all. The effect of such wasteful acquisitions can be significant. Alternatively, it is useful to consider utilities which capture the impact on clustering *configuration* caused by an acquisition. For example, utility can be measured by the number of instances for which cluster membership changes as the result of an acquisition [91].

Some clustering approaches do not employ a vectorial data representation;

instead, the proximity of pairs of instances is provided. Hence, for a dataset with N instances, the required information scales with $O(N^2)$. It has been shown [34, 15] that identifying the most informative proximity measures to acquire can be critical for overcoming the inherent data sparseness of proximity data, making such methods feasible in practice. For example, using the expected value of information to quantify the gain from additional information, [34] proposed an algorithm which identifies proximity values so as to minimize the risk from estimating clusters from the existing data. Thus, selected acquisitions aim to minimize the loss from deciding only based on the incomplete information instead of the optimal decision, when all proximity values are known.

Semi-supervised clustering also offers interesting opportunities to acquire limited supervision to improve clustering cost-effectively. For example, a subset of instances, must-link and cannot-link constraints, can specify instance pairs that must and must-not belong to the same cluster, respectively. Similarly, cluster-level constraints indicate whether or not instances in two different clusters ought to be assigned to the same cluster. To improve clustering, an information acquisition policy may suggest the constraints for which pairs would be most informative to acquire. Similar to active learning, the feature values, from which distances are derived, are known. Acquiring constraints for clustering may not bear much similarity to instance-level information acquisition for supervised learning. However, the uncertainly reduction principle has been effectively adapted to this setting as well. Specifically, for cluster-level constraint acquisition [39] proposes to acquire constraints when it is most difficult to determine whether two clusters should be merged. In contrast, for acquiring instance-level constraints, [7] proposes a policy which does not follow principles used in supervised settings. In particular, given the impact of initial centroids on clustering outcomes of the K-means clustering algorithm, they propose a constraint acquisition policy which improves the identification of cluster centroids and their neighborhoods with fewer queries. To accomplish this, they employ the farthest first traversal scheme to identify points from *different* clusters using fewer queries. A subsequent consolidation phase, acquires additional pair-wise constraints to explore the structure of each cluster's neighborhood.

In future work it would be interesting to consider policies that can consider different types of information, such as constraints information and feature values, which may be acquired at different costs. However, as reflected in the work we discuss above, and quite differently from the supervised setting, employing the Expected Utility framework for this task may not be the obvious choice in this case.

5.7.2   Class-Conditional Example Acquisition

In many model induction tasks, the amount of training data is constrained not by the cost of instance labels, but by the cost of gathering the independent covariates that are used to predict these labels. For example, in certain settings examples can be acquired by class, but gathering the feature values requires costly physical tests and experiments, large amounts of time or computation, or some other source of information that requires some budget outlay. Consider, for example, the problem of building predictive models based on data collected through an "artificial nose" with the intent of "sniffing out" explosive or hazardous chemical compounds [48, 50, 49]. In this setting, the reactivity of a large number of chemicals is already known, representing label-conditioned pools of available instances. However, producing these chemicals in a laboratory setting and running the resultant compound through the artificial nose may be an expensive, time-consuming process. This problem appears to face the inverse of the difficulties faced by active learning—labels essentially come for free, while the independent feature values are *completely* unknown and must be gathered at a cost (let's say, all at once). In this setting, it becomes important to consider the question: "In what proportion should classes be represented in a training set of a certain size?" [95]

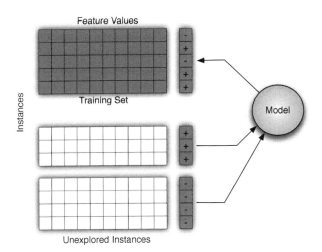

FIGURE 5.11: Active Class Selection: Gathering instances from random class-conditioned fonts in a proportion believed to offer greatest improvement in generalization performance.

Let's call the problem of proportioning class labels in a selection of n additional training instances, "Active Class Selection" (ACS) [48, 50, 49, 95]. This process is exemplified in Figure 5.11. In this setting, there is assumed to be large, class-conditioned (virtual) pools of available instances with completely hidden feature values. At each epoch, t, of the ACS process, the task is to leverage the current model when selecting examples from these pools in a proportion believed to have the greatest effectiveness for improving the generalization performance of this model. The feature values for each instance are then collected and the complete instances are added to the training set. The model is reconstructed and the processes is repeated until n examples are obtained (because the budget is exhausted or some other stopping criterion is met, such as a computational limit). Note that this situation can be considered to be a special case of the instance completion setting of Active Feature Acquisition (discussed above). It is a degenerate special case because, prior to selection, there is no information at all about the instances other than their classes.

For ACS, the extreme lack of information to guide selection leads to the development of unique uncertainty and utility estimators, which, in the absence of predictive covariates, require unique approximations. While alternative approaches to active class selection have emerged, for thematic clarity, uncertainty-based and expected utility-based approaches will be presented first. Note that because effective classification requires that both sides of a prediction boundary be represented, unlike typical active learning techniques, active class selection typically *samples* classes from their respective score distributions [72, 73].

5.7.2.1   Uncertainty-Based Approaches

This family of techniques for performing active class selection is based on the volatility in the predictions made about certain classes—those classes whose cross-validated predictions are subject to the most change between successive epochs of instance selection are likely to be based upon an uncertain predictor, and amenable to refinement by the incorporation of additional training data [48, 49]. Analogous to the case of more traditional uncertainty-based data acquisition, several heuristics have been devised to capture the notion of variability.

One measure of the uncertainty of a learned model is how volatile its predictive performance is in the face of new training data. For example, in Figure 5.8 we see various typical learning curves. With reasonably accurate training data, the modeling is much more volatile at the left side of the figure, showing large changes in generalization performance for the same amount of new training data. We can think that as the predictor gains knowledge of the problem space, it tends to solidify in the face of data, exhibiting less change and greater certainty. For ACS, we might wonder if the learning curves will be equally steep regardless of the class of the training data [48, 50, 49]. With this in mind, we can select instances at epoch t from the classes in proportion to their improvements in accuracy at $t-1$ and $t-2$. For example, we could use cross-validation to estimate the generalization performance of the classifier with respect to each class, $\mathcal{A}(c)$; class c can then be sampled according to:

$$p_{\mathcal{A}}^{t}(c) \propto \frac{\max\left\{0, \mathcal{A}^{t-1}(c) - \mathcal{A}^{t-2}(c)\right\}}{\sum_{c'} \max\left\{0, \mathcal{A}^{t-1}(c') - \mathcal{A}^{t-2}(c')\right\}}.$$

Alternatively, we could consider general volatility in class members' predicted labels, beyond improvement in the model's ability to predict the class. Again, by using cross-validated predictions at successive epochs, it is possible to isolate members of each class, and observe changes in the predicted class for each instance. For example, when the predicted label of a given instance changes between successive epochs, we can deem the instance to have been *redistricted* [48, 50, 49]. Again considering the level of volatility in a model's predictions to be a measurement of uncertainty, we can sample classes at epoch t according to each classes' proportional measure of redistricting:

$$p_{\mathcal{R}}^t(c) \propto \frac{\frac{1}{|c|} \sum_{x \in c} \mathbb{I}(f^{t-1}(x) \neq f^{t-2}(x))}{\sum_{c'} \frac{1}{|c'|} \sum_{x \in c'} \mathbb{I}(f^{t-1}(x) \neq f^{t-2}(x))},$$

where $\mathbb{I}(\cdot)$ is an indicator function taking the value of 1 if its argument is true and 0 otherwise. $f^{t-1}(x)$ and $f^{t-2}(x)$ are the predicted labels for instance x from the models trained at epoch $t-1$ and $t-2$, respectively [48, 50, 49].

5.7.2.2 Expected Class Utility

The previously described active class selection heuristics are reliant on the assumption that adding examples belonging to a particular class will improve the predictive accuracy with respect to that class. This does not directly estimate the utility of adding members of a particular class to a model's overall performance. Instead, it may be preferable to select classes whose instances' presence in the training set will reduce a model's misclassification cost by the greatest amount in expectation.

Let cost $(c_i|c_j)$ be the cost of predicting c_i on an instance x whose true label is c_j. Then the expected empirical misclassification cost over a sample dataset, $\mathbb{D}$, is:

$$\hat{R} = \frac{1}{|\mathbb{D}|} \sum_{x \in \mathbb{D}} \sum_i \hat{P}(c_i|x)\text{cost}(c_i|y),$$

where y is the correct class for a given x. Typically in the active class selection setting, this expectation would be taken over the training set (e.g. $\mathbb{D} = T$), preferably using cross-validation. In order to reduce this risk, we would like to select examples from class c leading to the greatest reduction in this expected risk [50].

Consider a predictive model $\hat{P}^{T \cup c}(\cdot|x)$, a model built on the training set, T, supplemented with an arbitrary example belonging to class c. Given the opportunity to choose an additional class-representative example to the training pool, we would like to select the class that reduces expected risk by the greatest amount:

$$\bar{c} = \arg \max_c U(c),$$

where

$$U(c) = \frac{1}{|\mathbb{D}|} \sum_{x \in \mathbb{D}} \sum_{i} \hat{P}^T(c_i|x)\text{cost}(c_i|y) - \frac{1}{|\mathbb{D}|} \sum_{x \in \mathbb{D}} \sum_{i} \hat{P}^{T \cup c}(c_i|x)\text{cost}(c_i|y).$$

Of course the benefit of adding additional examples on a test dataset is unknown. Furthermore, the impact of a particular class's examples may vary depending on the feature values of particular instances. In order to cope with these issues, we can estimate via cross-validation on the training set. Using sampling, we can try various class-conditional additions and compute the expected benefit of a class across that class's representatives in T, assessed on the testing folds. The above utility then becomes:

$$\hat{U}(c) = E_{x \in c} \left[\frac{1}{|\mathbb{D}|} \sum_{x \in \mathbb{D}} \sum_{i} \hat{P}^T(c_i|x)\text{cost}(c_i|y) - \frac{1}{|\mathbb{D}|} \sum_{x \in \mathbb{D}} \sum_{i} \hat{P}^{T \cup c}(c_i|x)\text{cost}(c_i|y) \right].$$

Note that it is often preferred to add examples in batch. In this case, we may wish to sample from the classes in proportion to their respective utilities:

$$p_{\hat{U}}^t(c) \propto \frac{\hat{U}(c)}{\sum_{c'} \hat{U}(c')}.$$

Note that diverse class-conditional acquisition costs can be incorporated as in Section 5.2, utilizing $\frac{\hat{U}(c)}{\omega_c}$ where ω_c is the (expected) cost of acquiring the feature vector of an example in class c.

5.7.2.3   Alternative Approaches to ACS

In addition to uncertainty-based and utility-based techniques, there are several alternative techniques for performing active class selection. Motivated by empirical results showing that barring any domain-specific information, when collecting examples for a training set of size n, a balanced class distribution tends to offer reasonable AUC on test data [92, 95], a reasonable baseline approach to active class selection is simply to select classes in balanced proportion.

Search strategies may alternately be employed in order to reveal the most effective class ratio at each epoch. Utilizing a nested cross-validation on the training set, the space of class ratios can be explored, with the most favorable ratio being utilized at each epoch. Note that it is not possible to explore all possible class ratios in all epochs, without eventually spending too much on one class or another. Thus, as we approach n we can narrow the range of class ratios, assuming that there is a problem-optimal class ratio that will become more apparent as we obtain more data [95].

It should be noted that many techniques employed for building classification models assume an identical or similar training and test distribution. Violating this assumption may lead to biased predictions on test data where classes preferentially represented in the training data are predicted more frequently. In particular "increasing the prior probability of a class increases the posterior probability of the class, moving the classification boundary for that class so that more cases are classified into that class" [76, 61]. Thus in settings where instances are selected specifically in proportions different from those seen in the wild, posterior probability estimates should be properly calibrated to be aligned with the test data, if possible [61, 26, 95].

5.7.3 Guided Selection

A much more general issue in selective data acquisition is the amount of control ceded to the "oracle" doing the acquisition. The work discussed so far assumes that an oracle will be queried for some specific value, and the oracle simply returns that value (or a noisy realization). However, if the oracle is actually a person, he or she may be able to apply considerable intelligence and other resources to "guide" the selection. Such guidance is especially helpful in situations where some aspect of the data is rare—where purely data-driven strategies are particularly challenged.

Let's continue thinking about the active class selection setting as a concrete case. In many practical settings, one class is quite rare. As a motivational example, consider building a predictive model from scratch designed to classify web pages containing a particular topic of interest. While large absolute numbers of such web pages may be present on the web, they may be outnumbered by uninteresting pages by a million to one or worse (take, for instance, the task of detecting and removing hate speech from the web [5]).

Unfortunately, when the class distribution is so skewed, active learning strategies can fail completely—and the failure is not simply due to the hurdles faced when trying to learn models in settings with skewed class distribution, a problem that has received a fair bit of attention [93, 4]. Rather, the problem faced by the active learner is far more treacherous: learning techniques cannot even concentrate on the rare instances as the techniques are unaware which instances to focus on.

Perhaps even more insidious is the difficulty posed by classes consisting of rare, disjunctive subconcepts. These disjuncts can emerge even in problems spaces without such an extreme class skew: when members of an important class do not manifest themselves as a simple, continuously dense region of the input space, but rather as many small disjoint clusters embedded throughout the input space [94]. For an active learner, these "small disjuncts" act like rare classes: when an active learner has not been exposed to instances of a subconcept, how can it best choose instances to label in order to properly distinguish that subconcept from its containing space?

While a plethora of techniques have been proposed for performing active learning specifically in the high-skew setting [89, 13, 104, 27] as well as techniques where the geometry and feature-density of the problem space are explicitly included when making instance selections [105, 33, 21, 59, 98, 53], these techniques, as initially appealing as they may seem, may fail just as badly as traditional active learning techniques. Class skew and subconcept rarity may be sufficient to thwart them completely [5, 4].

However, in these extremely difficult settings, we can task humans to search the problem space for rare cases, using tools (like search engines) and possibly interacting with the base learner. Consider the motivating example of hate speech classification on the web (from above). While an active learner may experience difficulty exploring the details of this rare class, a human oracle armed with a search interface is likely to expose examples of hate speech easily. In fact, given the coverage of modern web search engines, a human can produce interesting examples from a much larger sample of the problem space, far beyond that which is likely to be contained in a sample pool for active learning. This is critical due to hardware-imposed constraints on the size of the pool an active learner is able to choose from—e.g., a random draw of several hundred thousand examples from the problem space may not even contain any members of the minority class or of rare disjuncts!

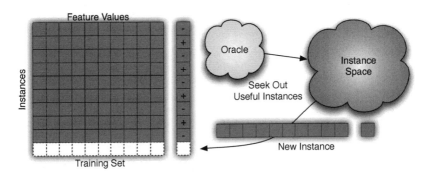

FIGURE 5.12: Guided Learning: An oracle selecting useful examples from the instance space.

Guided Learning is the general process of utilizing oracles to search the problem space, using their domain expertise to *seek* instances representing the interesting regions of the problem space. Figure 5.12 presents the general guided learning setting. Here, given some interface enabling search over the domain in question, an oracle searches for interesting examples, which are either supplemented with an implicit label by the oracle, or sent for explicit labeling as a second step. These examples are then added to the training set and a model is retrained. Oracles can leverage their background knowledge of the problem being faced. By incorporating the techniques of active class selection oracles can be directed to gather instances in a class-proportion believed to most strongly help train a model. Further, by allowing the oracle to interact with the base learner, confusing instances, those that "fool" the model can be sought out from the problem space and used for subsequent training in a form of human-guided uncertainty sampling.

While guided learning often presents an attractive and cost-effective alternative to active learning, particularly in difficult settings, the overall guided information acquisition paradigm is flexible, human intelligence and background knowledge can be used to *seek* a wide variety of information. As an example of alternative sources of information available through guided information acquisition, consider the problem of finding useful features when building classification models. In many settings, the choice of which features to use as a capable separator of classes may not be initially obvious. Simply including many features also is not an appealing option; with insufficient labeled examples, the underlying model or feature selection technique may confuse signal with noise, attributing predictive power to certain features simply due to noise and false-signals [65, 64].

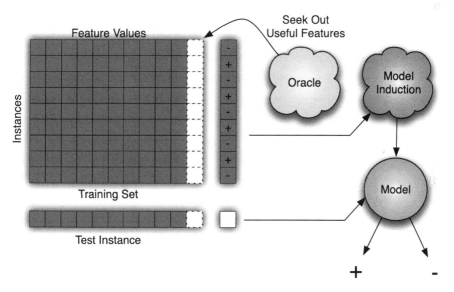

FIGURE 5.13: Guided feature selection: Tasking oracles with finding useful features.

However, human are often able to apply their background knowledge, suggesting discriminative features for a given problem or removing useless features currently being utilized by an existing model in order to approve predictive performance [65, 64, 17]. An example of this process can be seen in Figure 5.13. In this *guided feature selection* paradigm, human oracles describe additional features to the predictive system, in effect adding additional columns to the instance information matrix. Note that these features may be functions of existing feature values, or they may require explicit feature value acquisition as in Section 5.3.

Active feature labeling and active dual supervision are demonstrated to be effective techniques for reducing the total annotation effort required for building effective predictive models (see Section 5.4). However, while appropriately chosen feature labels may facilitate the construction of models able to effectively discriminate between classes, as with active learning, particularly difficult situations may stymie active feature selection and active dual supervision, wasting many queries on uninformative queries, simply because the base model has very little knowledge of the problem space [1]. However, just as in guided learning, human oracles may be requested to *seek* polarity labels for those features thought to most effectively discern between the classes. This process may be seen in Figure 5.14. Note that this process may be seamlessly incorporated with guided feature selection, adding new features and their associated label simultaneously. In the case of text classification, this may involve adding a term or phrase not originally considered, and assigning to that phrase a class polarity. This guided feature labeling has been demonstrated to offer much greater effectiveness than active feature labeling in "difficult" classification problems [1].

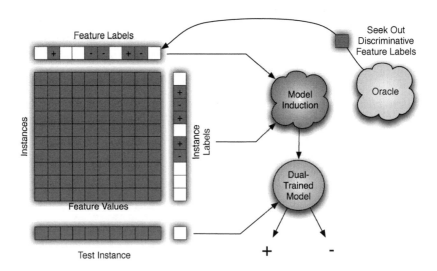

FIGURE 5.14: Guided Feature Labeling: Tasking oracles with finding features and their associated class polarity believed to be best able to discriminate between classes.

5.7.4 Beyond Improving a Single Model's Accuracy

Thus far, we have discussed different types of information that can be acquired. However, in the context of learning predictive models we have not considered settings in which the objective for information acquisitions differ from that of active learning policies, i.e., improving a single model's predictive accuracy (by some measure). As an example of such a setting, consider an application where the labels of training examples can be (actively) acquired in order to augment the training data of multiple classification models.

Combining the aspects of multi-task learning and active learning, selecting examples for Multiple Task Active Learning (MTAL) [69] can be approached in several ways. The first approach would be simply to alternate between acquisitions that benefit each of the models. The second approach would attempt to produce a single ranking of examples based on the benefits across the learning tasks. In this case, each prospective acquisition is first ranked by each of learning tasks, using traditional active learning policies. The overall rank for a prospective acquisition is then computed via the Borda aggregation procedure, i.e., by summing the prospective acquisition's rank numbers across all learning tasks. Both of these methods [69] are general, in that they can be used to learn different types of models. In fact, in principle, these policies can also apply when a different active learning policy is used to rank prospective acquisitions for different types of models (e.g., aggregation and classification models). However, their effectiveness has not been evaluated for these settings related to multiple active learning techniques. When multiple prediction tasks are related, such as when the labels of instances corresponding to each satisfy certain constraints, it is also possible to exploit these dependencies to improve the selection of informative instances [101].

An interesting scenario which implies yet another objective for information acquisition in practice arises when information acquisition aims to improve repetitive decisions, which are, in turn, informed by predictive models [74, 40]. Furthermore, many decisions are informed by multiple predictive models of different types. For instance, firms' sales tax audit decisions are typically informed by the predicted probability of tax fraud, but also by the predicted revenue that might be recovered. Note that prospective audit acquisitions will affect both predictive models. Interestingly, for each model, a different audit acquisition might be more desirable to improve the corresponding estimation. Hence, it is beneficial to understand how should an acquisition budget be allocated among them so as to benefit future audit decisions the most?

In principle, MTAL can be applied to cost-effectively improve the predictive accuracy of all the models informing the decisions. However, costly improvements in model accuracy do not necessarily yield better decisions [74]. Hence, more efficient policies can be derived if such greedy improvements in accuracy are avoided. Furthermore, exploiting knowledge of the decision's structure can yield significant benefits [74, 40, 41]. For example, when information is acquired for multiple models informing the decisions, it is useful to consider how changes in all of the models simultaneously will affect future decisions. This approach has been applied effectively when the same information can augment multiple models simultaneously [40, 41]. It will also be useful to study the effectiveness of this general principle when the training data of each of the models can be augmented by acquisition from a different source (i.e., the same acquisition cannot be used to train all models).

5.8 Conclusion

The vast majority of the information acquisition literature focuses on active learning, reflecting only a single setting—the selection of individual instances for the acquisition of a single, correct label with the objective of improving classification performance cost-effectively. However, as we outline in this chapter, a rich set of important practical problems arise once we consider the diverse set of information that is available to a machine learning system at some cost, and when the error-free assumptions typically used in such research are relaxed. In this chapter, we discussed three dimensions that define alternative information acquisition problems. Specifically these facets are: the different types of information that can be acquired to inform learning, the quality of the acquired information, and the different objectives which acquisitions ultimately aim to improve, cost-effectively. Since each of these facets can take a variety of settings in practice, cost-effective information acquisition gives rise to a diverse range of important problems.

In order to cope with the complexity of such a diverse range of problems, we have presented two general strategies for information acquisition. Namely, uncertainty reduction and expected utility approaches. While uncertainty-based approaches are appealing initially in that they are often simple to implement and have been subject to extensive study in the realm of traditional active learning, these techniques tend to fall short when faced with the more complex demands of general information acquisition. Combining effectiveness measures for diverse types of information seamlessly in concert with acquisition costs is often beyond the capability of uncertainty-based techniques. Fortunately, expected utility-based approaches offer a one-size-fits-all framework for integrating the empirical benefits of different acquisition types with the costs these acquisitions may incur. While expected utility approaches offer great promise, this is tempered by the difficulties associated with computing an accurate utility estimator in a way that is computationally tractable.

While we have demonstrated a wide range of use cases and settings for selective data acquisition, discussing applications ranging from marketing to medicine, there are innumerable scenarios yet to be explored; more complex combinations of data available at a cost, both at training and at use time, with relaxed assumptions regarding data cleanliness. Though it is difficult to speculate what new applications and future research into the realm of data acquisition will accomplish, we believe that the material presented here provides a solid foundation upon which this new work can build.

References

[1] Josh Attenberg, Prem Melville, and Foster Provost. Guided feature labeling for budget-sensitive learning under extreme class imbalance. In *BL-ICML '10: Workshop on Budgeted Learning*, 2010.

[2] Josh Attenberg, Prem Melville, and Foster J. Provost. A unified approach to active dual supervision for labeling features and examples. In *European Conference on Machine Learning*, 2010.

[3] Josh Attenberg and Foster Provost. Active inference and learning for classifying streams. In *BL-ICML '10: Workshop on Budgeted Learning*, 2010.

[4] Josh Attenberg and Foster Provost. Inactive learning? difficulties employing active learning in practice. *SIGKDD Explorations*, 12(2), 2010.

[5] Josh Attenberg and Foster Provost. Why label when you can search? Strategies for applying human resources to build classification models under extreme class imbalance. In *Conference on Knowledge Discovery and Data Mining (KDD)*, 2010.

[6] Arindam Banerjee, Chase Krumpelman, Sugato Basu, Raymond J. Mooney, and Joydeep Ghosh. Model-based overlapping clustering. In *Proc. of 11th ACM SIGKDD Intl. Conf. on Knowledge Discovery and Data Mining (KDD-05)*, 2005.

[7] Sugato Basu. Semi-supervised clustering with limited background knowledge. In *National Conference on Artificial Intelligence (AAAI)*, pages 979–980, 2004.

[8] Mustafa Bilgic and Lise Getoor. Voila: Efficient feature-value acquisition for classification. In *Proceedings of the Twenty-Second Conference on Artificial Intelligence (AAAI)*, pages 1225–1230, 2007.

[9] Mustafa Bilgic and Lise Getoor. Effective label acquisition for collective classification. In *Proceedings of the 14th ACM SIGKDD International Conference on Knowledge Discovery and Data Mining*, KDD '08, pages 43–51. ACM, 2008.

[10] Mustafa Bilgic and Lise Getoor. Reflect and correct: A misclassification prediction approach to active inference. *ACM Trans. Knowl. Discov. Data*, 3, December 2009.

[11] Mustafa Bilgic and Lise Getoor. Active Inference for Collective Classification. In *National Conference on Artificial Intelligence (AAAI)*, 2010.

[12] Catherine L. Blake and Christopher John Merz. UCI repository of machine learning databases. `http://www.ics.uci.edu/~mlearn/MLRepository.html`, 1998.

[13] Michael Bloodgood and K. Vijay Shanker. Taking into account the differences between actively and passively acquired data: the case of active learning with support vector machines for imbalanced datasets. In *North American Chapter of the Association for Computational Linguistics (NAACL)*, 2009.

[14] Carla E. Brodley and Mark A. Friedl. Identifying mislabeled training data. *Journal of Artificial Intelligence Research*, 11:131–167, 1999.

[15] Joachim M. Buhmann and Thomas Zöller. Active learning for hierarchical pairwise data clustering. In *International Conference on Pattern Recognition (ICPR)*, pages 2186–2189, 2000.

[16] Bob Carpenter. Multilevel Bayesian model of categorical data annotation, 2008. Available at: `http://lingpipe-blog.com/lingpipe-white-papers/`.

[17] Bruce Croft and Raj Das. Experiments with query acquisition and use in document retrieval systems. In *Proceedings of the ACM SIGIR Conference on Research and Development in Information Retrieval*, pages 349–368, 1990.

[18] B.V. Dasarathy, editor. *Information Fusion: An International Journal on Multi-Sensor, Multi-Source Information Fusion*. Elsevier, 2010.

[19] Alexander Philip Dawid and Allan M. Skene. Maximum likelihood estimation of observer error-rates using the EM algorithm. *Applied Statistics*, 28(1):20–28, September 1979.

[20] O. Dekel and O. Shamir. Vox populi: Collecting high-quality labels from a crowd. In *COLT 2009: Proceedings of the 22nd Annual Conference on Learning Theory*. Citeseer, 2009.

[21] P. Donmez and J. Carbonell. Paired sampling in density-sensitive active learning. In *Proc. 10th International Symposium on Artificial Intelligence and Mathematics*, 2008.

[22] Pinar Donmez and Jaime G. Carbonell. Proactive learning: Cost-sensitive active learning with multiple imperfect oracles. In *Proceedings of the 17th ACM Conference on Information and Knowledge Management (CIKM 2008)*, pages 619–628, 2008.

[23] Pinar Donmez, Jaime G. Carbonell, and Jeff Schneider. Efficiently learning the accuracy of labeling sources for selective sampling. In *Proceedings of the 15th ACM SIGKDD International Conference on Knowledge Discovery and Data Mining (KDD 2009)*, pages 259–268, 2009.

[24] G. Druck, G. Mann, and A. McCallum. Learning from labeled features using generalized expectation criteria. In *Special Interest Group in Information Retrieval (SIGIR)*, 2008.

[25] G. Druck, B. Settles, and A. McCallum. Active learning by labeling features. In *Conference on Empirical Methods in Natural Language Processing (EMNLP '09)*, pages 81–90. Association for Computational Linguistics, 2009.

[26] Charles Elkan. The foundations of cost-sensitive learning. In *Proceedings of the Seventeenth International Joint Conference on Artificial Intelligence*, pages 973–978, 2001.

[27] Seyda Ertekin, Jian Huang, Leon Bottou, and Lee Giles. Learning on the border: Active learning in imbalanced data classification. In *Conference on Information and Knowledge Management (CIKM)*, 2007.

[28] Jerome H. Friedman, Ron Kohavi, and Yeogirl Yun. Lazy decision trees. In *National Conference on Artificial Intelligence (AAAI)*, pages 717–724, 1996.

[29] G. M. Fung, O. L. Mangasarian, and J. W. Shavlik. Knowledge-based support vector machine classifiers. In *Advances in Neural Information Processing Systems 14*. MIT Press, 2002.

[30] Thomas George and Srujana Merugu. A scalable collaborative filtering framework based on co-clustering. In *IEEE International Conference on Data Mining (ICDM)*, pages 625–628, 2005.

[31] S. Godbole, A. Harpale, S. Sarawagi, and S. Chakrabarti. Document classification through interactive supervision of document and term labels. In *Practice of Knowledge Discovery in Databases (PKDD)*, 2004.

[32] R. Haertel, K. Seppi, E. Ringger, and J. Carroll. Return on investment for active learning. In *Proceedings of the NIPS Workshop on Cost-Sensitive Learning*, 2008.

[33] Jingrui He and Jaime G. Carbonell. Nearest-neighbor-based active learning for rare category detection. In *Neural Information Processing Systems (NIPS)*, 2007.

[34] Thomas Hofmann and Joachim M. Buhmann. Active data clustering. In *Proceedings of the 1997 Conference on Advances in Neural Information Processing Systems 10*, NIPS '97, pages 528–534, Cambridge, MA, 1998. MIT Press.

[35] P. Ipeirotis, F. Provost, V. Sheng, and J. Wang. Repeated labeling using multiple, noisy labelers. Technical Report Working Paper CeDER-10-03, Center for Digital Economy Research, NYU Stern School of Business, 2010.

[36] P.G. Ipeirotis, F. Provost, and J. Wang. Quality management on Amazon Mechanical Turk. In *Proceedings of the ACM SIGKDD Workshop on Human Computation*, pages 64–67, 2010.

[37] Pallika Kanani and Prem Melville. Prediction-time active feature-value acquisition for customer targeting. In *Proceedings of the Workshop on Cost Sensitive Learning, NIPS 2008*, 2008.

[38] Aloak Kapoor and Russell Greiner. Learning and classifying under hard budgets. In *European Conference on Machine Learning (ECML)*, pages 170–181, 2005.

[39] Dan Klein, Sepandar D. Kamvar, and Christopher D. Manning. From instance-level constraints to space-level constraints: Making the most of prior knowledge in data clustering. In *ICML*, pages 307–314, 2002.

[40] Danxia Kong and Maytal Saar-Tsechansky. Collaborative information acquisition. In *International Conference on Machine Learning Workshop on Budgeted Learning*, 2010.

[41] Danxia Kong and Maytal Saar-Tsechansky. A framework for collaborative information acquisition. In *Workshop on Information Technology and Systems*, 2010.

[42] Gautam Kunapuli, Kristin P. Bennett, Amina Shabbeer, Richard Maclin, and Jude W. Shavlik. Online knowledge-based support vector machines. In *European Conference on Machine Learning*, pages 145–161, 2010.

[43] Ludmila I. Kuncheva, Christopher J. Whitaker, Catherine A. Shipp, and Robert P.W. Duin. Limits on the majority vote accuracy in classifier fusion. *Pattern Analysis and Applications*, 6(1):22–31, April 2003.

[44] David Lewis and William Gale. A sequential algorithm for training text classifiers. In *Proceedings of 17th International ACM SIGIR Conference on Research and Development in Information Retrieval (SIGIR-94)*, 1994.

[45] R. Little and D. Rubin. *Statistical Analysis with Missing Data*. John Wiley & Sons, 1987.

[46] Bing Liu, Xiaoli Li, Wee Sun Lee, and Philip Yu. Text classification by labeling words. In *AAAI*, 2004.

[47] Dan Lizotte, Omid Madani, and Russell Greiner. Budgeted learning of naive-Bayes classifiers. In *Proc. of 19th Conf. on Uncertainty in Artificial Intelligence (UAI-2003)*, Acapulco, Mexico, 2003.

[48] R. Lomasky, C. Brodley, M. Aernecke, D. Walt, and M. Friedl. Active Class Selection. In *Machine Learning: ECML*, vol. 4701, pages 640–647, 2007.

[49] R. Lomasky, C. E. Brodley, S. Bencic, M. Aernecke, and D Walt. Guiding class selection for an artificial nose. In *NIPS Workshop on Testing of Deployable Learning and Decision Systems*, 2006.

[50] Rachel Lomasky. Active acquisition of informative training data. PhD thesis, Tufts University, 2010.

[51] Gabor Lugosi. Learning with an unreliable teacher. *Pattern Recognition*, 25(1):79–87, January 1992.

[52] Andrew McCallum and Kamal Nigam. A comparison of event models for Naive Bayes text classification. In *Papers from the AAAI-98 Workshop on Text Categorization*, pages 41–48, Madison, WI, July 1998.

[53] Andrew K. Mccallum and Kamal Nigam. Employing EM in pool-based active learning for text classification. In *International Conference on Machine Learning (ICML)*, 1998.

[54] Prem Melville, Wojciech Gryc, and Richard Lawrence. Sentiment analysis of blogs by combining lexical knowledge with text classification. In *Proceedings of the 15th Conference on Knowledge Discovery and Data Mining (KDD-09)*, 2009.

[55] Prem Melville and Raymond J. Mooney. Diverse ensembles for active learning. In *Proceedings of 21st International Conference on Machine Learning (ICML-2004)*, 2004.

[56] Prem Melville, Foster J. Provost, and Raymond J. Mooney. An expected utility approach to active feature-value acquisition. In *Proceedings of 5th IEEE International Conference on Data Mining (ICDM-05)*, pages 745–748, 2005.

[57] Prem Melville, Maytal Saar-Tsechansky, Foster J. Provost, and Raymond J. Mooney. Active feature-value acquisition for classifier induction. In *Proceedings of the IEEE International Conference on Data Mining (ICDM-04)*, pages 483–486, 2004.

[58] Prem Melville and Vikas Sindhwani. Active dual supervision: Reducing the cost of annotating examples and features. In *Proceedings of the NAACL HLT 2009 Workshop on Active Learning for Natural Language Processing*, 2009.

[59] Hieu T. Nguyen and Arnold Smeulders. Active learning using pre-clustering. In *International Conference on Machine Learning (ICML)*, 2004.

[60] Bo Pang, Lillian Lee, and Shivakumar Vaithyanathan. Thumbs up?: sentiment classification using machine learning techniques. In *Proceedings of the ACL-02 Conference on Empirical Methods in Natural Language Processing, Vol. 10*, pages 79–86. Association for Computational Linguistics, 2002.

[61] F. Provost. Machine learning from imbalanced datasets 101. In *Proceedings of the AAAI2000 Workshop on Imbalanced Data Sets*, 2000.

[62] Foster Provost and Andrea Pohoreckyj Danyluk. Learning from bad data. In *Proceedings of the ML-95 Workshop on Applying Machine Learning in Practice*, 1995.

[63] John Ross Quinlan. *C4.5: Programs for Machine Learning*. Morgan Kaufmann Publishers, 1992.

[64] Hema Raghavan, Omid Madani, and Rosie Jones. InterActive feature selection. In *Proceedings of the 19th International Joint Conference on Artificial Intelligence*, pages 841–846, 2005.

[65] Hema Raghavan, Omid Madani, Rosie Jones, and Leslie Kaelbling. Active learning with feedback on both features and instances. *Journal of Machine Learning Research*, 7, 2006.

[66] Matthew J. Rattigan, Marc Maier, and David Jensen. Exploiting Network Structure for Active Inference in Collective Classification. Technical Report 07-22, University of Massachusetts, Amherst, 2007.

[67] Vikas C. Raykar, Shipeng Yu, Linda H. Zhao, Anna Jerebko, Charles Florin, Gerardo Hermosillo Valadez, Luca Bogoni, and Linda Moy. Supervised learning from multiple experts: Whom to trust when everyone lies a bit. In *Proceedings of the 26th Annual International Conference on Machine Learning (ICML 2009)*, pages 889–896, 2009.

[68] Vikas C. Raykar, Shipeng Yu, Linda H. Zhao, Gerardo Hermosillo Valadez, Charles Florin, Luca Bogoni, and Linda Moy. Learning from crowds. *Journal of Machine Learning Research*, 11(7):1297–1322, April 2010.

[69] Roi Reichart, Katrin Tomanek, and Udo Hahn. Multi-task active learning for linguistic annotations. In *Annual Meeting of the Association for Computational Linguistics (ACL)*, 2008.

[70] Nicholas Roy and Andrew McCallum. Toward optimal active learning through sampling estimation of error reduction. In *Proceedings of the 18th International Conference on Machine Learning (ICML-2001)*, pages 441–448. Morgan Kaufmann, San Francisco, CA, 2001.

[71] Maytal Saar-Tsechansky, Prem Melville, and Foster J. Provost. Active feature-value acquisition. *Management Science*, 55(4):664–684, 2009.

[72] Maytal Saar-Tsechansky and Foster Provost. Active learning for class probability estimation and ranking. In *Proceedings of the Seventeenth International Joint Conference on Artificial Intelligence (IJCAI-2001*, pages 911–920, 2001.

[73] Maytal Saar-Tsechansky and Foster Provost. Active sampling for class probability estimation and ranking. *Machine Learning*, 54(2):153–178, 2004.

[74] Maytal Saar-Tsechansky and Foster Provost. Decision-centric active learning of binary-outcome models. In *Information Systems Research*, 2007.

[75] Maytal Saar-Tsechansky and Foster Provost. Handling missing values when applying classification models. *Journal of Machine Learning Research*, 8:1623–1657, December 2007.

[76] SAS Institute Inc. *Getting Started with SAS Enterprise Miner*. SAS Institute Inc, Cary, NC, 2001.

[77] Robert E. Schapire, Marie Rochery, Mazin G. Rahim, and Narendra Gupta. Incorporating prior knowledge into boosting. In *International Conference on Machine Learning (ICML)*, 2002.

[78] Andrew Schein and Lyle Ungar. Active learning for logistic regression: An evaluation. *Machine Learning*, 68(3):235–265–265, October 2007.

[79] B. Settles. Active Learning Literature Survey. Computer Sciences Technical Report 1648, University of Wisconsin–Madison, 2009.

[80] B. Settles, M. Craven, and L. Friedland. Active learning with real annotation costs. In *Proceedings of the NIPS Workshop on Cost-Sensitive Learning*, pages 1–10, 2008.

[81] Victor S. Sheng and Charles X. Ling. Feature value acquisition in testing: a sequential batch test algorithm. In *Proceedings of the 23rd International Conference on Machine Learning*, ICML '06, pages 809–816, New York, 2006.

[82] Victor S. Sheng, Foster Provost, and Panagiotis Ipeirotis. Get another label? Improving data quality and data mining using multiple, noisy labelers. In *Proceedings of the 14th ACM SIGKDD International Conference on Knowledge Discovery and Data Mining (KDD 2008)*, 2008.

[83] Bernard W. Silverman. Some asymptotic properties of the probabilistic teacher. *IEEE Transactions on Information Theory*, 26(2):246–249, March 1980.

[84] Vikas Sindhwani and Prem Melville. Document-word co-regularization for semi-supervised sentiment analysis. In *Proceedings of IEEE International Conference on Data Mining (ICDM-08)*, 2008.

[85] Vikas Sindhwani, Prem Melville, and Richard Lawrence. Uncertainty sampling and transductive experimental design for active dual supervision. In *Proceedings of the 26th International Conference on Machine Learning (ICML-09)*, 2009.

[86] Padhraic Smyth. Learning with probabilistic supervision. In Thomas Petsche, editor, *Computational Learning Theory and Natural Learning Systems, Vol. III: Selecting Good Models*. MIT Press, April 1995.

[87] Padhraic Smyth, Michael C. Burl, Usama M. Fayyad, and Pietro Perona. Knowledge discovery in large image databases: Dealing with uncertainties in ground truth. In *Conference on Knowledge Discovery and Data Mining (KDD)*, pages 109–120, 1994.

[88] Padhraic Smyth, Usama M. Fayyad, Michael C. Burl, Pietro Perona, and Pierre Baldi. Inferring ground truth from subjective labelling of Venus images. In *Neural Information Processing Systems (NIPS)*, pages 1085–1092, 1994.

[89] Katrin Tomanek and Udo Hahn. Reducing class imbalance during active learning for named entity annotation. In *K-CAP '09: International Conference on Knowledge Capture*, 2009.

[90] Geoffrey G. Towell and Jude W. Shavlik. Knowledge-based artificial neural networks. *Artificial Intelligence*, 70:119–165, 1994.

[91] Duy Vu, Mikhail Bilenko, Maytal Saar-Tsechansky, and Prem Melville. Intelligent information acquisition for improved clustering. In *Workshop on Information Technologies and Systems (WITS)*, 2007.

[92] G. Weiss and F. Provost. The Effect of Class Distribution on Classifier Learning. Rutgers technical report ml-tr-44, Rutgers, The State University of New Jersey, 2001.

[93] Gary M. Weiss. Mining with rarity: A unifying framework. *SIGKDD Explorations*, 6(1):7–19, 2004.

[94] Gary M. Weiss. The impact of small disjuncts on classifier learning. In Robert Stahlbock, Sven F. Crone, and Stefan Lessmann, editors, *Data Mining*, volume 8 of *Annals of Information Systems*, pages 193–226. Springer, 2010.

[95] Gary M. Weiss and Foster Provost. Learning when training data are costly: the effect of class distribution on tree induction. *Journal of Artificial Intelligence Research*, 19(1):315–354, 2003.

[96] Jacob Whitehill, Paul Ruvolo, Ting fan Wu, Jacob Bergsma, and Javier Movellan. Whose vote should count more: Optimal integration of labels from labelers of unknown expertise. In *Advances in Neural Information Processing Systems 22 (NIPS 2009)*, pages 2035–2043, 2009.

[97] Xiaoyun Wu and Rohini Srihari. Incorporating prior knowledge with weighted margin support vector machines. In *Conference on Knowledge Discovery and Data Mining (KDD)*, 2004.

[98] Zhao Xu, Kai Yu, Volker Tresp, Xiaowei Xu, and Jizhi Wang. Representative sampling for text classification using support vector machines. In *European Conference on Information Retrieval (ECIR)*, 2003.

[99] Y. Yan, R. Rosales, G. Fung, M. Schmidt, G. Hermosillo, L. Bogoni, L. Moy, J. Dy, and PA Malvern. Modeling annotator expertise: Learning when everybody knows a bit of something. In *International Conference on Artificial Intelligence and Statistics*, 2010.

[100] O. F. Zaidan and J. Eisner. Modeling annotators: A generative approach to learning from annotator rationales. In *Conference on Empirical Methods in Natural Language Processing (EMNLP)*, 2008.

[101] Yi Zhang. Multi-task active learning with output constraints. In *The Twenty-Fourth AAAI Conference on Artificial Intelligence*, 2010.

[102] Z. Zheng and B. Padmanabhan. On active learning for data acquisition. In *Proceedings of IEEE International Conference on Data Mining*, 2002.

[103] Zhiqiang Zheng and Balaji Padmanabhan. Selectively acquiring customer information: A new data acquisition problem and an active learning-based solution. *Management Science*, 52(5):697–712, May 2006.

[104] Jingbo Zhu and Eduard Hovy. Active learning for word sense disambiguation with methods for addressing the class imbalance problem. In *Conference on Empirical Methods in Natural Language Processing*, 2007.

[105] Jingbo Zhu, Huizhen Wang, Tianshun Yao, and Benjamin K. Tsou. Active learning with sampling by uncertainty and density for word sense disambiguation and text classification. In *International Conference on Computational Linguistics (COLING '08)*, 2008.

Part II

Cost-Sensitive Machine Learning Applications

Chapter 6

Minimizing Annotation Costs in Visual Category Learning

Sudheendra Vijayanarasimhan

Department of Computer Science University of Texas at Austin, Austin, Texas

Kristen Grauman

Department of Computer Science University of Texas at Austin, Austin, Texas

Visual recognition is the core problem of learning categories of objects, scenes, and activities, and then identifying new instances in image or video data. Robust recognition algorithms are crucial for many computer vision tasks, and also have potential applications touching many areas of artificial intelligence and information retrieval—including content-based image search, video data mining, or object identification for mobile robots.

Whereas "instance recognition" of particular objects is handled well by feature matching and geometric alignment, generic category-level recognition is more challenging due to the variable appearance among instances of the same class. Current approaches typically rely on supervised learning procedures to build object models, and thus demand some form of manually labeled data prepared by human annotators. This may range from identifying parts of objects, cropping and aligning images of objects to be learned, providing complete image segmentations or bounding boxes around objects, or giving weak image-level tags indicating an object's presence, as shown in Figure 6.1. Typically, the more informative the annotation is, the more manual effort is needed to provide it.

In practice, the accuracy of most current algorithms improves with larger labeled training sets and more detailed annotations. For example, the very best face detectors are trained with millions of manually labeled examples, and systems built with tedious pixel-level annotations generally outperform those with access only to image-level labels at training time.

While the standard supervised paradigm has certainly proven powerful, it is unlikely to scale for the upwards of tens of thousands of categories that

(a) All objects in the image are outlined and labeled.

(b) Individual object parts are outlined.

(c) Landmark points are marked.

(d) A bounding box is provided around the object of interest.

 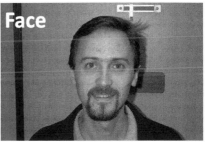

(e) Multiple image-level tags specify multiple objects present.

(f) An image-level tag specifies prominent object present within mild clutter.

FIGURE 6.1: Illustration of the standard kinds of supervision provided on image data to train classifiers for object recognition, approximately ordered in decreasing levels of manual effort.

humans can readily recognize. First, requiring such deliberate and plentiful attention from human annotators is costly. Second, the traditional means of collecting data can introduce unintended biases about what is learned. As such, researchers are actively exploring novel ways to reduce the role of human annotators in training visual recognition systems.

This chapter provides a detailed review of recent work in the area, with an emphasis on advances in active, semi-supervised, and unsupervised visual learning.

Strategies for reducing annotation costs can be broadly classified into three paradigms. First, some methods focus on reducing the *level* of supervision by using so-called "weakly" labeled data—which are easier for a human to provide, but leave some ambiguity. Such approaches treat some of the model parameters as hidden variables and try to automatically estimate them using powerful learning techniques.

A second group of approaches concentrates on reducing the *amount* or number of annotations required to train a visual model. In this domain, active learning strategies have been shown to exponentially improve the sample complexity over passive methods. Similarly, semi-supervised learning approaches use sparse labeled data along with a large amount of unlabeled data to obtain accurate models.

Finally, some work seeks to ease the *effort* required to provide supervision by designing innovative interfaces for obtaining annotations, and in some cases tempting human labelers to contribute data via games, access to datasets, or even monetary compensation.

We give an overview of each of these strategies in turn in Sections 6.1 through 6.3. Then, in Section 6.4 we describe a state-of-the-art cost-sensitive approach to object category learning that integrates all such types of reductions in supervision.

6.1 Reducing the Level of Supervision

This section overviews work in the object recognition literature aimed at reducing the *level* or granularity of supervision. We organize these ideas around three main themes: weak supervision (Section 6.1.1), noisy but cheap labels (Section 6.1.2), and unsupervised learning (Section 6.1.3). All share the theme of accepting less direct supervision for the sake of tapping widely available data and less human intervention.

6.1.1 Weakly Supervised Object Learning

Weakly supervised visual learning algorithms attempt to build category models from loosely or ambiguously labeled data. More specifically, most approaches in this genre assume that each image contains a single prominent object of interest, and the only supervision required is an image-level label saying what object that is. Whereas typical "strong" annotations mark the bounding box or segmentation for the object of interest, these labels are "weak" because they lack localization information. The general approach is to discover the common and/or discriminative portions of the weakly labeled exemplars for a given category. Robust models are then built to categorize *and* localize objects in novel images.

We summarize three variants of this approach: probabilistic part-based models, segmentation-based models, and classifiers trained with multiple-instance learning.

6.1.1.1 Part-Based Models Learned with EM

When faced with a set of cluttered training images, each of which is known to contain the object of interest, one learning strategy is to detect which *local parts* occur regularly throughout the examples—both in terms of their appearance similarity and the consistency of their geometric layout. The key assumption is that the backgrounds of the training images are mostly uncorrelated, and so by discovering a subset of local image patches that remain consistent in most views, the objects are extracted from the clutter at the same time the category's model parameters are fit.

This is the strategy for weakly supervised object category learning pioneered by Weber and colleagues for training the generative "constellation model" [144]. The constellation model uses a small fixed number of parts for a category, describes the appearance of each part in terms of the intensities within local patches, and represents geometry between the parts as a fully connected graph. The model parameters are the appearance descriptions at each of the parts and the relative 2D geometry between all pairs of parts; in their algorithm all distributions are modeled as Gaussians.

The model is trained through an Expectation Maximization (EM) procedure which iterates between i) the assignment of the parts to positions in the training images, and ii) the corresponding update to the model parameters. The E-step identifies promising object candidates within the cluttered images using the current parameters, while the M-step updates the model parameters based on the statistics from the E-step. The algorithm iteratively converges to a local maximum. Having learned a model for each category of interest, given a new image, the goal is to say whether each object is present. This decision is made by hypothesizing the assignment of parts to image locations, and then evaluating the likelihood ratio of the object being present or absent given the model.

While the initial approach in [144, 20] is not scale invariant and fixes the appearance of parts based on an initial quantization of the patches' intensities, work by Fergus et al. [44] shows how to use scale-invariant interest point detection to identify the candidate parts, and formulates the learning so that

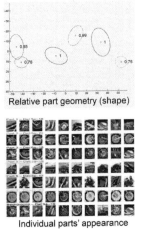

Relative part geometry (shape)

Individual parts' appearance

(a) Training images   (b) Learned model   (c)   Recognition   on novel images

FIGURE 6.2: An example of a weakly supervised constellation model for the Motorcycle category. (a) Example training images: each contains the object of interest, plus some background clutter. (b) Depiction of the learned model parameters. The top shows the mutual positions and variances of the learned six-part model; the bottom shows the appearance via the top 10 patches closest to the means of the appearance Gaussians for the six parts, plus background patches in the last row. (c) Example recognition results on novel images. (Figures are adapted from [44]. © 2003.)

the appearance and geometric parameters are fit simultaneously. Figure 6.2 shows an example model learned for the Motorcycle category.

The weak supervision paradigm introduced by this model has been influential in reconsidering how precise annotations must be for category learning.[1] Furthermore, a strength of this framework is its ability to accommodate classes with differing regularity in either appearance or geometry; for example, the model can learn and exploit the rather consistent layout of frontal faces, while it can learn that the shape of a deformable object like a leopard is widely varying but its texture is much tighter [44].

On the other hand, a weakness is its limitation to few parts in practice, given the fully connected graph's exponential increase in recognition time with respect to the number of parts. Furthermore, the 2D image plane representa-

---

[1]Note that the idea of part-based models has also been explored in a number of other approaches (e.g., [84, 42, 33, 100]), however, usually with stronger supervision in the form of localized training examples.

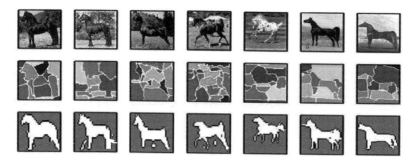

FIGURE 6.3: Weakly supervised *top-down segmentation algorithms* use a batch of images known to contain an object of interest to bring class-specific knowledge into the object segmentation procedure. This result from [13] shows that while the bottom-up segmentation into coherent regions (middle row) does not fully agree with the true boundaries of the horses (top row), a model-driven method can better extract the foreground object (bottom row). (Figure is taken from [13]. With kind permission from Springer Science + Business Media: Class-specific, top-down segmentation, 2002, Fig. 10.)

tion of shape restricts the training data to be pruned not only by the main object present, but also according to viewpoint (e.g., all motorbikes have their handlebars on the right side in the training views). Finally, by definition, with weak labels any local features consistent across training views are likely to be incorporated into the object model, even if on the background (e.g., the shadow cast by cars can be learned as a car part if it almost always is present).

6.1.1.2 Class-Specific Segmentation

A related class of model-driven object segmentation methods takes weakly supervised images (again, meaning a collection of exemplars where the object of interest is present, but so is background clutter) and extracts the foreground region of interest. In contrast to the above part-based strategy that extracts sparse patches based on their appearance and mutual positions, these approaches typically use regions produced from segmentation algorithms and contours produced from edge detection in order to pull out a *dense* connected area in each image. The segmentation-based methods are applicable for learning an object model, and also for the end goal of segmenting the input exemplar images.

A number of methods solve for a figure-ground assignment of pixels or superpixels, such that boundaries agree with a previously learned shape model or other class-based cue [13, 152, 146, 77, 32, 81, 2, 131]. Many rely on random field models to perform learning and/or inference. Such techniques generally work best when it is possible to construct a consistent shape prior for that category (e.g., side views of horses, see Figure 6.3), and when the objects are mostly unoccluded and prominent in the view.

Borenstein and colleagues were among the first to consider this class-specific segmentation problem, and they developed models that use the known shape of an object to guide segmentation [13, 14, 12]. Class-specific local patch matches are integrated with a global requirement for shape agreement. The LOCUS approach of [146] provides a generative pixel-based model that combines bottom-up color and edge cues with top-down shape and pose cues. Like the constellation model, it uses EM to optimize likelihood, but in this case the pose and segmentation of the objects are iteratively updated. In the OBJ-CUT algorithm of [77], the authors show how to insert prior knowledge about the object's shape (in the form of a part-based pictorial structure) into a Markov Random Field (MRF) model; this gives a prior over the shape of the segmentation that is global across the image plane, in contrast to traditional MRF models that only account for local interactions.

Conditional Random Fields (CRFs)—though more frequently employed for discriminative recognition when strong pixel-level supervision is available (e.g., [56, 124, 57])—are developed for the unsupervised segmentation setting in [2]. Hierarchical segmentations that capture the coherent bottom-up regions at multiple scales are integrated into the weakly supervised labeling task in [12, 131]. Hierarchical segmentations are valuable given the difficulty of choosing the region scales a priori in a single bottom-up segmentation.

Pushing the weak supervision even further, the Collect-Cut algorithm of [82] removes the assumption that one knows which objects are present per image. The algorithm discovers "pseudo" top-down cues among a collection of completely unlabeled images, and uses the shared structure to iteratively refine both the segmentation of each candidate region as well as the discovered object models. The technique designs an energy function amenable to graph cuts to revise the spatial extent of each initial segment. The energy function favors that pixels that agree with the appearance of any part of the cluster's ensemble model be included, while those that agree with the remaining background (or are likely attributable to another familiar object) be removed.

Co-segmentation algorithms are a special case of the weakly supervised class-specific segmentation task, in which one has a pair of images, each known to contain the exact same object amid background [114, 99]. This setting is relevant especially for interactive graphics applications or object tracking in video. An extension of these methods initializes the foreground automatically using probabilistic Latent Semantic Analysis (pLSA) [90].

While most methods in this group determine a region of interest per image based on shape and segmentation, the weakly supervised approach in [30] identifies a rectangular region of interest per training image. The model is initialized within the cluttered images using a set of local visual words found to be discriminative for the class, and then all windows are refined iteratively to increase their agreement in terms of the spatial layout of appearance patches and edges. See Figure 6.4.

FIGURE 6.4: Weakly supervised category learning with discovered rectangular regions of interest (ROI) [30]. A few of the training examples for two object categories, cars and bicycles, are shown. Top row: the ROIs are initialized via voting with discriminative local feature selection. Middle row: the same training instances after iterations aligning the spatially binned appearance features across all exemplars. Bottom row: after re-initialization by detection. (Figure is taken from [30]. ©2005.)

6.1.1.3   Single-Label Multiple-Instance Learning

Whereas the above techniques attempt to explicitly discover the commonalities among weakly labeled exemplars, methods based on multiple-instance learning (MIL) instead treat the supervision as a form of labeling known to be noisy [134, 95, 150, 141, 157, 36].

In the traditional binary supervised classification problem, the learner is provided a collection of N labeled data points $\{(x_i, y_i)\}_{i=1}^N$, where each $x_i \in \Re^d$ has a label $y_i \in \{+1, -1\}$, for $i = 1, \ldots, N$. The goal is to determine the function $f : \Re^d \to \{+1, -1\}$ that best predicts labels for new input patterns drawn from the same distribution as the training examples, such that the probability of error is minimized.

In MIL, the learner is instead provided with *sets* (or bags) of points, and is only told that at least one member of any *positive bag* is truly positive, while every member of any *negative bag* is guaranteed to be negative. The goal of MIL is to induce the function that will accurately label individual instances such as the ones within the training bags in spite of the label ambiguity: the ratio of negative to positive instances within every positive bag can be arbitrarily high. Figure 6.5 contrasts the two learning problems.

The MIL setting was first defined by Dietterich et al., who represented ambiguously labeled examples using axis-parallel hyper-rectangles and demonstrated applications for drug activity prediction [35]. More recently, MIL has received various treatments within the machine learning community using both probabilistic and margin-based approaches [157, 1, 47, 111, 19]. Some of these approaches offer iterative solutions that try to first estimate the membership of instances in a positive bag using the current model, followed by parameter estimation using the estimated probabilities.

Several scenarios where MIL is relevant to object recognition have been ex-

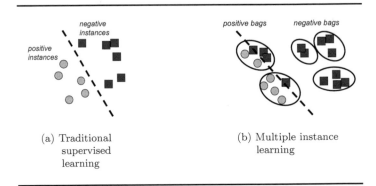

(a) Traditional supervised learning

(b) Multiple instance learning

FIGURE 6.5: In multiple-instance learning (MIL), labels are provided at the level of *bags* of instances. All items in a negative bag are negative, but for a positive bag we know only that at least one item is truly positive.

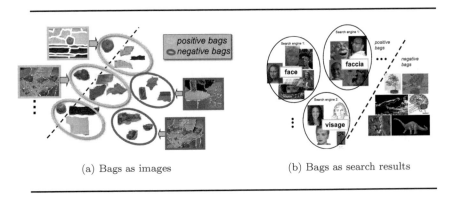

(a) Bags as images

(b) Bags as search results

FIGURE 6.6: Two example scenarios where MIL is applicable to low-supervision visual recognition.

plored. Most commonly, images are treated as bags of regions [95, 150, 46, 135]. As in earlier sections, the training images are labeled as to whether they contain the category of interest, but they also contain other objects and background clutter. Every image is represented by a bag of regions, each of which is characterized by its color, texture, shape, etc. as shown in Figure 6.6(a). For positive bags, we know that at least one of the regions contains the object of interest (i.e., an apple in Figure 6.6(a)). For negative bags, we know that the object is absent, and so all regions are negative instances (i.e., non-apples in Figure 6.6(a)). The goal is to predict when new image regions contain the object—that is, to learn to label regions as foreground or background.

For example, MIL is used in this "image as bag of regions" setting to classify natural scenes using very low resolution images in [95]. Content-based image retrieval is tackled using an MIL-based approach in [150, 155]. Weakly supervised object localization using a boosted MIL classifier is proposed in [46], where multiple stable segmentations represent the set of instances in a bag. A related MIL scenario is to accept stronger supervision in the form of bounding boxes around the object of interest, but then learn the objects' parts via MIL [36].

Exploiting MIL's ability to handle ambiguous labels in a different way, we can think of the image results from a keyword search as providing a positive bag of examples for an object we wish to learn [134], as depicted in Figure 6.6(b). The keyword associated with a category is used to download groups of images from multiple search engines in multiple languages. Each downloaded group is a bag, and the images within it are instances. For each positive bag, it is assumed that at least one image actually contains the object of interest, while many others may be irrelevant. Negative bags are constructed from images whose labels are known, or from unrelated searches. The goal is to predict the presence or absence of the category in new images.

6.1.1.4   Multi-Label Multiple-Instance Learning

The weak-supervision assumption in all methods discussed thus far (that a single prominent object appears on a variety of backgrounds in the training data) still entails some burden or pruning on the part of an annotator. In an even looser form of supervision, we want to accommodate images containing multiple objects of interest, together with some image-level labels, as depicted in Figure 6.1(e).

Multi-label variants of MIL that are suitable for this supervision setting have been considered [158, 154, 156, 136]. In this *multi-label multiple-instance learning* (MIML) case, instances within a bag can belong to any number of classes (as opposed to $\{+1, -1\}$ for MIL), but, similar to single-label MIL, only image-level labels or tags are available to the classifier. In [158], the MIML problem is transformed into a traditional supervised task by clustering instances within bags and computing a bag of words representation of the instances. More recently, the authors of [154, 156, 136] model the relation between instances and labels more explicitly using hidden variables or class-specific feature representations, with the goal of exploiting category co-occurrence cues.

In Section 6.4, we will define an MIML approach for active learning in detail, and present results applying it to object recognition.

6.1.2   Noisy Labels from Accompanying Text

Thus far, we have seen ways in which the level of supervision is reduced by limiting the amount of time a human has to spend annotating a single training example. In this section, we look at methods that instead reduce the

(a) Captioned images	(b) Scripted dialogue in video

(c) Tagged stock photos	(d) Keyword search results

FIGURE 6.7: Text naturally accompanying imagery can serve as a form of inexpensive loose labels. (Top right figure is courtesy of Everingham and colleagues [39]. Caption figure from [8]. © 2004 IEEE. Buffy figure from [39, 127]. © 2009 IEEE.)

level of supervision by exploiting existing data sources where text naturally accompanies images, thereby serving as free but noisy labels.

6.1.2.1 Captioned or Tagged Images

Sources include images embedded on web pages, captioned news photos, annotated stock photo collections, or scripted movie dialogues. See Figure 6.7. Any such images accompanied by naturally occurring text are an interesting source of data: they are very inexpensive to obtain, yet the noise and variability in the words near an image make their use as labels non-trivial.

One way to exploit tagged or captioned photos is to recover the correspondence (or "translation") between region descriptors and the keywords that appear alongside them [38, 65], or to model the joint distribution of words and regions [4, 97, 79] and scenes [88]. Recent work further shows how exploiting predicates (e.g., *isAbove*(A,B)) provides even stronger cues tying the two data views together [53]. Having learned such a model, one can predict the labels for new image examples.

For the special case of named people or faces, more direct associations can be successfully learned [8, 39, 68]. For example, in [8], news captions occurring alongside photographs are used to cluster faces occurring in the pictures, and natural language tools like named entity extraction can be used to parse the text meaningfully.

Another general strategy is to learn a new image representation (or similarly, distance function) that is bolstered by having observed many examples together with relevant text. To this end, variants of metric learning [107, 94], transfer learning [109], matrix factorization [92], and random field models [7] have all been explored. Previous work has also considered building a two-view "semantic space" using Kernelized Canonical Correlation Analysis (KCCA) for this purpose [55, 148, 10, 60].

While tags are most frequently treated as multi-label annotations specifying which objects may be present, recent work considers implicit cues that may be present in how humans provide the tags—for example, by naming the most prominent or important objects first [129, 61]. In [61], the tags on a novel test image are used to prime an object detector, given a prior for the scales and positions of the objects learned from rank and proximity cues extracted from the tag words. These methods hint at the possibility of vision systems that learn not just what each object looks like, but also "what to mention" about an image among those objects it predicts are present.

6.1.2.2 Keyword-Based Image Search

A number of techniques draw directly on keyword-based image search engines to provide an initial pool of images from which to learn models [151, 9, 119, 43, 87, 134, 31], and keyword-based image search (e.g., on Google Image Search or Flickr) is commonly used in practice to gather candidate images for benchmark datasets [22, 23, 40]. While for dataset creation the images are pruned manually, in recognition systems the search returns are dealt with automatically—for example by finding the most common visual themes using a topic model [43, 87], turning to MIL [134], bringing certain images to an annotator [70, 31], or pruning out cartoons or drawings with specialized classifiers [119].

6.1.3 Unsupervised Object Discovery

Apart from utilizing weak forms of supervision—whether from manually gathered images or textual cues—recent methods have also shown the possibility of discovering visual patterns from *unlabeled* image collections. In this group of methods, the only supervision an annotator would provide is to identify a single object's or a cluster's identity once the images have been automatically organized. Most are tested on benchmark object recognition datasets containing on the order of 10s of categories, with the labels withheld.

We organize these approaches into those based on latent topic models (Section 6.1.3.1), image clustering (Section 6.1.3.2), and mining for repeated semi-local feature configurations (Section 6.1.3.3).

6.1.3.1 Latent Topic Models

Several authors have studied probabilistic clustering methods originally developed for text—such as probabilistic Latent Semantic Analysis (pLSA), Latent Dirichlet Analysis (LDA), and Hierarchical Dirichlet Processes—to discover the hidden mixture of visual themes ("topics") in a collection of image data [126, 115, 43, 87]. The main idea is to use feature co-occurrence patterns in the images ("documents") to recover the relatively few underlying distributions that best account for the data. An image containing instances of several categories is modeled as a mixture of topics. The models are typically applied to images by using a visual analogue of a word, formed by vector quantizing local feature descriptors. Having discovered the topics, one can describe an image compactly based on the mixture of topics it contains, or gather those images with the most clear instances of a given topic. See Figure 6.8(a).

Recent extensions use segmentation to reduce the spatial extent of each "document" [115]. The authors decompose each image into multiple segmentations to increase the likelihood that each object in the image has a corresponding segment. The key idea is that the segments corresponding to coherent objects will produce strong matches, while the noisy segments will not produce any good matches. After discovering categories with LDA, the intra-cluster segments are sorted based on the Kullback-Leibler divergence to the cluster topic distribution to reveal the representative category instances. Other extensions show how to incorporate spatial constraints by jointly modeling location and appearance [43] or by using feature correspondences [91].

6.1.3.2 Image and Region Clustering

Other approaches treat the unsupervised visual category learning task as an image clustering problem. Given a collection of unlabeled images, various clustering methods offer a way of partitioning the data into a set of categories or clusters. However, the main challenge for such methods is to compute appropriate pairwise affinities between all pairs of unlabeled images such that semantically meaningful partitions can be obtained, and to isolate relevant features when dealing with multi-object or cluttered images. That is, simply clustering a global description of each image is unlikely to succeed for realistic natural images, or even the semi-controlled images in benchmark datasets.

Instead, a strategy considered by a number of researchers is to iterate between computing the foreground region of interest (or set of local features) per image, and the clusters resulting from those foreground selections [50, 80, 72, 73]. The goal is to simultaneously partition the images into the primary

(a) Visual topics   (b) Discovered common shapes

FIGURE 6.8: Example object discovery results. (a): Topics discovered with pLSA on the MIT scenes data [126]. Leftmost column shows original images, next column shows all detected local feature regions, and third column shows the topic-induced segmentation, where only visual words having a high probability of belonging to each of the selected (color-coded) topics are displayed. (b): Shapes discovered by identifying consistent contour patterns in unlabeled images [81]. Blue contours superimposed are those found to correspond well with others in the discovered cluster; rightmost column shows the automatically generated "prototype" shapes from the collection. For both results, the only supervision is the number of desired topics/clusters for the algorithm to find. (Figures from [126, 81]. © 2005, 2009.)

repeated objects, while also discovering the portions of each image that can be most consistently clustered with the rest. In this sense, the problem can be thought of as the weak-supervision setting (Section 6.1.1), but where the image-level label on each training image is an additional latent variable.

For example, in [50], affinities computed from local feature matches are used with spectral clustering to find object clusters and prototypes. Each image is represented as a set of local features, and feature correspondences are efficiently computed between all pairs of images using the Pyramid Match Kernel (PMK) [49]. Given an initial cluster, the best matching features are given the highest weights; this allows classifiers to be trained using the most representative instances for each cluster to finally predict the category of novel test images. See Figure 6.9.

In the "foreground focus" approach of [80], an initial image-level grouping is first computed based on feature correspondences, and then the cluster

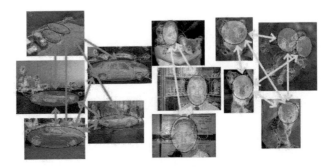

FIGURE 6.9: Graph partitioning algorithms can group sets of unlabeled images into semantically meaningful clusters if given appropriate pairwise affinity functions. This figure depicts how pairwise affinities based on partial feature correspondences between estimated foreground features can yield object-based partitions [50].

assignments are iteratively refined based on the evolving intra-cluster pattern of local matches. As a result, the significance attributed to each feature influences an image's cluster membership, while related images in a cluster affect the estimated significance of their features.

In a related approach [72], the authors build a large-scale network that captures the interactions of all visual features across the training set. They use link analysis techniques (e.g., PageRank [17]) to infer from the graph which features belong to which categories by analyzing the statistics of the link structure. Object categories are discovered using Normalized Cuts [123], and probable object regions are detected for each image. Recent work in [73] also shows how to detect the regions-of-interest (ROIs) in each unlabeled image by iteratively refining the selected exemplars across the dataset and ROI hypotheses in each image.

An alternative approach is to seek those images among the collection that best serve as prototypes. In [37], a message-passing algorithm propagates non-metric affinities to identify good exemplars. It takes as input measures of similarity between pairs of data instances and simultaneously considers all data instances as potential exemplars. Each pair of instances exchanges "messages" which signal how strongly a given instance favors the paired instance to be its exemplar compared to other candidate instances, and to what degree the paired instance is likely to be its cluster center factoring in the availability of that instance being an exemplar to other instances. The message-passing iterates until a set of exemplars and corresponding clusters emerge.

While most methods use local appearance matches (e.g., based on SIFT patches [93]) due to their distinctiveness amidst cluttered images, some recent work considers object discovery from shape cues [81], which is important to find and summarize objects without regular textures (e.g., swans, mugs, etc.). See Figure 6.8(b) for example discoveries.

There are some tradeoffs between the topic modeling and matching-based clustering approaches. Both strategies essentially discover feature co-occurrence patterns in images. However, the latter computes explicit correspondences between local image features, which makes it possible to isolate the most distinctive features within some partition, and assign a confidence value to each feature reflecting how relevant it is to one of the discovered categories. In contrast, latent topic models produce soft cluster assignments, where an image is explained as a mixture of all the discovered topics; a feature's confidence is thus influenced by the visual word distribution of the entire dataset. See [133] for further analysis of the tradeoffs.

6.1.3.3   Feature Configuration Mining

Some work considers scalable techniques for mining common semi-local feature configurations in large image collections [108, 103, 29, 102]. The idea is to mine the data for those local feature patterns that co-occur with some spatial regularity. Typically those patterns will belong to objects or parts of objects; in contrast to techniques discussed above, however, the local component features are usually allowed some flexibility in their relative spatial configuration.

For example, in [108], the method discovers the features that frequently occur on the foreground object and rarely on the background for each intra-category image. The algorithm relies on frequent item-set mining to efficiently mine for recurring patterns in large image collections. In [102], unsupervised learning of hierarchical spatial structures is performed using a rule-based model capturing spatial patterns, where each rule is represented by a star-graph.

Tackling the important challenge of mining massive collections of images, in [29], the authors propose a novel hashing scheme called Geometric min-Hashing that combines visual appearance with semi-local geometric information. In contrast to the widely used unordered bag-of-visual-words model, their method's incorporation of geometric information provides a discriminative description of the object while preserving repeatability (high probability that similar instances collide in the same hash bin). They demonstrate the method for small object discovery with large datasets (on the order of 10^5).

6.2   Reducing the Amount of Supervision

Whereas the work discussed thus far strives to loosen the *specificity* of labels required to learn object models, another class of techniques aims to reduce the total *amount* of supervision. Specifically, this includes semi-supervised, active, and transfer learning approaches for object recognition. Compared to the breadth of weak supervision object recognition work, at this point much less work has been done in this direction in the vision community.

6.2.1 Semi-Supervised Visual Learning

Semi-supervised learning approaches build classifiers using a large amount of unlabeled data, together with a small amount of labeled data.[2] Many existing algorithms use the well-known "cluster assumption," which says that points are likely to originate from the same class if they are near one another or are connectable via a path through regions of high density in the feature space. This assumption means that the information from sparse labeled points can be propagated among the many unlabeled points clustered around them.

These concepts transfer well to sparsely labeled image examples. For example, a constrained semi-supervised learning approach is developed in [76] to address the data association problem, where one needs to associate image regions to the appropriate image-level object labels. Further extensions show how a conditional random field model can propagate label information across adjacent superpixels in the image, essentially applying the cluster assumption to spatial nearness in the image plane [25]. While many semi-supervised algorithms—for example, those based on the max-margin principle—deal with multi-class problems by combining multiple binary classifiers, some recent work considers an efficient multi-class semi-supervised boosting algorithm amenable to object categorization [117].

In addition to a sparse set of labeled images, semi-supervised learning can exploit similarity (dissimilarity) constraints that record a sparse set of *pairs* of examples that should be in the same (different) class. This general idea is shown to significantly improve object category discovery in a constrained clustering approach in [50], and to boost image retrieval and object comparisons in the metric learning methods of [122, 58, 63]. Such algorithms typically entail measuring pairwise affinities between the data points, which can become prohibitive to do exhaustively for very large image collections. To address this limitation, recent work develops a linear-time approximation for the eigenvectors of the normalized graph Laplacian, which makes it possible to efficiently propagate labels through collections of as many as 80 million images [45]. See Figure 6.10.

6.2.1.1 Self-Training

A form of semi-supervised learning called "self-training" first trains a classifier with a small amount of labeled data, and then uses that model to predict labels on the unlabeled data. The most confident predictions are then treated

---

[2]See [159] for a survey of semi-supervised learning algorithms.

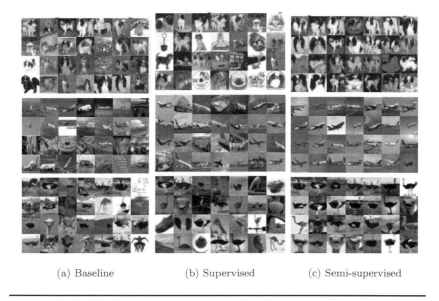

(a) Baseline   (b) Supervised   (c) Semi-supervised

FIGURE 6.10: An efficient semi-supervised learning approach can exploit unlabeled images together with a small number of labeled images to propagate small amounts of human-provided information. This result from Fergus and colleagues [45] shows examples of the improvement for re-ranking images of object categories: (a) the baseline top images retrieved by a search engine (from top to bottom, for "Japanese spaniel," "airbus," and "ostrich"), (b) the re-ranked results using only supervised learning, and (c) the results using the semi-supervised learner. (Figures from [45]. Figure courtesy of Fergus et al.)

as newly labeled points and inserted into the training set, and the classifier is retrained.

This notion is leveraged in the OPTIMOL system of [87], where object categories are learned from a combination of labeled seed examples and unlabeled images downloaded from the Web. In this case, the unlabeled pool is automatically obtained by searching for the category's name in several image search engines (e.g., Google Image Search), which helpfully focuses the scope of the unlabeled pool. In this way, limited training data is used to incrementally collect larger training sets and update the category model. Self-training is also explored to incrementally improve an object detector in [112]; as desired, the results show it is possible to use much less labeled data and still learn models as accurate as those trained with a larger set of labeled images.

6.2.1.2   Co-Training

Whereas self-training relies only on a single feature space for the image data, co-training is a related form of semi-supervised learning applicable when we have access to two "views" or channels for the instances. The idea is that two independent classifiers constructed in the two feature spaces can train each other by classifying disjoint sets of unlabeled data [11]. Ideally, each view should be conditionally independent (i.e., the two feature sets of each instance are conditionally independent given the class) and sufficient (i.e., the class of an instance can be accurately predicted from either view alone). Co-training first learns a separate classifier for each view using any labeled examples; the most confident predictions of each classifier on the unlabeled data are then used to iteratively construct additional labeled training data.

A co-training algorithm suitable for margin-based classifiers is developed in [86] and used to train object detectors. In this case, a small amount of manually labeled data is used to train a pair of object detectors, and the most certain predictions from either one is used to bolster the training set. The results with car detection for traffic surveillance video data show significant improvements due to the effective use of unlabeled data. More recently, a Bayesian co-training approach that simultaneously discovers the amount of noise per view while also solving the classification problem is developed in [28]. The algorithm is robust to noise and view disagreement (e.g., sample corruption via occlusion in some camera view), and results for multi-view object detection show its strength for detection in a low-fidelity sensor network.

While the above algorithms exploit two *visual* views of the instances, multiple modalities are also an attractive source of data for co-training. Gupta and colleagues show its power for exploiting images or videos accompanied by textual annotations (captions or commentary) to efficiently learn scene and action categories [54]. Note that in contrast to those methods treating accompanying text as *labels* (discussed in Section 6.1.2.1), this strategy instead exploits the predictors learned in two distinct but coupled modalities.

6.2.1.3   Semi-Supervision with Disjoint Labels

The standard semi-supervised learning setting assumes that both the labeled and unlabeled data belong to the same set of labels, naturally allowing for a transfer of information on labeled points to those that are unlabeled. However, in the visual category learning domain, another form of semi-supervision is possible, where the labeled data and unlabeled data are from *disjoint* sets of classes, but the knowledge from the classes for which we have supervision can assist in better learning and discovering novel categories among the unlabeled data.

This form of *context-aware discovery* is proposed in [83], where knowledge about previously learned categories enables more accurate unsupervised learning of objects. The approach introduces a novel object-graph descriptor to encode the layout of object-level co-occurrence patterns relative to an unfa-

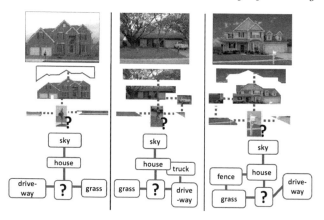

FIGURE 6.11: Context-aware visual discovery leverages the context provided by familiar (known) categories relative to unknown objects in order to perform better unsupervised grouping. In this example, the unknown regions are the mailboxes. The goal is to form clusters on the basis of the similarity of the unknown regions appearance, as well as the similarity between the "object-graphs" implied by surrounding familiar objects. This can be seen as a form of semi-supervised learning with disjoint label spaces. (Figure from [83]. © 2010 IEEE.)

miliar region. By using it to model the interaction between an image's known and unknown objects, one can better detect the existence of new (untrained) visual categories. For example, as depicted in Figure 6.11, if the system is familiar with objects like "sky," "house," and "driveway," treating those objects as context can facilitate the discovery of the new class "mailbox," for which it has no training exemplars. Thus, rather than mine for all categories from scratch, this approach identifies new objects while drawing on useful cues from familiar ones. This setting is well suited, for example, for a continuously learning agent that can be initialized with knowledge of some common objects in the world, but must also be able to explore new scenes and capture compact models for the novel objects it encounters.

6.2.2 Active Visual Learning

Active learning is another useful way to reduce the amount of human supervision required to learn category models. Active learning strategies analyze unlabeled data to select informative examples for which labels should be obtained from a human annotator. The classifiers are initialized with some labeled data, and then the system repeatedly forms label queries to feed to the annotators; given their reply, the classifiers are updated, and the cycle repeats. See Figure 6.12 for a depiction of the standard active learning loop. While a "passive" learner that waits for whatever labeled data the annotator chooses

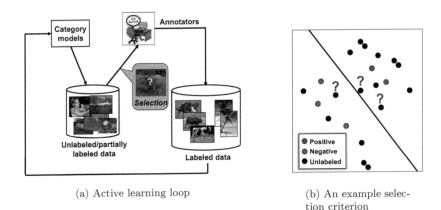

(a) Active learning loop

(b) An example selection criterion

FIGURE 6.12: (a) In active learning, the classifier is initially trained on a small set of examples, and then a selection criterion is repeatedly applied to all unlabeled data to choose potentially informative examples for which labels should be requested next. (b) For example, the simple margin selection criterion [132, 118, 24] selects those unlabeled points nearest the current decision boundary for labeling.

to provide will learn more slowly, active learners pinpoint the weaknesses in the model and thereby learn more efficiently.

A variety of selection criteria for choosing the right example to query have been explored in the machine learning literature, including uncertainty sampling, margin-based criteria, entropy or version space reduction, and decision-theoretic value of information measures.[3] For example, a simple margin-based criterion aimed at reducing the version space identifies those unlabeled points that are nearest the current decision boundary (see Figure 6.12(b)). Intuitively, these are the points that may most change the classifier, and therefore are expected to give the most benefit for the labeling expense. Some work in vision exploits existing strategies, but often the complexity of image annotations and object learning necessitates novel labeling scenarios and new active selection methods, as we will describe below.

6.2.2.1   Interactive Content-Based Retrieval

Active forms of *query refinement* for content-based retrieval have been explored in a number of systems. There the goal is to treat the user as the annotator, and have him or her give positive or negative feedback on well-chosen images to better revise the ranking measure being used to pull up the candidate relevant images for that specific query [27, 101, 149]. In a sense,

---

[3]See [121] for a survey.

these methods learn a "one-time" visual category model meant to capture the user's model of relevant content during that search session. This is in contrast to visual category learning methods discussed below, which instead aim to actively train a generic object model with a human answering labeling queries.

6.2.2.2 Active Labeling: Images as Data Points

Active learning strategies for object recognition have only recently begun to be explored. The first methods directly treat images as data points and show how to actively seek labels for image recognition. Specifically, an uncertainty-based approach for Gaussian Process classifiers is developed in [70] and shown to quicken learning for 101 object categories, while a labeled dataset is actively generated using confidence-weighted boosting in [31].

While selection functions are often easier to formulate in the binary class setting, given the importance of multi-class category learning for object recognition, vision researchers have also developed novel selection methods well suited to multi-class data. A probabilistic nearest neighbor strategy drawing on kernel learning is proposed in [62], and an uncertainty measure generalizing SVM margin-based selection functions to multi-class tasks is given in [69].

6.2.2.3 Active Image Annotation: Multi-Label and Multi-Question

When the unlabeled image pool does not consist only of single-object images, the selection problem also becomes more challenging, since the selection function must evaluate informativeness in the face of intermingled clutter and multiple object instances. Multiple-instance learning strategies have been proposed to address this setting [120, 135]. As reviewed above, in the MIL setting, images are bags of regions, and so the ambiguity of image-level labels can be appropriately modeled.

With multi-label data, one can also account for the correlations between objects that commonly appear together; such context is exploited in the "two-dimensional" active learning method of [106], in which the algorithm chooses both the label dimension and the instance dimension to query. The intuition is that the active learner should be less likely to ask whether an object is present if another object commonly co-occurring with it is already labeled (e.g., table and chair).

The richness of image annotations also necessitates targeting wider types of requests to annotators, which calls for active selection criteria that weigh the examples and the possible questions to be asked in a unified manner. For example, the annotator may be asked to provide a bounding box around all objects of interest, or to label a specific region, or to provide manual segmentations on some image. We first introduced this idea of "multi-question" active learning in [135], and generalized it to multi-label data with predicted costs in [136]. Further work in this direction shows how to generate questions about relationships and context [125]. (Note: We review the cost-sensitive multi-question approach in detail below in Section 6.4.)

6.2.2.4 Non-Myopic and Batch-Mode Active Selection

Most active learning work (in vision or otherwise) has focused on myopic selection algorithms that pose a single query to the annotator before retraining the model, or, similarly, that make multiple annotation requests based only on the current model's view of the data. This is restrictive, since retraining after each single label is expensive, and it is often preferable to farm out a *batch* of good queries at once. Systems such as Mechanical Turk or LabelMe [116] provide access to multiple distributed annotators simultaneously, but an active learning system that needs to repeatedly go offline and compute the next annotation request cannot take advantage of such resources.

To counter this, a few "batch-mode" active learning strategies have been proposed recently [118, 18, 74, 52, 59, 139], including novel methods developed specifically for image retrieval [59] and visual recognition [139]. Batch selection calls for more than a selection of the N-best queries at a given iteration, since such a greedy strategy does not account for possible overlap in information. Instead, most batch selection functions balance informativeness with the so-called *diversity* among the selected set [18, 59, 74].

By relying on the current classifier to estimate uncertainty, however, these functions' performance can degrade with very large batches; balancing uncertainty and diversity properly can also require good heuristics. Batch selection algorithms that account for changes in the model predicted to occur after obtaining the new labels can better cope with this issue [52, 139]. The algorithm in [139] is both far-sighted and sensitive to the costs of labeling, optimizing the selection of a batch so as to meet a prescribed *budget* of annotation time/money. Results on multiple object and activity recognition datasets show that the ability to compute such variably-sized batches is critical to have real advantages when data have varying labeling costs (i.e., the longer a video, the more we must pay an annotator to determine whether a given action occurs).

6.2.2.5 Active Classification

While the above approaches use active strategies for acquiring label information when training a classifier, a distinct set of approaches perform *active classification* by allowing the classifier to actively acquire features. During classification, an active classifier can—at some cost—obtain the values of some unspecified features, before deciding upon a class label. Thus, rather than building a classifier for later use, the goal is to handle the given test case in an online manner. Such strategies are important when trying to manage the cost of acquiring features.

This scenario is clearly valuable for medical diagnosis: one chooses which tests to run while weighing their cost and expected benefit toward reducing uncertainty [66, 51]. Though perhaps less immediately apparent, the setting is also of interest in image recognition, where one wants to avoid extracting expensive descriptors when they are not critical to making the category decision [48, 140], or one wants to pinpoint questions to a human in the loop so that the system and human arrive at the right label collaboratively [16].

In the active classification problem, researchers are also interested in developing non-myopic criteria. This leads naturally to formulations with Partially Observable Markov Decision Processes (POMDPs). In object detection, recent work frames visual search as a POMDP in order to actively schedule eye fixations for a foveal camera that provides high-resolution images near the fovea [21]. POMDPs are also useful to obtain myopic or non-myopic strategies for feature acquisition when sensing concealed targets [67].

6.2.3   Transfer and Domain Adaptation

Finally, a recognition system can make do with less total training data by transferring knowledge of some categories to more efficiently learn others [41, 5, 78, 110, 130]. A common theme in object recognition transfer learning work is to identify the shared visual aspects of different object categories.

One form of transfer learning for object recognition learns object models from just a few images by incorporating "generic" knowledge obtained from previously learned models of unrelated categories [41, 96]. In [41], object categories are represented using probabilistic constellation models, and the prior knowledge is represented as a probability density function on the appearance and geometry parameters of the models. The posterior of the model for an object category is obtained by updating the prior in the light of one or more observations. In this way knowledge learned from a large number of training examples on unrelated categories is transferred in order to learn new categories with few training images. In related work, a distribution over the set of *transforms* that can jointly bring images into correspondence is used as prior knowledge to train image classifiers with as few as one example [96]. More recently, a shape-based model is developed that allows parameter-based transfer of individual shape and appearance information, transfer of local symmetry between parts, and transfer of part topology [130].

Rather than use prior knowledge over the model parameters, another approach is to explicitly identify local visual features that can be shared across multiple categories [5], or to exploit known class relationships to identify likely useful features [85]. Related to the idea of shared features, shared prototype examples can help transfer knowledge [110]. The assumption is that related problems may share a significant number of relevant prototypes. Therefore, a concise representation is found by performing a joint loss minimization over the training sets of the related problems, with a shared regularization penalty that minimizes the total number of prototypes involved in the approximation.

A very different form of transfer is proposed in [78], where intermediate visual *attributes* make it possible to learn models for novel object categories with zero training examples. The idea is that having learned to predict the

otter
```
black:     yes
white:     no
brown:     yes
stripes:   no
water:     yes
eats fish: yes
```

polar bear
```
black:     no
white:     yes
brown:     no
stripes:   no
water:     yes
eats fish: yes
```

zebra
```
black:     yes
white:     yes
brown:     no
stripes:   yes
water:     no
eats fish: no
```

FIGURE 6.13: Transfer learning with visual attributes: a set of high-level attributes are learned. Then, by describing a novel object category with this attribute vocabulary, one can detect it even without any training images, based on which attribute description a test image best matches. (Figure from [78]. © 2009 IEEE.)

presence of certain attributes shared among different subsets of object categories (e.g., furry, white, toothed), a human can then define a novel category model through its actual semantic attributes. This means, for example, that if we have classifiers for a large menu of visual attributes, then we can define a new model for "cats" by simply stating that they are furry, have a tail, may be striped, etc. See Figure 6.13. Because such properties transcend the specific learning task at hand, they can be pre-learned from image datasets unrelated to the new task. In this way attributes are an encouraging new way to transfer and share cues across traditional object categories.

6.3   Reducing the Effort Required in Supervision

The previous algorithms largely reduced the level and amount of supervision via their machine learning strategies. In this section, we briefly describe innovative interfaces and segmentation tools that instead aim to reduce the *effort* a human annotator must expend when providing an image or video label.

6.3.1   Online Annotation Interfaces

Online labeling interfaces make it possible to leverage the many web users who are willing to contribute annotations for fun or money. The LabelMe project [116, 153] entails an evolving dataset of images and annotations. Users are free to upload content and add polygonal object boundaries and labels as they like, and others can download the data to create specialized datasets (see Figure 6.14, left). More recently, the possibility of directly compensating annotators with cash in a distributed framework has arisen with crowdsourcing services such as Mechanical Turk [128, 34, 136, 105, 145, 138]. While fairly elaborate image annotation jobs are usually quickly accepted and executed by Mechanical Turk workers, quality control is of course a challenge. As such, some recent research examines how to optimize the way image labeling jobs are given to workers in order to manage consistency of labels obtained online [105].

6.3.2   Image Labeling Games

Aside from money, entertainment can entice people to label images online. The "games with a purpose" work of von Ahn and colleagues has contributed several image-based two-person games that as a side effect produce labeled image data potentially useful to object recognition.

In the online ESP game [142], two people are paired by the system randomly. Players are not told who their partners are, nor are they allowed to communicate with their partners. The only thing partners have in common is an image they can both see. (See Figure 6.14, right.) From the player's perspective, the goal of the game is to guess what his partner is typing for each image. Once both players have typed the same string, they move on to the next image. The words that two players agree on are treated as valid labels for the image.

In the Peekaboom game [143], the goal is to obtain a form of localization information rather than image tags. One player sees the entire image, the other player sees none of it to begin. The first player reveals small regions of the image in sequence, and the second player must guess the object with as few revealed regions as possible.

In any such game, the built-in motivation to win the game with a partner serves as a valuable form of quality control in the resulting annotations. While in principle a suitable source of data for vision researchers, however, to our knowledge no recognition work thus far has leveraged such data.

6.3.3   Interactive Segmentation Algorithms

Interactive segmentation algorithms make it easier for an annotator to specify a region of interest. Such tools allow a user to segment complex foreground objects without having to trace the outline in detail. The basic idea is to let the human in the loop guide the process, but leave the low-level pixel

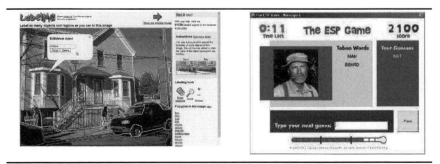

FIGURE 6.14: Left: the LabelMe labeling tool in use. The user is shown an image along with possibly one or more existing annotations drawn on the image. The user has the option of annotating a new object by clicking along the boundary of the desired object and indicating its identity, or editing an existing annotation. The users may annotate as many objects in the image as they wish. (From [116]. With kind permission from Springer Science + Business Media: Labelme: a database and web-based tool for image annotation, IJCV 2005, Figure 1.) Right: the ESP Game for image tagging. (Figure from [142]. © 2004 Association for Computing Machinery, Inc. Reprinted by permission.)

alignment of boundaries to the algorithm. Figure 6.15 shows the required user interaction of some popular tools and their corresponding results. There is extensive work in this area; here we touch only on a few representative examples.

The Intelligent Scissors approach allows a user to use the mouse to rapidly identify the minimum cost contour that traces out the object's boundary [98]. The method works by continually updating the shortest path between the current cursor position and a previously marked seed point, with path costs measured in terms of gradient strength and image distance. This allows the interactively generated contour to "snap" to the likely boundaries in the image.

Boykov and colleagues investigate segmentation objectives efficiently solvable with graph cuts algorithms [15]. The user marks some pixels that serve as hard constraints for segmentation (i.e., pixels that must be foreground/background). Additional soft constraints can encode boundary and region cues. Then, graph cuts is used to find the globally optimal split into two regions that satisfies the constraints.

The GrabCut algorithm [113] extends graph-cuts segmentation to iteratively optimize the segmentation and parameters of the color model, and introduces a method for border matting that estimates both the alpha-matte around the object boundary and the foreground colors. Recent work provides an interactive form of co-segmentation, and actively guides the annotator's attention to regions of the images most likely to reduce segmentation uncer-

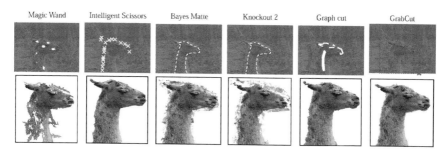

FIGURE 6.15: Tools for interactive segmentation. The top row shows the user interaction required to complete the segmentation or matting process, which can be brush/lasso marks to indicate foreground or background pixels or marks to pinpoint a boundary. The bottom row illustrates the resulting segmentation. (Figure from [113]. © 2004 Association for Computing Machinery, Inc. Reprinted by permission.)

tainty [6]. All such techniques facilitate faster annotations, and are relevant both for the cost-sensitive tasks we highlight here and otherwise.

6.4   Cost-Sensitive Multi-Level Active Learning

So far, we have surveyed approaches in the object recognition literature that aim to reduce annotation costs, either in terms of the "level," the "amount," or the "effort" involved in providing supervision. This final section presents our approach for cost-sensitive visual category learning, which brings together all three components.[4]

The goal is to learn category models with minimum supervision under the realistic setting where each potential training image can contain multiple object classes. Throughout, our assumption is that human effort is more scarce and expensive than machine cycles; thus our method prefers to invest in computing the best queries to make, rather than bother human annotators for an abundance of less useful labels.

As seen in the previous sections, a variety of supervisory information can be obtained in order to train object classifiers: some images are labeled as containing the category of interest (or not), some have both a class label and object outlines, while others have no annotations at all. We consider three

---

[4]We summarize ideas originally presented in [135, 136, 137]. This section is a condensed overview of that work; the interested reader should see the original papers for additional details on the algorithms and results.

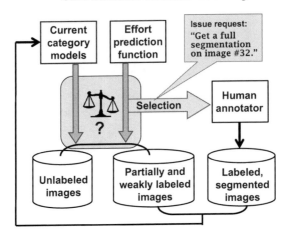

FIGURE 6.16: Summary of the approach. After learning from a small initial set of labeled images, all available unlabeled and partially labeled data are surveyed. The worth of every candidate annotation is estimated across all images using a value of information criterion that rewards reductions in misclassification risk while penalizing the predicted annotation effort costs. The annotation type *and* example with the largest worth are then selected, and the task is posed to a human annotator. Then, based on the annotator response, the example is moved from the unlabeled or partially labeled pool into the partially or fully labeled pool, as appropriate. The process repeats until there are no more examples with positive worth, or once the allowed annotation cost budget has been spent. (Figure from [137]; reprinted courtesy of Springer.)

specific types of annotations: a label on an image region, an image-level tag specifying a category that is present, and a complete segmentation of the entire image (see Figure 6.17). We refer to these types as "levels," since they correspond to different levels of detail in the annotation. A key question we wish to address in our approach is how to effectively balance a *mixture* of such annotation levels when actively training an object recognition system.

We first show how an extension of the multiple-instance learning problem to multi-label data can accommodate all three types of supervisory information defined above. We then derive an active learning criterion that predicts how informative further annotation on any particular unlabeled image or region would be, while accounting for the variable expense associated with the different annotation types using a decision-theoretic value of information (VOI) criterion.

The algorithm uses this criterion at every iteration in order to choose the best question to ask a human supervisor, such as an annotator working through an online labeling service. As long as the information expected from further annotations outweighs the cost of obtaining them, the algorithm will request the next valuable annotation, re-train the classifier, and repeat. Thus, our framework simultaneously balances the candidate "levels" of annotations, minimizes the "amount" of supervision via active selection, and reduces the "effort" required by formulating a sequence of annotation tasks suitable to post on a labeling service. The overall process is depicted in Figure 6.16.

6.4.1 Multi-Label Multiple-Instance Learning

In the MIL setting, as noted in Section 6.1.1.3, the learner is given bags of instances and told that at least one example from a positive bag is positive, while none of the members in a negative bag is positive. MIL is well suited for the image classification scenario where training images are labeled as to whether they contain the category of interest, but they also contain background clutter. An image can be represented by a bag of regions, each of which is characterized by its properties such as color, texture, shape, etc. ([95, 150]). For positive bags, at least one of the regions contains the object of interest. In this usual two-class setting, the goal is to predict when new image regions contain the object—that is, to learn to label regions as foreground or background. Since a positive instance is a positive bag containing a single instance, MIL can accommodate both region labels (instance-level) and image tags (bag-level).

In the more general multiple-instance multi-label (MIML) setting, each instance within a bag can be associated with one of C possible class labels; therefore each bag is associated with multiple labels—whichever labels at least one of its instances has. In this case, multi-class classifiers can be constructed using a series of one-vs.-one or one-vs.-all classifiers for the C labels.

Formally, let $\{(X_1, L_1), (X_2, L_2), \ldots, (X_N, L_N)\}$ denote a set of training bags and their associated labels. Each bag consists of a set of instances $X_i = \{x_1^i, x_2^i, \ldots, x_{n_i}^i\}$, and a set of labels $L_i = \{l_1^i, l_2^i, \ldots, l_{m_i}^i\}$, where n_i denotes the number of instances in X_i, and m_i denotes the number of labels in L_i. Note that often a bag has fewer unique labels than instances ($m_i \leq n_i$), since multiple instances may have the same label. Every instance x_j^i is associated with a description $\phi(x_j^i)$ in some kernel embedding space and some class label $l_k^i \in \mathbb{L} = \{1, \ldots, C\}$, but with only the bag-level labels it is ambiguous which instance(s) belongs to which label. In particular, a bag X_i has label l if and only if it contains at least one instance with label l. Note that a labeled instance is a special case of a bag, where the bag contains only one example ($n_i = 1$), and there is no label ambiguity.

For our purposes, an image is a bag, and its instances are the overseg-mented regions within it found automatically with a segmentation algorithm (see Figure 6.19). A bag's labels are tags naming the categories present within the image; a region (instance) label names the object in the particular region. Each region has a feature vector describing its appearance. This follows the common use of MIL for images ([95, 154, 135]), but in the generalized multiple-instance multi-label case.

We define a Multi-Label Set Kernel that weights the membership contribution of each instance within the bag according to the estimated probability that the instance belongs to the class. That way if an instance has a high chance of belonging to the given class, its feature vector will dominate the representation. Let X_1 and X_2 be bags associated with labels l_1 and l_2, respectively, that are currently being used to construct a classifier separating classes l_1 and l_2. Then the kernel value between bags X_1, X_2 is given by

$$\mathcal{K}(X_1^{(l_1)}, X_2^{(l_2)}) = \sum_{i=1}^{n_1} \sum_{j=1}^{n_2} p(l_1|x_i^1)\, p(l_2|x_j^2)\, \mathcal{K}(x_i^1, x_j^2), \qquad (6.1)$$

where $\mathcal{K}(x_i^1, x_j^2) = \phi(x_i^1)^T \phi(x_j^2)$ is the kernel value computed for instances x_i^1 and x_j^2, and $p(l_1|x_i^1), p(l_2|x_j^2)$ are the membership probabilities of instances x_1, x_2 belonging to classes l_1, l_2, respectively. These probabilities can be obtained directly from the posteriors of the classifiers that can distinguish between classes l_1, l_2. Note that because the kernel is parameterized by the label under consideration, a multi-label bag can contribute multiple different ⟨feature,label⟩ pairs to the training sets of a number of the one-vs.-one classifiers.

The proposed kernel in (6.1) is valid for both instances and bags, and thus can be used to build kernel-based classifiers such as support vector machines (SVMs) to distinguish bags and instances of all pairs of classes. To map the SVM's decision values to multi-class posterior probabilities, we use Platt's algorithm [104], followed by the pairwise coupling approach [147].

6.4.2 Active Multi-Level Selection of Multi-Label Annotations

Thus far we have defined the multi-label learner, the basic classifier which can learn from both weakly supervised (bag) and strongly supervised (instance) data. Next we shall describe the strategy to perform active selection among candidate annotations.

In order to choose among annotations that require different levels of supervision, we want to establish quantitative measures that can directly compute both the informativeness of the annotation and the effective cost or effort involved in obtaining it. Then, we can design a Value of Information (VOI) selection function to score each candidate according to its informativeness minus its cost; i.e., the most cost-effective queries are those where informativeness most outweighs effort. Other VOI-based active learners and selective sampling algorithms have been explored previously in [71, 89, 75], but none considers optimizing the request across label types or strengths.

In the following, we first address how to predict the cost of an annotation (Section 6.4.2.1), followed by its informativeness (Section 6.4.2.2) for the candidate annotation types mentioned above and shown in Figure 6.17.

  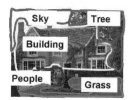

| (a) Name an object in the image (unlabeled bag). | (b) Label the specified region (unlabeled instance). | (c) Segment the image and name all objects (label all instances). |

FIGURE 6.17: The three candidate annotation types (or "levels") that our approach chooses from when formulating a request. (Figures from [137]; reprinted courtesy of Springer.)

FIGURE 6.18: Which image would you rather annotate? Humans can easily glance at an image and roughly gauge the difficulty. This appears to be true even without prior knowledge about the specific objects present in the image (right pair).

6.4.2.1 Predicting the Cost of an Annotation

There are three possible types of annotation request: the classifier can ask for a label on a bag, a label on an instance within a bag, or a label on all instances within a bag. A label on a bag serves as a "flag" for class membership, which is ambiguous because we do not know which of the instances in the bag are associated with the label. A label on an instance unambiguously names the class in a single image region, while labeling all instances within a bag corresponds to fully segmenting and labeling an image (see Figure 6.17).

Traditional active learning methods assume equal manual effort per label, and thus try to minimize the total number of queries made to the annotator. In reality, annotation costs can vary substantially from image to image, and from type to type. If we consider the total time required to provide an annotation as a measure of the effort involved, which seems reasonable given that many real world jobs involving human labor are measured this way (e.g., hourly rates), then we would expect complex images containing a large number of objects to require more annotation time. Thus, the standard "flat cost" implied by traditional active learners is inadequate.

Instead, our system needs to be able to view an unlabeled image and estimate the effort it will entail. That is, without actually obtaining the annotation, we need to estimate how long it will take a typical annotator to complete it. As Figure 6.18 suggests, humans are able to predict the difficulty of annotating an image even without prior knowledge about the objects occurring in the image (second row) or other high-level cues. Therefore, it seems plausible that the difficulty level of an image could be predicted based on the image's low-level features. For an extreme example, if an image contains a single color it most likely contains only one object, and so it should not be difficult to segment. If the image has significant responses to a large number of filters, then it may be highly cluttered, and so it could take a long time.

We use supervised learning to estimate the difficulty of segmenting an image. It is unclear which features will optimally reflect annotation difficulty, and admittedly high-level recognition itself plays some role. We begin with some generic features that may be decent indicators of image complexity: a histogram of oriented gradients, a gray-scale histogram, and two new features based on the edge density and color uniformity in a local area. The features are designed to indicate the density of boundaries possibly present, and in turn to reflect the fact that more objects could lead to more annotation time. Then, we use a multiple kernel learning algorithm to select those most useful for the task.

We gather training data for the cost predictor online, using Amazon's Mechanical Turk system, where we can pay anonymous workers to segment images of our choosing. The users are given a polygon-drawing tool to superimpose object boundaries, and are instructed to name and outline every major object. The system times their responses. Thus the labels on the training images will be the times that annotators needed to complete a full annotation. To account for noise in the data collection, we collect a large number of user responses per image. Even if users generally have the same relative speeds (faster on easy ones, slower on harder ones), their absolute speeds may vary. Therefore, to make the values comparable, we normalize each user's times by his/her mean and use the average time taken on an image to be its target label.

We construct a χ^2 RBF kernel over the training examples per image feature. Based on the timing obtained from the anonymous users we divide the set of training images into a discrete range of "easy" and "hard" images using the mean time over all the images. We then use the MKL approach of [3] to learn the weights on the image features for the binary classification problem of classifying images into "easy" and "hard" categories. Using the obtained combined kernel, we also learn a cost predictor function using Support Vector Regression (SVR).

From this we can build a cost function $\mathcal{C}(\mathbf{z})$ that takes a candidate annotation $\mathbf{z}$ as input, and returns the predicted time requirement (in seconds) as output. When $\mathbf{z}$ is a candidate full segmentation, we apply the learned function to the image. When $\mathbf{z}$ is a request for a tag (bag-level label), we set $\mathcal{C}(\mathbf{z})$ as the cost estimated using similar time-based experiments. Finally, when **z** entails outlining a single object, we estimate the cost as the full image's predicted time, divided by the number of segments in the image.

6.4.2.2 Predicting the Informativeness of an Annotation

Given this learned cost function, we can now define the complete MIML active learning criterion. Inspired by the classic notion of the *value of information* (VOI), we derive a measure to gauge the relative risk reduction a new multi-label annotation may provide. The main idea is to evaluate the candidate images and annotation types, and predict which combination (of image + type) will lead to the greatest net decrease in risk for the current classifier, when each choice is penalized according to its expected manual effort. In contrast to previous VOI methods, this measure enables the multi-label setting and selects from among multiple types of annotations.

At any stage in the learning process the dataset can be divided into three different pools: $\mathcal{X}_U$, the set of unlabeled examples (bags and instances); $\mathcal{X}_L$, the set of labeled examples; and $\mathcal{X}_P$, the set of partially labeled examples, which contains all bags for which we have only a partial set of bag-level labels. The four types of examples are shown in Figure 6.19.

Let r_l denote the risk associated with misclassifying an example belonging to class l. The risk associated with $\mathcal{X}_L$ is:

$$\mathcal{R}(\mathcal{X}_L) = \sum_{X_i \in \mathcal{X}_L} \sum_{l \in L_i} r_l \left(1 - p(l|X_i)\right), \tag{6.2}$$

where $p(l|X_i)$ is the probability that X_i is classified with label l, and r_l is the risk associated with misclassifying an example belonging to class l. Here, X_i is again used to denote both instances and bags and L_i its label(s). If X_i is a training instance it has only one label, and we can compute $p(l|X_i)$ via the current MIML classifier.

If X_i is a multi-label bag in the training set, we compute the probability it receives label l as follows:

$$p(l|X_i) = p\left(l|x_1^i, \ldots, x_{n_i}^i\right) = 1 - \prod_{j=1}^{n_i} (1 - p(l|x_j^i)). \tag{6.3}$$

The above reflects the fact that for a bag to *not* belong to a class, it must be the case that none of its instances belong to the class. Thus the probability of a bag *not* having a label is equivalent to the probability that *none* of its instances has that class label.

The MIML classifier implicitly assumes that every image/instance can be classified into one of C labels. However, in the more general case, the dataset can also contain images that do not necessarily belong to the C classes. Such images are given a "negative" label which specifies that none of the instances/regions in the image belongs to any of the classes in $\{1, \ldots, C\}$,

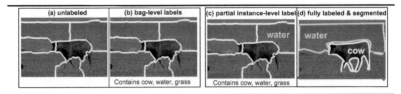

FIGURE 6.19: In the MIML scenario, images are multi-label bags of regions (instances). Unlabeled images are oversegmented into regions (a). For an image with *bag-level* labels, we know which categories are present in it, but we do not know in which regions (b). For an image with some *instance-level* labels, we have labels on some of the segments (c). For a *fully annotated* image, we have true object boundaries and labels (d). (Figure is from [137]; reprinted courtesy of Springer.)

similar to the "negative" label in a standard MIL formulation. In this case, we weight $p(l|X_i)$ with the probability that X_i belongs to any one of the C classes as opposed to the "negative" class, which is obtained by training a standard MIL classifier. Note that when $C = 1$, a single foreground class, the above reduces to the standard MIL solution since $p(l|X_i)$ is trivially 1. Similarly, in the absence of a "negative" class the above reduces to the MIML solution.

The corresponding risk for the unlabeled data is:

$$\mathcal{R}(\mathcal{X}_U) = \sum_{X_i \in \mathcal{X}_U} \sum_{l=1}^{C} r_l (1 - p(l|X_i)) \Pr(l|X_i), \qquad (6.4)$$

where we compute the probabilities for bags using Equation 6.3, and $\Pr(l|X_i)$ is the true probability that unlabeled example X_i has label l, approximated as $\Pr(l|X_i) \approx p(l|X_i)$.

For the partially labeled data, the risk is:

$$\mathcal{R}(\mathcal{X}_P) = \sum_{X_i \in \mathcal{X}_P} \sum_{l \in L_i} r_l (1 - p(l|X_i)) + \sum_{l \in U_i} r_l (1 - p(l|X_i)) p(l|X_i),$$

where $U_i = \mathbb{L} \setminus L_i$.

The value r_l is the risk associated with misclassifying an example belonging to class l, specified in the same units as the cost function defined in Section 6.4.2.1. Intuitively, it should reflect the real cost of a classification mistake, as the algorithm directly trades off the cost of the manual labeling against the damage done by misclassification. In general, r_l should be set based on realistic system requirements; we interpret it as the cost of manually fixing a classification error (e.g., an average segmentation requires 50 seconds). If one preferred to avoid errors on a particular class, that could be encoded with variable r_l values per class label l. Note that r_l is not a parameter that needs to be optimized for performance; rather, it gives flexibility for situations that have real costs associated with the task.

In the next section we bring together the effort predictions and misclassification risk reduction estimates to compute the VOI-based active selection criterion.

6.4.2.3 Computing the MIML Value of Information (VOI)

The total cost $T(\mathcal{X}_L, \mathcal{X}_U, \mathcal{X}_P)$ associated with a given snapshot of the data is the total misclassification risk, plus the cost of obtaining all the labeled data thus far:

$$T(\mathcal{X}_L, \mathcal{X}_U, \mathcal{X}_P) = \mathcal{R}(\mathcal{X}_L) + \mathcal{R}(\mathcal{X}_U) + \mathcal{R}(\mathcal{X}_P) + \sum_{X_i \in \mathcal{X}_B} \sum_{l \in L_i} \mathcal{C}(X_i^l),$$

where $\mathcal{X}_B = \mathcal{X}_L \cup \mathcal{X}_P$, and $\mathcal{C}(\cdot)$ is defined in Section 6.4.2.1.

We measure the utility of obtaining a particular annotation by predicting the change in total cost that would result from the addition of the annotation to $\mathcal{X}_L$. Therefore, the value of information for an annotation $\mathbf{z}$ is:

$$
\begin{aligned}
VOI(\mathbf{z}) &= T(\mathcal{X}_L, \mathcal{X}_U, \mathcal{X}_P) - T\left(\hat{\mathcal{X}}_L, \hat{\mathcal{X}}_U, \hat{\mathcal{X}}_P\right) \qquad (6.5) \\
&= \mathcal{R}(\mathcal{X}_L) + \mathcal{R}(\mathcal{X}_U) + \mathcal{R}(\mathcal{X}_P) \\
&\quad - \left(\mathcal{R}(\hat{\mathcal{X}}_L) + \mathcal{R}(\hat{\mathcal{X}}_U) + \mathcal{R}(\hat{\mathcal{X}}_P)\right) - \mathcal{C}(\mathbf{z}),
\end{aligned}
$$

where $\hat{\mathcal{X}}_L, \hat{\mathcal{X}}_U, \hat{\mathcal{X}}_P$ denote the set of labeled, unlabeled and partially labeled data after obtaining annotation $\mathbf{z}$. Note that $\mathbf{z}$ could be any one among the three annotation types described in Figure 6.17. If all the labels in the example have been obtained through $\mathbf{z}$ then the example is moved to the labeled pool, i.e., $\hat{\mathcal{X}}_L = \mathcal{X}_L \cup \mathbf{z}$. On the other hand, if the example contains instances (regions) with no label information even after obtaining annotation $\mathbf{z}$ then the example is moved to the set of partially labeled data, i.e., $\hat{\mathcal{X}}_P = \mathcal{X}_P \cup \mathbf{z}$. Similarly, the example associated with $\mathbf{z}$ is removed from $\mathcal{X}_U$ or $\mathcal{X}_P$ as appropriate.

A high VOI for a given input denotes that the total cost would be decreased by adding its annotation. So, the classifier seeks annotations that give maximal VOI values.

The VOI function relies on estimates for the risk of yet-unlabeled data, so we must predict how the classifier will change given the candidate annotation, without actually knowing its label(s). We estimate the total risk induced by incorporating a candidate annotation $\mathbf{z}$ using the expected value:

$$\mathcal{R}(\hat{\mathcal{X}}_L) + \mathcal{R}(\hat{\mathcal{X}}_U) + \mathcal{R}(\hat{\mathcal{X}}_P) \approx E[\mathcal{R}(\hat{\mathcal{X}}_L) + \mathcal{R}(\hat{\mathcal{X}}_U) + \mathcal{R}(\hat{\mathcal{X}}_P)], \qquad (6.6)$$

henceforth denoted by $\mathbb{E}$.

If the annotation $\mathbf{z}$ will label an unlabeled instance (Figure 6.17(b)), computing the expectation is straightforward, since that instance can simply be removed from $\mathcal{X}_U$ and added to $\mathcal{X}_L$ to evaluate the risk were it assigned each of the L possible labels in turn:

$$\mathbb{E} = \sum_{l \in \mathbb{L}} \left(\mathcal{R}(\mathcal{X}_L \cup \mathbf{z}^{(l)}) + \mathcal{R}(\{\mathcal{X}_U, \mathcal{X}_P\} \setminus \mathbf{z}) \right) \Pr(l|\mathbf{z}), \qquad (6.7)$$

where $\mathbb{L} = \{1, \dots, C\}$ is the set of all possible label assignments for $\mathbf{z}$. The value $\Pr(l|\mathbf{z})$ is obtained by evaluating the current classifier on $\mathbf{z}$ and mapping the output to the associated posterior, and risk is computed based on the (temporarily) modified classifier with $\mathbf{z}^{(l)}$ inserted into the labeled set. Similarly, if the candidate annotation $\mathbf{z}$ will add an image-level label to an unlabeled or partially labeled bag (Figure 6.17(a)), then $\Pr(l|\mathbf{z})$ is calculated using Equation 6.3.

In the final case, the annotation $\mathbf{z}$ entails fully segmenting and labeling an image. Recall that we break an unlabeled image into M estimated regions using an automatic bottom-up segmentation algorithm (Figure 6.17(c)). Using these regions, we approximate the utility of obtaining the joint set of labels for the generated segments (the bag's instances). The segmentation is fixed (i.e., it is unaffected by the evolving class models). Note that while the generated segments will not usually correspond perfectly to the underlying object boundaries, they nonetheless serve as a good approximation to the actual worth of a full segmentation. If an unlabeled image is selected for full segmentation and labeling, when presenting the image to a human we directly request the true outlines on all the objects and their corresponding labels; that is, once an image is labeled, we disregard its automatically segmented regions.

To obtain the utility of a bag containing M instances, we need to consider C^M possible labelings: $\mathbb{L} = \{1, \dots, C\}^M$. Therefore, a direct computation of the expectation is impractical. Instead, we use a form of Gibbs sampling to draw samples of the label assignment from the joint distribution over the M instances' descriptors and approximate the expected value over these samples. Let $\mathbf{z} = \{z_1, \dots, z_M\}$ be the bag's instances, and let $\mathbf{z}^{(\mathbf{a})} = \left\{ (z_1^{(a_1)}), \dots, (z_M^{(a_M)}) \right\}$ denote the label assignment we wish to sample, with $a_j \in \{1, \dots, C\}$. To generate samples from the joint label assignment of the M instances, we cycle through the M variables in turn as follows:

1. Initialize $\{a_i : i = 1, \dots, M\}$ according to maximum posteriors

2. For iterations $\tau = 1, \dots T$:
    - Sample $a_1^{\tau+1} \sim p(a_1|a_2^\tau, a_3^\tau, \dots, a_M^\tau)$.
    - Sample $a_2^{\tau+1} \sim p(a_2|a_1^\tau, a_3^\tau, \dots, a_M^\tau)$.

    $\vdots$

    - Sample $a_j^{\tau+1} \sim p(a_j|a_1^\tau, \dots, a_{j-1}^\tau, a_{j+1}^\tau, \dots, a_M^\tau)$.

$\vdots$

- Sample $a_M^{\tau+1} \sim p(a_M | a_1^\tau, a_2^\tau, ..., a_{M-1}^\tau)$.

To sample from the conditional distribution of one instance's label given the rest $(p(a_j | a_1^\tau, ..., a_{j-1}^\tau, a_{j+1}^\tau, ..., a_M^\tau))$—the basic procedure required by Gibbs sampling—we first retrain the classifier with the given labels added to the labeled pool, i.e.,

$$\mathcal{X}_L = \mathcal{X}_L \cup \{(z_1, a_1), ..., (z_{j-1}, a_{j-1}), (z_{j+1}, a_{j+1}), ..., (z_M, a_M)\}.$$

We then draw the remaining label according to $a_j \sim \Pr(l|z_j)$, for $l \in \{1, ..., C\}$, where z_j denotes the one instance currently under consideration. For bag $\mathbf{z}$, the expected total risk is then the average risk computed over all generated samples:

$$
\begin{aligned}
\mathbb{E} \quad = \quad & \frac{1}{S} \sum_{k=1}^{S} (\mathcal{R}(\{\mathcal{X}_L \smallsetminus \mathbf{z}\} \cup \{z_1^{(a_1)_k}, ..., z_M^{(a_M)_k}\}) \\
+ \quad & \mathcal{R}(\mathcal{X}_U \smallsetminus \{z_1, z_2, ..., z_M\}) + \mathcal{R}(\mathcal{X}_P)),
\end{aligned}
\tag{6.8}
$$

where k indexes the S samples. As usual, we can expect more samples (higher values of S) to lead to more reliable estimates of the expected value; in practice we find about 25 samples to be sufficient for our data. We compute the risk on $\mathcal{X}_L$ for each fixed sample by removing the bag $\mathbf{z}$ from the unlabeled or partially labeled pool, and inserting its instances with the label given by the sample's label assignment.

We stress that when computing the VOI of a candidate annotation we have no supervision information on that example, including the object outlines. Hence, the computation of VOI is performed using segments/regions generated using an automatic segmentation algorithm. Once we obtain a complete segmentation of an image from the annotator, we use the actual region outlines and labels to retrain the classifier.

Computing the VOI values for all unlabeled data, especially for the positive bags, requires repeatedly solving the classifier objective function with slightly different inputs; to make this manageable we employ incremental SVM updates [26].

6.4.3   Summary of the Algorithm

We can now actively select multi-label, multi-level image annotations so as to maximize the expected benefit relative to the manual effort expended. The MIML classifier is initially trained using a small number of tagged images. To get each subsequent annotation, the active learner surveys all remaining unlabeled and partially labeled examples, computes their VOI, and requests the label for the example with the maximal value. After the classifier is updated with this label, the process repeats. The final classifier can predict image- and region-level labels, in binary or multi-class settings. Refer back to Figure 6.16 for a summary of the approach.

6.4.4 Illustrative Results

In the following subsections, we evaluate three main aspects of the approach: (1) its effectiveness as an active learner when selecting from three different types of annotations on a multi-label image recognition problem, (2) its ability to accurately predict annotation costs, and (3) the effect of introducing the cost predictor in the active selection function. For additional in-depth results, please see [137].

We experiment with the publicly available MSRC[5] dataset. We choose the MSRC dataset because it is a common benchmark for multi-class object segmentation. The MSRC v2 dataset contains 591 images from 21 classes and a variable number of objects per image, with 240 images and 14 classes in the (subset) v1. We use an RBF kernel with $\gamma = 10$, and set the SVM parameters based on cross-validation.

6.4.4.1 Active Selection with Multi-Label Multiple-Instance Data

First we demonstrate the impact of using the proposed selection function in the general multi-label setting where an image contains multiple objects of interest plus clutter, while choosing from different types of annotations.

We divide the examples into five folds containing an equal number in each, and use the first part for training and the rest for testing. We construct the initial training set such that each class appears in at least five images, and use image-level labels. The rest of the training set forms the unlabeled pool of data. The active learner can request either complete segmentations or region-level labels from among the initial training examples, or image-level labels from any unlabeled example.

We set $r_l = 50$ for all classes, which means that each misclassification is worth 50 s of user time. The parameter r_l should reflect the real cost of a classification mistake, and in our case we find that an error made by the automatic labeling would take around 50 s to manually fix for the average image. For this experiment we fix the costs per type using the mean times from real annotators: 50 s for complete segmentations, 10 s for a region outline, and 3 s for a flag.

We compare the approach to a "passive" selection strategy, which uses the same classifier but picks labels to receive at random, as well as a single-level active baseline (traditional active learning) that uses the VOI function, but only selects from unlabeled regions. All methods are given a fixed manual effort budget and are allowed to make a sequence of label requests until the budget is used up.

Figure 6.20 shows the resulting learning curves. Accuracy is measured

---

[5] http://research.microsoft.com/en−us/projects/objectclassrecognition/.

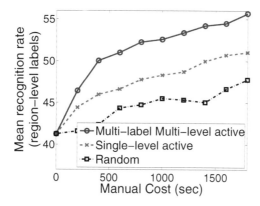

FIGURE 6.20: Learning curves when actively or randomly selecting multi-level and single-level annotations. The plot shows the region-level accuracy as a function of annotation effort expended. Our multi-level active selection approach yields the steepest learning curves while random selection lags behind, wasting annotation effort on less informative examples. More importantly, we see that it outperforms traditional active learning, which is limited to questions at a single-level of granularity. (Figure appears in [137]; reprinted courtesy of Springer.)

as the average value of the diagonal of the confusion matrix for region-level predictions on the test set. All results are averaged over five random trials. The proposed multi-level active selection yields the steepest learning curves. Random selection lags behind, wasting annotation effort on less informative examples. Traditional or single-level active selection is preferable to random selection, yet we get best results when the active learner can choose between multiple types of annotations, including segmentations or image flags. The total gains after 1800 seconds of annotator effort are significant, given the complexity of the 21-way classification problem. On the whole, our active approach requires 47% less effort than the passive learner to reach the maximum prediction accuracy for this dataset.

Figure 6.21 shows annotation queries selected by our approach during the first 12 iterations of an example run starting from a small training set consisting of two image tags per class. These qualitative examples indicate a number of interesting things. First, we see that the annotations automatically requested are dominated by image tags, which is reasonable considering they are the least expensive labels among the three types. At the same time, the images for which tags are requested appear to consist of a small number of clearly defined objects ("sky," "water," in the second and third images, "water," "building" in the first image, etc.). On more complex images, such as the sixth image of the airplane, a complete segmentation is requested. Also a region label on the "tree" region is requested on the tenth image, even though

(a) Initial training set.

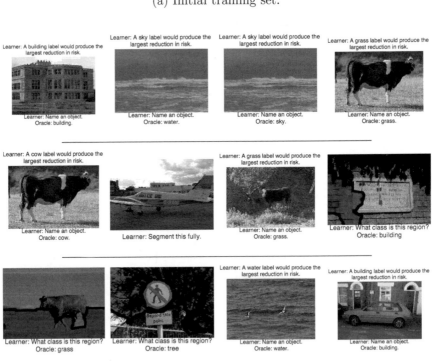

(b) Annotations selected by the active learner in order (row major).

FIGURE 6.21: (a) A small training set containing two examples per class. (b) The first annotation queries selected by our method due to their VOI scores. The active learning query (one among a region label, an image tag or a complete segmentation) is displayed at the bottom of the image along with the oracle's answer. For a query on a region, the corresponding region is highlighted in the image; for an image tag, the text on the top of the image represents what label is expected to produce the best reduction in risk (the l with the largest value in the summation of (6.7)). (Figure from [137]; reprinted courtesy of Springer.)

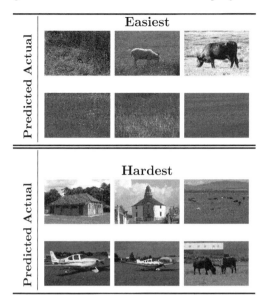

FIGURE 6.22: The easiest and hardest images to annotate based on actual annotators' timing data (top rows), and the predictions of our cost function on novel images (bottom rows). (Figure appears in [137]; reprinted courtesy of Springer.)

a tree image tag is already available on the same image in the training set. This illustrates that in some cases stronger annotations might be required, even when the classifier already contains weaker information about a class. Finally, the examples selected are also diverse. For example, in the images selected that contain the region "sky," the appearance of the region is distinct from the examples of "sky" already available in the training set.

6.4.4.2 Image Annotation Effort Prediction

Next, we isolate how well we can learn to predict the difficulty of segmenting images based on image features. To train the cost function, we gather data with Amazon's Mechanical Turk. Users are required to completely segment images from the 14-class MSRC v1 dataset while a script records the time taken per image. We collect 25–50 annotations per image from different users. Users could skip images they preferred not to segment; each user was allowed to label up to 240 images.

Figure 6.22 shows examples that were easiest and hardest to segment, as measured by the ground truth actual time taken for at least eight annotators. Alongside, we show the examples that the regressor predicts to be easiest and hardest (from a separate partition of the data). These examples are intuitive,

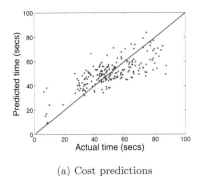

(a) Cost predictions

| % imp. | Cost(secs) | | % Cost |
	CP	NC	saved
5	11.40	11.52	+1.07
10	24.52	31.41	+21.94
15	45.25	63.24	+28.45
20	165.85	251.10	+33.95
25	365.73	543.69	+32.73

(b) Impact on active selection

FIGURE 6.23: (a) Scatter plot of the actual time taken by users to segment an image vs. the value predicted by the cost function. The predicted and actual times are highly correlated, showing that the cost predictor has learned how difficult an image is to segment using only low-level image features. (b) Savings in cost when using cost prediction within the active learner. CP refers to using cost prediction, and NC is the same active selection criterion but without cost prediction. Overall, the active selection takes less effort to attain the same level of accuracy as a cost-blind active learner.

as one can imagine needing a lot more clicks to draw polygons on the many objects in the "hardest" set.

Figure 6.23(a) plots the actual time taken by the annotators for each image against the value predicted by our cost function, as obtained with leave-one-out cross-validation for all 240 images. The root mean squared difference between the actual and predicted times is 11.1 s, with an average prediction error of 22%. In comparison, predicting a constant value of 50 s (the mean of the data) yields an average prediction error of 46%. Given that the actual times vary from 8 to 100 s, and that the average cross-annotator disagreement was 18 s, an average error of 11 s seems quite good.

6.4.4.3 Active Selection with a Learned Effort Prediction Function

Thus far we have fixed the costs assigned per annotation type; now we show the impact of using the predicted cost while making active choices. We train a binary multi-instance classifier for each MSRC category using image labels on $\frac{4}{5}$-th of the data per class, in five different runs. The rest is used for testing. We compare two MIL active learners: one using cost prediction, and one assigning a flat cost to annotations. At test time, both learners are "charged" the ground truth cost of getting the requested annotation.

Figure 6.23(b) shows the cost required to improve the base classifier to different levels of accuracy. The fourth column shows the relative time savings the cost prediction enables over a cost-blind active learner that uses the same selection strategy. For larger improvements, predicting the cost leads to noticeably greater savings in manual effort—over 30% savings to attain a 25% accuracy improvement. We also observe that for a few classes that are more homogeneous in appearance (e.g., "sky"), the predicted cost function has only a minor impact on the active selection quality. This is likely because the images within such class are fairly consistent, and equally informative and easy to label.

6.4.5   Summary

While traditional active learning restricts supervision to yes/no questions (binary labels), these results show that accommodating supervision at multiple levels and choosing targeted questions for annotators allows us to more efficiently build accurate low-cost recognition models. The algorithm itself, while tested extensively for object recognition, is in fact general enough to accept other types of annotations or classifiers, as long as the cost and risk functions can be appropriately defined.

In ongoing work, we are exploring other aspects of cost-sensitive learning for object recognition. This includes budgeted selection techniques that choose a *batch* of useful tasks to give annotators working in parallel [139], and algorithms to make the selection scalable over millions of unlabeled data instances [64].

Our work overviewed here also suggests interesting extensions to target the selected annotation tasks in an annotator-specific manner, to further maximize effort spent. Furthermore, while we have worked solely with bottom-up segmentations to compose the bags of regions, it would be interesting to consider how to continuously refine a top-down segmentation model while learning the object categories actively.

6.5   Conclusion

This chapter described how recent research in vision and machine learning is tackling the "supervision bottleneck" in learning visual object categories. We saw how techniques ranging from unsupervised topic modeling to transfer learning can play a role in minimizing human intervention, and examined in detail a recently introduced cost-sensitive active learning algorithm. Problems in this area will continue to be important to visual recognition research, as we determine the most effective ways to transfer human knowledge about objects into reliable predictive systems.

Acknowledgments

This work was supported in part by Google Research, a Microsoft Research New Faculty Fellowship, NSF EIA-0303609, and the Henry Luce Foundation.

References

[1] S. Andrews, I. Tsochantaridis, and T. Hofmann. Support Vector Machines for Multiple-Instance Learning. In *Neural Information Processing Systems (NIPS)*, 2002.

[2] H. Arora, N. Loeff, D. Forsyth, and N. Ahuja. Unsupervised Segmentation of Objects Using Efficient Learning. In *Proceedings of the IEEE Conference on Computer Vision and Pattern Recognition (CVPR)*, 2007.

[3] Francis R. Bach, Gert R. G. Lanckriet, and Michael I. Jordan. Fast Kernel Learning Using Sequential Minimal Optimization. Technical Report UCB/CSD-04-1307, University of California at Berkeley, Feb 2004.

[4] K. Barnard, P. Duygulu, N. de Freitas, D. Forsyth, D. Blei, and M. Jordan. Matching Words and Pictures. *Journal of Machine Learning Research*, 3:1107–1135, 2003.

[5] E. Bart and S. Ullman. Cross-Generalization: Learning Novel Classes from a Single Example by Feature Replacement. In *Proceedings of the IEEE Conference on Computer Vision and Pattern Recognition (CVPR)*, 2005.

[6] D. Batra, A. Kowdle, D. Parikh, J. Luo, and T. Chen. iCoseg: Interactive Co-segmentation with Intelligen Scribble Guidance. In *Proceedings of the IEEE Conference on Computer Vision and Pattern Recognition (CVPR)*, 2010.

[7] R. Bekkerman and J. Jeon. Multi-modal Clustering for Multimedia Collections. In *Proceedings of the IEEE Conference on Computer Vision and Pattern Recognition (CVPR)*, 2007.

[8] T. Berg, A. Berg, J. Edwards, M. Maire, R. White, Y. Teh, E. Learned-Miller, and D. Forsyth. Names and Faces in the News. In *Proceedings of the IEEE Conference on Computer Vision and Pattern Recognition (CVPR)*, 2004.

[9] T. Berg and D. Forsyth. Animals on the Web. In *Proceedings of the IEEE Conference on Computer Vision and Pattern Recognition (CVPR)*, 2006.

[10] M. B. Blaschko and C. H. Lampert. Correlational Spectral Clustering. In *Proceedings of the IEEE Conference on Computer Vision and Pattern Recognition (CVPR)*, 2008.

[11] A. Blum and T. Mitchell. Combining Labeled and Unlabeled Data with Co-training. In *COLT: Proceedings of the Workshop on Computational Learning Theory*, 1998.

[12] E. Borenstein, E. Sharon, and S. Ullman. Combining Top-down and Bottom-up Segmentation. In *CVPR Workshop*, 2004.

[13] E. Borenstein and S. Ullman. Class-Specific, Top-Down Segmentation. In *Proceedings of European Conference on Computer Vision (ECCV)*, 2002.

[14] E. Borenstein and S. Ullman. Learning to Segment. In *Proceedings of European Conference on Computer Vision (ECCV)*, 2004.

[15] Y. Y. Boykov and M. P. Jolly. Interactive Graph Cuts for Optimal Boundary & Region Segmentation of Objects in n-d Images. In *Proceedings of the Eighth IEEE International Conference on Computer Vision*, 2001.

[16] S. Branson, C. Wah, B. Babenko, F. Schroff, P. Welinder, P. Perona, and S. Belongie. Visual Recognition with Humans in the Loop. In *Proceedings of European Conference on Computer Vision (ECCV)*, 2010.

[17] S. Brin and L. Page. The Anatomy of a Large-Scale Hypertextual Web Search Engine. In *WWW*, 1998.

[18] K. Brinker. Incorporating Diversity in Active Learning with Support Vector Machines. In *Proceedings of International Conference on Machine Learning (ICML)*, 2003.

[19] R. Bunescu and R. Mooney. Multiple Instance Learning for Sparse Positive Bags. In *Proceedings of International Conference on Machine Learning (ICML)*, 2007.

[20] M. Burl, M. Weber, and P. Perona. A Probabilistic Approach to Object Recognition Using Local Photometry and Global Geometry. In *Proceedings of European Conference on Computer Vision (ECCV)*, 1998.

[21] Nicholas J. Butko and Javier R. Movellan. Optimal Scanning for Faster Object Detection. In *Proceedings of the IEEE Conference on Computer Vision and Pattern Recognition (CVPR)*, 2009.

[22] Caltech 101 Image Database. *http://www.vision.caltech.edu/Image-Datasets/Caltech101/*, 2004.

[23] Caltech 256 Image Database. *http://www.vision.caltech.edu/Image-Datasets/Caltech256/*, 2007.

[24] C. Campbell, N. Cristianini, and A. Smola. Query Learning with Large Margin Classifiers. In *Proceedings of International Conference on Machine Learning (ICML)*, 2000.

[25] P. Carbonetto, G. Dorko, C. Schmid, H. Kuck, and N. de Freitas. A Semi-Supervised Learning Approach to Object Recognition with Spatial Integration of Local Features and Segmentation Cues. In *Toward Category-Level Object Recognition*, Springer, Berlin, 2006.

[26] G. Cauwenberghs and T. Poggio. Incremental and Decremental Support Vector Machine Learning. In *Neural Information Processing Systems (NIPS)*, 2000.

[27] E. Chang, S. Tong, K. Goh, and C.-W. Chang. Support Vector Machine Concept-Dependent Active Learning for Image Retrieval. *IEEE Transactions on Multimedia*, 2005.

[28] C. Mario Christoudias, R. Urtasun, A. Kapoor, and T. Darrell. Co-training with Noisy Perceptual Observations. In *Proceedings of the IEEE Conference on Computer Vision and Pattern Recognition (CVPR)*, 2009.

[29] O. Chum, M. Perdoch, and J. Matas. Geometric min-Hashing: Finding a (Thick) Needle in a Haystack. In *Proceedings of the IEEE Conference on Computer Vision and Pattern Recognition (CVPR)*, 2009.

[30] O. Chum and A. Zisserman. An Exemplar Model for Learning Object Classes. In *Proceedings of the IEEE Conference on Computer Vision and Pattern Recognition (CVPR)*, 2007.

[31] B. Collins, J. Deng, K. Li, and L. Fei-Fei. Towards Scalable Dataset Construction: An Active Learning Approach. In *Proceedings of European Conference on Computer Vision (ECCV)*, 2008.

[32] T. Cour and J. Shi. Recognizing Objects by Piecing Together the Segmentation Puzzle. In *Proceedings of the IEEE Conference on Computer Vision and Pattern Recognition (CVPR)*, 2007.

[33] D. Crandall, P. Felzenszwalb, and D. Huttenlocher. Spatial Priors for Part-Based Recognition using Statistical Models. In *Proceedings of the IEEE Conference on Computer Vision and Pattern Recognition (CVPR)*, 2005.

[34] J. Deng, W. Dong, R. Socher, L.-J. Li, K. Li, and L. Fei-Fei. Imagenet: A Large-Scale Hierarchical Image Database. In *Proceedings of the IEEE Conference on Computer Vision and Pattern Recognition (CVPR)*, 2009.

[35] T. Dietterich, R. Lathrop, and T. Lozano-Perez. Solving the Multiple Instance Problem with Axis-Parallel Rectangles. *Artificial Intelligence*, 89(1-2):31–71, 1997.

[36] P. Dollár, B. Babenko, S. Belongie, P. Perona, and Z. Tu. Multiple Component Learning for Object Detection. In *Proceedings of European Conference on Computer Vision (ECCV)*, 2008.

[37] D. Dueck and B. Frey. Non-Metric Affinity Propagation for Unsupervised Image Categorization. In *Proceedings of the IEEE International Conference on Computer Vision (ICCV)*, 2007.

[38] P. Duygulu, K. Barnard, N. de Freitas, and D. Forsyth. Object Recognition as Machine Translation: Learning a Lexicon for a Fixed Image Vocabulary. In *Proceedings of European Conference on Computer Vision (ECCV)*, 2002.

[39] M. Everingham, J. Sivic, and A. Zisserman. Hello! My Name is ... Buffy — Automatic Naming of Characters in TV Video. In *British Machine Vision Conference*, 2006.

[40] M. Everingham, L. Van Gool, C. K. I. Williams, J. Winn, and A. Zisserman. The PASCAL Visual Object Classes Challenge 2008 (VOC2008) Results. http://www.pascal-network.org/challenges/VOC/voc2008/workshop/index.html.

[41] L. Fei-Fei, R. Fergus, and P. Perona. A Bayesian Approach to Unsupervised One-Shot Learning of Object Categories. In *Proceedings of the IEEE International Conference on Computer Vision (ICCV)*, 2003.

[42] P. Felzenszwalb and D. Huttenlocher. Pictorial Structures for Object Recognition. *International Journal of Computer Vision (IJCV)*, 61(1), 2005.

[43] R. Fergus, L. Fei-Fei, P. Perona, and A. Zisserman. Learning Object Categories from Google's Image Search. In *Proceedings of the IEEE International Conference on Computer Vision (ICCV)*, 2005.

[44] R. Fergus, P. Perona, and A. Zisserman. Object Class Recognition by Unsupervised Scale-Invariant Learning. In *Proceedings of the IEEE Conference on Computer Vision and Pattern Recognition (CVPR)*, 2003.

[45] R. Fergus, Y. Weiss, and A. Torralba. Semi-Supervised Learning in Gigantic Image Collections. In *Neural Information Processing Systems (NIPS)*, 2009.

[46] Carolina Galleguillos, Boris Babenko, Andrew Rabinovich, and Serge Belongie. Weakly Supervised Object Localization with Stable Segmentations. In *ECCV '08: Proceedings of the 10th European Conference on Computer Vision*, pages 193–207. Springer-Verlag, Heidelberg, 2008.

[47] T. Gartner, P. Flach, A. Kowalczyk, and A. Smola. Multi-Instance Kernels. In *Proceedings of International Conference on Machine Learning (ICML)*, 2002.

[48] D. Geman and B. Jedynak. An Active Testing Model for Tracking Roads from Satellite Images. *IEEE Transactions on Pattern Analysis and Machine Intelligence (PAMI)*, 18:1–14, 1996.

[49] K. Grauman and T. Darrell. The Pyramid Match Kernel: Discriminative Classification with Sets of Image Features. In *Proceedings of the IEEE International Conference on Computer Vision (ICCV)*, 2005.

[50] K. Grauman and T. Darrell. Unsupervised Learning of Categories from Sets of Partially Matching Image Features. In *Proceedings of the IEEE Conference on Computer Vision and Pattern Recognition (CVPR)*, 2006.

[51] R. Greiner, A. Grove, and D. Roth. Learning Cost-Sensitive Active Classifiers. *Artificial Intelligence*, 139(2):137–174, 2002.

[52] Y. Guo and D. Schuurmans. Discriminative Batch Mode Active Learning. In *Neural Information Processing Systems (NIPS)*, 2007.

[53] A. Gupta and L. Davis. Beyond Nouns: Exploiting Prepositions and Comparative Adjectives for Learning Visual Classifiers. In *Proceedings of European Conference on Computer Vision (ECCV)*, 2008.

[54] S. Gupta, J. Kim, K. Grauman, and R. Mooney. Watch, Listen & Learn: Co-training on Captioned Images and Videos. In *Proceedings of the European Conference on Machine Learning and Principles and Practice of Knowledge Discovery in Databases (ECML PKDD)*, 2008.

[55] D. Hardoon and J. Shawe-Taylor. KCCA for Different Level Precision in Content-Based Image Retrieval. In *Third International Workshop on Content-Based Multimedia Indexing*, 2003.

[56] X. He, R. Zemel, and M. Carreira-Perpinan. Multiscale Conditional Random Fields for Image Labeling. In *Proceedings of the IEEE Conference on Computer Vision and Pattern Recognition (CVPR)*, 2004.

[57] G. Heitz and D. Koller. Learning Spatial Context: Using Stuff to Find Things. In *Proceedings of European Conference on Computer Vision (ECCV)*, 2008.

[58] T. Hertz, A. Bar-Hillel, and D. Weinshall. Learning Distance Functions for Image Retrieval. In *Proceedings of the IEEE Conference on Computer Vision and Pattern Recognition (CVPR)*, 2004.

[59] S. Hoi, R. Jin, J. Zhu, and M. Lyu. Semi-Supervised SVM Batch Mode Active Learning with Applications to Image Retrieval. *ACM Transactions on Information Systems*, 1(1), 2009.

[60] S. J. Hwang and K. Grauman. Accounting for the Relative Importance of Objects in Image Retrieval. In *British Machine Vision Conference*, 2010.

[61] S. J. Hwang and K. Grauman. Reading Between the Lines: Object Localization Using Implicit Cues from Image Tags. In *Proceedings of the IEEE Conference on Computer Vision and Pattern Recognition (CVPR)*, 2010.

[62] P. Jain and A. Kapoor. Active Learning for Large Multi-Class Problems. In *Proceedings of the IEEE Conference on Computer Vision and Pattern Recognition (CVPR)*, 2009.

[63] P. Jain, B. Kulis, and K. Grauman. Fast Image Search for Learned Metrics. In *Proceedings of the IEEE Conference on Computer Vision and Pattern Recognition (CVPR)*, 2008.

[64] P. Jain, S. Vijayanarasimhan, and K. Grauman. Hashing Hyperplane Queries to Near Points with Applications to Large-Scale Active Learning. In *Neural Information Processing Systems (NIPS)*, 2010.

[65] M. Jamieson, A. Fazly, S. Dickinson, S. Stevenson, and S. Wachsmuth. Learning Structured Appearance Models from Captioned Images of Cluttered Scenes. In *Proceedings of the IEEE International Conference on Computer Vision (ICCV)*, 2007.

[66] Shihao Ji and Lawrence Carin. Cost-Sensitive Feature Acquisition and Classification. *Pattern Recognition*, 2007.

[67] Shihao Ji, R. Parr, and L. Carin. Nonmyopic Multiaspect Sensing with Partially Observable Markov Decision Processes. *IEEE Transactions on Signal Processing*, 2007.

[68] L. Jie, B. Caputo, and V. Ferrari. Who's Doing What: Joint Modeling of Names and Verbs for Simultaneous Face and Pose Annotation. In *Neural Information Processing Systems (NIPS)*, 2009.

[69] A. Joshi, F. Porikli, and N. Papanikolopoulos. Multi-Class Active Learning for Image Classification. In *Proceedings of the IEEE Conference on Computer Vision and Pattern Recognition (CVPR)*, 2009.

[70] A. Kapoor, K. Grauman, R. Urtasun, and T. Darrell. Active Learning with Gaussian Processes for Object Categorization. In *Proceedings of the IEEE International Conference on Computer Vision (ICCV)*, 2007.

[71] A. Kapoor, E. Horvitz, and S. Basu. Selective Supervision: Guiding Supervised Learning with Decision-Theoretic Active Learning. In *International Joint Conference on Artificial Intelligence (IJCAI)*, 2007.

[72] G. Kim, C. Faloutsos, and M. Hebert. Unsupervised Modeling of Object Categories Using Link Analysis Techniques. In *Proceedings of the IEEE Conference on Computer Vision and Pattern Recognition (CVPR)*, 2008.

[73] G. Kim and A. Torralba. Unsupervised Detection of Regions of Interest using Link Analysis. In *Neural Information Processing Systems (NIPS)*, 2009.

[74] A. Krause and C. Guestrin. Nonmyopic Active Learning of Gaussian Processes: an Exploration-Exploitation Approach. In *Proceedings of International Conference on Machine Learning (ICML)*, 2007.

[75] A. Krause and C. Guestrin. Optimal Value of Information in Graphical Models. *Journal of Artificial Intelligence Research (JAIR)*, 35:557–591, 2009.

[76] H. Kuck, P. Carbonetto, and N. de Freitas. A Constrained Semi-Supervised Learning Approach to Data Association. In *Proceedings of European Conference on Computer Vision (ECCV)*, 2004.

[77] M. P. Kumar, P. H. S. Torr, and A. Zisserman. OBJ CUT. In *Proceedings of the IEEE Conference on Computer Vision and Pattern Recognition (CVPR)*, 2005.

[78] C. Lampert, H. Nickisch, and S. Harmeling. Learning to Detect Unseen Object Classes by Between-Class Attribute Transfer. In *Proceedings of the IEEE Conference on Computer Vision and Pattern Recognition (CVPR)*, 2009.

[79] V. Lavrenko, R. Manmatha, and J. Jeon. A Model for Learning the Semantics of Pictures. In *Neural Information Processing Systems (NIPS)*, 2003.

[80] Y. J. Lee and K. Grauman. Foreground Focus: Unsupervised Learning from Partially Matching Images. *International Journal of Computer Vision (IJCV)*, 85(2), May 2009.

[81] Y. J. Lee and K. Grauman. Shape Discovery from Unlabeled Image Collections. In *Proceedings of the IEEE Conference on Computer Vision and Pattern Recognition (CVPR)*, 2009.

[82] Y. J. Lee and K. Grauman. Collect-Cut: Segmentation with Top-Down Cues Discovered in Multi-Object Images. In *Proceedings of the IEEE Conference on Computer Vision and Pattern Recognition (CVPR)*, 2010.

[83] Y. J. Lee and K. Grauman. Object-Graphs for Context-Aware Category Discovery. In *Proceedings of the IEEE Conference on Computer Vision and Pattern Recognition (CVPR)*, 2010.

[84] B. Leibe, A. Leonardis, and B. Schiele. Combined Object Categorization and Segmentation with an Implicit Shape Model. In *Workshop on Statistical Learning in Computer Vision*, 2004.

[85] K. Levi, M. Fink, and Y. Weiss. Learning from a Small Number of Examples by Exploiting Object Categories. In *Workshop of Learning in Computer Vision (LCVPR)*, 2004.

[86] A. Levin, P. Viola, and Y. Freund. Unsupervised Improvement of Visual Detectors Using Cotraining. In *Proceedings of the IEEE International Conference on Computer Vision (ICCV)*, 2003.

[87] L. Li, G. Wang, and L. Fei-Fei. OPTIMOL: Automatic Online Picture Collection via Incremental Model Learning. In *Proceedings of the IEEE Conference on Computer Vision and Pattern Recognition (CVPR)*, 2007.

[88] L.-J. Li, R. Socher, and L. Fei-Fei. Towards Total Scene Understanding: Classification, Annotation and Segmentation in an Automatic Framework. In *Proceedings of the IEEE Conference on Computer Vision and Pattern Recognition (CVPR)*, 2009.

[89] M. Lindenbaum, S. Markovitch, and D. Rusakov. Selective Sampling for Nearest Neighbor Classifiers. *Machine Learning*, 54(2), 2004.

[90] D. Liu and T. Chen. Background Cutout with Automatic Object Discovery. In *Proceedings of the International Conference on Image Processing (ICIP)*, 2007.

[91] D. Liu and T. Chen. Unsupervised Image Categorization and Object Localization using Topic Models and Correspondences between Images. In *Proceedings of the IEEE International Conference on Computer Vision (ICCV)*, 2007.

[92] N. Loeff and A. Farhadi. Scene Discovery by Matrix Factorization. In *Proceedings of European Conference on Computer Vision (ECCV)*, 2008.

[93] D. Lowe. Distinctive Image Features from Scale-Invariant Keypoints. *International Journal of Computer Vision (IJCV)*, 60(2), 2004.

[94] A. Makadia, V. Pavlovic, and S. Kumar. A New Baseline for Image Annotation. In *Proceedings of European Conference on Computer Vision (ECCV)*, 2008.

[95] O. Maron and A. Ratan. Multiple-Instance Learning for Natural Scene Classification. In *Proceedings of International Conference on Machine Learning (ICML)*, 1998.

[96] E. Miller, N. Matsakis, and P. Viola. Learning from One Example through Shared Densities on Transforms. In *Proceedings of the IEEE Conference on Computer Vision and Pattern Recognition (CVPR)*, 2000.

[97] F. Monay and D. Gatica-Perez. On Image Autoannotation with Latent Space Models. In *ACM Multimedia*, 2003.

[98] E. Mortensen and W. Barrett. Intelligent Scissors for Image Composition. In *SIGGRAPH*, 1995.

[99] L. Mukherjee, V. Singh, and C. R. Dyer. Half-Integrality Based Algorithms for Cosegmentation of Images. In *Proceedings of the IEEE Conference on Computer Vision and Pattern Recognition (CVPR)*, 2009.

[100] A. Opelt, A. Pinz, and A. Zisserman. A Boundary-Fragment-Model for Object Detection. In *Proceedings of European Conference on Computer Vision (ECCV)*, pages 575–588, 2006.

[101] N. Panda, K. Goh, and E. Chang. Active Learning in Very Large Image Databases. *Journal of Multimedia Tools and Applications: Special Issue on Computer Vision Meets Databases*, 31(3), December 2006.

[102] Devi Parikh, C. Lawrence Zitnick, and Tsuhan Chen. Unsupervised Learning of Hierarchical Spatial Structures in Images. In *IEEE Conference on Computer Vision and Pattern Recognition*, 2009.

[103] J. Philbin and A. Zisserman. Object Mining using a Matching Graph on Very Large Image Collections. In *Proceedings of the Indian Conference on Computer Vision, Graphics and Image Processing*, 2008.

[104] J. Platt. Probabilistic Outputs for Support Vector Machines and Comparisons to Regularized Likelihood Methods. In *Advances in Large Margin Classifiers*. MIT Press, Cambridge, MA, 1999.

[105] P.Welinder and P. Perona. Online Crowdsourcing: Rating Annotators and Obtaining Cost-Effective Labels. In *Workshop on Advancing Computer Vision with Humans in the Loop at CVPR*, 2010.

[106] G. Qi, X. Hua, Y. Rui, J. Tang, and H. Zhang. Two-Dimensional Active Learning for Image Classification. In *Proceedings of the IEEE Conference on Computer Vision and Pattern Recognition (CVPR)*, 2008.

[107] G. J. Qi, X. S. Hua, and H. J. Zhang. Learning Semantic Distance from Community-Tagged Media Collection. In *Multimedia*, 2009.

[108] T. Quack, V. Ferrari, B. Leibe, and L. Van Gool. Efficient Mining of Frequent and Distinctive Feature Configurations. In *Proceedings of the IEEE International Conference on Computer Vision (ICCV)*, 2007.

[109] A. Quattoni, M. Collins, and T. Darrell. Learning Visual Representations Using Images with Captions. In *Proceedings of the IEEE Conference on Computer Vision and Pattern Recognition (CVPR)*, 2007.

[110] A. Quattoni, M. Collins, and T. Darrell. Transfer Learning for Image Classification with Sparse Prototype Representations. In *Proceedings of the IEEE Conference on Computer Vision and Pattern Recognition (CVPR)*, 2008.

[111] S. Ray and M. Craven. Supervised v. Multiple Instance Learning: An Empirical Comparison. In *Proceedings of International Conference on Machine Learning (ICML)*, 2005.

[112] C. Rosenberg, M. Hebert, and H. Schneiderman. Semi-Supervised Self-Training of Object Detection Models. In *Seventh IEEE Workshop on Applications of Computer Vision*, 2005.

[113] C. Rother, V. Kolmogorov, and A. Blake. Grabcut: Interactive Foreground Extraction Using Iterated Graph Cuts. In *ACM Transactions on Graphics*, 2004.

[114] C. Rother, V. Kolmogorov, T. Minka, and A. Blake. Cosegmentation of Image Pairs by Histogram Matching — Incorporating a Global Constraint into MRFs. In *Proceedings of the IEEE Conference on Computer Vision and Pattern Recognition (CVPR)*, 2006.

[115] B. Russell, A. Efros, J. Sivic, W. Freeman, and A. Zisserman. Using Multiple Segmentations to Discover Objects and their Extent in Image Collections. In *Proceedings of the IEEE Conference on Computer Vision and Pattern Recognition (CVPR)*, 2006.

[116] B. Russell, A. Torralba, K. Murphy, and W. Freeman. LabelMe: A Database and Web-Based Tool for Image Annotation. Technical report, Massachusetts Institute of Technology, Cambridge, MA 2005.

[117] A. Saffari, C. Leistner, and H. Bischof. Regularized Multi-Class Semi-Supervised Boosting. In *Proceedings of the IEEE Conference on Computer Vision and Pattern Recognition (CVPR)*, 2009.

[118] G. Schohn and D. Cohn. Less is More: Active Learning with Support Vector Machines. In *Proceedings of International Conference on Machine Learning (ICML)*, 2000.

[119] F. Schroff, A. Criminisi, and A. Zisserman. Harvesting Image Databases from the Web. In *Proceedings of the IEEE International Conference on Computer Vision (ICCV)*, 2007.

[120] B. Settles, M. Craven, and S. Ray. Multiple-Instance Active Learning. In *Neural Information Processing Systems (NIPS)*, 2008.

[121] Burr Settles. Active Learning Literature Survey. Technical Report 1648, University of Wisconsin–Madison, 2009.

[122] G. Shakhnarovich, P. Viola, and T. Darrell. Fast Pose Estimation with Parameter-Sensitive Hashing. In *Proceedings of the IEEE International Conference on Computer Vision (ICCV)*, 2003.

[123] J. Shi and J. Malik. Normalized Cuts and Image Segmentation. *IEEE Transactions on Pattern Analysis and Machine Intelligence (PAMI)*, 22(8):888–905, August 2000.

[124] J. Shotton, J. Winn, C. Rother, and A. Criminisi. Textonboost: Joint Appearance, Shape and Context Modeling for Multi-Class Object Recognition and Segmentation. In *Proceedings of European Conference on Computer Vision (ECCV)*, 2006.

[125] B. Siddiquie and A. Gupta. Beyond Active Noun Tagging: Modeling Contextual Interactions for Multi-Class Active Learning. In *Proceedings of the IEEE Conference on Computer Vision and Pattern Recognition (CVPR)*, 2010.

[126] J. Sivic, B. Russell, A. Efros, A. Zisserman, and W. Freeman. Discovering Object Categories in Image Collections. In *Proceedings of the IEEE International Conference on Computer Vision (ICCV)*, 2005.

[127] Josef Sivic, Mark Everingham, and Andrew Zisserman. "Who Are You?" — Learning Person Specific Classifiers from Video. In *Proceedings of the IEEE Conference on Computer Vision and Pattern Recognition (CVPR)*, 2009.

[128] A. Sorokin and D. Forsyth. Utility Data Annotation with Amazon Mechanical Turk. In *Proceedings of the CVPR Workshop on Internet Vision*, 2008.

[129] M. Spain and P. Perona. Some Objects Are More Equal Than Others: Measuring and Predicting Importance. In *Proceedings of European Conference on Computer Vision (ECCV)*, 2008.

[130] M. Stark, M. Goesele, and B. Schiele. A Shape-Based Object Class Model for Knowledge Transfer. In *Proceedings of the IEEE International Conference on Computer Vision (ICCV)*, 2009.

[131] S. Todorovic and N. Ahuja. Extracting Subimages of an Unknown Category from a Set of Images. In *Proceedings of the IEEE Conference on Computer Vision and Pattern Recognition (CVPR)*, 2006.

[132] S. Tong and D. Koller. Support Vector Machine Active Learning with Applications to Text Classification. In *Proceedings of International Conference on Machine Learning (ICML)*, 2000.

[133] T. Tuytelaars, C. Lampert, M. Blaschko, and W. Buntine. Unsupervised Object Discovery: A Comparison. *International Journal of Computer Vision (IJCV)*, 2009.

[134] S. Vijayanarasimhan and K. Grauman. Keywords to Visual Categories: Multiple-Instance Learning for Weakly Supervised Object Categorization. In *Proceedings of the IEEE Conference on Computer Vision and Pattern Recognition (CVPR)*, 2008.

[135] S. Vijayanarasimhan and K. Grauman. Multi-Level Active Prediction of Useful Image Annotations for Recognition. In *Neural Information Processing Systems (NIPS)*, 2008.

[136] S. Vijayanarasimhan and K. Grauman. What's It Going to Cost You?: Predicting Effort vs. Informativeness for Multi-Label Image Annotations. In *Proceedings of the IEEE Conference on Computer Vision and Pattern Recognition (CVPR)*, 2009.

[137] S. Vijayanarasimhan and K. Grauman. Cost-Sensitive Active Visual Category Learning. *International Journal of Computer Vision (IJCV)*, 91(1), 2011.

[138] S. Vijayanarasimhan and K. Grauman. Large-Scale Live Active Learning: Training Object Detectors with Crawled Data and Crowds. In *Proceedings of the IEEE Conference on Computer Vision and Pattern Recognition (CVPR)*, 2011.

[139] S. Vijayanarasimhan, P. Jain, and K. Grauman. Far-Sighted Active Learning on a Budget for Image and Video Recognition. In *Proceedings of the IEEE Conference on Computer Vision and Pattern Recognition (CVPR)*, 2010.

[140] S. Vijayanarasimhan and A. Kapoor. Visual Recognition and Detection Under Bounded Computational Resources. In *Proceedings of the IEEE Conference on Computer Vision and Pattern Recognition (CVPR)*, 2010.

[141] P. Viola, J. Platt, and C. Zhang. Multiple Instance Boosting for Object Detection. In *Neural Information Processing Systems (NIPS)*, 2005.

[142] L. von Ahn and L. Dabbish. Labeling Images with a Computer Game. In *Proceedings of the ACM Conference on Human Factors in Computing Systems*, 2004.

[143] L. von Ahn, R. Liu, and M. Blum. Peekaboom: A Game for Locating Objects in Images. In *SIGCHI*, 2006.

[144] M. Weber, M. Welling, and P. Perona. Unsupervised Learning of Models for Recognition. In *Proceedings of European Conference on Computer Vision (ECCV)*, 2000.

[145] P. Welinder, S. Branson, S. Belongie, and P. Perona. The Multidimensional Wisdom of Crowds. In *Neural Information Processing Systems (NIPS)*, 2010.

[146] J. Winn and N. Jojic. LOCUS: Learning Object Classes with Unsupervised Segmentation. In *Proceedings of the IEEE International Conference on Computer Vision (ICCV)*, 2005.

[147] Ting-Fan Wu, Chih-Jen Lin, and Ruby C. Weng. Probability Estimates for Multi-Class Classification by Pairwise Coupling. *JMLR*, 2004.

[148] O. Yakhnenko and V. Honavar. Multiple Label Prediction for Image Annotation with Multiple Kernel Correlation Models. In *Workshop on Visual Context Learning, in conjunction with CVPR*, 2009.

[149] R. Yan, J. Yang, and A. Hauptmann. Automatically Labeling Video Data using Multi-Class Active Learning. In *Proceedings of the IEEE International Conference on Computer Vision (ICCV)*, 2003.

[150] C. Yang and T. Lozano-Perez. Image Database Retrieval with Multiple-Instance Learning Techniques. In *ICDE*, 2000.

[151] T. Yeh, K. Tollmar, and T. Darrell. Searching the Web with Mobile Images for Location Recognition. In *Proceedings of the IEEE Conference on Computer Vision and Pattern Recognition (CVPR)*, 2004.

[152] S. Yu, R. Gross, and J. Shi. Concurrent Object Recognition and Segmentation by Graph Partitioning. In *Neural Information Processing Systems (NIPS)*, 2002.

[153] J. Yuan, B. Russell, C. Liu, and A. Torralba. LabelMe Video: Building a Video Database with Human Annotations. In *Proceedings of the IEEE Conference on Computer Vision and Pattern Recognition (CVPR)*, 2009.

[154] Zheng-Jun Zha, Xian-Sheng Hua, Tao Mei, Jingdong Wang, Guo-Jun Qi, and Zengfu Wang. Joint Multi-Label Multi-Instance Learning for Image Classification. In *Proceedings of the IEEE Conference on Computer Vision and Pattern Recognition (CVPR)*, 2008.

[155] C. Zhang, X. Chen, M. Chen, S. Chen, and M. Shyu. A Multiple Instance Learning Approach for Content Based Image Retrieval Using One-Class Support Vector Machine. In *ICME*, 2005.

[156] Min L. Zhang and Zhi H. Zhou. Multi-Label Learning by Instance Differentiation. In *Proceedings AAAI*, 2007.

[157] Q. Zhang and S. Goldman. EM-DD: An Improved Multiple-Instance Learning Technique. In *Neural Information Processing Systems (NIPS)*, 2002.

[158] Zhi H. Zhou and Min L. Zhang. Multi-Instance Multi-Label Learning with Application to Scene Classification. In *Neural Information Processing Systems (NIPS)*, 2006.

[159] Xiaojin Zhu. Semi-Supervised Learning Literature Survey. Technical Report 1530, University of Wisconsin–Madison, 2005.

Chapter 7

Reliability and Redundancy: Reducing Error Cost in Medical Imaging

Xiang Sean Zhou, Yiqiang Zhan, Zhigang Peng, Maneesh Dewan, Bing Jian, Arun Krishnan

Siemens Healthcare, Malvern, Pennsylvania

Martin Harder, Raphael Schwarz, Lars Lauer, Heiko Meyer

Siemens Healthcare, Erlangen, Germany

Stefan Grosskopf, Ute Feuerlein, and Hendrik Ditt

Siemens Healthcare, Forchheim, Germany

7.1 Introduction

Cost-sensitive learning is a very relevant topic in the domain of medical decision support. There are many types of costs, both monetary and non-monetary. The non-monetary costs include factors that may be difficult to quantify, such as side effects of drugs, tests, or therapy, or quality of life (QoL) [18] impact due to medical interventions, etc.

7.1.1 Cost-Sensitive Learning for Medical Decision Support

In the literature, two important categories of costs have been discussed: the first is the cost of (medical) tests; the second is the asymmetric costs associated with different errors [7].

7.1.1.1 Cost of Tests

All medical tests have associated monetary costs. Aside from that, some medical tests are not completely safe or free of side effects. Such potential harm should be considered as cost for the test as well, although in many cases it is difficult to quantify. On the monetary side, costs vary greatly from one test to another. For example, a magnetic resonance imaging (MRI), computed tomography (CT), or positron emission tomography (PET) scan typically cost much more than a x-ray or ultrasound scan. On the non-monetary side, some tests cause direct or accumulative harm to the patient. For example, the ionizing radiation associated with a x-ray, CT or PET scan are hazardous to the human body and excessive exposure can cause cancer or other diseases. We typically avoid such modalities on pregnant mothers (for whom ultrasound is the safer choice) or sensitive organs such as the brain (for which repeated scientific studies are often conducted using MRI).

Of course, all tests are not the same, and the applicability and benefit vary greatly from one test to another. For example, ultrasound is both low-cost and safe, but its resolution, sensitivity, or specificity are in many cases limited as compared to CT or MRI.

For an example analysis of how to incorporate such test costs in a classification framework, see [4].

7.1.1.2 Cost of Errors

The second category of cost is the cost of errors [7]. The two common types of errors (false positives and false negatives) have rather different implications. If a computer algorithm (or a human doctor) missed an early sign of a cancer that would have been curable in its initial stage, this could lead to the unnecessary early loss of life for the patient. This is obviously the kind of "deadly" cost one should try very hard to avoid. On the other hand, if the algorithm (or the doctor) made the mistake of sounding a false alarm, the cost could be high as well, because a false alarm often leads to unnecessary follow-up tests, additional procedures such as biopsies which can be excruciatingly painful, emotional stress for the patient and family, lost time and income, etc.

7.1.1.3 To Learn, or Not to Learn

When quality of life (QoL) [18] factors are taken into consideration, sometimes even non-errors (i.e., correct classification/diagnosis) can carry exceedingly high cost due to its negative consequences in terms of QoL. This can be the case, for example, for someone getting to know about an uncontrollable and incurable disease. In this case, it is not a matter of *how to do learning* (either cost-sensitive or not), but rather *whether one wants to learn (about the painful truth) at all*. Such type of analysis will be complex and can be controversial, especially if it ventures into the domain of public policy recommendations.

7.1.2 Can Self-Awareness Reduce the Cost of Errors?

In this chapter, we focus only on the cost of errors. In particular, we ask the question whether a computer algorithm can be aware of its own errors so that it can alert the human user whenever an error occurs. This way, a high level of automation can be achieved which can reduce human fatigue and errors. And the human intelligence and alertness are best utilized on those uncertain cases raised by the computer.

Overall, the cost associated with errors can be eliminated or at least dramatically reduced. This scenario is relevant for applications in which a computer program is used to automate or speed up an otherwise tedious or time-consuming task for a human user.

Unfortunately, such self-awareness is not a very meaningful concept in classification. For example, in the case of two-class classification, if the algorithm knows or believes that it is making a mistake, it would have just switched the output class label.

However, there is a class of image analysis or computer vision problems for which such a self-awareness concept would be useful. These are the problems of pattern localizations in images, for which an algorithm could be designed to achieve some self-awareness of errors. Reliable alerts of potential algorithmic errors can trigger corrective steps by a human user, thus reducing the overall error cost.

Below, we describe an example scenario in medical imaging, and motivate our proposed new concept of *reliability* as a new performance measure for self-awareness.

7.1.3 Self-Awareness for Pattern Localization in Medical Images

For medical imaging applications, the operator often needs to find certain anatomical structures such as the pelvis, heart, liver, or knee meniscus from scout images.[1] Based on the target location (and orientation), with the patient instructed to stay still, the operator can then acquire high-resolution 3D images focused on (and aligned with) the target structure.

An algorithm that can automatically find these anatomical structures would make the imaging process faster and more consistent, eliminating potential human errors or variabilities.

The users of such pattern localization algorithms often ask, in a wishful tone, "*Can your algorithm alert me when it fails?*" Because this would then truly improve the user experience: the user can sit back and relax, and steps in to intervene *only* when the algorithm stops and pops up an alert.

Indeed, *know-thy-failure* would be a very desirable property for any computer vision algorithms. However, is this a meaningful requirement? In other words, is it possible to achieve at all?—A classifier may know it is *unsure* based on, e.g., a small margin [19], but as mentioned earlier, it would not know its own *failures*. If it knew it was making a mistake, it would have switched its answer to avoid that error. For pattern localization problems though, this is indeed a meaningful concept and requirement. The question is how, and to what degree, it can be satisfied.

We try to answer these questions in more detail in Section 7.3 by first defining in Section 7.2 a quantitative measure for this *know-thy-failure* requirement. We then discuss algorithmic strategies toward satisfying such a requirement in Section 7.4.

7.2   A Measure of Reliability

7.2.1   Self-Assessment

To report its own failures, an algorithm should add a self-assessment step and provide a categorical assessment for each of its outputs. Probabilities

---

[1]A scout scan, 2D or 3D, is conducted as the first step during a CT or MR scan to establish an anatomical reference to the internal organ or structure of interest.

and margins can be very informative [19, 3] but a clear-cut judgment has to be made for each output of the algorithm because *to alert, or not to alert (the user), that is the question.* A "40% of chance that the output is a false positive" is not very actionable.

A naive but actionable self-assessment, for those algorithms that output probabilities or margins, is to declare all decisions with small margins, or on-the-fence probabilities, as "failures." This strategy, however, is more "knowing-thy-uncertainty" than "knowing-thy-failure," and can have a high false alarm rate.

Ideally, *the self-assessment should be based on new information beyond that used already for deriving the original answer.* This may not be possible in a classification setting with a fixed feature space. But for computer vision applications, new information can always be extracted from the images (*"An image is worth a thousand words"*) and they do help—for example, a *"tree"* or *"monkey"* detector should be helpful in assessing *"human face"* detection results by resolving ambiguities, e.g., faces detected on tree barks or monkeys.

Definition 1 (Integrated assessment and **postmortem assessment)** An **integrated assessment** is a self-assessment fed back and fused with the original answer. This is, however, not always possible if, for example, an initial answer is required in a timely manner and its assessment can only be computed afterward or the assessment uses information from future cases or accumulated population statistics. In this case the assessment is **postmortem** in nature.

7.2.2 The Reliability Measure

Table 7.1 shows the traditional confusion matrix for actual and predicted positives P and $\tilde{P}$, and negatives N and $\tilde{N}$, respectively. The cells in the matrix contain the numbers of test cases in four different categories: true positives (TP), false positives (FP), true negatives (TN), and false negatives (FN).

The algorithm's performance in terms of *sensitivity* S, *specificity* C, and *accuracy* A are defined as follows:

$$S = TP/P, \quad C = TN/N, \quad A = (TP + TN)/(P + N), \quad (7.1)$$

where $P = TP + FN$ and $N = FP + TN$.

Denoting the algorithm's self-assessments of the four output types as

TABLE 7.1:
Confusion matrix.

	P	N
$\tilde{P}$	TP	FP
$\tilde{N}$	FN	TN

TABLE 7.2:   Reliability confusion matrix.

	TP	FP	TN	FN
$\mathcal{E}(TP)$	n_1	n_5	0	0
$\mathcal{E}(FP)$	n_6	n_2	0	0
$\mathcal{E}(TN)$	0	0	n_3	n_7
$\mathcal{E}(FN)$	0	0	n_8	n_4

$\mathcal{E}(TP)$, $\mathcal{E}(FP)$, $\mathcal{E}(TN)$, and $\mathcal{E}(FN)$, a confusion matrix can be constructed between the actual performance and self-assessed performance as in Table 7.2.

Here, n_2, for example, is the total number of all those test cases that the algorithm has labeled as "Positive" *incorrectly* (i.e., these are actual *FP*s) while the assessment module of the algorithm believes the output is "Incorrect." Although the algorithm is wrong in its judgment of the cases, it is nevertheless correct in judging itself—it knows about its own failures. Whereas n_6 is the number of cases that the algorithm labeled as "Positive" *correctly* (i.e., these are actual *TP*s) while the assessment module still believed them to be "Incorrect." For these cases, the algorithm is actually correct in its outputs, but wrong in its self-assessment—it does not know its successes.

Similarly, n_3 is the number of cases that the algorithm labeled as "Negative" *correctly* (i.e., these are actual *TN*s) while its assessment module labeled these outputs as "Correct." These are examples of "knowing thy successes" (this is the case for n_1 as well). Whereas n_7 is the number of cases that the algorithm labeled as "Negative" *incorrectly* (i.e., these are *FN*s) while its assessment module believed such outputs to be "Correct." The algorithm does not know its failures in these cases.

The 0s in this matrix indicate situations that are not meaningful. For example, if the algorithm labels a test case "Negative," its assessment module will only need to judge whether this labeling is "Correct" (i.e., $\mathcal{E}(TN)$) or "Incorrect" (i.e., $\mathcal{E}(FN)$).

Based on this table, a *reliability* measure, $\mathcal{R}$, can be simply defined as the ratio of the diagonal sum (i.e., all the cases for which the algorithm knows its failures or its successes) over the matrix sum (i.e., all cases, including those cases where the algorithm misjudged its failures or its successes):

$$\mathcal{R} = \frac{\sum_{i=1}^{4} n_i}{\sum_{j=1}^{8} n_j}. \tag{7.2}$$

With this formulation, all assessments are equally weighted: a false alert (that labels a good output as bad) is equally bad as an uncaught error, and a recognition of success is as good as a detection of failure.

Remark 1. *In general, high $\mathcal{R}$ does not necessarily mean high $\mathcal{S}$, $\mathcal{C}$, or $\mathcal{A}$, and vice versa.*

An algorithm can perform poorly, but achieve high reliability. For example, a bad algorithm for iris (or heart) localization with many misses (*FN*s) may have a high reliability if a very good face (or lung) detector is employed as part of the self-assessment: the algorithm will know that many "$\tilde{N}$s" are "*FN*s" ($n_4 \gg 0$). If n_4 dominates Eq. 7.2, the reliability score will be high. Conversely, an overly cautious assessment module for a highly *accurate* algorithm may spew out many false alerts.

Remark 2. *Assuming* **integrated assessment,** *for a pure two-class classification problem,* $\mathcal{R} = \mathcal{A}$.

This is because the classifier would not report any $\mathcal{E}(FP)$ or $\mathcal{E}(FN)$ because it would have simply switched the class label for those cases, thus lumping n_2 into n_3, n_6 into n_7, n_4 into n_1, and n_8 into n_5. The *reliability* $\mathcal{R} = (n_1 + n_3)/(n_1 + n_5 + n_3 + n_7)$ reduces to the traditional *accuracy* measure $\mathcal{A}$ of Eq. (7.1). In other words, *what the algorithm knows can be* fully *integrated into its outputs.* The *reliability* measure will not provide any new information. Similar can be said of multi-class classification.

However, whenever the algorithm's knowledge (i.e., self-assessment) cannot be *fully* integrated into its output, the *reliability* score becomes meaningful and informative. This is the case for pattern localization: the algorithm may know that the heart should be in the image according to the scene context, but just could not locate it *directly* because of, for example, diseases—see Figure 7.3 (h). Here *knowing an error does not automatically correct it.*

7.3 Reliability of Pattern Localization: Asymmetric Cost for *FP*s and *FN*s

Definition 2 (Pattern detection vs. **Pattern localization)** The goal of **pattern detection** is to detect all instances of a pattern in a given image, in which the number of instances k is unknown, $k \in \{0, 1, 2, ...\}$. If $k \in \{1\}$, it is specifically referred to as **pattern localization**.

Examples of **pattern localization** problems are common in the medical imaging domain—one use case was defined at the beginning of this chapter, and more are discussed in Section 7.4. One example of non-medical use cases is a vision-based driver detection system equipped in an intelligent car, where the number of driver will always be one: $k \in \{1\}$.

Note that for this class of problems, a localization error in a *TP* image yields both an *FP* and an *FN*.

Figure 7.1 illustrates some examples of *TP*, *FP*, *TN*, and *FN* from a face detection algorithm.

Remark 3. *Assuming* **integrated assessment,** *for a pattern detection problem:* $n_2 = n_6 = 0$.

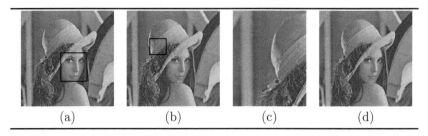

(a)   (b)   (c)   (d)

FIGURE 7.1: Possible outputs of a face detection algorithm. (a) a *TP* detection/localization (black box); (b) an *FP* detection (black box) and an *FN* or missed detection; (c) a *TN*; (d) an *FN* or missed detection.

If the algorithm believed that an original answer of "$\tilde{P}$" was actually wrong, it would have modified it to an "$\tilde{N}$." As a result, n_2 and n_6 would be lumped into n_3 and n_7. More precisely, n_6 would be lumped into n_7, n_2 would move into n_3 (for *TN* cases) or n_7 (for *FN* cases)—the last scenario is possible when, for example, an *FP* face detection on a tree trunk was discovered, but a real face existed in another part of the image. Going one step further, if the assessment of an *FP* case prompted the algorithm logic to select a new location as a positive return, n_2 would actually shift into n_1. In any case, n_2 will end up being zero.

Remark 4. *Assuming **integrated assessment**, for a pure pattern localization problem: $n_3 = n_7 = n_8 = 0 \Longrightarrow \{\mathcal{R} = 100\% \Longleftrightarrow FP \; rate = 0\}$.*[2]

It is easy to see that $n_3 = n_7 = n_8 = 0$ because for a pure pattern localization problem, there are no *TN*s, therefore, in Table 7.2 the whole third row (*TN*) and third column ($\mathcal{E}(TN)$) should be empty.

From remark 3 we also have $n_2 = n_6 = 0$. Therefore, $\mathcal{R} = \frac{n_1+n_4}{n_1+n_4+n_5}$, and $\mathcal{R} = 100\%$ iff $n_5 = 0$.

Remark 4 points a path to high *reliability*: pick the operating point on the ROC curve so that the *FP* rate is as low as possible, while maintaining an acceptable level of accuracy $\mathcal{A}$. A *reliability*-demanding user would rather prefer, for example, a system with 0% *FP*s and 5% *FN*s over one with 2% *FP*s and 2% *FN*s, because the former system is mostly autonomous, while the latter requires continuous human supervision just to catch those 2% *FP*s. When pushed to the extreme, one reaches a trivial and "lazy" solution to achieve a zero *FP* rate thus 100% *reliability*: The algorithm can just give up and alert the user that "I have failed to find the target" for *all* cases ($n_1 = n_5 = 0$). But of course this is of no practical interest because $\mathcal{A} = 0$.

In real-world situations, however, $k \in \{1\}$ is never guaranteed and there is always exceptions. When a car is moving, a driver should be there. But he or she may be so tall or so short that the face or eyes are out of the field of view

---

[2]Also true is that the positive predictive value $PPV = TP/(TP + FP) = 100\%$.

of the monitoring camera. When a patient is scanned, the technologist could have incorrectly registered the patient position, and the algorithm would end up searching for a knee inside an image of the brain.

To summarize, in order to push toward a 100% reliability, one has to reduce off-diagonal terms in Table 7.2. This boils down to two requirements in a typical real-world use case as discussed above:

1. No false positives ($n_5 = 0$);
2. Know false negatives from true negatives ($n_7 = n_8 = 0$).

An algorithm's ability to detect and recognize those relatively rare *TN* cases would be very useful, especially if different handling were to be applied, such as customized logic in the host application or specific messages to the user. For example, when a wrong body part or orientation is scanned, it is important for the algorithm to recognize it and alert the operator for correction, instead of a general fail-to-locate message or even worse, a false positive finding.

7.4 Implications and Learning Strategy for Medical Imaging Applications

In natural image understanding, humans achieve high *reliability* through a logical understanding of the whole scene. As an **integrated assessment** step, this effectively removes *FPs* ($n_5 \to 0$) and confirms *TNs* ($n_7, n_8 \to 0$). This step is, in general, not easy to imitate by an algorithm because natural images have unlimited variability in scene composition and lighting variations[3][26].

However, for medical images, scene understanding is much more feasible due to the constrained nature of the imaging process and redundancies in the images. This is especially true for anatomical imaging based on x-ray, CT, MRI, etc.

7.4.1 Anatomical Pattern Localization for Medical Imaging

Figures 7.2–7.4 show three example applications. For all three, the goal is to find in a 2D or 3D image a target anatomical structure, e.g., the meniscus of the knee, the bounding box for the pelvis, or the center of each vertebra. In some cases, the scale and/or orientation of the target are needed as well. Undetected mistakes can be harmful to the patient, in which case they should be avoided at all cost. For example, for Application II, a bigger-than-necessary box will result in an unnecessarily high level of radiation to the patient and less voxel resolution. On the other hand, a smaller-than-necessary box means

---

[3]In ambiguous cases, even human vision can be fooled: our eyes often fail to connect all the dots (e.g., of a Dalmatian dog [10], p.14) when visual cues are sparse.

missing information, which may prompt the need for a rescan, resulting in waste of time and added radiation to the patient, again.

Although these applications are specific and well constrained, they are still very challenging due to the unusually high requirements of medical applications [29], and the very nature of medical imaging that *anomaly is the norm*. Some of the difficult cases are shown in Figures 7.2–7.4.

How does a human learn and perform these tasks with such high reliability? It is important to notice that when a disease or an artifact affects an anatomical structure, the remaining portions of the structure or other anatomical structures would hint at its existence and extent. It is *redundancy* that the human visual recognition system exploits to *reliably* recognize a scene, simultaneously with its structure and components.

7.4.2 The Whole is *Less* Than the Sum of Its Parts

When it comes to visual object recognition and localization, *the whole is less than the sum of its parts*. In other words, one does not need to see *all* the trees in order to see the forest. A subset of all the parts is often sufficient to reveal the whole. This is a general rule but in medical imaging, the subset can be even smaller due to well-defined imaging protocols and strong prior knowledge. Humans can make a well-educated guess of the extent of the target anatomies in most of Figure 7.3 because sufficient evidence of its parts is present within the image.

Furthermore, there are "long-range" or "distant" relationships or constraints, all the way from head to toe, that provide strong redundancies for anatomical modeling: kidneys do not exist in a head and neck scan; and in a whole body scan, the pelvis is always *below* the lung in a predictable way. These are just simple examples of a very rich set of anatomical constraints that could be employed to improve reliability.

7.4.3 Improving Reliability through a Spatial Ensemble Method

Based on the above analysis, we adopt a relatively straightforward strategy to achieve high *reliability*: The basic idea is to collect a more-than-necessary amount of evidence, not only on and around the target, but also (far) away from the target, and fuse them using a voting algorithm constrained by spatial configuration models [28]. This is analogous to existing ensemble methods such as bagging predictors [2] which make *redundant* use of the training set by resampling. We call our strategy spatial ensemble through realignment, or SERA. More details are given below.

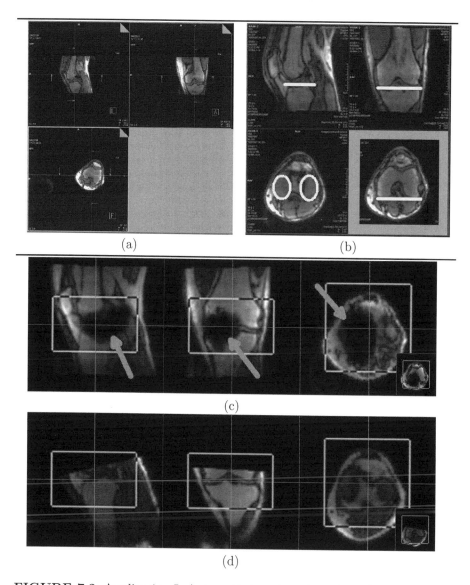

FIGURE 7.2: Application I: Automatic imaging plane detection in 3D MR scout images. (a) Input: Scout scan of a knee; (b) Desired output: aligned for optimal imaging of the menisci; (c) Examples of disease/artifact occluding target (arrow); and (d) Missing anatomy. Images are "straightened" or re-oriented in 3D. Rectangles show desired localization.

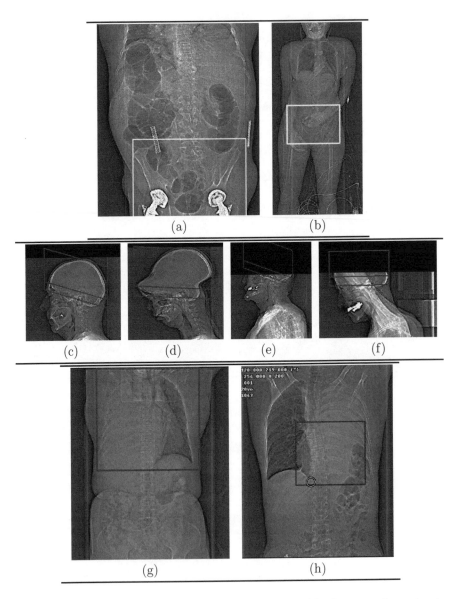

FIGURE 7.3: Application II: Automatic organ and body parts detection in CT topograms.

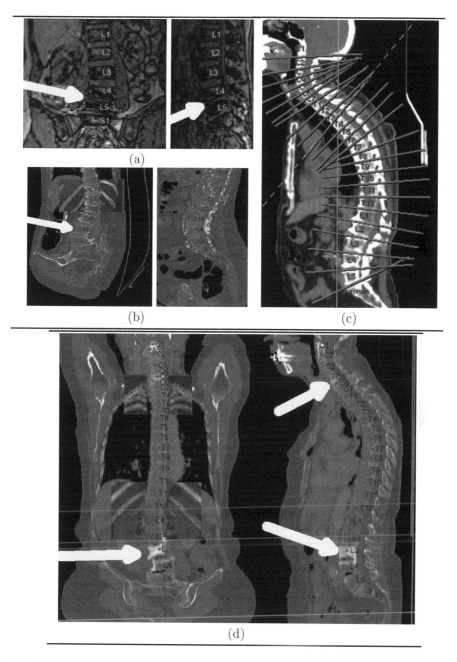

FIGURE 7.4: Application III: Automatic vertebra localization and labeling for MR (a) and CT (b–d). Notice that with abnormal patient positioning (b) and diseases (arrows) and at very low resolution and low CT dose (d), the algorithm can perform faster and more consistently than humans.

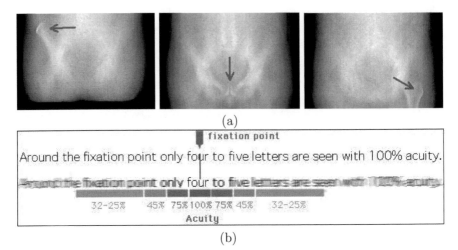

FIGURE 7.5: Realigned spatial ensemble resembles the foveal vision system, with each bag collecting a specific piece of foveal evidence. (a) Medians of *foveal* evidence around pelvis from about 300 CT topograms. Arrows indicate the points of "foveal fixation" achieved by realigning the training set. (b) Human foveal vision takes in only local evidence with a blurred peripheral context [23, 11].

7.4.3.1   Spatial Ensemble through Realignment (SERA)

Given a training set $\mathcal{L} = \{(y_n, \boldsymbol{x}_n), n = 1, ..., N\}$ where the ys are the class labels and $\boldsymbol{x}$s are the inputs, and a learning algorithm that uses this set to form a predictor $\varphi(\boldsymbol{x}, \mathcal{L})$, a bagging predictor can be formulated as below [2]:

$$\varphi_B(\boldsymbol{x}) = av_B\varphi(\boldsymbol{x}, \mathcal{L}^{(B)}). \tag{7.3}$$

where $\mathcal{L}^{(B)}$s are the bootstrap samples or bags, and av_B denotes averaging or voting.

In the context of this chapter, $\boldsymbol{x}$ is an image (or a volume). We redefine the bootstraping step *spatially* instead of *sample-wise*, with each bag using *all* the images in the training set, but realigned by different anatomical landmarks. Denoting the realignment process of the training set as $A_i \circledast \mathcal{L}$, with A_i representing the ith alignment parameters and $\circledast$ the alignment operation, we have:

$$\varphi_A(\boldsymbol{x}) = vote_i\varphi(\boldsymbol{x}, A_i \circledast \mathcal{L}), \tag{7.4}$$

with a similar number of realignment as the typical number of bags: $|A| \approx |B|$ (Breiman [2] suggests about 20 and our experiments confirmed this number to be reasonable).

Figure 7.5(a) shows medians of some of the realigned bags based on some landmarks around the pelvis. The spatial ensemble makes sense because it somewhat resembles the human's foveal vision system [21, 23], which makes repeated examinations of the same scene with different focus points. Figure 7.5(b) is an illustration of how the human visual system works at any given time point: only a small neighborhood is in focus and the context is blurred [11]. Repeated examinations of multiple focal points in the scene eventually arrives at, and confirms, a consensus recognition of the scene. Figure 7.6 compares the spatial ensemble with classic ensemble methods. For each "bag" of a re-aligned training set, a separate *foveal* detector is trained in the form of a classifier C_i (see Figure 7.6). Several existing algorithms can be used for this, including AdaBoost-based algorithms or the random forest/ferns algorithms (e.g., [16, 13]). It is interesting to note that, for matching objects in natural images and video, Lepetit and Fua [13] also used a large set of local evidence to ensure robustness. (The difference is that they could assume a known space of variations and thus synthesize as many training data as needed. This is not possible in our case in that we have neither unlimited training data nor anticipated variations.)

Once the foveal evidence is gathered, a majority vote can robustly answer the question as to whether the target is in the image or not, and roughly where. To be more precise, we employ data-driven spatial configuration models to further remove potential error detections, and use the remaining confirmed evidences to predict the target parameters.

7.4.3.2 Data-Driven Sparse Configuration Models

The aim of this module is to detect outliers robustly (i.e., with a high breakdown point), by learning from the annotated landmarks on the training dataset. Denote the conditional probability of one piece of foveal evidence or landmark location $\mathbf{p}_i$ given other landmarks as $P(\mathbf{p}_i|\mathbf{P}_{\bar{i}})$. If all the $\mathbf{p}_j$s in the set $\mathbf{P}_{\bar{i}}$ are correct, this probability can be used to measure the quality of $\mathbf{p}_i$. However, since it is not known which of the $\mathbf{p}_j$s are erroneous, we resort to a RANSAC-type strategy by sampling many subsets of landmarks and detecting the outliers from the samples.

To address the potential challenge that the majority portion of a target anatomical pattern may be missing or occluded or altered by disease or artifacts—see for example Figure 7.2(c) and Figure 7.3(b, e–h)—we suggest the use of small or *sparse* $\mathbf{P}_{\bar{i}}$s. In other words, a landmark is judged by only a small subset of others every time. In this chapter, we take every pair or triple of landmarks to form a voting group and construct predictors only among themselves. This kind of *sparsity*, and *"democracy"* (i.e., aggregation of many *small* decisions), has two advantages: a decision can be made even when only a scarce set of evidence is available; and the final decision is robust to a potentially high percentage of erroneous detections, as long as they are *inconsistent* with one another.

The vote received by landmark point $\mathbf{p}_i$ is denoted by $\eta(\mathbf{p}_i|\mathbf{P}_v)$, where $\mathbf{P}_v$ is a voting group. The vote is defined as $\mathbf{p}_i$'s likelihood of being accepted or predicted by $\mathbf{P}_v$ based on the conditional distribution estimated using the

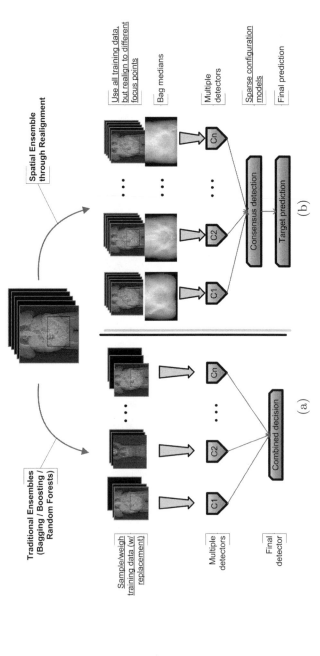

FIGURE 7.6: Spatial ensemble through realignment. (a) Traditional ensemble; (b) SERA: Spatial ensemble based on different focus points, with each bag reusing *all* images and *all* context.

annotated training set. Assuming Gaussianity with mean ν_i and covariance Σ, the vote is simply

$$\eta(\mathbf{p}_i|\mathbf{P}_v) = \frac{1}{(2\pi)^{D/2}|\Sigma|^{1/2}} e^{-\frac{1}{2}(\mathbf{p}_i-\nu_i)^T \Sigma^{-1}(\mathbf{p}_i-\nu_i)}, \tag{7.5}$$

where $D \in \{2,3\}$ is the dimensionality of the image. A non-parametric approach would also work where a training database is used to provide nearest neighbors as references on the fly.

The collection of all groups is an overly redundant representation of the spatial relationship among the parts of an anatomical structure—even if severe diseases affect many landmarks resulting in wrong or missed detections, a consensus can still form among the remaining landmarks.

7.4.3.3 Rule-Based Evidence Fusion

This is a commonly applied strategy for improving traditional performance measures such as *accuracy*. This strategy should be utilized for self-assessment to improve *reliability* as well. For example, for App-III, whether the algorithm has failed to detect the fifth lumbar vertebra (L5)—i.e., an *FN*, in which case it must alert the user—or the patient has a sacralization of L5—i.e., a normal anatomical variant thus a *TN*, in which case the algorithm should not report a failure—can be disambiguated by evidence gathered from other vertebrae (including those of the cervical spine all the way on top) and from surrounding anatomical structures, such as ribs and the sacroiliac joints. The fusion of this evidence can be quite complicated, and sometimes requires the coding of extensive clinical knowledge. Nevertheless, this is exactly the way human experts achieve their high reliability. We have implemented as much knowledge as possible in App-III and have found out that this is the single most important component in our system for achieving high reliability. This is probably due to the fact that the spine is the most "knowledge-rich" anatomy among the three applications.

7.4.4 What Level of Reliability Can We Achieve?— Experiments and Results

To see what reliability scores we could achieve, we collected and tested on several relatively large datasets. Specifically we have 744 MR T1 scout scans of the knee, 198 head topograms, 120 MR T1 scout scans of the spine, and 1225 CT scans of various types, including about 30% of low-dose, low-resolution CTs from PET-CT scans and 20% lung scans with few or no cervical or lumbar vertebrae present in the images—these are challenging because vertebra counting is difficult if one cannot see either end of the spine.

Table 7.3 lists the reliability (and accuracy) of the proposed redundancy-exploiting algorithm (SERA) for the three applications. The baseline algorithms for each of the applications are, respectively, a predecessor algorithm

TABLE 7.3:   Reliabilities ($\mathcal{R}$) achieved for the three applications.

	App-I (MR)		App-II (Topogram)		App-III (MR/CT)	
Methods	*Baseline*	*SERA*	*Baseline*	*SERA*	*Baseline*	*SERA*
# cases	744	744	198	198	60(MR)	120/1225)
$\mathcal{A}$	84.8%	99.6%	88.4%	97.0%	90%	98.3%/93.5%
$\mathcal{R}$	90.1%*	**99.73%**	89.9%*	**98.0%**	90%	**98.3%/96.8%**

*: No separate self-assessment, based on only *FPs*—may be overestimated.

based on femur segmentation, the active appearance model (AAM [5]) approach, and the method and results reported in [17]. For algorithms that do not provide a self-assessment, it is assumed that they have no *self-doubts*, i.e., the second and last row in Table 7.2 contain only zeros.

From the results, it is apparent that the 3D problem (App-I) is easier than the 2D projective problem (App-II), and spine labeling for arbitrary CT is a tricky problem (some cases are ambiguous to human experts as well). There is much to do before we can approach 100% reliability.

In most cases our algorithm runs in a few seconds on a regular PC (2.8GHz CPU with 2GB RAM), satisfying or exceeding user requirements.

7.5   Related Work and Discussions

7.5.1   Related Concepts—Defect and Reliability; Confidence by Margin; Reliability Diagram

Traditional analysis of device defect rate [20] defined reliability as the probability of failure-free operation for a specific time. This definition is not comparable to our second-order performance measure $\mathcal{R}$ as defined in Equation 7.2; it is actually closer to the traditional first-order measurement of accuracy $\mathcal{A}$.

Classification confidence can be derived from margins, and it was shown by Shawn-Taylor [19] that a large margin indicates high confidence in classification. This is indeed a very useful observation. However, not much can be said about samples with small margins. Without new information or new training data, there is no way to boost the margin for those cases. "Knowing-thy-confidence" is not nearly as useful for the human user as "knowing-thy-failure."

Reliability diagram is a tool for assessing the reliability of probabilistic forecast systems [3]. It is more of a probabilistic postmortem assessment, rather than an actionable supplement to the original decision. Our reliability measure is based on the categorical answer to the question: *Has a mistake been made or not?* A reliability diagram does not directly provide a quantitative reliability measure and can be misleading [3].

7.5.2   Related Algorithms—Bag-of-Visual-Words; Spatial Bagging

The use of bag-of-visual-words is common nowadays for scene classification [8, 24]. Here the term "bag" signifies the fact that the visual words are mixed without considering spatial origin. The same can be said about the spatial bagging method proposed by Vucetic et al. [22], where an image is broken up into patches and randomly sampled as bags. In both cases, the *throw-'em-in-a-bag-and-shake-it* philosophy seems ill-fitted for medical imaging applications because we should try to take advantage of the strong spatial dependencies or redundancies in human anatomy and in medical images.

7.5.3   Related Strategies—Object Recognition by Parts

In the broader research field of object detection and recognition, many methods based on the use of local features have been proposed. The objects of interest were in many cases faces, cars, or people [6, 1, 25, 14, 15, 12]. The techniques include boosted detector with a statistical shape model [6], "part-based representation" of the object with global shape constraint learned using the Sparse Network of Winnows [1], and SVM classifiers for detecting as well as integrating parts [15], etc. Compared to existing methods, including the most recent learning-based detection methods (e.g., [9, 27]), the proposed algorithm gains reliability through redundancy, with much more redundant use of the image content at the part level, from both within and (far) beyond the target. In addition, an overly redundant set of sparse predictors are used to remove outliers and errors. Our tests showed that such redundancies notably improve decision confidence and reliability as defined in this chapter, especially for multi-class problems and for unusual and challenging inputs. Another important difference, in our view, is the fact that we have formulated the *recognition-by-parts* intuition in a more principled way as a spatial ensemble, so that we no longer need to worry about what context to use for each part, or which parts to pick—just use the whole image as context, and use as many pieces of foveal evidence as you can computationally afford.

7.5.4   Automation and Its Legal and Cost Implications

In the medical domain, automation is a sensitive topic due to safety and legal concerns. Today, user-in-the-loop is required for every case. However, as the algorithm becomes more and more reliable (although can we ever claim 100% reliability?), at what point can we take the leap of faith and really let the user out of the loop? The answer, from a pure economical point of view, is to weigh the cost savings (coming from, say, 99.9% of the reliable cases) against the cost increase (from the 0.01% undetected failures). In some countries, legislation on punitive damages can severely skew this balance. Nevertheless, the day of paradigm shift may come sooner for MR than CT, simply because no harm is caused by an MR imaging process.

7.5.5 Extensions

The reliability measure, along with the proposed strategies to improve it can be applied to many other applications within and beyond the medical domain.

References

[1] S. Agarwal, A. Awan, and D. Roth. Learning to detect objects in images via a sparse, part-based representation. *IEEE Trans. Pattern Anal. Machine Intell.*, 26(11):1475–1490, 2004.

[2] L. Breiman. Bagging predictors. *Machine Learning*, 24:123–140, 1996.

[3] J. Brocker and L. A. Smith. Increasing the reliability of reliability diagrams. *Weather and Forecasting*, 22(3):651–661, 2007.

[4] X. Chai, L. Deng, Q. Yang, and C. X. Ling. Test-cost sensitive naive Bayes classification. In *Proc. Fourth IEEE Int'l Conf. on Data Mining*, pages 51–58. IEEE Computer Society, 2004.

[5] T. F. Cootes, G. J. Edwards, C. J. Taylor, et al. Active appearance models. *IEEE Trans. Pattern Anal. Machine Intell.*, 23(6):681–685, 2001.

[6] D. Cristinacce and T. Cootes. Facial feature detection using AdaBoost with shape constraints. In *British Machine Vision Conference*, pages 231–240, 2003.

[7] C. Elkan. The foundations of cost-sensitive learning. In *International Joint Conference on Artificial Intelligence*, volume 17, pages 973–978. Citeseer, 2001.

[8] L. Fei-Fei and P. Perona. A bayesian hierarchical model for learning natural scene categories. In *Proc. IEEE Conf. on Computer Vision and Pattern Recog.*, San Diego, CA, volume 2, 2005.

[9] B. Georgescu, X. S. Zhou, D. Comaniciu, and A. Gupta. Database-guided segmentation of anatomical structures with complex appearance. In *Proc. IEEE Conf. on Computer Vision and Pattern Recog.*, San Diego, CA, II: 429–436, 2005.

[10] R. L. Gregory. *The Intelligent Eye.* McGraw-Hill, 1970.

[11] H. W. Hunziker. Im Auge des Lesers—foveale und periphere Wahrnehmung: vom Buchstabieren zur Lesefreude (The eye of the reader: foveal and peripheral perception—from letter recognition to the joy of reading). *Transmedia Zurich*, 2006.

[12] B. Leibe, A. Leonardis, and B. Schiele. Robust object detection with interleaved categorization and segmentation. *Int'l J. of Computer Vision*, 77(1):259–289, 2008.

[13] V. Lepetit and P. Fua. Keypoint recognition using randomized trees. *IEEE Trans. Pattern Anal. Machine Intell.*, 28(9):1465, 2006.

[14] T. K. Leung, M. C. Burl, and P. Perona. Finding faces in cluttered scenes using random labeled graph matching. In *Proc. Intl. Conf. on Computer Vision*, Cambridge, MA, pages 637–644, 1995.

[15] A. Mohan, C. Papageorgiou, and T. Poggio. Example-based object detection in images by components. *IEEE Trans. Pattern Anal. Machine Intell.*, 23(4):349–361, 2001.

[16] M. Ozuysal, P. Fua, and V. Lepetit. Fast keypoint recognition in ten lines of code. In *Proc. IEEE Conf. on Computer Vision and Pattern Recog.*, Minneapolis, MN, volume 1, pages 1–8, 2007.

[17] V. Pekar, D. Bystrov, H. Heese, S. Dries, S. Schmidt, R. Grewer, C. den Harder, R. Bergmans, A. Simonetti, and A. van Muiswinkel. Automated planning of scan geometries in spine MRI scans. *Medical Image Computing and Computer-Assisted Intervention*, pages 601–608, 2007.

[18] H. Schipper. Quality of life. *Journal of Psychosocial Oncology*, 8(2):171–185, 1990.

[19] J. Shawe-Taylor. Confidence estimates of classification accuracy on new examples. In *Computational Learning Theory*, pages 260–271. Springer, 1997.

[20] F. T. Sheldon, K. M. Kavi, R. C. Tausworthe, J. T. Yu, R. Brettschneider, and W. W. Everett. Reliability measurement: from theory to practice. *IEEE Software*, 9(4):13–20, 1992.

[21] N. S. Sutherland. Outlines of a theory of visual pattern recognition in animals and man. *Proc. Royal Soc. of London. Series B, Biological Sciences*, 171(1024):297–317, 1968.

[22] S. Vucetic, T. Fiez, and Z. Obradovic. A data partitioning scheme for spatial regression. In *Proc. IEEE/INNS Int'l Joint Conf. on Neural Networks*, 1999.

[23] B. A. Wandell. *Foundations of Vision.* Sinauer Associates, Inc., 1995.

[24] J. Yang, Y. G. Jiang, A. G. Hauptmann, and C. W. Ngo. Evaluating bag-of-visual-words representations in scene classification. In *Proc. Int'l Workshop on Multimedia Inform. Retrieval,* pages 197–206, 2007.

[25] K. C. Yow and R. Cipolla. Feature-based human face detection. *Image and Vision Computing,* 15(9):713–735, 1997.

[26] A. Yuille and D. Kersten. Vision as Bayesian inference: Analysis by synthesis? *Trends in Cognitive Sciences,* 10(7):301–308, 2006.

[27] Y. Zheng, X. Lu, B. Georgescu, A. Littmann, E. Mueller, and D. Comaniciu. Robust object detection using marginal space learning and ranking-based multi-detector aggregation. In *Proceedings of the IEEE Conference on Computer Vision and Pattern Recognition,* Miami, FL, 2009.

[28] X. S. Zhou, Z. Peng, Y. Zhan, M. Dewan, B. Jian, A. Krishnan, Y. Tao, M. Harder, S. Grosskopf, and U. Feuerlein. Redundancy, redundancy, redundancy: The three keys to highly robust anatomical parsing in medical images. In *MIR '10: Proc. Int'l Conf. Multimedia Info Retrieval,* pages 175–184, New York, NY, 2010. ACM.

[29] X. S. Zhou, S. Zillner, M. Moeller, M. Sintek, Y. Zhan, A. Krishnan, and A. Gupta. Semantics and CBIR: A medical imaging perspective. In *Proc. Int'l Conf. Content-Based Image and Video Retrieval,* pages 571–580, 2008.

Chapter 8

Cost-Sensitive Learning in Computational Advertising

Deepak Agarwal

Yahoo! Research, Sunnyvale, California

8.1 Introduction

Users interact with the web by visiting web sites and issuing queries to search engines. Showing advertisements (ads) to users during such interactions is a multi-billion dollar industry. The main goal is to match user visits to ads in a given context (web search, visiting a news site, checking e-mail, and so on). *What makes this match making task different than other recommender problems like movie recommendation, content recommendation on a website, document recommendation in web search, product recommendation on a shopping site?* The primary reason is due to the cost and utility functions that are involved in matching ads—they are distinct from those used in other recommender problems. For instance, in web search and content recommendation, success of a matching algorithm is typically measured as improvement in user engagement metrics. In advertising since the ad links are sponsored by advertisers, publisher revenue and advertiser return on investment (ROI) are crucial for success. In fact, although most large-scale recommender problems can be abstractly formulated as algorithmically matching users to items in different contexts, constructing matching algorithms is an ill-posed problem in the absence of a well-defined notion of optimality that is quantified through some objective function. While the long-term objective is to maximize profit, online advertising systems typically depend on metrics that are measurable in the short term. For instance, although high-quality and topically relevant ads may not necessarily lead to significant improvements in click-rates, it may have favorable long-term impact like improving the return rate of users to web sites, which in turn leads to an increase in long-term revenue. Constructing objective functions that are based on short-term metrics involves identifying and appropriately quantifying various utilities and costs, and then striking a balance among several objectives, some of which may compete with each other. In this chapter we discuss the utilities and costs involved in one such algorithmic match making problem—online advertising. An effective *match-making* solution in such applications require strong interplay among various disciplines like computer science, economics, information retrieval, machine learning, optimization and statistics. This has given rise to a new scientific discipline that is now referred to as *Computational Advertising* [14, 12].

We shall refer to any instance where one could display an ad in some context as an *opportunity*. Then broadly speaking, there are three main entities involved in online advertising—buyers of opportunites, sellers of opportunities, and commercial intermediaries that connect buyers and sellers either for a flat fee or profit through arbitrage. Depending on the context and the revenue model pursued, the role of intermediaries are different. In the context of web search, sponsored ad links are matched to user queries. Such a matching depends on several factors, the important ones being the keywords (bidded phrases) specified by the advertiser, the amount of money an advertiser is willing to pay for an ad click, and performance of the ad that is typically measured via click-rates (CTR). This keyword-based matching in the context of web search is called *Sponsored Search*(SS), it revolutioned web search and online advertising in the early part of the 21st century and gave rise to a multi-billion dollar industry. A later variation of this model pioneered by Google provided sponsored links to users visiting web sites, this is often referred to as *Contextual Match* (CM). For instance, a user visiting a sports page like www.espn.com may see ads about Rolex watches.

For both SS and CM, the primary pricing model is pay-per-click where advertisers pay only if there is a click on their ads. For major web search engines like Google, Bing, and Yahoo!, the intermediaries who match ads on the search page are often providers of web search results. In CM, the intermediary is often some ad network that matches ads to opportunities on publisher pages and shares a percentage of the accrued revenue with the publisher. For instance, when ESPN signs up with an intermediary like Google Adsense, it allows Google to display ads when a user visits ESPN. When there is an ad click, revenue is obtained from the advertiser and the proceeds are shared between the intermediary (Google in this case) and the content provider (ESPN in this case). The ecosystem may get more nuanced when an intermediary on the publisher side aggregates content from small contributors. In this case, the content aggregator signs up content with the intermediary on the ad side, the proceeds are shared by the ad intermediary, the content aggregator (yet another intermediary) and the original content producer. Several such aggregators exist, Associated Content (owned by Yahoo!) is a good example.

Both SS and CM are performance-based advertising models where payment is typically made when a positive feedback like ad-click or conversion (user buying some product on the advertiser site post-click) is obtained from the user. Such a model may not be suitable for advertisers who are more interested in creating long-term brand awareness for their products than boosting immediate sales. Creating brand awareness often promotes future sales (offline and online) and leads to loyal customers, especially when ads are properly targeted to appropriate user segments. This is similar in spirit to advertising on television, popular magazines, and newspapers, and is referred to as online *display* advertising. Unlike performance-based advertising, the revenue model in display advertising is typically Cost-per-Milli (CPM) whereby ad opportunities are priced in bundles of thousands and are paid for by the advertiser irrespective of user actions. It is useful to note that in performance-based advertising since the advertiser pays only if the user reacts positively to the ad, the risk is taken by the publisher; with a CPM model in display advertising the risk is entirely on the advertiser. For instance, even if a CPM-based display advertising campaign does not perform well in terms of clicks and conversions, the publisher gets paid.

In recent times, display advertising has however evolved from the traditional CPM model of media buy into a more sophisticated marketplace. Broadly speaking, display advertising follows two different models—*guaranteed delivery* and *non-guaranteed delivery*. A large fraction of online display advertising is sold in the form of *guaranteed contracts* where an advertiser enters into an agreement with a publisher to guarantee some user visits at a future time point [6, 20]. For instance, a shoe manufacturer may wish to purchase a guaranteed contract to display a new sports shoe ad 100 million times to Males in California who visit Yahoo! Sports during Superbowl 2011, and Yahoo! as a publisher will guarantee such contracts. Typically, advertisers pay higher CPM to procure such a guarantee.

As the name suggests, non-guaranteed delivery does not provide a guarantee on visit volumes, marketers working on behalf of advertisers negotiate deals with different publishers to target audience segments they are interested in. Commercial intermediaries like ad networks facilitate such a process by aggregating publisher inventory and matching advertisers to the desired inventory. Beyond ad networks, "ad exchanges" have become popular in recent times as they provide a unified marketplace for buyers and sellers to transact across network boundaries (e.g., RightMedia exchange, Double-click exchange). This is sometimes also referred to as the "network-of-networks" model. In an ad exchange, ads are sold for each opportunity through an auction as in performance advertising. Ad campaigns may choose different pricing models like CPM, pay-per-click, pay-per-conversion, and so on. In fact, exchanges like RightMedia provide more options whereby advertisers pay only upon receiving a certain number of clicks/conversions (e.g., dynamic CPM model in RightMedia); the publishers are, however, paid for each opportunity in the exchange. The match-making algorithms that power auctions in such an ad exchange normalize across different pricing types to create a "single currency" that is used to select auction winners. The ultimate goal is to maximize publisher revenue but at the same time ensure good ROI for advertisers. A schematic diagram of different advertising models is given in Figure 8.1. In

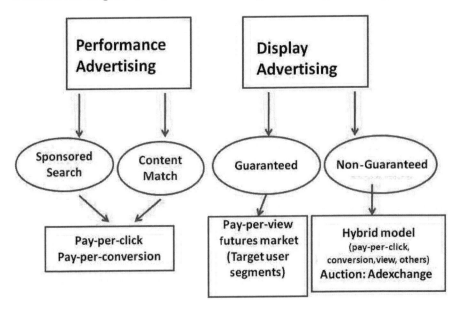

FIGURE 8.1: Computational advertising variants.

the rest of this chapter, we will provide a detailed account of various computational advertising models and point out tradeoffs involved in matching ads to opportunities. A key ingredient in all performance-based advertising are machine learning methods that learn response rates when ads are displayed for opportunities. We will show that this is not a supervised learning problem; instead, it is an explore/exploit problem where the goal is to actively experiment and selectively learn response rates to maximize overall revenue subject to various constraints.

8.2 Performance Advertising: Sponsored Search and Contextual Matching

We first provide an overview of different ad matching components in Sponsored Search and Contextual Matching. We describe the keyword-based ad matching process, the explore/exploit tradeoffs involved in ranking ads, the pricing formula, and how these components are connected. This is followed by a brief review of existing research in these areas.

8.2.1 Sponsored Search

We begin by describing the match-making process in Sponsored Search; for more details and history we refer the reader to [19, 11]. To advertise in the context of a certain query, an advertiser creates a campaign that consists of one or more ads. Along with details like title and URL, the advertiser submits the following information—set of keywords that are relevant to the ads (called bidded phrases), a bid associated with each keyword that reflects the amount the advertiser is willing to pay per click, and the total advertising budget dedicated to the campaign. When an opportunity arrives (user enters a query in the search box), we retrieve a set of candidate ads that match the normalized query. Ads that bid less than some small pre-specified amount (called reserve price) are removed. After the first stage pruning that is based on matching bidded phrases to the query, the candidate ads participate for ad slots through an auction. The ads are typically ranked based on some function of bid and performance measure like click-rate (CTR). For instance, it is customary to use a function like *expected revenue*, i.e., $bid \times CTR$, but other functions like $bid^\alpha \times CTR$ that controls the tradeoff between performance and advertiser willingness to pay are also used. In some cases additional measures like ad quality and engagement on landing page are also included in the ranking formula (see [35] for an example). Such measures are secret sauces of search engines and not revealed, hence we only consider ranking based on expected revenue. Of course the CTRs are not known and have to be estimated from historical data, this is done through machine learning methods. Once the ad rankings are obtained and there is a click on some ad, a pricing scheme decides the amount to be paid by the advertiser. Since large scale SS systems conduct billions of auctions on a daily basis, it is important to have a pricing model that avoids vindictive bidding by antisocial participants. Incentive compatibility (IC) is an attractive property; it guarantees that bidders maximize their payoffs by bidding the true value of their perceived profit from ad click. First-price auction where the advertiser pays the bidded amount is not incentive compatible, it is prone to vindictive bidding. This can encourage advertisers not to bid their true value which may reduce revenue in the long run. Hence, most search engines follow the generalized second-price auction formula (GSP) where payoff per click is a function of other bids and CTRs [9]. According to GSP, a click on the ith ranked ad obtains a payout of

$$bid_{i+1} CTR_{i+1}/CTR_i.$$

This is the minimum bid for the ith ranked ad to be ranked above the $(i+1)^{st}$ ad.

8.2.1.1   Ranking Ads Is an Explore/Exploit Problem

We show that the optimization problem of maximizing revenue with unknown CTR is an explore/exploit problem. For simplicity, let us assume we allocate only one ad to a query on the search engine result page (SERP). We also assume the first-price auction model whereby the winner pays the highest bid, this makes the exposition easier. Consider a hypothetical scenario where we consider a single query that is expected to occur N times in a certain time period of interest (e.g., a month). Let us assume there are K candidate ads for this query with fixed bids $b_i, i = 1, \cdots, K$. If $p_i, i = 1, \cdots, K$ denotes the true CTR, we select $\mathrm{argmax}_{i=1,\cdots,K} p_i b_i$ to display on all N instances and maximize total expected revenue, which in this case is $N \max_i b_i p_i$. But the p_is are unknown and have to be estimated from data. In such a scenario, what is the best online ad serving policy for N opportunities that minimize the expected *regret* (expected deviation from maximum possible revenue) given by

$$R(N) = N \max_i b_i p_i - \sum_{i=1}^{K} b_i p_i E(T_i(N))? \qquad (8.1)$$

In Equation 8.1, $T_i(N)$ is a random variable that denotes the number of times ad i is selected as winner. This is an instance of the classic multi-armed bandit problem and illustrates the so-called "explore/exploit" dilemma inherent in performance advertising applications. At any stage, the choice of which ad to show next involves a fundamental tradeoff between "exploit" (show the ad that appears to be doing well so far) and "explore" (show the ad that may appear to be inferior now but could be potentially good).

For instance, suppose $K = 2$ and $b_i = \$1$ for each i, assume all advertisers have large budgets, and the estimated odds of obtaining a click by showing ad 1 and ad 2 are 10:5 and 2:3, respectively. It is tempting to show ad 1 thereafter on all opportunities but this will starve ad 2. This is not the best strategy since the true odds for the second ad can be higher, and the system may have had an unlucky streak due to random fluctuations. But how much exploration is optimal to ensure maximum total revenue on average after N displays? For instance, should we keep showing an ad until it fails to provide a click and then switch to others? Or can we do better with alternate explore/exploit strategies? The precise mathematical answers to these innocuous-looking questions is notoriously difficult and it took a few decades before Gittins provided a solution in his landmark paper [21]. Since then, this area has witnessed rapid progress with extensive research done in the last four decades [27, 22, 17, 10, 30]. Although a comprehensive mathematical treatment is beyond the scope of this chapter, it is possible to describe the structure of the best-serving strategy which is as follows — based on data accumulated so far from previous displays, we independently assess the *future potential* of each ad to be the best and play the one that has maximum potential. For instance, one can measure the potential of an ad by using $(\text{mean} + 2\sqrt{(\text{variance})})$ based on payoffs obtained from previous displays, this is an instance of what are known as upper confidence bound schemes [27]. The key insight here is the fact that if one could assess the potential of each ad independently and play the one with the best potential, it provides the optimal strategy. Of course computing the potential is non-trivial and depends on the application.

We point out that constructing ad ranking in SS is not a supervised machine learning problem where the main goal is to minimize out-of-sample predictive error through a learned model on retrospective data. In SS, we need machine learning methods that inform the system on how to construct the ad serving scheme itself to collect future data. Hence, the ranking problem is more related to active learning [36], but there are important differences. In active learning the goal is to sample points judiciously to minimize the out-of-sample predictive error of a classifier/regressor. In advertising our goal is to sample points sequentially to maximize total revenue. To illustrate this difference, we appeal to our example of a single query and two ads. Let us assume it is possible to construct a machine learning model to predict the CTRs of ads based on ad features (see [32] for an example of such a model). Let's assume $p_2 b_2 - p_1 b_1 = \delta > 0$. Active learning strives to sample points to minimize the prediction error on both p_1 and p_2, explore/exploit methods would sample to ensure the sign of δ is predicted correctly with a high probability using a small number of samples. Intuitively, the moment we can infer an ad is inferior to the best one, it is removed and not shown again. The goal is to achieve such a convergence rapidly by minimizing the cost of exploration.

Having interpreted ad ranking for a single query as a multi-armed bandit problem, a straightforward generalization is to treat each query as a separate bandit. If we consider the user dimension, then each (query, user) pair is a separate bandit. Clearly this is more challenging, the large number of bandits and the heavy tailed distribution associated with categorical variables like query and user leads to enormous data sparsity in practice. Also, the ad inventory is not static since new campaigns are introduced and old ones run out of budget, this exacerbates the data sparsity problem. There is a delay in receiving feedback for two reasons: (1) the users take time to click after the ad is displayed, and (2) data transfer from web servers to backend clusters where model parameters get updated incurs some latency. Classical bandit settings assume instantaneous feedback and do not account for such a delay, which is important in advertising applications. For a practical solution, it is attractive to reduce the dimension of the problem by expressing the large number of CTRs through a smaller number of parameters. For instance, CTR of sports ads for sports queries can be assumed to be correlated. This expedites the learning process and reduces the amount of exploration required to converge to the best ads. Also, since the payout in the GSP formula depends on the bids and CTRs of other ads, converging to the best ad is not sufficient to maximize revenue. In fact, optimal explore/exploit schemes to maximize revenue for the GSP auction needs more research.

The impact of the first phase matching algorithm that selects a smaller set of candidate ads based on keywords is also significant since search engines typically provide two kinds of keyword matching options to advertisers: *exact* match and *broad* match. In broad match, if a keyword is conceptually related to the query, the ad is admissible for the auction. For instance, a bid on keyword "shoe" can make an ad eligible to participate in an auction for a query "Nike." The broad match option is good for advertisers since it eliminates the need to carefully craft keywords for an ad campaign which could be a tedious task in practice. It is also good for the intermediary (search engine provider) since it provides a scope to expand the size of the candidate pool that participates in an auction and increases competition. In general, high-volume queries typically have high demand, and broad match provides a mechanism to divert some of this demand to tail queries that are related. But the algorithms used to determine broad match have a significant impact on performance. Increasing candidates in auctions have two effects: (1) chances of obtaining a better paying ad increases, and (2) the number of inferior ads also increases. While every low payoff ad incurs additional exploration cost since it has to be shown a few times before being eliminated, if the likelihood of introducing high payoff ads is significant, the exploration cost is offset by gains obtained from exploiting better ads. In a nutshell, the first phase keyword matching algorithms, the machine learning algorithms used to rank ads in an auction, and the pricing formula that determines payoff are all tightly connected and have to be considered together for obtaining an optimal solution.

8.2.2 Contextual Matching

The issues in CM are similar to SS but the context, which in this case is a web page, is more noisy. This changes the solution of the two components – keyword match and ad ranking models. Broad match becomes more important and has to be done by looking at various properties of the web page, such as the text, title, anchor text of incoming links and so on. Also, the allocation of ad positions depends on the page layout: the high-dimensional context features and lower click-rates add more noise and makes the ad ranking problem harder. Since the intermediary in this case (the ad-network) is often not the content publisher, chances of click fraud by unscrupulous publishers in collusion with third-party sources increases, special efforts have to be made to monitor the system continuously and carefully. All issues on explore/exploit tradeoffs described in the context of SS also apply to CM, and the pricing formula is still based on GSP.

8.2.3 Overview of Existing Literature in SS and CM

We briefly review existing work in the area of broad match and machine learning approaches for ranking ads, the literature on pricing and auction theory will not be covered in this chapter.

8.2.3.1 Broad Match Methods

We can classify existing broad match methods into two types — *Relevance* based and *Click* based. The simplest relevance-based approach is to treat context and ads as documents and then use classical information retrieval (IR) methods. But in SS both queries and keywords are short; in CM web pages are heterogeneous and noisier than usual text corpora analyzed in information retrieval (IR) literature. For instance, the lexicon includes documents that vary in length, the topics covered are diverse. Hence, better IR methods are generally required to improve relevance-based broad match. A natural solution is to find similar queries $\mathcal{N}_Q$ for each query Q based on relevance. One can then use $\mathcal{N}_q \cup Q$ to find exact matches for a query Q online. This approach was investigated in [26] where a query Q' is defined to be related to query Q if Q and Q' co-occur together more often than expected under independence. The deviation from independence is measured through a likelihood ratio test. The queries are also split into phrases using mutual information on the co-occurence statistics and the phrases in the expanded query set are used for broad match. However, the approach did not return many additional ads and led to poor coverage. To ameliorate this, [31] followed a supervised learning approach. For a set of head queries, they first perform query expansion by using bag-of-words representation of the top documents returned by a search engine. A set of top ads are collected based on relevance measure between bag-of-words from queries and ads. These ads are then presented to editors to obtain labels, a machine learning model based on features is learned to predict editorial labels. At run time, relevant broad matches are retrieved based on relevance score from machine learned model and also the bid of second-highest ad. This ensures better coverage of high revenue ads and leads to significant improvement in offline analysis. Along similar lines, [13] augments both queries and advertiser keywords with top search results and extract four kinds of features — words, classification into a taxonomy trained through editorial labels, entities, and phrases. The similarity score between a query and ad is then computed using a weighted average of cosine similarities for words, categories, entities, and phrases. This score is used to expand the ad set online for a given query. The authors applied a similar approach to CM.

It is also quite natural to expand the ad set by analyzing historical click-logs and inferring matches based on query and ad features that are correlated with CTR. An item-item similarity approach was taken in [8] where relevant ads for a query were inferred based on marginal correlation to ads. Along similar lines, [25] developed a predictive model based on clicks but using a more feature-based approach. They proposed an online perceptron algorithm to estimate the feature weights and showed significant improvement on a live MSFT ad system. More research in this area may lead to better selection of ads in the broad match stage that can potentially lead to significant improvement in performance.

8.2.3.2   Explore/Exploit Methods for Ad Ranking

A large body of existing research in machine learning has focused on building explore/exploit methods for ranking ads that survive the keyword matching phase. As discussed before, the explore/exploit problem here is high dimensional and methods to share data across bandits by reducing dimension is important. One attractive way is to use supervised learning methods like regression that exploits similarities in the CTR of query-ad pairs through features.

More precisely, let y_{ij} denote the binary response when ad j is shown to opportunity i which a combination of some (query, user) pair. Also, let $\boldsymbol{x}_i$ and $\boldsymbol{x}_j$ denote features extracted from the opportunity and ad, respectively. These typically include text features extracted from queries/ads, ad keywords, topical information on queries/ads, and so on. Then,

$$
\begin{aligned}
y_{ij} &\sim \text{Bernoulli}(p_{ij}) \\
h(p_{ij}) &= \boldsymbol{x}_i' A \boldsymbol{x}_j,
\end{aligned}
$$

where A is a matrix of weights associated with features. A large body of existing work in this area follows this strategy to reduce the dimension of the multiple bandit problems. (See [32, 15, 16, 24].) In most cases the methods are based on logistic regression where $h(x) = log(\frac{x}{1-x})$, except in [24] where the authors use probit regression, i.e., $h(x) = \Phi^{-1}(x)$ (Φ is the CDF of a standard normal variate). In most advertising applications, the number of all possible features are large and hence estimating all elements in A is prohibitive. Some form of feature selection is often used when conducting the regression. In practice, some pre-filtering followed by methods based on forward selection or $L_p(p = 1, 2)$ regularization on the elements of A are used.

Another class of methods have explored CTR estimation from a collabortive filtering perspective where the goal is to estimate CTR for each (i, j) pair. This is difficult since a large fraction of pairs have little data and no positive response which leads to noisy estimates. To avoid sparsity, these methods exploit the natural hierarchy that is often available for both query and ads to obtain a good fallback model. For instance, [2, 38] consider a contextual matching problem where both queries and ads are organized into a topic taxonomy. They show that borrowing strength from data at coarser resolution to smooth CTR estimates at finer resolutions leads to significant improvement in accuracy. It is also possible to build a hybrid model where a feature-based model is augmented with hierarchical corrections [1]. In other words, we assume

$$p_{ij} = h^{-1}(\boldsymbol{x}_i' A \boldsymbol{x}_j)\phi_{ij},$$

where ϕ_{ij}s are latent variables that capture the residual variation for cell (i,j). Estimating the ϕ_{ij}s need careful attention due to data sparsity at the cell resolution, a large fraction of (i,j) pairs have small sample size, and zero clicks. In computational advertising, the queries and ads are often organized hierarchically. The ads are part of campaigns run by advertisers. Hence, click-rates (rather residuals ϕ_{ij}) of ads within the same campaign are expected to be correlated, similarly ads belonging to the same advertiser are expected to be correlated. On the query side, in CM there is a natural hierarchy where URLs are nested within domains, which are in turn organized into categories, and so on. In SS, queries can be classified into query classes. It is attractive to estimate the "corrections" ϕ_{ij}s by exploiting such hierarchical correlations. To provide an example of a model that uses such correlations, let us assume the opportunity i is organized into a hierarchy of two levels $i \to i_1$(query nested within query classes) and the ad j is in a three-level hierarchy $j \to j_1 \to j_2$ (ad is nested within a campaign, which in turn is nested within advertiser). Then, the cell (i,j) has three parents $((i,j_1),(i,j_2),(i_1,j))$ to estimate corrections at finer resolutions by pooling data at coarser resolution. One assumes

$$\phi_{ij} = \delta_{ij}\delta_{ij_1}\delta_{ij_2}\delta_{i_1j}, \tag{8.2}$$

where each node combination has a parameter δ. To avoid over-fitting, one can assume δs are iid drawn from some prior $\mathcal{D}$ with mean 1 and some scale parameter. For more details on fitting such a model to massive datasets, we refer the reader to [1].

Many existing machine learning papers in computational advertising only discuss modeling to reduce the dimension of the explore/exploit problem. A complete solution that combines both modeling and explore/exploit is considered in a few papers [24, 34]. In general, explore/exploit schemes used in large systems are often simple. For instance, ϵ-greedy where complete randomization (or some form of restricted randomization) is done for a small fraction of opportunities and pure exploitation based on a model is often used for the rest due to its inherent simplicity and robust performance. When working in a Bayesian paradigm, randomization induced by drawing from the posterior instead of ranking by posterior means is often quite attractive [37]. Other solutions include upper confidence bound (UCB) policies [30, 27], and a rigorous Bayesian solution discussed in [3]. This is an active research area both in computational advertising and several other recommender problems. Since the main focus of this chapter is to provide an overview of various costs and utilities involved in computational advertising applications, we do not provide a detailed description of various CTR estimation methods here, but in general this is a component where machine learning plays a major role. As we remarked before, although supervised learning methods are crucial to reduce the dimension of the bandit problem, this is not a supervised learning problem and the explore/exploit costs should be taken into consideration. This brings us to another important question of how to evaluate new explore/exploit algorithms. The best way of course is to run controlled experiments on a randomized subset of traffic in the real system (control vs new algorithm), this is often easy to do in a well-designed engineering system. However, testing several methods could become quite expensive, hence offline evaluation metrics are important. Several recent papers that have developed such metrics, we refer the readers to [28] for complete details. Based on our experience with real applications, we believe that evaluating the quality of a new explore/exploit algorithm should be conducted by looking at multiple metrics, slicing and dicing the data, and creating visual plots to examine the output of models. A procedure that looks promising can then be tried out on real opportunites through controlled experiments before coming to a final conclusion.

We also note that most advertising applications are dynamic where new ads and opportunities get introduced routinely. It is important to have a model that can update parameters frequently (e.g., every 5 to 10 minutes). This reduces the impact of cold-start. In fact, good feature-based initialization through an offline model and fast online updates at the (ad, opportunity) resolution provides an effective modeling strategy [4].

8.3 Display Advertising

Since performance advertising is based on keywords, it is an effective way to target users who are looking for something specific. It is also primarily used by advertisers to increase short-term online sales. However, there are scenarios where advertisers are interested in increasing the reach of their products to a larger audience. For instance, Nike may want to target the youth population in metropolitan India with the goal of enhancing future sales. Performance advertising is not suitable for such a task since the target audience may not even be aware of the product, so there is little chance they will click on a small text link to buy the product online. Such reach or brand awareness advertising is similar in spirit to marketing campaigns pursued by corporations on media like TV, magazines, and newspapers. Display advertising provides a similar medium online when users are browsing web pages in different verticals on a portal like Yahoo!, checking emails, chatting with friends, logging into Facebook, Twitter, and so on. Unlike performance advertising, the ads here are not only text based but instead include text, logo, pictures, and more recently rich media. Rich media, synonymous for interactive multimedia, is enhanced media that utilizes a combination of text, audio, still images, animation, video, and interactivity content for active participation from the recipient of the ad. Display advertising also has a significant advantage over advertising in magazines, newspapers, and TVs. Targeting options such as demographic and behavioral targeting are available to laser in on the audience of choice and, advertisers can track the performance of campaigns to measure metrics such as impressions, clicks, and conversions to calculate ROI.

But the important question is — Does display advertising really work? A couple of recent studies clearly show the answer is in the affirmative [29, 23]. The authors show display advertising leads to the following impacts: (1) it increases offline sales; (2) it increases the number of search queries issuing advertiser-branded terms; (3) it increases online sales for the advertiser; and (4) it increases the number of visits to the advertiser's web site. This is good news because typically the click-rates on display ads are quite low. According to [23] it was roughly 0.1% in 2008.

8.3.1 Guaranteed Display Advertising

As mentioned in the introductory section, display advertising is sold in two forms — guaranteed and non-guaranteed. Guaranteed display is more akin to traditional advertising on TV, in magazines, and in newspapers. In this setting a large publisher, such as Yahoo!, enters into contracts with big advertisers like ScottTrade and Netflix to show their ads to a prespecified number of users matching prespecified advertiser targeting constraints. For instance, ScottTrade may book a contract to target 100M males from San Francisco on Yahoo! Finance in January. The publisher takes on the risk of uncertainty in supply and guarantees the delivery of these impressions. Since there are penalties associated with under-delivering, it is in the best interest of the publisher to ensure such guarantees are met. Advertisers pay significantly more to procure guarantees, hence they expect the publisher to deliver, both in terms of quantity and quality. Other than uncertainty in supply, a big publisher typically sells impressions to a large number of advertiser and hence signs up several contracts simultaneously. The targeting constraints associated with these contracts are not independent and tend to overlap. For instance, a young male from San Francisco visiting Yahoo! Finance could be served ads from both ScottTrade and Fidelity since the latter may only specify young males as their targeting constraints. The notion of *overlapping* inventory plays a crucial role in guaranteed display advertising systems.

We now provide a high-level description of various components in a guaranteed delivery display advertising system. Actual systems operated by organizations may differ substantially from our description in terms of implementation details, but the basic issues involved are well covered. First, we separate the components as *offline* and *online*. Offline components are used in booking

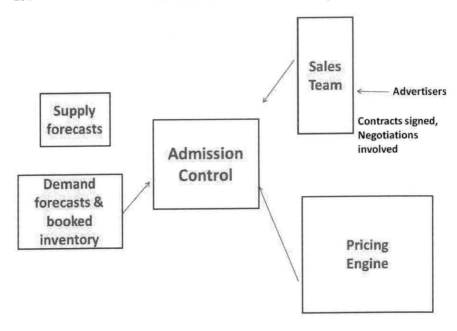

FIGURE 8.2: Offline components in a typical guaranteed delivery advertising system.

contracts, online components help in making ad serving decisions in a split second when new opportunities arrive.

8.3.1.1 Offline Components

Figure 8.2 provides a schematic of various offline components. The process typically begins with a sales representative connecting with an advertiser interested in booking contracts on some publisher network through an ad network. Based on advertiser request, the sales person queries the system to determine the feasibility of signing a contract with targeting constraints at the price specified by the advertiser. The *admission control* component determines such feasibility based on inputs from supply forecasts, demand forecasts, existing bookings, and information from pricing engines. Availability of targeted inventory is generally obtained by solving an optimization problem. The ad network forecasts supply for the time period of interest on a large number of disjoint supply nodes. These supply nodes could be some representative user samples as in [5], or a partition obtained through a clustering methodology. The demand nodes consist of existing bookings and future anticipated demand. Each supply node is connected to a set of demand nodes since the targeting constraints are not independent. To see if a new hypothetical contract is feasible, an additional psuedo-node can be added and feasibility can be obtained through linear/non-linear programming techniques. Once feasibility is guaranteed, the *pricing engine* provides a price based on the amount of contention for the targeted inventory. At this stage, offline negotiations are possible and depends on the relationship of the advertiser with the ad network's sales representative.

8.3.1.2 Online Components

When an opportunity arrives, the ad server makes a decision on what ads to serve in a few milliseconds. This is done by the online system, it is a sequential algorithm that serves ads such that contracts booked offline are successfully delivered. Constructing such a serving algorithm is complex and challenging. Contracts booked in the system vary in terms of targeting constraints, time period, start and end dates, and several other things. Thus, when an opportunity i arrives at time t, a set of contracts $\mathcal{C}_i$ are eligible to get served. Each eligible contract is at a different stage in its lifetime — some may have just started, some are close to completion, and others might be somewhere in between. The contracts also differ in terms of their delivery profile — some may be on track, some may have fallen far behind and could be at risk of under-delivering. Other than targeting, contracts may also involve other constraints. Two such constraints are commonplace — (1) frequency capping that limits the number of repeat displays of an ad to a user, and (2) uniform delivery which constrains the variation in total delivery volume over time. For instance, a contract booked over 6 months and scheduled to end around Christmas cannot be starved during the holiday season and front-loaded to deliver earlier. The ad-serving algorithm has to take all such criteria into consideration and decide on what ads to serve for opportunity i at t to reduce loss due to under-delivery. An efficient ad-serving algorithm also encourages the sales team to take more risks and book finely targeted and highly priced contracts that lead to increases in revenue.

Actual ad-serving algorithms deployed by organizations in practice are complex and implementation details are secret sauces that are not revealed. Typically, there is a component that takes supply forecasts, booked contracts, and other contract statistics as input and performs some computation in near real time to produce a fresh serving allocation plan. Figure 8.3 provides a schematic diagram showing the main online components of a typical guaranteed delivery system.

8.3.1.3 Objectives in Guaranteed Delivery System

We discuss objectives that are typically considered in determining the allocation of inventory in guaranteed display advertising. Unlike Sponsored Search and Contextual Matching, advertiser objectives in display advertising varies. The primary objective, especially for big advertisers interested in booking premium guaranteed delivery, is to create brand awareness to increase future product sales. But there are other advertisers like mortgage lenders that

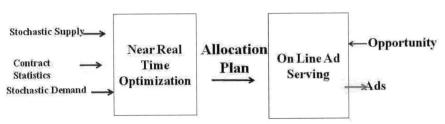

FIGURE 8.3: Online components of a typical guaranteed delivery advertising system.

are primarily interested in immediate sales and book campaigns to maximize clicks/conversions. There are some that are interested both in promoting the brand and obtaining leads to increase immediate sales (e.g., car companies). Also, since guaranteed delivery typically costs more than non-guaranteed, the ad network has to take steps to maintain a superior quality that justifies the additional mark-up in guaranteed delivery prices. The optimization problem that determines allocation subjects to various constraints should consider these multiple objectives to obtain a good solution from the feasible ones.

To formulate the objectives, we begin with some notations. Let us fix some future time period, and let s_i denote the supply forecast for the ith supply cluster, d_j denote the volume of contract j and p_j denotes the price per impression of node j. Let C_i denote the set of contracts that qualify for supply node i based on targeting constraints, referred to as neighborhood of i. With slight abuse of notations, let C_j denote the set of supply nodes that are eligible for contract j. Let x_{ij} denote the fraction of supply in node i that is allocated to contract j.

Underdelivery cost — Denoting by $P_j(d)$ the additional under-delivery penalty function for contract j, the cost of underdelivery is given as

$$\text{UND}(\boldsymbol{x}) = \sum_j (p_j + P_j)(d_j - \sum_{i \in C_j} s_i x_{ij}) 1(d_j > \sum_{i \in C_j} s_i x_{ij}). \quad (8.3)$$

The goal is to determine $\boldsymbol{x}$ that minimizes the under-delivery cost.

8.3.1.4 Non-Guaranteed Revenue

Some user visits on a publisher network may not have high demand in the guaranteed marketplace and could be sold in the non-guaranteed market (e.g., ad-exchange). Hence, one of the objectives would be to determine allocation of opportunities to contract such that we minimize under-delivery but also maximize revenue by selling high paying opportunities in the non-guaranteed market. For instance, a young male user from San Francisco interested in cars may obtain a premium in non-guaranteed marketplace but none of the existing contracts may have specified such fine grained targeting attributes. If the existing contracts could be satisfied by using other opportunities, one may want to sell this high-valued impression non-guaranteed to maximize overall revenue. Mathematically, let $e_i = s_i(1 - \sum_{j \in C_i} x_{ij})1(\sum_{j \in C_i} x_{ij} < 1)$ denote the excess supply after allocation to guaranteed contracts, let q_i denote the expected price for opportunity i in non-guaranteed market. Profit from selling leftovers in non-guaranteed is given by

$$\text{NGDP}(\boldsymbol{x}) = \sum_i q_i e_i. \tag{8.4}$$

Our goal is to determine $\boldsymbol{x}$ that maximizes $\text{NGDP}(\boldsymbol{x})$.

8.3.1.5 Brand Value/Representativeness

The next objective is more subtle and protects the guaranteed delivery marketplace by discouraging "cherry-picking" of high-valued and often highly targeted non-guaranteed opportunities away from guaranteed contracts. Ideally, every guaranteed contract should receive a representative mix of opportunities from the entire publisher network subject to targeting constraints, the non-representativeness induced in the delivery profile should only be due to contention by other guaranteed contracts that are willing to pay more for some of the targeted opportunities. This is essential to maintain a healthy mark-up of guaranteed display price over non-guaranteed. If advertiser ROI from non-guaranteed exceeds guaranteed then there is no incentive for them to pay more. This is all the more important because guaranteed is typically used by big advertisers who spend significant sums of money with the network, so a few unhappy advertisers can cost the publisher dearly. Thus, if θ_{ij} denotes the ideal allocation that ensures a representative allocation (e.g., $\theta_{ij} = s_i d_j / \sum_{k \in C_j} s_k$), the goal would be to minimize some distance measure $D(\boldsymbol{x}, \boldsymbol{\theta})$. One simple distance function would be $D(\boldsymbol{x}, \boldsymbol{\theta}) = \sum_{ij}(x_{ij} - \theta_{ij})^2/\theta_{ij}$.

The three objectives considered so far (minimizing under-delivery, maximizing non-guaranteed revenue from remnant opportunities, maximizing representativeness for guaranteed contracts) cannot be optimized simultaneously since they compete with each other. For instance, maximizing non-guaranteed revenue will hurt representativeness. Hence, one takes recourse to multi-objective optimization and obtains a Pareto optimal solution that represents the best compromise among objectives [33]. Other objectives like click-rates/conversion rates can also be added similarly. We refer the reader to [18] for a case study on a Yahoo! application. For more motivation on representativeness from an economic perspective, we refer the reader to [7].

8.3.2 Non-Guaranteed Display Advertising

Guaranteed delivery is typically used by big advertisers with large budgets on high-volume publisher networks like Yahoo!, MSN, and so on. In some sense, guaranteed delivery represents the premium inventory in display. But this is often not good enough to satisfy the advertising demand of marketers who are interested in increasing audience reach across different publisher sites as cheaply as possible in a fragmented display advertising marketplace. Booking ads across different publisher sites using different platforms is tedious and time consuming; an automated and efficient system is desirable. Ad networks aggregate publisher inventory across different publishers and provide such a facility to some extent, but this is still not sufficient since different networks tend to focus on specific aspects. In recent times, ad exchanges have bought new levels of efficiencies to the online display ad market, making it easier for marketers to find the opportunities they need at the right price. Like a stock exchange, an ad exchange provides a unified marketplace to connect buyers (advertisers) and sellers (publishers) in an automated fashion, eliminating the need for marketers to book inventory through a tedious and often manual process that involves working with several systems. The exchange enables this transparency by selecting a winner for every single opportunity through an auction. As in a stock exchange, the key issue with successful functioning of an ad exchange is liquidity. Once there are enough opportunities, connecting the right buyers and sellers is automatic and efficient through the laws of demand and supply. Intermediaries like ad networks play the same role as stock brokers in a stock exchange helping the advertisers trade and find the best inventory at a reasonable price. Publishers can specify the minimum payout for an opportunity, thereby eliminating low bids. The transparency and efficiency provided by the exchange is beneficial for both publishers and advertisers. For publishers, it provides a clearinghouse to sell inventory at the right price. Advertisers get the audience they need from a large and diverse collection of inventory at the best price in an almost automated fashion. Ad exchanges have finally gained significance in recent times, primarily due to the launch of the long-promised exchanges by Google, MSFT, and others. The more mature ones like Yahoo!'s RightMedia exchange have further strengthened their position by focusing more on quality instead of just quantity and providing new functionalities like real-time bidding (RTB).

We now provide a high-level overview of how auctions are conducted in the RightMedia exchange. Unlike performance advertising, the first phase selection of candidate ads depends on targeting constraints specified by the ad campaigns; there is no option like broad match. However, the targeting constraints are typically coarse and qualify for a large fraction of opportunities on the exchange. The second phase ranking problem is more challenging in this scenario. The ad campaigns can participate using different pricing types like CPM, CPC (cost-per-click), CPA (cost-per-conversion) and dCPM (dynamic CPM). For CPA, there are two different kinds of models: conversion after a click (CPA-PC) and conversion attributed to a page view of an ad on some publisher site (CPA-PV). Dynamic CPM is a pricing model that allows the advertisers to buy clicks/conversions in bulk without taking as much risk as in CPM. An advertiser specifies a CPM bid but in addition also specifies a conversion/click goal the campaign should meet. For instance, a dCPM campaign could have \$1 CPM bid but specify a goal of \$5 per conversion. This effectively specifies the total number of conversions an advertiser is expecting from the campaign. The exchange uses this information and dynamically bids on behalf of the advertiser to ensure that the ROI goals of the advertiser are met. The fundamental question is: *Given different pricing types that specify advertiser willingness to pay in different currencies, how should one conduct an auction in a unified way?* The solution currently pursued is to convert all pricing type specifications into a single currency, expected CPM (eCPM). For instance, if the click-rate is .005 and the bid per click is \$1, the eCPM is $1000 \times .005 \times 1 = \$5$. Thus, the machine learning problem here is to construct explore/exploit methods that can estimate click/conversion rates so that we maximize revenue in the eCPM based auctions. One important thing in this application is the need to obtain accurate estimate of absolute probabilities, which makes the estimation problem more challenging. While we will not discuss various machine learning challenges involved in performing explore/exploit on the exchange, we refer the reader to [1] for an example of a modeling solution and the nature of data obtained from the RightMedia exchange. The issues with explore/exploit discussed in the context of performance advertising all apply, except that the first phase candidate selection criteria and the utilities involved in conducting the auctions are different. The use of models like dCPM that promote buying clicks/conversions in bundles introduces new technical challenges for the explore/exploit problem. We also note that the bid used to compute the eCPM is adjusted for the *cuts* that are shared by various intermediaries in the exchange that connect buyers to sellers.

8.4   Discussion

Computational advertising is a multi-billion industry. It can be thought of as a recommender problem where the goal is to match opportunities to ads to maximize revenue. Depending on the goal of the advertisers, it comes in various flavors and has given rise to a complex ecosystem of publishers, advertisers, and various intermediaries. The costs and utilities involved in connecting an ad to a given opportunity vary and depend critically on the context. We also showed that a performance-based advertising problem can be formulated as a set of parallel multi-armed bandit problems, one for each opportunity. However, the bandit problems involved in performance-based advertising are far more complex than classical ones. The large number of parallel bandits leads to extreme data sparsity and it is difficult to converge to the best ad through vanilla bandit algorithms. Further, the bandit arms (ads) are not fixed; old ones are retired and new ones are introduced on a routine basis. The payoff per opportunity does not depend on the winner alone, but also on the performance of other ads that participate. This further complicates the solution of the bandit problem. Using supervised learning techniques to reduce the dimension and blending it with simple explore/exploit problems like UCB, ϵ-greedy, posterior draws, are generally used and they perform reasonably well. However, a combined solution that incorporates the initial candidate selection (broad match), dimension reduction through supervised learning, and auction payout simultaneously to achieve optimality is still an open problem and requires more work. In fact, it clearly shows there is significant room for improving performance advertising through future research.

In display advertising, forecasting supply is a challenging machine learning problem. However, unlike classical forecasting problems, the cost of forecasting error in this problem varies and depends on the targeting constraints used by existing bookings, future demand, and price (which depends on supply and demand). For instance, error in forecasting supply for an attribute combination that has more contention from bookings and demand is more costly. Machine learning methods that can improve accuracy in supply forecasts after incorporating the demand and pricing constraints in the system are important. Stochastic optimization that can incorporate uncertainty in both demand and supply when solving for admission control and ad-serving are also important problems that need more research. Although the machine learning challenges in non-guaranteed delivery are similar in nature to those in performance advertising, the utilities and costs involved are more complex. Moreover, the click and conversion rates in non-guaranteed are significantly lower and there is more data heterogeneity, which makes the explore/exploit problem more challenging. The move toward real-time bidding by major ad exchanges also adds statistical variation to the bid distribution that needs to be modeled and further complicates the explore/exploit tradeoffs.

Other contexts in which computational advertising models are being practiced include mobile devices and social media. Although still at an early stage, it is not clear that solutions from other contexts like Sponsored Search and Content Match apply to mobile devices. For instance, the additional location information, limited real-estate, and differences in what users are looking for in mobile devices may make the match-making solutions quite different. For advertising based on social connections, it is important to exploit the network information to perform ad targeting. Both problems mentioned above entail several challenges.

References

[1] Deepak Agarwal, Rahul Agrawal, Rajiv Khanna, and Nagaraj Kota. Estimating rates of rare events with multiple hierarchies through scalable

log-linear models. In *Knowledge Discovery and Data Mining '10*, pages 213–222, 2010.

[2] Deepak Agarwal, Andrei Zary Broder, Deepayan Chakrabarti, Dejan Diklic, Vanja Josifovski, and Mayssam Sayyadian. Estimating rates of rare events at multiple resolutions. In *Knowledge Discovery and Data Mining '07*, pages 16–25, 2007.

[3] Deepak Agarwal, Bee-Chung Chen, and Pradheep Elango. Explore/exploit schemes for web content optimization. In *International Conference on Data Mining*, pages 1–10, 2009.

[4] Deepak Agarwal, Bee-Chung Chen, and Pradheep Elango. Fast online learning through offline initialization for time-sensitive recommendation. In *Knowledge Discovery and Data Mining*, pages 703–712, 2010.

[5] Deepak Agarwal, Datong Chen, Long-ji Lin, Jayavel Shanmugasundaram, and Erik Vee. Forecasting high-dimensional data. In *Proceedings of the 2010 International Conference on Management of Data*, SIGMOD '10, pages 1003–1012. ACM, 2010.

[6] D. K. Agarwal and J. A. Tomlin. Optimal allocation of overlapping inventory in on-line advertising. Presented at INFORMS, 2008.

[7] A. Ghosh, P. Macafee, K. Papineni, and S. Vassilvitskii. Bidding for representative allocations for display advertising. In *Proceedings of the 4th International Workshop on Internet and Network Economics*, 2009.

[8] Tasos Anastasakos, Dustin Hillard, Sanjay Kshetramade, and Hema Raghavan. A collaborative filtering approach to ad recommendation using the query-ad click graph. In *International Conference on Information and Knowledge Management*, pages 1927–1930, 2009.

[9] B. Edelman, M. Ostrovsky, and M. Schwarz. Internet advertising and the generalized second-price auction: Selling billions of dollars worth of keywords. *American Economic Review, American Economic Association*, 97(1):242–259, 2007.

[10] D. Berry and B. Fristedt. *Bandit Problems: Sequential Allocation of Experiments*. Chapman & Hall, 1985.

[11] B. J. Jansen and T. Mullen. Sponsored search: An overview of the concept, history and technology. *International Journal of Electronic Business*, 6:114–131, 2008.

[12] Andrei Broder. Computational advertising. In *SODA '08: Proceedings of the Nineteenth Annual ACM-SIAM Symposium on Discrete Algorithms*, pages 992–992, 2008.

[13] Andrei Z. Broder, Peter Ciccolo, Marcus Fontoura, Evgeniy Gabrilovich, Vanja Josifovski, and Lance Riedel. Search advertising using web relevance feedback. In *International Conference on Information and Knowledge Management*, pages 1013–1022, 2008.

[14] A. Z. Broder. Computational advertising and recommender systems. In *Proceedings of the 2008 ACM Conference on Recommender Systems*, pages 1–2. ACM, 2008.

[15] Deepayan Chakrabarti, Deepak Agarwal, and Vanja Josifovski. Contextual advertising by combining relevance with click feedback. In *International Conference on World Wide Web*, pages 417–426, 2008.

[16] Haibin Cheng and Erick Cantú-Paz. Personalized click prediction in sponsored search. In *Web Search and Data Mining*, pages 351–360, 2010.

[17] M. H. DeGroot. *Optimal Statistical Decisions*. John Wiley & Sons, 2004.

[18] E. Vee, S. Vassilvitski, and J. Shanmugasundaran. Optimal online assignment with forecasts. In *Electronic Commerce*, 2010.

[19] D. C. Fain and J. O. Pederson. Sponsored search: A brief history. *Bulletin of American Society of Information and Technology*, 32:12–13, 2006.

[20] U. Feige, N. Immorlica, V. Mirrokni, and H. Nazerzadeh. A combinatorial allocation mechanism with penalties for banner advertising. Presented at INFORMS, 2008.

[21] J. C. Gittins. Bandit processes and dynamic allocation indices. *Journal of the Royal Statistical Society, B*, 41, 1979.

[22] K. D. Glazebrook, P. S. Ansell, R. T. Dunn, and R. R. Lumley. On the optimal allocation of service to impatient tasks. *Journal of Applied Probability*, 2004.

[23] G. M. Fulgoni and M. P. Morn. How online advertising works: Wither the click? Empirical Generalizations in Advertising Conference for Industry and Academia, 2008.

[24] T. Graepel, J. Q. Candela, T. Borchert, and R. Herbrich. Large-scale Bayesian click-through rate prediction for sponsored search advertising in microsoft's bing search engine. In *International Conference on Machine Learning*, 2010.

[25] Sonal Gupta, Mikhail Bilenko, and Matthew Richardson. Catching the drift: learning broad matches from clickthrough data. In *Knowledge Discovery and Data Mining*, pages 1165–1174, 2009.

[26] Rosie Jones, Benjamin Rey, Omid Madani, and Wiley Greiner. Generating query substitutions. In *Proceedings of the 15th International Conference on World Wide Web*, WWW '06, pages 387–396, New York, NY, 2006. ACM.

[27] T. L. Lai and Herbert Robbins. Asymptotically efficient adaptive allocation rules. *Advances in Applied Mathematics*, 1985.

[28] John Langford, Alexander Strehl, and Jennifer Wortman. Exploration scavenging. In *Proceedings of the 25th International Conference on Machine learning*, ICML '08, pages 528–535, New York, NY, 2008. ACM.

[29] R. Lewis and D. Reiley. Retail advertising works! measuring the effects of advertising on sales via a controlled experiment on yahoo! Yahoo! Research Technical Report, 2009.

[30] P. Auer, N. Cesa-Bianchi, and P. Fischer. Finite-time analysis of the multiarmed bandit problem. *Machine Learning*, 2002.

[31] Filip Radlinski, Andrei Z. Broder, Peter Ciccolo, Evgeniy Gabrilovich, Vanja Josifovski, and Lance Riedel. Optimizing relevance and revenue in ad search: a query substitution approach. In *SIGIR*, pages 403–410, 2008.

[32] Matthew Richardson, Ewa Dominowska, and Robert Ragno. Predicting clicks: Estimating the click-through rate for new ads. In *International Conference on World Wide Web '07*, 2007.

[33] R. Steuer. *Multi-Criteria Optimization: Theory, Computation, and Application*. Wiley, 1986.

[34] P. Sandeep, D. Agarwal, D. Chakrabarti, and V. Josifovski. Bandits for taxonomies: A model-based approach. In *SDM*, 2007.

[35] D. Sculley, Robert G. Malkin, Sugato Basu, and Roberto J. Bayardo. Predicting bounce rates in sponsored search advertisements. In *KDD*, pages 1325–1334, 2009.

[36] S. Dasgupta and J. Langford. Active learning tutorial. Presented at ICML, 2009.

[37] W. R. Thompson. On the likelihood that one unknown probability exceeds another in view of the evidence of two samples. *Biometrika*, 25:285–294, 1933.

[38] Liang Zhang and Deepak Agarwal. Fast computation of posterior mode in multi-level hierarchical models. In *NIPS*, pages 1913–1920, 2008.

Chapter 9

Cost-Sensitive Machine Learning for Information Retrieval

Martin Szummer

Microsoft Research, Cambridge, UK

Filip Radlinski

Microsoft, Vancouver British Columbia, Canada

9.1   Introduction

Information retrieval systems aim to help users find relevant information quickly and efficiently. A typical session with such a system starts with a user posing a query, in response to which the system presents a ranking of documents retrieved from a large collection, such as the web or a company document store. The user interacts with these results by examining and possible selecting (clicking on) some. The user can also follow up by reformulating the query to continue searching or can abandon the search. When finished, the user may or may not be satisfied.

There are multiple costs at play in this interaction, reflecting both the user and the system. First, there is a *user utility* (utility being the negative of cost) measuring the degree to which the information need is satisfied: high if the desired document or documents were found quickly, low if finding the documents took a lot of effort, and perhaps negative if effort was spent without finding anything. The retrieval system aims to maximize user utility. Second, there is cost to the system. In order to build and evaluate a system, one typically requires examples of interactions with low and high utility. In particular, many systems today use machine learning and are trained on collections of user interactions with known utility. Determining the utility of an interaction usually requires the judgment of a paid expert. Since a large number of examples are necessary to build a good retrieval system, the acquisition of training data represents a major *system cost*. We exclude non-machine-learning related costs such as development and operational costs.

As information retrieval systems balance user utility against system cost, they provide a rich stage for cost-sensitive machine learning techniques. General techniques such as active, semi-supervised, adaptation, and online learning apply. The information retrieval domain offers a special setting for these techniques, however, as the task is to rank results into an ordered list, rather than more standard classification or regression tasks. Moreover, the training data may consist of preferences among items, rather than absolute labels for individual items. In addition, the data is grouped by query, with multiple training documents per query.

Algorithms that measure, optimize, or reduce these costs are a central topic in information retrieval. The challenge is that the user utility cannot be directly observed, and involves the non-tangible satisfaction of users' individual information needs. The field relies heavily on the notion of *relevance* of a document to a query as a proxy for user utility. Not surprisingly, there are many ways of defining relevance; Mizzaro's survey [41] covers 160 works, listing many types such as topical relevance and relevance to a task. However, as a first approximation, we will treat relevance simply as a binary relation between a query and a document.

We will later study another proxy for user utility, namely *user behavior*, in particular user clicks on search results. A common assumption is that users click on results that are more likely to meet their information need than on other results. Confusingly, while clicks may indicate relative utility, they do not constitute utility in themselves. In fact, we want to minimize the number of clicks required to find the desired documents. We may also want to minimize more general measures, such as time-till-found, but the "found" event again is usually not directly observable.

Unlike user utility, the system cost is directly observable. One substantial cost is the relevance judgment cost. Expert judges need to be trained and paid, with typical collections often consisting of millions of judgments over tens of thousands of queries (e.g., [14]) collected at significant expense. For instance, judges involved in assessing documents for one of the tasks for the annual Text Retrieval Conference (TREC) in 2008 took on average around two minutes to select and understand each query to judge, followed by ten to twenty seconds per judged document [1]. Considering additional expenses in maintaining representative query collections (i.e., requiring judgments to be collected for all queries in a sample), and ensuring that judgments are current with respect to the intent of actual users, the costs can be substantially higher. Crowd-sourced judgments appear significantly cheaper, but multiple judges are necessary to maintain quality, and judge training to ensure consistency of judgments is often impractical. In comparison, the cost of obtaining user behavior data is negligible.

Even though system costs are easy to quantify, they are non-trivial to manage. Judgments are required for multiple purposes, such as training and evaluating the system. These tasks differ in what queries should be judged, how many documents to judge per query, how many judges to ask to reduce noise, among other differences. For example, to evaluate which of two systems is better, it is not useful to judge documents that the systems rank identically (see work on minimal test collections [10]), whereas it could be useful for training purposes. Allocating judgments to minimize system cost while maximizing user utility is thus a complex problem.

9.2   Utility in Information Retrieval

We now formalize user utility employing decision theory. Decision theory was present in retrieval as early as the 1960s (surveyed in [54]); in the early days, users had to pay for querying retrieval systems, which perhaps focused attention on costs. Decision theory has among many applications been used for active learning for retrieval [21], and as a framework for complex cost functions, such as those encouraging diverse results or coverage of multiple subtopics [57].

Decision theory is a framework for choosing an *action* under uncertainty in order to maximize expected utility. In retrieval, the action is the ranking of documents for a given user query. In other words, an action is a permutation of documents in the collection. The utility depends on how the user interacts with the results list; for example, how many documents the user *examines* (looks at the summary for) or clicks, and how many of those are relevant. When choosing a ranking, the system is uncertain about how the user will behave in response to that ranking, and maintains a distribution over possible behaviors. The best action is that which maximizes expected utility under the uncertainty.

For brevity, our description is for a single query, which is left implicit. Hence, we only discuss actions and rankings for that query. All examinations and relevance are with respect to that query.

We describe the possible actions (permutations) by $\boldsymbol{\pi}$, where $\boldsymbol{\pi}(r) = i$ denotes that rank r is assigned item i. We refer to the ranked list of documents by $\boldsymbol{x}_{\boldsymbol{\pi}}$. We shall use the subscript notation (r) to implicitly mean $\boldsymbol{\pi}(r)$, so that we can refer to rth element in the ranking by $\boldsymbol{x}_{(r)}$. Let $\boldsymbol{y}_{\boldsymbol{\pi}}$ describe the user actions, which consists of binary indicators $e_{(r)}$ and $c_{(r)}$ which are 1 when the user examined and clicked a document at rank r, respectively. The uncertainty over user actions is described by the distribution $P(\boldsymbol{y}_{\boldsymbol{\pi}} \mid \boldsymbol{x}_{\boldsymbol{\pi}})$. The system maximizes expected utility by selecting an action

$$\boldsymbol{\pi} = \operatorname*{argmax}_{\boldsymbol{\pi}} E_{P(y_{\boldsymbol{\pi}}|x_{\boldsymbol{\pi}})}[U(\boldsymbol{y}_{\boldsymbol{\pi}}, \boldsymbol{x}_{\boldsymbol{\pi}})]. \tag{9.1}$$

This model is very general. We will refer to the expected utility of a ranking as the *value* $V(\boldsymbol{\pi}) = E_{P(y_{\boldsymbol{\pi}}|x_{\boldsymbol{\pi}})}[U(\boldsymbol{y}_{\boldsymbol{\pi}}, \boldsymbol{x}_{\boldsymbol{\pi}})]$. As real user interactions are too complex to model precisely, we simplify the model in three steps. Firstly, we consider utilities that depend only on a single modality, in particular the relevance l of documents, and possibly the content $\boldsymbol{x}$ of the documents. At training time, relevance ground truth is provided by human judges, and at test time, relevance is estimated by the system. We will defer utilities based on clicks to Section 9.4.2 or both relevance and clicks to Section 9.5.

Secondly, we model the user as sequentially examining the results list from the top, with a probability $P(e_{(r)})$ of examining the rth rank, where the probability is high at the top but decays monotonically to 0 further down the list. The uncertainty is only whether the user examines the document, and depends only on the rank r. We also assume that relevance is a deterministic function of the document, hence the utility is deterministic given examination. Thirdly, we assume that the utility of the whole ranking decomposes over each rank position, given the previous ranks, in one of these three ways:

$$V_{\text{dep}}(\boldsymbol{\pi}) = \sum_{r} P(e_{(r)})U(l_{(r)}, \boldsymbol{x}_{(r)} \mid l_{(r-1)}, \boldsymbol{x}_{(r-1)}, \ldots, l_{(1)}, \boldsymbol{x}_{(1)}), \tag{9.2}$$

$$V_{\text{indep-lab}}(\boldsymbol{\pi}) = \sum_r P(e_{(r)})U(l_{(r)} \mid l_{(r-1)}, \dots, l_{(1)}), \tag{9.3}$$

$$V_{\text{indep}}(\boldsymbol{\pi}) = \sum_r P(e_{(r)})U(l_{(r)}). \tag{9.4}$$

V_{indep} is fully independent and the utility of each document only depends on its relevance. $V_{\text{indep-lab}}$ allows the utility to depend on the relevance of previously examined documents, for example, on how many there were. Finally, V_{dep} is a dependent utility, whose value can be a function of both the relevance and identity of the document $x_{(r)}$, e.g., taking into account whether the document is a duplicate or redundant in light of previously examined documents.

9.2.1 The Probability Ranking Principle

Having chosen a suitable utility function, the question becomes how to find the ranking $\boldsymbol{\pi}$ that maximizes expected utility (Equation 9.1). The naive approach is to evaluate all possible rankings, but there is an infeasible exponential number of them. Fortunately, there exists a simple efficient scheme for value functions that decompose as V_{indep} and $V_{\text{indep-lab}}$. This scheme is the probability ranking principle (PRP) [46], which states that an optimal ranking is achieved by ordering documents in decreasing probability of relevance. It assumes that the relevance $l_{(r)}$ of a document is independent of other documents; however, the utility can depend on the number of previously examined documents. It justifies a greedy ranking scheme, where the next highest utility document is picked one by one. The probability $P(e_{(r)})$ of examining documents does not influence the optimal ranking (so long as it decays monotonically).

9.2.2 Common Utility Formulations

We now interpret popular retrieval cost functions (metrics) using the utility formalism from the previous section. These metrics are based on the relevance of retrieved documents. The relevance can be absolute and assigned to individual items, or it can be relative and apply to pairs of items.

Nearly all metrics emphasize the top of the ranking, as they implicitly presume the sequential browsing model, in which a user is more likely to look at top results. Hence, errors at the top of the ranking are more costly to users. There are two common choices for the browsing model $P(e_{(r)})$. In the *cutoff at K* model (abbreviated as @K), the user is assumed to examine the top K documents with equal probability, and none below that, i.e., $P(e_{(r)}) = \frac{1}{K}\mathbb{I}_{r \in [1,K]}$. In the discount model, the probability of examination decays according to a *discount* function of rank r, such as $P(e_{(r)}) \propto 1/\log_2(r+1)$, although this function is often eventually truncated at some rank r.

TABLE 9.1: Some popular metrics written in the utility framework.

Metric	Relevance	$P(e_{(r)})$	$U(l_{(r)} \mid l_{(r-1)}, \ldots)$
Precision @K	$\{0,1\}$	$\frac{1}{K}\mathbb{I}_{r\in[1,K]}$	$l_{(r)}$
Recall @K	$\{0,1\}$	$\frac{1}{K}\mathbb{I}_{r\in[1,K]}$	$l_{(r)} \cdot K/\text{Nrel}$
AP @K	$\{0,1\}$	$\frac{1}{K}\mathbb{I}_{r\in[1,K]}$	$\frac{1}{r}\sum_{r'=1}^{r} l_{(r')}$
DCG	$\{0,\ldots,R\text{-}1\}$	$\frac{1}{\log_2(r+1)}$	$2^{l_{(r)}} - 1$
ppref @K	$r' \succ r$	$\frac{1}{K}\mathbb{I}_{r\in[1,K]}$	$\frac{2}{K(K-1)}\sum_{r'=1}^{r-1}\mathbb{I}_{r'\succ r}$

The four columns detail the metric, the domain of the relevance label, the examination model, and the formula for the utility. Nrel is the total number of relevant documents for the query.

9.2.2.1   Absolute User Utilities

Absolute relevance can be described using labels l_i of individual items. The relevance can be binary, in which case $l_i = 1$ denotes relevant and $l_i = 0$ non-relevant. Alternatively, relevance can be *graded*, $l_i \in [0, \ldots, L_{\max}-1]$.

For binary relevance, two basic metrics are precision and recall at a cutoff K. Precision @K is the fraction of relevant documents out of the top K. Recall @K is the fraction of relevant documents in the top K out of the total number of relevant documents for that query in the collection. Note that these two metrics are invariant to the ranking within the top K, treating the documents above the cutoff as a set.

Average precision (AP) is a metric that is more sensitive to the ranking. It is defined as an average of precision @i, where i are the ranks of relevant documents. It is typically applied with very large or no cutoffs.

For graded relevance, a popular metric is discounted cumulative gain (DCG) and its normalized version (NDCG) [29]. It assigns each graded label l_i a utility called a label gain L_i, e.g., $L_i = 2^{l_i} - 1$, reflecting that excellent high-grade documents contribute much more utility than only fairly relevant ones. The metric focuses on the top of the ranking by weighting rank positions according to a discount function R_i of the rank r_i, a model for $P(e_{(r)})$. DCG is often truncated at relatively low cutoffs. NDCG is obtained by dividing the DCG value by $\text{DCG}_{\max}$, the maximum value of the sum achieved by an ideal ranking, so that the ideal NDCG score is 1.

Precision, recall, and NDCG can all be written in the form $\sum_i L_i R_i$, with the appropriate discount R_i and label gains L_i, corresponding to the browsing examination model and utility parts (Table 9.1).

The above formulas are used to calculate the metrics for a single query. To train or evaluate a retrieval system, the metrics are typically averaged over a large number of different queries. The average of AP over queries is explicitly referred to as *mean average precision* (MAP), and is one of the most common metrics.

9.2.2.2 Preference-Based User Utilities

The above metrics require absolute relevance labels. Sometimes only relative relevance preferences between pairs of documents are available. One metric for this case is precision of preferences (*ppref*) @K, which is simply the fraction of document pairs correctly ordered in the top K (see also Table 9.1). This metric is strongly related to others, such as Kendall's τ [36, 25], the Spearman Footrule [22], and ROC Area [42]. Analogously to absolute judgments metrics, one can also define recall of preferences and average precision of preferences [12], which are more rank sensitive.

9.2.3 Ambiguity, Diversity, and Dependent Utility

Until now, we have a single, universal relevance. This is unrealistic when considering multiple users. First, note that information retrieval queries are often inherently ambiguous, for example *jaguar*. In such cases, different users can consider the same document to have different relevance, with the relevance of documents being anti-correlated with document similarity. To obtain maximal utility, the ranking shown to users must present a *diverse* range of results about different possible information needs. Second, even when the meaning of a query is certain, multiple results may contain redundant information. While some redundancy may increase user utility (for example, providing the same facts from independent sources), redundant documents generally do not add any utility to users. These two challenges make estimating the probability of relevance without considering previously ranked documents impossible, meaning that the probability ranking principle does not apply. This will lead us to a number of *dependent* utility functions.

For evaluating diversity, queries are often defined in terms of *subtopics* [16] or information *nuggets* [18] (intuitively, different aspects relevant to the query). For example, subtopic recall @K is the fraction of subtopics for a given query retrieved by rank K [16]. Similarly, subtopic precision is a function of the number of documents that a user must examine before observing a specified fraction of subtopics [16]. The nugget approach gives reduced credit as nuggets of information are repeated, parameterized with a parameter α, giving a metric α–NDCG [18]. Finally, Novelty- and Ranked-Biased Precision (NRBP) is a complex metric that considers novelty, redundancy, and query ambiguity [19].

Most interestingly from a decision theoretic aspect, Wang and Zhu argue that expected utility must be traded against variance in utility due to uncertainty from query ambiguity, idiosyncratic user preferences, and errors made by the ranking function [33]. They propose to optimize $E[U] - b \cdot \text{Var}[U]$ with a choice of b determined by the ranking task.

9.2.4 Utilities for Generalization

The retrieval community has worked hard to develop algorithms that directly optimize various user utilities on training data (Section 9.3). Optimizing ranking objectives does give better performance than optimizing classification or regression objectives in retrieval applications [43]. However, such direct optimization on training data is an example of empirical risk minimization (ERM), and is not usually optimal, as it ignores the need for generalization to new test data. In particular, ERM assumes that the true data distribution consists of exactly the given training points, and nothing else.

Generalization suffers particularly when the utility ignores large parts of the training data. For example, utilities with aggressive cutoffs, such as NDCG@5, only depend on a few top-ranked results, and are invariant to the ranking beyond the cutoff. This effectively ignores most of the training data. Usually, better generalization is obtained by training without cutoffs, and with a slowly decaying discount function. For example, training with a linearly decaying discount is better than the standard logarithmic decay used for evaluation at test time [52]. Furthermore, it is better to train with informative metrics that are sensitive to the order of all items (such as AP and NDCG), rather than with precision and recall @K, which are invariant to permutations of the top K.

9.2.5 Label Collection

Judgments (labels) are required both for training a system, and for evaluating its utility. Judgments are typically made by paid assessors, at significant cost. The TREC community has been developing evaluation collections for many years. In these evaluations, typically the top 100 results for 50 chosen queries retrieved by about 20 systems were pooled and judged, requiring about 73,000 judgments annually [47]. Recently, much larger web collections have been released by Microsoft, Yahoo, and Yandex, with 30,000 queries and more than half a million judgments. However, test collections have exceeded 1 billion unjudged documents, and thus only a tiny fraction of possible queries and available documents are assessed. Hence, strategies for choosing representative documents and queries to judge are essential.

Firstly, we consider different types of judgments: absolute or relative. Absolute judgments consist of a relevance label that is assigned to individual documents for a query. The labels are typically binary (indicating relevant/non-relevant), or graded up to five levels of relevance. Multiple grades capture fine distinctions in relevance, but calibration across judges and queries becomes difficult. Preference judgments offer a flexible alternative: judges indicate their relative preference of one document versus another. Studies show that humans produce judgments that are more consistent and do so quicker when giving preferences rather than absolute labels [11]. Label collection schemes also vary in whether judges formulate their own queries, or whether they judge other users' queries, in which case they have to infer the underlying information needs [47]. Moreover, judges have varying levels of expertise about the query topic, and topic experts often assign harsher judgments than novices do [3]. Preference judgments may help here, but have not been extensively applied yet.

Secondly, we must decide what queries and what documents to judge. The actual query distribution follows a power law: there are a few exceedingly popular queries, but there is a long tail of rare queries that amount to a significant fraction of the total volume observed by a retrieval system, and thus cannot be ignored. It appears useful to follow the distribution and include the popular queries in training sets, but it is unknown how to find representative tail queries.

For a given query, documents must be selected for judging. For evaluation purposes, it is common to judge a pool of top-K documents from multiple systems. For training purposes, it is important to include sufficient examples from many regions of the test distribution of different levels of relevance. A common strategy is to use old evaluation sets for training, but care must be taken to avoid biased training sets. Bias can occur for example when only the top results from a simple ranker (e.g., a TF-IDF variant such as BM25) are included [40]; it is important to also include samples of lower-ranking results. Active learning (Section 9.4.3.2) offers more informed strategies for document and query selection.

9.3 Learning to Rank

Most modern retrieval systems rely on machine learning to learn a ranking function that optimizes user utility. The training set consists of multiple queries, each with an associated partial ranking of documents (where the partial ranking may be empty). For a new test query, the goal is to rank all the documents in the collection.

9.3.1 Problem Setting

Consider the ranking problem for a single query; this consists of a set $X = \{x_i \in \mathbb{R}^n\}$ of items (documents) with feature vectors, to which we would like to assign a ranking $\mathbf{r}$, a permutation of the numbers $1, \ldots, |X|$. Here r_i refers to the rank of item i and the top (preferred) rank is 1.

In ranking, label information can take several forms as we have seen, such as absolute labels for individual items, preference relations, partial orderings, or complete orderings. Here, we will focus on pairwise preference relations of the form "item i is preferred to j," and denoted by $i \succ j$. This is a pragmatic choice, as preference relations arise naturally from user choices from lists (e.g., clicks on search results). Moreover, absolute labels can be trivially translated into preferences on pairs, but not vice versa. Ranking algorithms usually rely on pairwise comparisons internally, thus models of preference play a central role, unlike in classification and ordinal regression algorithms.

Let D^L be a set of labeled items. Our task is to learn a function $f(\boldsymbol{x})$ that ranks the items X for a query. We will consider rankers that assign a score $s_i = f(\boldsymbol{x}_i)$ to each item, where higher scores indicate preference. A ranking can be produced simply by sorting the scores (we assume there are no ties). We will consider probabilistic models that assign a probability of preference $P(i \succ j)$ based on score differences.

For notational convenience, we will display a ranking for a single query (consisting of a single set of items, preferences with respect to that query, yielding a single rank ordering); in practice, we will have training data consisting of multiple document sets with associated orderings, $\{X^{(q)}, \mathbf{r}^{(q)}\}$, from which we learn a single ranking function f.

9.3.2   Learning Algorithms

We need a probabilistic model and an algorithm that learns a ranker from pairwise preferences, or individually labeled items that induce preferences on pairs. The algorithm should be able to optimize the established user utilities (e.g., MAP, NDCG), including their emphasis of top rank positions, and be scalable to large datasets.

We will focus on the LambdaRank algorithm [8], as it is a very effective and practical algorithm, and is extensible to semi-supervised learning and adaptation. We begin by looking at probabilistic models for rankings.

9.3.2.1   Bradley-Terry Model

We now introduce a model that makes probabilistic predictions, such as assigning a probability to one item being preferred to another. Moreover, given training data, we can infer parameters of the model, to learn a ranker.

We employ the Bradley-Terry model, a long-standing model in the literature [6, 38]. It associates a parameter s_i to each item, which can be thought of as a score. Then it defines the probability $P(i \succ j)$ that item i is preferred to j to be the logistic function of their score difference:

$$P(i \succ j) = 1/(1 + \mathrm{e}^{-(s_i - s_j)}). \tag{9.5}$$

For example, if $s_i > s_j$, then $P(i \succ j) > 0.5$. By construction, pairwise preferences from the model are transitive, so that $P(i \succ j) > 0.5$ and $P(j \succ k) > 0.5$ implies $P(i \succ k) > 0.5$; in fact, $P(i \succ j)$ and $P(j \succ k)$ uniquely determine $P(i \succ k)$ [7].

Learning to Rank Algorithm. Given scores, the Bradley-Terry model defines probabilities of preference, but our task is to go all the way from item features to a ranking function. We can choose a neural network for assigning the scores $s_i = f(\boldsymbol{x}_i; \boldsymbol{w})$ for the Bradley-Terry model, and in this way we obtain the RankNet model [7]. We do not have to use a neural network, however; any differentiable function will do for our purposes. This model can be learned by maximizing a sum of log likelihoods over the observed preference pairs D^L, as indicated by $\mathbb{I}_{i \succ j}$ (ordered pairs (i, j) and (j, i) are both included in the sum):

$$\max_{\boldsymbol{w}} \sum_{(i,j) \in D^L} \mathbb{I}_{i \succ j} \log P(i \succ j). \tag{9.6}$$

The maximization can be done via stochastic gradient descent with respect to the parameters $\boldsymbol{w}$. This objective can be seen as a smooth approximation to pairwise accuracy (ppref), is easy to optimize, and gives good retrieval results. Although it is not a common metric in retrieval benchmarks, the Bradley-Terry model will figure as a smoothness factor in other retrieval utilities, which we will discuss next.

9.3.2.2 LambdaRank

The challenge in learning a ranker tailored to NDCG, MAP, and most retrieval metrics is that these metrics depend only on the rank of items, rather than their underlying scores. This reflects the fact that the user is shown only a ranked list. Moreover, the ranker should be able to incorporate the metrics' emphasis on correctly ranking the top documents, since these are the documents the user is most likely to see.

Recall that many utilities can be written as $U = \sum_i L_i R_i$. This may appear simple, but the ranks r_i are discontinuous functions in the parameters $\boldsymbol{w}$; in particular, the ranking is determined by sorting by the scores $\{s_i\}$. The ranks only change when one score overtakes another, in which case the metric makes a step change; otherwise it remains constant.

LambdaRank [8] is an algorithm that has been empirically shown to optimize NDCG and MAP [23] and works with other independent metrics too. LambdaRank is state of the art in ranking: for instance, the winning entry in the recent Yahoo ranking competition [14] was based on the LambdaRank principle, with $f()$ chosen to be an ensemble of boosted decision trees. It is a practical algorithm with excellent generalization and speed on web-scale information retrieval tasks [52]. Other popular learning to rank algorithms include RankSVM [30] and RankBoost [27].

We now describe how LambdaRank can optimize any utility that decomposes into a sum over document pairs. This includes utilities of the form $\sum_i L_i R_i$ (as shown below), as well as mean average precision (MAP) (using results from [23]).

There are a few ways to present LambdaRank. Firstly, we can see it as a Bradley-Terry model of pairwise preferences where the log likelihood of each pair has been weighted by the magnitude of change in the metric if the items in that pair are swapped. It is a very intuitive way to weight pairs, but it does not explain why this actually optimizes the desired metric.

The second way is how LambdaRank was originally presented [8]. It observes that it can be easier to optimize an implicit objective defined by a gradient function with respect to the sorted scores, rather than working with the original cost function. This gradient function can be discontinuous. This viewpoint suggests searching over valid gradient functions for one that generalizes well on the metric, but offers no guidance for which functions to search over for a given objective.

The third explanation of LambdaRank is our derivation that starts from the original metric, rewritten in terms of pairs, and then smoothed in order to be differentiable. We can write U in terms of pairs:

$$U = \sum_i L_i R_i \stackrel{\circ}{=} 2N \sum_i L_i R_i - \sum_i L_i \sum_j R_j - \sum_j L_j \sum_i R_i \qquad (9.7)$$

$$= \sum_{(i,j)} \left(L_i R_i + L_j R_j - L_i R_j - L_j R_i \right) \stackrel{\triangle}{=} \sum_{(i,j)} \Delta_{ij}. \qquad (9.8)$$

Here $\stackrel{\circ}{=}$ refers to equality for purposes of maximization with respect to $\boldsymbol{w}$, which is invariant to multiplication by $2N$, where N is the number of items in the ranking, as well as to subtraction of products of the constants $\sum_i L_i$ and $\sum_j R_j = N(N+1)/2$ (a sum over all possible ranks). We observe that the first summand in Equation 9.8 equals the metric value of the ranking minus the metric value of the ranking if i and j were to be swapped. We denote this change in metric due to the swap by Δ_{ij}. After some algebra, it can be shown to be equivalent to maximize

$$U \stackrel{\circ}{=} \sum_{(i,j)\in D^L} |\Delta_{ij}| \, \mathbb{I}_{i \succ j} \, \mathbb{I}_{P(i \succ j) > 0.5}. \qquad (9.9)$$

This expression involves two indicators (step functions). The first one indicates the observed preferences (e.g., as given by judges). The second one is a step function of the preferences $P(i \succ j)$ output by the model. For learning and optimization, we would prefer this to be a smooth function, and therefore we replace the step by a logarithm, over the [0,1] domain of the argument $P(i \succ j)$.[1]

$$U \cong \sum_{(i,j)\in D^L} |\Delta_{ij}| \, \mathbb{I}_{i \succ j} \log P(i \succ j), \qquad (9.10)$$

with gradient $\quad dU/ds_i = \sum_{\{j|(i,j)\in D^L\}} |\Delta_{ij}| \left(\mathbb{I}_{i \succ j} - P(i \succ j) \right). \qquad (9.11)$

---

[1] Since $P(i \succ j) = \sigma(s_i - s_j)$ (a logistic of score difference) we can also interpret the approximation as replacing a step loss of score difference by a logistic loss of score difference $(\log \sigma(s_i - s_j))$.

We have taken the derivative of a sigmoid $dP(i \succ j)/ds_i = P(i \succ j)(1 - P(i \succ j)) = P(i \succ j)P(j \succ i)$.

LambdaRank gradients can also be intuitively visualized as "forces" acting on each pair of documents (Figure 9.1), pushing the more relevant document up in the ranking, and the other one down. The resultant force on document i, shown in dU/ds_i, is a sum over forces from other documents j. The forces depend on the current ranks and scores (which in turn depend on the parameters w), as well as the labels of the documents. The gradient with respect to parameters can then be calculated as $dU/dw = \sum_i (dU/ds_i)(ds_i/dw)$, and this is used for gradient descent training.

9.3.2.3 Optimizing Non-Independent Utilities

So far, the algorithms presented optimize a *fully independent* utility function, as described in Section 9.2. We now turn to dependent utilities. Most algorithms for dependent utilities are based on the idea of maximal marginal relevance (MMR) [9]. MMR picks the top-ranked document according to a given independent ranking function f. However, MMR then greedily picks the next document that best trades off a high independent score with low document similarity g to previously picked documents. At rank r, the algorithm picks a document satisfying

$$\operatorname*{argmax}_{x_i} \left(f(x_i) - \lambda \max_{r' < r} g(x_i, x_{(r')}) \right). \tag{9.12}$$

A variety of models have been learned for this setting (for example, [16, 33]).

An alternative greedy selection formulation involves sequentially picking documents while always assuming that all previously selected documents are non-relevant [15],

$$\operatorname*{argmax}_{x_i} U(x_i \mid \forall r' : r' < r, \ U(x_{(r')}) = 0). \tag{9.13}$$

This requires training a new model for scoring documents at each rank, and is only practical when the ranking model can be updated incrementally.

A non-greedy approach that optimizes non-independent metrics has also been proposed [55]. Instead of relying on document similarity, or learning at every position, it involves explicitly learning weights for word occurrence features in documents to optimize the utility of the entire set of documents retrieved.

9.4 Reducing Labeling Cost

We have argued that the labeling cost is a significant factor when building a retrieval system. In this section, we examine ways of reducing this cost. One way is to use fewer labeled items, but to supplement these with unlabeled items that can be obtained in large quantities at low cost. This approach is used in *semi-supervised ranking* (Section 9.4.1). Second, we can collect cheaper types of labels; instead of paying professional assessors to make explicit judgments, we can derive *implicit labels* based on user clicks (9.4.2). Third, we can selectively label items that are the most informative to the system at a point in time; this is *active learning to rank* (9.4.3). Finally, we can use labels from one task for related tasks, for example in *ranking adaptation* (9.5) from one corpus of documents to another.

9.4.1 Semi-Supervised Ranking

Semi-supervised learning involves learning from partially labeled data, commonly including a small amount of labeled data and a large amount of unlabeled data. There is a wealth of work in semi-supervised classification and regression. The problem setting also occurs in retrieval. One instance is *relevance feedback*, in which a user issues a query, and labels a few of the resulting documents from a (typically) hand-tailored ranker (BM25 or language modeling). The ranker then incorporates the partially labeled results to produce refined results.

Here we employ semi-supervised data for learning a better ranking function. This is applicable both to learning a general ranker for new queries (a non-transductive case), or to improving a ranker for specific queries as in the relevance feedback scenario (a transductive case where the test query is given at training time). A training query may come with only unlabeled documents, or with some labeled and some unlabeled. The labeled data D^L for a query consists of individually labeled documents or preference relationships between documents, whereas the unlabeled data D^U is a set of documents which will be used in an unsupervised way (and whose labels may not be available). The unlabeled items for a query are typically taken from its retrieved results (for some standard retrieval methods) and from near the top of their rankings for that query. Such items are more likely to reveal some structure useful for learning ranking functions emphasizing top ranks, unlike random items that would generally be non-relevant and spread out thinly in the space, having little in common with one another.

9.4.1.1 Overview of Semi-Supervised Ranking

Existing semi-supervised work falls in two broad classes: self-training and graph-based regularization. The self-training approach, termed *pseudo relevance feedback*, is very popular in retrieval [37]. It assumes that the top k retrieved results from the ranker are relevant, and uses them to retrain the ranker. A variation of this is to take the results below rank k to be negative (non-relevant); this is a fairly safe assumption, as the vast majority of items are non-relevant, and including such items improves ranker training in practice. Other self-training approaches assign labels via a nearest neighbor classifier [2].

Graph-based regularization is another way to combine labeled and unlabeled data, via a manifold regularizer (the second term below) [4]. In the context of regression, we have

$$\min_f \sum_{i \in D^L} \|f(\boldsymbol{x}_i) - y_i\|^2 + \beta \sum_{i,j \in D^U} W_{ij} \|f(\boldsymbol{x}_i) - f(\boldsymbol{x}_j)\|^2. \qquad (9.14)$$

This formulation fits the function f to target labels y_i while also making sure that function values of similar items $\boldsymbol{x}_i$ and $\boldsymbol{x}_j$ are close, according to a similarity measure W_{ij}, typically defined in terms of graph Laplacians.

The approach has been extended to ranking by handling input given as pairwise preference relations [49], and the function f can be a Gaussian process [17]. Moreover, these works have been limited to a single query (corresponding to a single graph, a transductive case), and have high computational cost $O(|D^U|^3)$. We will therefore focus on a more general graph-based regularization approach that extends LambdaRank, that can optimize ranking metrics (NDCG or MAP), and is very scalable. We will begin by stepping back to discuss regularization principles for ranking.

9.4.1.2 Ranking Regularization

The key to semi-supervised learning is a principle connecting the structure of the unlabeled data with the function to be learned. In classification, a commonly used principle is the cluster assumption [48], which states that data points in each high-density region (cluster) should have the same labels. In regression, a principle is to assume that the function value changes slowly in high-density regions (as formalized by Equation 9.14). In retrieval, it has been observed that closely related documents tend to be relevant to the same query. We interpret this in a ranking context, and require that similar documents be similar in preference to each other with respect to a query. Specifically, neither document should be much preferred to the other; ideally, they should tie in preference.

This preference similarity assumption is weaker than the classification one, as it only constrains relative item order, and not absolute score or class. For a similar pair of documents, it does not assume which document is preferred, or where in the overall ranking the pair will place.

We quantify the similarity between documents i and j as the probability of transitioning between them under a noise model. We base the transition probability on the exponentiated distance $d_{ij}^2 = \|\boldsymbol{x}_i - \boldsymbol{x}_j\|^2$ between the document feature vectors. However, we only allow transitions to K-nearest neighbors $N_K(i)$, as we want to follow the local manifold relying only on local distances. The probability of an i to j transition is

$$\hat{q}_{j|i} = \begin{cases} \mathrm{e}^{-d_{ij}^2/\sigma_i} / \sum_{k \in N_K(i)} \mathrm{e}^{-d_{ik}^2/\sigma_i} & \text{if } j \in N_K(i), \\ 0 & \text{otherwise.} \end{cases} \qquad (9.15)$$

The probability of going there and back is then $\hat{q}_{ij} = \hat{q}_{i|j}\hat{q}_{j|i} \, / \, Z$, where Z normalizes $\hat{q}_{ij}$ to sum to one over all pairs.

We also quantify the probability that neither document is preferred to the other. This is given by $P(i \nsucc j)P(j \nsucc i)$, where $P(i \nsucc j) = 1 - P(i \succ j) = P(j \succ i)$. The lowest possible preference is a tie, when $P(i \succ j) = P(j \succ i) = 0.5$. These probabilities are given by the Bradley-Terry model, and depend on the ranking function with parameters $\boldsymbol{w}$.

To form the regularizer, we must link the document similarity to the preference similarity. Recall the manifold regularizer for regression (Equation 9.14) that penalized the output difference between a pair of items (i, j) according to their input similarity. In the ranking case, for every pair (i, j) we have a probabilistic preference similarity, and a probabilistic input similarity. We shall penalize the difference between these two distributions according to their KL divergence. This penalty is the same as the stochastic neighbor embedding (SNE) objective [53], which ensures that probabilistic neighborhood relations in a high-dimensional space are preserved when the points are embedded in a low-dimensional space. One can think of this regularizer as penalizing bad embeddings from the input space to the low-dimensional rank space.

The ranking regularizer becomes $\sum_{(i,j)} \hat{q}_{ij} \log P(i \nsucc j)P(j \nsucc i)$. It strongly penalizes models for which similar documents (high $\hat{q}_{ij}$) have dissimilar preference (probabilities close to 0 and 1, yielding a low product $P(i \nsucc j)P(j \nsucc i)$). However, it only weakly penalizes the converse: dissimilar documents can be similar in preference. This behavior springs from the asymmetry of the KL-divergence. It is desirable, as we can assume more about preferences between similar documents than about dissimilar ones.

Semi-Supervised LambdaRank. The ranking regularizer does not use label information, thus it can be used for all documents, both labeled and unlabeled ones. Most user utilities place an extra emphasis on top ranks, and we can incorporate this into the regularizer by weighting document pairs according to their absolute difference in discount $|\Delta_{ij}^U| = |R_i - R_j|$.

We obtain a semi-supervised ranker by adding the regularizer to the supervised LambdaRank objective (Equation 9.10),

$$U \cong \sum_{(i,j) \in D^L} |\Delta_{ij}||\mathbb{I}_{i \succ j}| \log P(i \succ j) + \beta \sum_{i,j \in D^U} |\Delta_{ij}^U| \hat{q}_{ij} \, \log P(i \nsucc j)P(j \nsucc i),$$

$$dU/ds_i = \sum_{\{j|(i,j) \in D^L\}} |\Delta_{ij}| \, (\mathbb{I}_{i \succ j} - P(i \succ j)) + \beta \sum_{j \in D^U} |\Delta_{ij}^U| \hat{q}_{ij} \, (0.5 - P(i \succ j)).$$

$$(9.16)$$

Comparing the labeled and unlabeled terms, one sees that the document similarity probability $\hat{q}_{ij}$ serves a role similar to preferences $\mathbb{I}_{i \succ j}$ in the labeled data. One difference between the labeled and unlabeled gradients is that the unlabeled gradient always tries to reduce the difference in ranks between i and j; the gradient sign is controlled by $0.5 - P(i \succ j)$ which is positive if $i \prec j$, or 0 if equal, or negative otherwise. In contrast, the labeled gradients

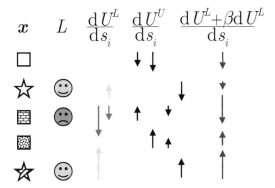

FIGURE 9.1: Example gradients for labeled data, unlabeled data, and both during a run of LambdaRank. All gradients are with respect to document scores s_i, pushing the documents up or down the ranking.

can either increase or decrease the rank difference depending on the labels, as the sign is positive when $i \succ j$ or negative when $j \succ i$, regardless of their ranking position. Figure 9.1 illustrates the construction of labeled and unlabeled gradients for LambdaRank. The column marked $\boldsymbol{x}$ shows the items in the training data, where items with similar shapes are assumed similar to each other (squares and stars). The L column shows the labels of the items in the training data (positive and negative), and $\mathrm{d}U^L/\mathrm{d}s_i$ shows the magnitude and direction of the labeled gradients. For each pair of items, positive items are pulled up and negative items are pushed down in the ranking. The force magnitude is dictated by the difference in rank between the two items. Similarly, $\mathrm{d}U^U/\mathrm{d}s_i$ shows the unlabeled gradients for the data. Similar items are pulled toward each other. The last column in the figure shows the total semi-supervised gradient.

The labeled part of LambdaRank scales linearly in the number of labeled training queries, and effectively gives an algorithm that is near-linear in the total number of labeled items for typical workloads [8]. The semi-supervised algorithm is also linear in the total number of training queries. Since we are regularizing only with respect to the K-nearest neighbors of each item in the input space, the overall algorithm is approximately linear in the total number of data points.

In experiments, semi-supervised LambdaRank shows significant gains over supervised LambdaRank even for relatively large supervised training sets, including several thousands of labeled preference pairs [51]. The algorithm scales well to large sets of unlabeled examples: training with tens of millions of preferences takes approximately an hour.

9.4.2   Implicit Labels

The natural conclusion of reducing labeling cost is to eliminate paid judges completely from the process of collecting relevance labels. Instead, we can rely on users to provide relevance judgments. As an added benefit, this can increase the fidelity of the labels, as users are better placed to know the intent of their query and thus the relevance of individual documents.

However, using the same judgment approach with users as with expert judges, requesting *explicit* relevance labels, is usually too disruptive to users. While some ranking settings have users who are willing to provide absolute relevance judgments for free (for example, many movie recommendation systems rely on users' explicit relevance judgments), typical information retrieval settings such as web search cannot expect to obtain such labels from users. Hence, this section studies approaches to obtain relevance judgments from users *implicitly*, while they naturally interact with a web search system.

9.4.2.1   User Search Actions

Given a web search setting, the first question we must ask is how much of user behavior can we practically observe. Kelly and Teevan [34] provided a detailed survey of the many user actions that can be observed including browsing, bookmarking, printing, and so forth. A growing fraction of web browsers can record many aspects of user behavior, such as queries submitted and reformulated, what web pages were viewed and their viewing times, and clicks, together with a unique user-id and IP address that provides an approximate user location. Here, we will focus on clicks on search results.

9.4.2.2   Absolute Click Interpretation

Given observations of web search queries and clicks on search results, how can we infer relevance labels that can be used for learning? The simplest model is that a click on a web document implies that the document is relevant to the user's query [5, 35]. More sophisticated models employ clicks across an entire user session to infer absolute relevance labels for documents [24, 58].

However, this can lead to incorrect relevance labels, as shown by Joachims et al. [32]. In particular, they asked users to perform web searches and presented the users with the search results either in the order returned by a popular web search engine, or reversing the top ten results. They found that the users exhibit a *trust bias* where users trust that documents presented high by the search engine are most relevant, and second a *quality-of-context bias* where users are more likely to click on less relevant documents if they are embedded in a poorer quality ranking. Together, these types of bias are usually referred to as *presentation bias*, in that result presentation affects users' choices in addition to document relevance.

9.4.2.3   Preference Click Interpretation

An alternative interpretation of user clicks was proposed by [20, 31]: as preference judgments. Intuitively, selection of web search results may be much like the selections people make when purchasing products, where they must select among the available options. Perhaps users choose to click on a search result not because it is relevant, but because it is more likely to be relevant than any other option they are aware of. This idea is known as revealed preferences in economics. Interpreting clicks as preferences can additionally be motivated by the observation that humans inherently find it difficult to assess relevance reliably on an absolute scale.

To infer preferences about documents from user clicks, we start from the sequential browsing model from Section 9.2: The users examine lists of web search results in order from the top. Whenever the user examines a document that appears relevant to his information need, he may choose to click. However, this is not an indication of satisfaction with the document. Rather, it is interpreted as an indication that the clicked document appears more promising than any documents the user has already examined but did not click. A number of such strategies that make various assumptions about previously considered documents are shown in the top part of Table 9.2. These strategies provide reliable preference judgments with agreement rates with respect to explicit expert judgments almost as high as those between different expert assessors providing explicit judgments [32]. In particular, we see that the strategies that take into account presentation bias, i.e., the order in which users view search results, are more accurate.

Extending this approach to span multiple queries from a user session yields further improvements. In particular, if a user issues two queries in sequence for the same information need, and does not click on any results for the first query, but does click for the second, then a further strategy obtains even higher agreement rates with judges as shown at the bottom of Table 9.2. This allows preference judgments to be collected at almost no cost from users during their natural interactions with a search engine.

9.4.3   Active Implicit Preferences

Although the implicit label collection approach described above provides a very large amount of training data at minimal cost, there are a number of limitations with the approach. First, all the inferred preferences that avoid presentation bias *oppose* the original ranking order. This means that only a biased fraction of possible preference pairs can be collected in this way. In fact, a learning algorithm could simply return the reverse of the original ranking to satisfy all the preferences. Moreover, if data are collected continuously and the ranking function is retrained periodically, the ranking function never

TABLE 9.2: Implicit labeling strategies and their accuracy [32].

Strategy and Description	Accuracy (%)
CLICK ≻ SKIP ABOVE: A clicked-on document is more relevant than one presented higher but not clicked on.	78.2 ± 5.6
LAST CLICK ≻ SKIP ABOVE: The last clicked document is more relevant than any presented higher and skipped.	80.9 ± 5.1
CLICK ≻ EARLIER CLICK: A clicked document is more relevant than any presented higher that were clicked.	64.3 ± 15.4
CLICK ≻ SKIP PREVIOUS: A clicked document is more relevant than the preceding document, if it was not clicked.	80.7 ± 9.6
CLICK ≻ NO-CLICK NEXT: A clicked document is more relevant than the next document, if it was not clicked.	67.4 ± 8.2
CLICK ≻ TOPTWO NO CLICK EARLIER QUERY A clicked document is more relevant than the top two documents of the ranking for an earlier query with the same information need that received no clicks.	84.5 ± 6.1

A *skip* occurs when the user examines but does not click a document. The preference judgments used to assess accuracy have an inter-judge agreement rate of 86.4%.

converges to an optimal ranking.[2] Second, preferences can only be collected over documents that are already retrieved, and further will mostly be collected over documents that are already at a high rank because web search users predominantly click on documents in top positions.

We address these limitations by using an *active* data collection approach, in which the system selects the rankings to show users to elicit user preferences that are unbiased and most informative to the learning process.

9.4.3.1   Minimal Randomization

One active experimentation condition commonly made by search engines is that user utility for a given query must not be degraded substantially even while collecting more useful training data. Subject to this constraint, one method to allow preferences that both oppose and support the original ranking order is to perturb the search results randomly.

Given a ranked result list such as $(x_{(1)}, x_{(2)}, x_{(3)}, x_{(4)}, x_{(5)}, \dots)$, the FairPairs algorithm [44] randomly considers the results as adjacent pairs $((x_{(1)}, x_{(2)}), (x_{(3)}, x_{(4)}), (x_{(5)}, x_{(6)}), \dots)$ or $(x_{(1)}, (x_{(2)}, x_{(3)}), (x_{(4)}, x_{(5)}), \dots)$.

---

[2]To see why, observe that for any learned ranking any time a user skips over any result and clicks on a lower one (for example after entering an ambiguous query) this will generate preferences that oppose the ranking order. Given enough users, there will eventually be enough opposing preferences that the learning algorithm will change the ranking.

Each pair of results is then independently flipped with 50% probability. For example, the final ranking might end up as $(\boldsymbol{x}_{(1)}, \boldsymbol{x}_{(2)}, \boldsymbol{x}_{(4)}, \boldsymbol{x}_{(3)}, \boldsymbol{x}_{(5)}, \ldots)$ with only $\boldsymbol{x}_{(3)}$ and $\boldsymbol{x}_{(4)}$ flipped. In expectation half the results will be presented at their original rank and all results will be presented within one rank of their original position, satisfying the constraint that results must not be degraded substantially.

Subject to two simple assumptions (particularly that the probability of clicking on an examined document depends only on its relevance), the Fair-Pairs algorithm combined with the CLICK $\succ$ SKIP ABOVE strategy within each pair is guaranteed to give preference data that are unaffected by presentation bias [44]. Furthermore, by considering the frequency with which a preference judgment is collected in either direction based on search engine user clicks, we can measure the confidence with which a particular document is considered more relevant than another particular document. However, in practice clicking behavior depends on more than the relevance of the documents (for example, it also depends on the result summary shown to users), although this can be compensated for [56].

9.4.3.2 Greedy Training Data Collection

We now relax the constraint that all documents must be presented within one position of their original rank. As a result, it is possible to collect more informative training data. Here, we assume that we are permitted to show any two documents at the top two positions, but the remainder of the ranking must be preserved. We start with the Bradley-Terry model introduced earlier, where $S^* = (s_1^*, \ldots, s_N^*)$ denotes the (unknown) true relevance scores for the documents $\{\boldsymbol{x}_1, \ldots, \boldsymbol{x}_N\}$. The learning to rank problem in this setting becomes learning an estimate of S^* given preferences D^L.

Formally, our goal is to find an $S = (s_1, \ldots, s_N)$ that produces a ranking with maximal utility. However, for notational convenience we formulate the problem as minimizing the *loss* $\mathcal{L}$ of S with respect to the true scores S^*.

$$\mathcal{L}(S, S^*) = U(S^*) - U(S). \tag{9.17}$$

Noting that S^* is unknown, we find the ranking that minimizes the expected loss given what we know about S^*, namely $P(S \mid D^L)$:

$$\hat{S} \triangleq \underset{S}{\operatorname{argmin}} \, E_{S^* \sim P(S|D^L)} \left[\mathcal{L}(S, S^*) \right], \tag{9.18}$$

where S^* is drawn from the probability distribution $P(S \mid D^L)$.

We assume that $P(S \mid D^L)$ is multivariate normal with diagonal covariance, and that $\mathcal{L}$ can be decomposed as pairwise losses $\mathcal{L}_{ij}$ over documents i, j in our collection:

$$E_{S^* \sim P(S|D^L)} \left[\mathcal{L}(S, S^*) \right] = \sum_{i=1}^{N} \sum_{j=i+1}^{N} E_{S^* \sim P(S|D^L)} \left[\mathcal{L}_{ij}(S, S^*) \right]. \tag{9.19}$$

In this setting, for many loss functions (such as pair accuracy ppref) the mode of $P(S \mid D^L)$ is often the minimum in Equation 9.18 [45].

Next, we need an algorithm to estimate $P(S \mid D^L)$ given preference pairs observed from clicks. As clicking behavior is often noisy, we model the probability of obtaining pairwise comparisons using the Bradley-Terry model. If we also assume that the document relevances are distributed according to a Gaussian prior, we can use the Glicko chess rating system [28] to estimate the relevance of each document and the uncertainty in the relevance. In particular, this provides a set of closed form approximate online updates to $P(S \mid D^L)$ as comparisons are observed [45].

We can now return to our initial goal: determine which ranking should be shown to the users of our search system to minimize the loss most quickly. One approach is to perform approximate gradient descent on the loss function: Each time a user arrives, we find the pair of documents whose contribution to the expected loss is likely to decrease most following a pairwise comparison. We present these two documents at the top of the ranking shown. Due to users more often considering top results, this makes it most likely we obtain a preference between the documents from this user, thus improving our estimate of the relative relevance of these two documents. The expected loss contribution of a pair after a comparison of documents x_i and x_j can be estimated as a weighted sum of the contribution for the two possible outcomes (either x_i wins the comparison or x_j wins). We can use $P(S \mid D^L)$ to estimate the probability of each of these two possible outcomes. More formally, letting $D_{ij}^{L'}$ be the training data after including the outcome of the comparison of x_i and x_j, and $\hat{S}'_{ij}$ be minimum in Equation 9.18 given $D_{ij}^{L'}$, we select the pair x_i and x_j that satisfies:

$$\operatorname*{argmax}_{x_i, x_j \in X,\ i \neq j} \left(E_{P(S^* \mid D^L)} \left[\mathcal{L}_{ij}(\hat{S}, S^*) \right] - E_{P(\hat{S}'_{ij})} \left[E_{P(S^* \mid D_{ij}^{L'})} \left[\mathcal{L}_{ij}(\hat{S}'_{ij}, S^*) \right] \right] \right),$$

(9.20)

where $P(S^* \mid D^L)$ is shorthand for $S^* \sim P(S \mid D^L)$. The first term is the expected loss before the comparison, and the second is the expected loss over the two possible outcomes after the comparison. Note that in the interest of tractability, this formulation ignores the change in contribution from interactions of each document (e.g. x_i) with all other documents $(X - \{x_i, x_j\})$. Alternative strategies for this setting are described by [45].

9.4.3.3 Online Learning and Label Collection

In this section, we consider what happens if we entirely remove the requirement that the rankings shown must be similar to the current best-estimate ranking of documents. This allows us to address the most general active learning to rank formulation: Suppose we wish to show users rankings such that the total utility obtained by all users over all time is maximized, irrespective of whether in the short term users are presented with poor rankings.

Formally, we want to learn an optimal ranking of documents $X = \{x_1, \ldots, x_n\}$ for one fixed query. For simplicity, we will only use the identity of the documents, and do not require any document features or measure of document similarity to the query. Suppose we have a population of users (who may differ in the relevance they assign to each document for this potentially ambiguous query), where each user u_c considers some subset of documents $A_c \subset X$ as relevant to the query (with utility 1), and the remainder of the documents as non-relevant (with zero utility). Intuitively, users with different interpretations for the query would have different relevant sets, while users with similar interpretations would have similar relevant sets.

At time t, the system interacts with user u_t with relevant set A_t. We present an ordered set of k documents. The user examines the results in order, and clicks on up to one document. In the simplest case, we could model users as always clicking on the first relevant document, and never clicking on a non-relevant document, although the results below also hold if users click probabilistically.

We observe utility 1 if the user clicks, 0 if not. The goal is to maximize the total utility, summing over all time. This total utility represents the number of users who clicked on any result, i.e., who found at least one relevant document.

As an introduction to the learning approach, first consider the trivial case of finding the best single document to show users. Clearly, this is the document that is relevant to the largest fraction of users. However, as users arrive in sequence from some unknown distribution (where different users find different documents relevant), finding the best document is non-trivial.

One strategy to find the best document is to show each document a fixed number of times (to a random sample of the users), and thus estimate the expected utility of each document. However, this approach is suboptimal in the long run, as an unlucky sequence of users may result in a suboptimal document being permanently selected. This would result in a constant amount of utility being lost in each iteration. The optimal solution to maximize the total utility has been addressed in the literature as a Multi-Armed Bandit (MAB) problem, modeled on casino slot machines, sometimes also called one-armed bandits (e.g., [13]). In the MAB setting, we assume that there are many one-armed bandits, and at each time step the algorithm must choose an arm (i.e., bandit to play). Each time a bandit arm is selected, the payoff received is a sample from an unknown probability distribution of which we wish to estimate the expected payoff. In the information retrieval setting, the payoff (utility) of the bandit arm (document) selected is 1 if the current user finds the document relevant and clicks, and 0 otherwise. An MAB algorithm then maintains a score for every document, representing its historical payoff and the uncertainty in this estimate (for example, the UCB1 algorithm [13] maintains an upper confidence bound on the mean payoff of each bandit, always selecting the bandit with highest upper confidence bound). This leads to a *sublinear* difference between the optimal and expected utility collected.

Returning to the problem of selecting a ranking of k documents, the best sequence of rankings to show users can be modeled similarly [39, 26]. Intuitively, the ranked bandits algorithm proposed by [26] selects the document to show at each rank using a copy of the same multi-armed bandit algorithm from the one-document setting. The MAB algorithm instance MAB_i at each rank i thus independently selects the document to show at that rank. This online approach learns the optimal ranking with almost the same total utility as the best polynomial time offline learning algorithm that is given the same sequence but with users known up front [39, 26]. By additionally assuming that a similarity function between documents is known, and by sharing information between MAB instances at different ranks, [50] showed how to scale the Ranked Bandits algorithm to much larger document collections. Nevertheless, the scalability of such optimal approaches remains limited and the utility obtained in realistic time scales is usually inferior to approaches that optimize independent utility.

9.5   Multiple Utilities

So far, we have discussed retrieval utilities based on a single type of data, such as expert judgments, or user click behavior. None of these modalities equals the actual user utility, and each has different strengths and weaknesses. Here we show how the utilities are complementary, and show how to learn a ranker that considers multiple utilities.

We will exemplify the common scenario of combining expert judgments with user clicks. These reflect *relevance* and *popularity*. As our understanding of user utilities evolves, many more aspects of utilities will emerge. For example, *freshness*, the degree to which an item is up to date, and *accessibility*, whether the presentation is appropriate to the user (e.g., due to age and background).

Judgments and user behaviors are complementary in several ways. Judgments are limited to relatively few queries, due to the expense involved in collecting them. Judgments are currently made by a few individuals, and may differ from actual users that formulated the query. However, the judgment process, judgment type, and quality can be controlled: we can request judgments for particular documents, possibly deep in the ranking, and can judge many documents for the same query. For clicks there is significant noise due to only a small snippet from the document being visible prior to the user deciding whether to click, user mistakes, and potential malicious noise. On the other hand, click noise may be uncorrelated to the judgment noise, and one modality can therefore serve to correct the other. Clicks are cheap to obtain and can cover huge sets of queries. They can provide more fine-grained relevance information and thereby resolve judgment ties. Clicks tend to occur mostly on top-ranked documents; to learn about the click appeal of an item, we need to place it in top ranks. Unfortunately, putting non-relevant documents in top ranks hurts the user experience, thus, limiting the scope of items for which we can collect clicks.

We can combine judgment and click utilities via a convex combination

$$U(y) = (1 - \alpha)U_{\text{relevance}}(y) + \alpha U_{\text{clicks}}(y), \qquad (9.21)$$

with α determining the tradeoff. Here we will take an approach that allows us to vary α, or to consider more general combinations of utilities, without having to retrain the main model [59]. In other words, we will separate the choice of utility from the learned model, so that the two can be developed independently. This allows a retrieval system to support multiple, possibly user-specific utilities. It is unlike the previous direct optimization of a specific utility as performed by LambdaRank.

Instead, we will learn multiple models that given a document, predict each input to the utility. Then we can evaluate any utility based on these inputs. In particular, for the case above, we learn a judgment model $P(l \mid \boldsymbol{x}, \boldsymbol{w})$ and a click model $P(c \mid \boldsymbol{x}, \boldsymbol{w})$, based on features $\boldsymbol{x}$ for a query-document pair.

The judgment model can be any probabilistic classifier, such as a neural network. The click prediction model has special requirements. It should take into account the proportion of actual clicks for documents that were previously shown, as well as generalizing from query-document match features (such as TF-IDF) that are necessary for documents that have not been shown a sufficient number of times. This can be achieved by a Bayesian linear classifier with an individual mean and variance parameter for each query-document pair, representing its click statistics, as well as parameters for query-document match features, document features, and rank position at which the click occurred. The Bayesian formulation captures uncertainty in the weight estimates, and properly accounts for weights relating to a single or many query-document click observations.

Experiments with this model [59] show that training with a combined utility gives better results than training with a pure judgment or pure click utility, even when evaluated using either of those pure utilities. In a concrete example with web search data, for the query "adobe" the model predicted that the page www.adobe.com was the most relevant, but that the acrobat reader download page was the most clicked. For intermediate values of α, the combined utility places www.adobe.com at the top and acrobat reader second, getting the best of both worlds. A practical application is the adaptation of a search engine built for one collection to another collection. It may be feasible to collect both judgments and clicks on the original collection, but judgments may be more costly than clicks for the second, since a judgment process is cumbersome to set up. The model can still rely on clicks to adapt: For example, a search engine deployed at an accounting firm may observe an above-average fraction of clicks on spreadsheet results, and infer that spreadsheet files should be ranked high at this firm.

9.6 Conclusion

Information retrieval has long been concerned with evaluating and optimizing user and system utility. The field offers a distinctive setting for cost-sensitive learning in that the problems involve rankings. The challenge is to capture user utility in the retrieval process, as well as to control the training cost of the retrieval system. We have covered common utilities, learning algorithms for these utilities, and several ways to reduce system training cost, e.g., by employing semi-supervised data, and by exploiting user clicks as a cheap form of training data.

Nevertheless, many questions remain open for future research. Importantly, we need more accurate user utilities that come closer to measuring user satisfaction. For example, we have treated the queries as independent. In reality, the user often reformulates a query in response to retrieval results, and the context of previous queries and the history of interaction can be exploited. Ultimately, we should take advantage of user interaction to learn a personalized model and elicit an individual utility for each user, representing their interests, behaviors, and values.

We also require better learning algorithms for complex utilities. Existing approaches for dependent utilities and online learning are either greedy approximations, or not scalable to practical problems, neither at training nor at test time. Moreover, even though many models provide distributions over rankings, the majority of algorithms simply return the mode ranking, ignoring the uncertainty when making decisions. In summary, retrieval systems are still in their infancy, and we believe they provide unique challenges and opportunities for cost-sensitive learning.

References

[1] James Allan, Javed A. Aslamy, Ben Carterette, Virgil Pavlu, and Evangelos Kanoulas. Million query track 2008 overview. In *Proceedings of Text REtrieval Conference*, 2008.

[2] Massih Reza Amini, Tuong Vinh Truong, and Cyril Goutte. A boosting algorithm for learning bipartite ranking functions with partially labeled data. In *Proceedings of the ACM Conference on Research and Development in Information Retrieval (SIGIR)*, pages 99–106, 2008.

[3] Peter Bailey, Nick Craswell, Ian Soboroff, Paul Thomas, Arjen P. de Vries, and Emine Yilmaz. Relevance assessment: Are judges exchangeable and

does it matter? In *Proceedings of the ACM Conference on Research and Development in Information Retrieval (SIGIR)*, pages 667–674, 2008.

[4] Mikhail Belkin, Partha Niyogi, and Vikas Sindhwani. Manifold regularization: A geometric framework for learning from labeled and unlabeled examples. *Journal of Machine Learning Research*, (7):2399–2434, 2006.

[5] Justin Boyan, Dayne Freitag, and Thorsten Joachims. A machine learning architecture for optimizing web search engines. In *AAAI Workshop on Internet Based Information Systems*, 1996.

[6] R. A. Bradley and M. E. Terry. The rank analysis of incomplete block designs. 1. The method of paired comparisons. *Biometrika*, 39:324–345, 1952.

[7] Chris Burges, T. Shaked, E. Renshaw, A. Lazier, M. Deeds, N. Hamilton, and G. Hullender. Learning to rank using gradient descent. In *Proceedings of the International Conference on Machine Learning (ICML)*, pages 89–96, 2005.

[8] Christopher J. C. Burges, Robert Ragno, and Quoc Viet Le. Learning to rank with nonsmooth cost functions. In *Proceedings of the International Conference on Advances in Neural Information Processing Systems (NIPS)*, pages 193–200, 2006.

[9] Jamie Carbonell and Jade Goldstein. The use of MMR, diversity-based reranking for reordering documents and producing summaries. In *Proceedings of the ACM Conference on Research and Development in Information Retrieval (SIGIR)*, pages 335–336, 1998.

[10] Ben Carterette, James Allan, and Ramesh Sitaraman. Minimal test collections for retrieval evaluation. In *Proceedings of the ACM Conference on Research and Development in Information Retrieval (SIGIR)*, pages 268–275, New York, NY, 2006.

[11] Ben Carterette, Paul Bennett, David Chickering, and Susan Dumais. Here or there: Preference judgments for relevance. In *Proceedings of the European Conference on Information Retrieval (ECIR)*, pages 16–27, 2008.

[12] Ben Carterette and Paul N. Bennett. Evaluation measures for preference judgments. In *Proceedings of the ACM Conference on Research and Development in Information Retrieval (SIGIR)*, pages 685–686, 2008.

[13] Nicolo Cesa-Bianchi and Gabor Lugosi. *Prediction, Learning, and Games.* Cambridge University Press, 2006.

[14] Olivier Chapelle, Yi Chang, and Tie-Yan Liu, editors. *Yahoo! Learning to Rank Challenge*, 2010. http://learningtorankchallenge.yahoo.com/.

[15] Harr Chen and David R. Karger. Less is more: Probabilistic models for retrieving fewer relevant documents. In *Proceedings of the ACM Conference on Research and Development in Information Retrieval (SIGIR)*, pages 429–436, 2006.

[16] Cheng Zhai, William W. Cohen, and John Lafferty. Beyond Independent Relevance: Methods and Evaluation Metrics for Subtopic Retrieval. In *Proceedings of the ACM Conference on Research and Development in Information Retrieval (SIGIR)*, pages 10–17, 2003.

[17] Wei Chu and Zoubin Ghahramani. Extensions of Gaussian processes for ranking: Semi-supervised and active learning. In *NIPS Workshop on Learning to Rank*, 2005.

[18] Charles L. A. Clarke, Maheedhar Kolla, Gordon V. Cormack, Olga Vechtomova, Azin Ashkan, Stefan Büttcher, and Ian MacKinnon. Novelty and diversity in information retrieval evaluation. In *Proceedings of the ACM Conference on Research and Development in Information Retrieval (SIGIR)*, pages 659–666, 2008.

[19] Charles L. A. Clarke, Maheedhar Kolla, and Olga Vechtomova. An effectiveness measure for ambiguous and underspecified queries. In *Proceedings of the International Conference on the Theory of Information Retrieval (ICTIR)*, pages 188–199, 2009.

[20] William W. Cohen, Robert E. Shapire, and Yoram Singer. Learning to order things. *Journal of Artificial Intelligence Research*, 10:243–270, 1999.

[21] I.J. Cox, M.L. Miller, T.P. Minka, T.V. Papathomas, and P.N. Yianilos. The Bayesian image retrieval system, PicHunter: Theory, implementation, and psychophysical experiments. *IEEE Transactions on Image Processing*, 9(1):20–37, January 2000.

[22] P. Diaconis and R. Graham. Spearman's Footrule as a Measure of Disarray. *Journal of the Royal Statistical Society, Series B*, 39(2):262–268, 1977.

[23] Pinar Donmez, Krysta M. Svore, and Christopher J. C. Burges. On the local optimality of Lambdarank. In *Proceedings of the ACM Conference on Research and Development in Information Retrieval (SIGIR)*, pages 460–467, 2009.

[24] Georges Dupret and Ciya Liao. A model to estimate intrinsic document relevance from the clickthrough logs of a web search engine. In *WSDM '10: Proceedings of the Third ACM International Conference on Web Search and Data Mining*, pages 181–190, New York, NY, 2010.

[25] Ronald Fagin, Ravi Kumar, and D. Sivakumar. Comparing top k lists. *SIAM Journal of Discrete Math*, 17(1):134–160, 2003.

[26] Filip Radlinski, Robert Kleinberg, and Thorsten Joachims. Learning diverse rankings with multi-armed bandits. In *Proceedings of the International Conference on Machine Learning (ICML)*, pages 784–791, 2008.

[27] Y. Freund, R. Iyer, R.E. Schapire, and Y. Singer. An efficient boosting algorithm for combining preferences. *Journal of Machine Learning Research*, 4:933–969, 2003.

[28] Mark E. Glickman. Parameter estimation in large dynamic paired comparison experiments. *Applied Statistics*, 48:377–394, 1999.

[29] Kalervo Järvelin and Jaana Kekäläinen. IR evaluation methods for retrieving highly relevant documents. In *Proceedings of the ACM Conference on Research and Development in Information Retrieval (SIGIR)*, pages 41–48, 2000.

[30] Thorsten Joachims. Optimizing search engines using clickthrough data. In *International Conference on Knowledge Discovery and Data Mining (KDD)*, pages 133–142, 2002.

[31] Thorsten Joachims. Optimizing Search Engines Using Clickthrough Data. In *Proceedings of the ACM International Conference on Knowledge Discovery and Data Mining (KDD)*, pages 132–142, 2002.

[32] Thorsten Joachims, Laura Granka, Bing Pan, Helene Hembrooke, Filip Radlinski, and Geri Gay. Evaluating the accuracy of implicit feedback from clicks and query reformulations in web search. *ACM Transactions on Information Science (TOIS)*, 25(2), 2007. Article 7.

[33] Jun Wang and Jianhan Zhu. Portfolio Theory of Information Retrieval. In *Proceedings of the ACM Conference on Research and Development in Information Retrieval (SIGIR)*, pages 115–122, 2009.

[34] Diane Kelly and Jaime Teevan. Implicit Feedback for Inferring User Preference: A Bibliography. *SIGIR Forum*, 32(2):18–28, 2003.

[35] Charles Kemp and Kotagiri Ramamohanarao. Long-Term Learning for Web Search Engines. In *Proceedings of the European Conference on Principles and Pratice of Knowledge Discovery in Databases (PKDD)*, pages 263–274, 2002.

[36] M. Kendall and J. D. Gibbons. *Rank Correlation Methods*. Edward Arnold, London, 1990.

[37] Christopher D. Manning, Prabhakar Raghavan, and Hinrich Schütze. *Introduction to Information Retrieval*. Cambridge University Press, 2008.

[38] John Marden. *Analyzing and Modeling Rank Data.* Chapman & Hall, 1995.

[39] Matthew Streeter and Daniel Golovin. An Online Algorithm for Maximizing Submodular Functions. Technical Report CMU-CS-07-171, School of Computer Science, Carnegie Mellon University, December 2007.

[40] Tom Minka and Stephen Robertson. Selection bias in the LETOR datasets, *SIGIR 2008 Workshop on Learning to Rank for Information Retrieval,* 2008.

[41] Stefano Mizzaro. Relevance: The whole history. *Journal of the American Society for Information Science,* 48:810–832, 1997.

[42] Foster Provost and Tom Fawcett. Analysis and visualization of classifier performance: Comparison under imprecise class and cost distributions. In *Proceedings of the ACM International Conference on Knowledge Discovery and Data Mining (KDD),* pages 43–48, 1997.

[43] Tao Qin, Tie-Yan Liu, Jun Xu, and Hang Li. LETOR: A benchmark collection for research on learning to rank for information retrieval. *Information Retrieval Journal,* 13(4):346–374, 2010.

[44] Filip Radlinski and Thorsten Joachims. Minimally invasive randomization for collecting unbiased preferences from clickthrough logs. In *Proceedings of the National Conference on Artificial Intelligence (AAAI),* pages 1406–1412, 2006.

[45] Filip Radlinski and Thorsten Joachims. Active exploration for learning rankings from clickthrough data. In *Proceedings of the ACM International Conference on Knowledge Discovery and Data Mining (KDD),* pages 570–579, 2007.

[46] S. E. Robertson. The probability ranking principle in IR. *Journal of Documentation,* 33:294–304, 1977.

[47] Mark Sanderson. Test collection based evaluation of information retrieval systems. *Foundations and Trends in Information Retrieval,* 4(4):247–375, 2010.

[48] Matthias Seeger. Learning with labeled and unlabeled data. Unpublished. http://www.dai.ed.ac.uk/homes/seeger/, February 2001.

[49] Agarwal Shivani. Ranking on graph data. In *Proceedings of the International Conference on Machine Learning (ICML),* pages 25–32, 2006.

[50] Aleksandrs Slivkins, Filip Radlinski, and Sreenivas Gollapudi. Learning optimally diverse rankings over large document collections. In *Proceedings of the International Conference on Machine Learning (ICML),* pages 983–990, 2010.

[51] Martin Szummer and Emine Yilmaz. Semi-supervised ranking. In preparation.

[52] Michael Taylor, John Guiver, Stephen Robertson, and Tom Minka. Softrank: Optimizing non-smooth rank metrics. In *Proceedings of ACM International Conference on Web Search and Data Mining (WSDM)*, pages 77–86, 2008.

[53] L.J.P. van der Maaten and G.E. Hinton. Visualizing data using t-SNE. *Journal of Machine Learning Research*, 9:2579–2605, 2008.

[54] C. J. van Rijsbergen. *Information Retrieval*. Butterworth & Co, 2nd edition, 1979.

[55] Yisong Yue and Thorsten Joachims. Predicting diverse subsets using structural SVMs. In *Proceedings of the International Conference on Machine Learning (ICML)*, pages 1224–1231, 2008.

[56] Yisong Yue, Rajan Patel, and Hein Roehrig. Beyond position bias: Examining result attractiveness as a source of presentation bias in clickthrough data. In *WWW '10: Proceedings of the 19th International Conference on World Wide Web*, pages 1011–1018, New York, NY, 2010.

[57] ChengXiang Zhai and John Lafferty. A risk minimization framework for information retrieval. *Information Processing & Management*, 42(1):31–55, 2006.

[58] Feimin Zhong, Dong Wang, Gang Wang, Weizhu Chen, Yuchen Zhang, Zheng Chen, and Haixun Wang. Incorporating post-click behaviors into a click model. In *SIGIR '10: Proceeding of the 33rd International ACM SIGIR Conference on Research and Development in Information Retrieval*, pages 355–362, New York, NY, 2010.

[59] Onno Zoeter, Michael Taylor, Ed Snelson, John Guiver, Nick Craswell, and Martin Szummer. A decision theoretic framework for ranking using implicit feedback. In *SIGIR 2008 Workshop on Learning to Rank for Information Retrieval*, 2008.

Index

0/1-loss, 15–16

A

Absolute log-odds ratio, 116
Accessibility, 288
Accuracy
　classifiers, 117
　cost *vs.*, 96–97
　generalization, 111, 123
　improving, 145–146
　rule-based evidence fusion and,
　　235
　SERA, 235–236
　single model, 145–146
Acquisition; *see also* Active
　　feature-value acquisition;
　　Information acquisition;
　　Selective data acquisition
　cost, 88
　data, 102–103
　features, 89, 183
　label, 122–124
　policy, 110, 112–113
　sources, 126
　value, 102–103
　viral marketing, 131
ACS. *see* Active class selection
Active class selection (ACS),
　　137–138, 140–141
Active feature-value acquisition
　　(AFA), 109–113
　class labels and, 112–113
　instance completion setting, 138
　prediction time, 133–135
Active interleaving, 119
Active learning, 3, 23–24
　AFA *vs.*, 110

batch-mode, 182
cost-sensitive multi-level,
　　187–189
cycle, 5
decision theory and, 267–268
guided learning *vs.*, 143
illustrated example of, 8–9
loop, 180
pool-based, 9
ranking, 278
scenarios, 5–8
stream-based, 7
visual, 179–183
VOI-based, 190
AdaBoost, 52, 67–68, 91
Ad exchanges, 244, 258
Admission control, 254
Ad networks, 243–244, 258
Ad ranking
　CTR and, 246–248
　explore/exploit method, 250–252
　feedback delays in, 247–248
　SS and, 246–248
Ad server logs, 131
Advertising, 241–245; *see also*
　　Candidate ads; Display
　　advertising
　campaigns, 244
　ecosystem, 259
　guaranteed delivery, 243
　matching, 242
　non-guaranteed delivery, 243
　online active inference and, 131
　performance, 243, 245–252
　positioning, 248
　variants, 244

Printed and bound by CPI Group (UK) Ltd, Croydon, CR0 4YY

23/10/2024

01777674-0014